CONQUEST AND CHRISTIANIZATION

Following its violent conquest by Charlemagne (772–804), Saxony became both a Christian and a Carolingian region. This book sets out to re-evaluate the political integration and Christianization of Saxony and to show how the success of this transformation has important implications for how we view governance, the institutional church and Christian communities in the early Middle Ages. A burgeoning array of Carolingian regional studies are pulled together to offer a new synthesis of the history of Saxony in the Carolingian empire and to undercut the narrative of top-down Christianization with a more grassroots model that highlights the potential for diversity within Carolingian Christianity. This book is a comprehensive and accessible account which will provide students with a fresh view of the incorporation of Saxony into the Carolingian world.

INGRID REMBOLD is Junior Research Fellow at Hertford College, Oxford. Her research to date has examined themes relating to governance, monasticism and Christianization in the early medieval world. She has published articles in *Early Medieval Europe,* the *Journal of Medieval History* and *History Compass*, as well as various contributions to forthcoming edited volumes. She has been awarded the Early Medieval Europe Essay Prize and the Prince Consort & Thirlwall Prize and Seeley Medal.

Cambridge Studies in Medieval Life and Thought
Fourth Series

General Editor:
ROSAMOND MCKITTERICK
Emeritus Professor of Medieval History, University of Cambridge,
and Fellow of Sidney Sussex College

Advisory Editors:
CHRISTINE CARPENTER
Emeritus Professor of Medieval English History, University of Cambridge

MAGNUS RYAN
University Lecturer in History, University of Cambridge, and Fellow of Peterhouse

The series *Cambridge Studies in Medieval Life and Thought* was inaugurated by G.G. Coulton in 1921; Professor Rosamond McKitterick now acts as General Editor of the Fourth Series, with Professor Christine Carpenter and Dr Magnus Ryan as Advisory Editors. The series brings together outstanding work by medieval scholars over a wide range of human endeavour extending from political economy to the history of ideas.

This is book 108 in the series, and a full list of titles in the series can be found at:
www.cambridge.org/medievallifeandthought

CONQUEST AND CHRISTIANIZATION

Saxony and the Carolingian World, 772–888

INGRID REMBOLD
University of Oxford

CAMBRIDGE
UNIVERSITY PRESS

University Printing House, Cambridge CB2 8BS, United Kingdom

One Liberty Plaza, 20th Floor, New York, NY 10006, USA

477 Williamstown Road, Port Melbourne, VIC 3207, Australia

314–321, 3rd Floor, Plot 3, Splendor Forum, Jasola District Centre, New Delhi - 110025, India

79 Anson Road, #06-04/06, Singapore 079906

Cambridge University Press is part of the University of Cambridge.

It furthers the University's mission by disseminating knowledge in the pursuit of
education, learning and research at the highest international levels of excellence.

www.cambridge.org
Information on this title: www.cambridge.org/9781316647202
DOI: 10.1017/9781108164597

© Ingrid Rembold 2018

First published 2018
First paperback edition 2020

A catalogue record for this publication is available from the British Library

Library of Congress Cataloging in Publication data
NAMES: Rembold, Ingrid, 1988- author.
TITLE: Conquest and Christianization : Saxony and the Carolingian world, 772–888 / Ingrid
Rembold, University of Oxford.
DESCRIPTION: New York : Cambridge University Press, 2017. | Series: Cambridge
studies in medieval life and thought. Fourth series ; book 108 | Includes bibliographical
references and index.
IDENTIFIERS: LCCN 2017030490 | ISBN 9781107196216 (hardback)
SUBJECTS: LCSH: Europe–Church history–600-1500. | Church history–9th century. |
Church history–8th century. | Conversion–Christianity–History. | Saxons–History. |
Carolingians–History.
CLASSIFICATION: LCC BR253 .R46 2017 | DDC 274.3/03–dc23
LC record available at https://lccn.loc.gov/2017030490

ISBN 978-1-107-19621-6 Hardback
ISBN 978-1-316-64720-2 Paperback

To my family, with thanks and love

CONTENTS

vii

FIGURES

MAPS

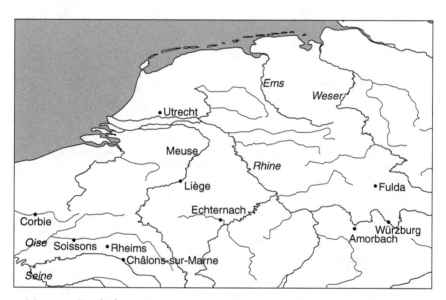

Map 1.   Frankish missionary sponsors. For practical reasons, modern river systems and coastlines have been depicted; these have however shifted, sometimes dramatically, over time

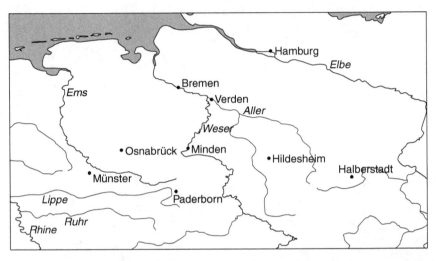

Map 2. Bishoprics in Carolingian Saxony

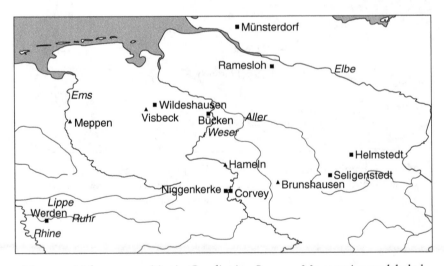

Map 3. Male communities in Carolingian Saxony. Monasteries are labeled
with squares; dependent monastic cells, with triangles

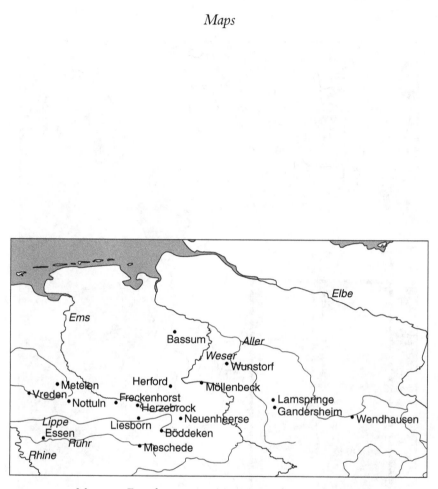

Map 4. Female communities in Carolingian Saxony

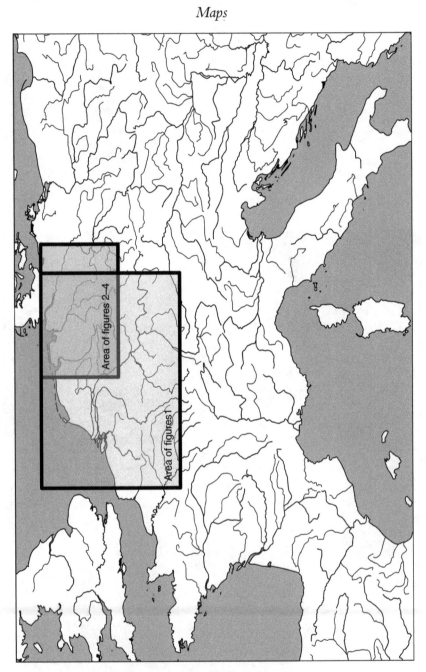

Map 5.   The European Context

ACKNOWLEDGEMENTS

This book could not have been completed without the generous assistance and support of my benefactors, colleagues, family and friends. I am especially grateful to John Osborn, whose endowment of a doctoral studentship enabled me to pursue this research, and likewise to Sidney Sussex College, the Faculty of History, the Lightfoot Scholarship, the Bibliographic Society and the German Historical Society for their support of my doctoral research. My postdoctoral work, which has allowed me to complete the revisions to this book, was generously funded by Hertford College, Oxford and the Deutscher Akademischer Austauschdienst.

My doctoral supervisor, Rosamond McKitterick, has offered unflagging guidance and support, and it is to her that I give my greatest thanks. Her advice and friendship have proved invaluable. I am also grateful to Hedwig Röckelein for her mentorship during my time in Göttingen, and to Christopher Tyerman and John Nightingale for their guidance here in Oxford. The process of adapting my doctoral thesis into a book was greatly aided by the comments and advice of both my anonymous peer reviewers and my doctoral examiners, Matthew Innes and Ian Wood, to whom I extend my sincere thanks. I am likewise grateful to my editor, Liz Friend-Smith, and all those at Cambridge University Press, for their support throughout this process.

My work has further benefited enormously from the suggestions of a broad range of colleagues, both at conferences, seminars and workshops and beyond. In particular, I would like to thank Nora Berend, Philippa Byrne, Robert Flierman, Eric Goldberg, Bernard Gowers, Eliza Hartrich, Elisabeth Kristofferson, Max McComb, Jinty Nelson, Rachel Stone, Graeme Ward and Chris Wickham, who generously offered their time to comment on chapters. My thanks are doubly owed to Chris, Max and Elisabeth, who all provided me with unpublished articles or thesis drafts, and especially to Robert, whose excellent work on early

Acknowledgements

medieval Saxony has been an inspiration, and whose comments, suggestions, and many insights have been extremely helpful. His recent book, *Saxon Identities, AD 150–900*, will no doubt shape the field for some time to come. Finally, I would like to thank the medieval graduate community at Cambridge, both for their encouragement and for their friendship.

This book is dedicated to my family – my parents, Chris and Kristen; my sister, Karen; and especially my husband, Robin – for their love and support.

NOTE ON TRANSLATIONS

The translations included in this book are my own, with the exception of biblical quotations, for which I have largely employed the Douay-Rheims translation. I have, however, consulted other translations extensively in the course of my research and in the drafting of my translations. Accordingly, many of my translations are deeply indebted to existing English-language translations; in particular, my translations of passages from the *Heliand* are greatly indebted to the excellent translation of Tonya K. Dewey (T. K. Dewey, tr., *An Annotated English Translation of the Old Saxon Heliand: A Ninth-Century Biblical Paraphrase in the Germanic Epic Style* (Lewiston, NY, 2011)). Both in order to acknowledge such debts and to inform the reader of these useful aids, I have included a bibliography of primary sources which have been translated into English. While it is by no means comprehensive, I hope that this short guide will prove useful to teachers and students alike.

ABBREVIATIONS

AfD	*Archiv für Diplomatik, Schriftgeschichte, Siegel- und Wappenkunde*
Cap.	*Capitularia regum Francorum*
Cap. episc.	*Capitula episcoporum*
Conc.	*Concilia*
DA	*Deutsches Archiv für Erforschung des Mittelalters*
D Arn	*Arnolfi diplomata*
D Kar. 1	*Caroli magni diplomata*
D Kar. 2	*Ludovici pii diplomata*
D Karl	*Karoli III. diplomata*
D LD	*Ludovici Germanici diplomata*
D LJ	*Ludovici iunoris diplomata*
D LK	*Ludovici infantis diplomata*
D Lo I	*Lotharii I. diplomata*
D O I	*Ottonis I. diplomata*
D Zw	*Zwentiboldi diplomata*
EME	*Early Medieval Europe*
Epp.	*Epistolae (in Quart): Epistolae Merowingici et Karolini aevi*
Fontes iuris	*Fontes iuris Germanici antiqui in usum scholarum separatim editi*
Francia	*Francia: Forschungen zur Westeuropäischen Geschichte*
Freise, *Vita*	E. Freise (ed.), *Die Vita sancti Liudgeri: Vollständige Faksimile-Ausgabe der Handschrift Ms. Theol. lat. fol. 323 der Staatsbibliothek Berlin – Preußischer Kulturbesitz. Text, Übersetzung und Kommentar, Forschungsbeiträge* (Graz: Akadem. Druck- und Verlagsanstalt, 1999)

Godman, Jarnut, and Johanek, *Am Vorabend*	P. Godman, J. Jarnut and P. Johanek (eds.), *Am Vorabend der Kaiserkrönung: das Epos "Karolus Magnus et Leo papa" und der Papstbesuch in Paderborn 799* (Berlin: Akademie, 2002)
Green and Siegmund, *Saxons*	D. H. Green and F. Siegmund (eds.), *The Continental Saxons from the Migration Period to the Tenth Century: An Ethnographic Perspective* (Studies in Historical Archaeoethnology 6) (Woodbridge: Boydell, 2003)
GSNF	Germania Sacra Neue Folge
Hässler, Jarnut, and Wemhoff, *Sachsen*	H. J. Hässler, J. Jarnut and M. Wemhoff (eds.), *Sachsen und Franken in Westfalen: zur Komplexität der ethnischen Deutung und Abgrenzung zweier frühmittelalterlicher Stämme* (Studien zur Sachsenforschung 12) (Oldenburg: Isensee, 1999)
Lintzel, *Schriften*	M. Lintzel (ed.), *Ausgewählte Schriften*, 2 vols. (Berlin: Akademie, 1961)
MGH	*Monumenta Germaniae Historica*
NJ	*Niedersächsisches Jahrbuch für Landesgeschichte*
Poet.	*Poetae Latini medii aevi*
Settimane	Settimane di Studio del Centro italiano di studi sull' alto medioevo
SRG	*Scriptores rerum Germanicarum in usum scholarum separatim editi*
SRG NS	*Scriptores rerum Germanicarum, Nova series*
SRM	*Scriptores rerum Merovingicarum*
SS	*Scriptores (in Folio)*
Stiegemann and Wemhoff, *799*	C. Stiegemann and M. Wemhoff (eds.), *799: Kunst und Kultur der Karolingerzeit. Karl der Grosse und Papst Leo III. in Paderborn: Katalog der Ausstellung, Paderborn 1999*, 3 vols. (Mainz: von Zabern, 1999)
SzGS	Studien zur Germania Sacra
WZ	*Westfälische Zeitschrift*
ZfG	*Zeitschrift für Geschichtswissenschaft*

INTRODUCTION

This war, which had been drawn out over so many years, was concluded on the condition – proposed by the king, and accepted by the Saxons – that they, having cast aside demonic worship and abandoned the ceremonies of their fathers, were to receive the sacraments of Christian faith and religion, and then, having been united to the Franks, to become one people (*populus*) with them.[1]

So wrote Einhard in his *Life of Charlemagne*.[2] The Saxon conquest had concluded in 804, following thirty-three years of intermittent conflict. It had already been memorialized and endowed with unique prominence in the Carolingian annalistic tradition, most notably in the *Royal Frankish Annals* and their revision. Even Einhard, writing with the benefit of hindsight, explicitly marked out the conquest of Saxony as the most important war which Charlemagne ever fought.[3] The extraordinary attention paid to Saxony in those years of protracted campaigning did not last; rather, Saxony fell off the map after 804. The main-line Carolingian historiographical texts are silent about its subsequent history. Interest was piqued by the *Stellinga* revolt in the mid-ninth century, but then, equally swiftly, it fades away once more.[4] Not until the rise of the Ottonians did interest in contemporary Saxon history resurface.

Widukind of Corvey, the great historical writer of the mid-tenth century, gives only the following:

---

[1] Einhard, *Vita Karoli Magni*, ed. O. Holder-Egger, *MGH SRG* 25 (Hanover: Hahn, 1911), c. 7, p. 10: 'Eaque conditione a rege proposita et ab illis suscepta tractum per tot annos bellum constat esse finitum, ut, abiecto daemonum cultu et relictis patriis caerimoniis, Christianae fidei atque religionis sacramenta susciperent et Francis adunati unus cum eis populus efficerentur.'
[2] For the dating of this work, see below, pp. 13–14.
[3] Einhard, *Vita Karoli Magni*, ed. Holder-Egger, c. 13, p. 15.
[4] For a similar point, see H. Röckelein, *Reliquientranslationen nach Sachsen im 9. Jahrhundert: über Kommunikation, Mobilität und Öffentlichkeit im Frühmittelalter* (Beihefte der Francia 48) (Sigmaringen: J. Thorbecke, 2002), p. 24.

Just as Charlemagne was the most powerful of kings, so too was he vigilant with no less wisdom. Certainly, because he was more prudent than all other mortals in his time, he decided that it was not right for a neighbouring, noble people to be held back in empty error; he strove in every way, that they might be led to the true path. He compelled them first by pleasant persuasions, then by the fury of wars, and eventually in the thirtieth year of his empire – indeed, he, formerly a king, was made an emperor – he prevailed in that which he had spent so many years to achieve: so that those who were formerly friends and allies of the Franks were made brothers as if one people (*gens*) in the Christian faith, just as we see them now.

The last of the Carolingians who ruled the Eastern Franks was Louis, of Arnulf, the nephew of Charles [the Fat], the great-grandfather of King Lothar ... As King Louis did not have a son, all the people of the Franks and Saxons sought to place the royal crown upon Otto.[5]

Without a single nod to the ninth century, Widukind thus jumped straight from Carolingian conquest to Ottonian ascendancy, leaving a gaping lacuna. Much historiography on the subject has done exactly the same: while there is abundant scholarship on the conquest of Saxony and on the Ottonians (and on their forebears, the Liudolfinger family), the intervening period is often overlooked.

It is difficult to see how a narrative as expedited as that of Widukind can be justified. There are ample signs that this intervening period was one of profound transformation. The Saxony we glimpse before the conquest period is an entirely different entity from that which crops up in Ottonian historiography. Pre-conquest Saxony appears to have lacked any unity as a region, either in terms of politics, religion, ethnicity or material culture; even its borders were ill-defined.[6] Its inhabitants practised 'paganism', and, despite earlier missionary efforts, the institutional structures of Christianity, that is, churches, monasteries and bishoprics,

---

[5] Widukind of Corvey, *Res Gestae Saxonicae*, eds. P. Hirsch and H. E. Lohmann, *MGH SRG* 60 (Hanover: Hahn, 1935), I:15–16, pp. 25–6: 'Magnus vero Karolus cum esset regum fortissimus, non minori sapientia vigilabat. Enimvero considerabat, quia suis temporibus omni mortali prudentior erat, finitimam gentem nobilemque vano errore retineri non oportere; modis omnibus satagebat, quatinus ad veram viam duceretur. Et nunc blanda suasione, nunc bellorum inpetu ad id cogebat, tandemque tricesimo imperii sui anno obtinuit – imperator quippe ex rege creatus est – , quod multis temporibus elaborando non defecit: ob id qui olim socii et amici erant Francorum, iam fratres et quasi una gens ex Christiana fide, veluti modo videmus, facta est. Ultimus vero Karolorum apud orientales Francos imperantium Hluthowicus ex Arnulfo fratruele Karoli, huius Lotharii regis proavi, natus erat . . . . Regi autem Hluthowico non erat filius, omnisque populus Francorum atque Saxonum quarebat Oddoni diadema imponere regni.' For this passage, see also M. Becher, *Rex, Dux und Gens: Untersuchungen zur Entstehung des sächsischen Herzogtums im 9. und 10. Jahrhundert* (Historische Studien 444) (Husum: Matthiesen, 1996), pp. 43–4.

[6] For this, see above all M. Springer, 'Location in space and time' in Green and Siegmund, *Saxons*, pp. 11–36; M. Springer, *Die Sachsen* (Stuttgart: W. Kohlhammer, 2004), pp. 131–52.

were entirely absent.[7] There was little social stratification, and the entire region was economically underdeveloped.[8] This is not the picture we see emerging from Ottonian Saxony, which functioned as a fully Christian polity and boasted a clearly defined elite and expanding economy, and whose dynasty would come to constitute the clearest successor to the Carolingians that tenth-century Europe could offer.[9] These developments may have been set in motion by the conquest, but they were crucially built upon and consolidated in the succeeding period.

A long-term perspective, therefore, is instructive: it informs us that major political, cultural and socio-economic processes had occurred in ninth-century Saxony. At the same time, however, such a perspective must not be allowed to slip into teleology: foreknowledge of the end-point of these developments should not direct research into this intervening period. Ninth-century Saxony was not simply a preamble to Ottonian ascendancy. To approach Carolingian Saxony primarily as a precursor to the Ottonian state is to privilege the political above the religious, the emergence of a dynasty above a wide-scale religious reorientation. The Christianization of the region was arguably the greatest realignment of early medieval Saxon history, and has the signal benefit of surprisingly extensive documentation in the extant source material. Nevertheless, the Christianization of Saxony has yet to be studied *in toto*: while excellent recent studies have addressed parts of this process, whether thematically or in specific localities, a large-scale assessment of this important development has not been forthcoming. This book attempts to fill this lacuna through a systematic study of politics, society and Christianization in Carolingian Saxony.

In its progression from an undeveloped, pagan and hitherto disunified territory to a Christian region of the Carolingian polity, Saxony represents an important test case for the nature of Christianization and Christian reform in the early medieval world. In spite of a growing consensus on the decentralized and regionalized nature of early medieval governance, these processes continue to be approached as operating in a

---

[7] On the difficulties in using 'paganism' to denote religious observance, see below, pp. 190–1.

[8] See, for example, the comments of S. Epperlein, 'Sachsen im frühen Mittelalter: Diskussionsbeitrag zur Sozialstruktur Sachsens im 9. Jahrhundert und seiner politischen Stellung im frühen Mittelalter', *Jahrbuch für Wirtschaftsgeschichte*, 7(1) (1966), 189–212; F. Siegmund, 'Social relations among the Old Saxons' in Green and Siegmund, *Saxons*, pp. 77–111; H. Steuer, 'The beginnings of urban economies among the Saxons' in Green and Siegmund, *Saxons*, pp. 159–92; R. Wenskus, 'Die ständische Entwicklung in Sachsen im Gefolge der fränkischen Eroberung' in *Angli e Sassoni al di qua e al di là del mare: 26 aprile-10 maggio 1984* (Settimane 32:2) (Spoleto: Il Centro, 1986), pp. 587–616.

[9] For outline treatments of Ottonian Saxony, see especially K. Leyser, *Rule and Conflict in an Early Medieval Society: Ottonian Saxony* (London: Arnold, 1979); K. Leyser, *Medieval Germany and Its Neighbours, 900–1250* (London: Hambledon, 1982).

top-down manner. This is especially the case in Saxony, where the process of Christianization, which began with forced wartime conversions, has been viewed as a foreign, even colonial, imposition. According to this perspective, it was left to Carolingian kings and outside missionaries to convert a recalcitrant populace who assumed, at best, a lukewarm Christianity patterned by 'pagan' elements. Yet in contrast to previous views, this book argues that the brutality of the Saxon wars did not preclude acceptance of Christianity and Carolingian rule. With a fresh reading of a wide range of Latin and Old Saxon sources, it explores the manner in which Saxony was incorporated into the Carolingian political order and the Christian *ecclesia*. What implications did Carolingian rule have for the exercise of power within Saxony? To what and to whom can the development of a Christian landscape in Saxony be attributed? How did communities in Saxony make sense of their past and present? Carolingian Saxony provides a case study of social transformation. The nature of this transformation, and how successfully it was achieved, has important implications for how we view governance, the institutional church and Christian communities in the early Middle Ages.

THE SAXONS AND SAXONY BEFORE CONQUEST

Before turning to Carolingian Saxony, however, it may be helpful to give a general overview of pre-conquest Saxon history, and likewise of the terms 'Saxon' and 'Saxony' themselves. Here, it important to note that there is no evidence of any internal 'Saxon' coherence prior to the conquest, whether in terms of politics, ethnicity, religion, law or material culture. Borders were ill-defined, and contacts with neighbouring territories, and especially with Francia and Frisia, were extensive.[10] In what follows, then, 'Saxony' and 'Saxon' will be employed, following contemporary Carolingian usage, as terms of convenience to refer to the region conquered by Charlemagne and to the inhabitants of that region respectively. The extent to which 'Saxon' as a term meaningfully represents the self-identification of those who lived in this region is, at least at the beginning of this period, questionable; therefore it is used here principally as a useful term of art.[11]

---

[10] For connections to Frisia, see below, pp. 42–4, 189; see also J. T. Palmer, 'Beyond Frankish authority: Frisia and Saxony between the Anglo-Saxons and Carolingians' in H. Sauer and J. Story (eds.), *Anglo-Saxon England and the Continent* (Essays in Anglo-Saxon Studies 3) (Tempe: Arizona Center for Medieval and Renaissance Studies, 2011), pp. 139–62; I. N. Wood, 'Beyond satraps and ostriches: political and social structures of the Saxons in the early Carolingian period' in Green and Siegmund, *Saxons*, pp. 271–97, here p. 281.

[11] See here especially the helpful comments of Röckelein, *Reliquientranslationen nach Sachsen*, pp. 19–23.

As is often the case with ethnonyms, the term 'Saxon' was used to refer to a diverse range of peoples, including, but not limited to, the continental Saxons in Saxony, the (Anglo-)Saxons in Britain and other itinerant groups of Saxons, often pirates, in Gaul and Italy.[12] The term, then, was not specific to those who lived in Saxony; correspondingly, those who lived in the region of Saxony often appear to have had other, more local forms of identity. The most important of these, at least in the late eighth century, were the groups known as the Westphalians, Eastphalians and Angarians. These groups formed political units with leaders, had their own distinctive legal traditions and corresponded to geographic areas within 'Saxony'. They do not, however, appear to have been stable configurations; Matthias Becher in particular has argued that these confederations first appear in late eighth-century sources, and may be the result of Frankish warfare.[13] Nor were they the only groups in Saxony: further afield were the inhabitants of the Bardengau (the region around present-day Bardowick, near the eastern frontier) and the Nordliudi (literally, the 'northern people'), among others.[14] The term 'Saxon' comprehended all of these diverse peoples in Frankish sources; whether those labelled as Saxons prior to the conquest would have identified themselves as such remains far from certain.

If 'the Saxons' are elusive, so too is 'Saxony'; descriptions of the region are few and far between. In terms of physical geography, Saxony encompassed a large section of modern-day northwestern Germany; it corresponded roughly to the German federal state of Lower Saxony (Niedersachsen), with significant portions of North Rhine-Westphalia (Nordrhein-Westfalen), Schleswig-Holstein and Saxony-Anhalt (Sachsen-Anhalt) thrown in (notably, it did not stretch to modern-day Saxony in northeastern Germany). It extended west almost as far as the Rhine and east beyond the Elbe; it was traversed internally by the Ems, the Weser, the Aller and the Lippe rivers, alongside smaller tributaries. In the south, the Teutoburg Forest and Harz Mountains served as a natural

---

[12] For this point, see especially Springer, 'Location in space and time', pp. 11–20; see also R. Flierman, *Saxon Identities, AD 150–900* (London: Bloomsbury Academic, 2017), pp. 32–6, 63–73; Springer, *Die Sachsen*, pp. 47–56, 100–11.

[13] M. Becher, '*Non enim habent regem idem Antiqui Saxones* ... Verfassung und Ethnogenese in Sachsen während des 8. Jahrhunderts' in Hässler, Jarnut and Wemhoff, *Sachsen*, pp. 1–31; see also M. Becher, 'Die Sachsen im 7. und 8. Jahrhundert: Verfassung und Ethnogenese' in Stiegemann and Wemhoff, *799*, vol. I: pp. 188–94, here pp. 190–2; Flierman, *Saxon Identities*, p. 98; Wood, 'Beyond satraps and ostriches', p. 276; see also J. T. Palmer, 'Anskar's imagined communities' in H. Antonsson and I. H. Garipzanov (eds.), *Saints and Their Lives on the Periphery* (Cursor mundi 9) (Turnhout: Brepols, 2010), pp. 171–88, here pp. 173–4.

[14] For these, and other peoples, see Becher, 'Die Sachsen im 7. und 8. Jahrhundert', p. 192; Wood, 'Beyond satraps and ostriches', p. 276.

border; further north, the terrain flattened out, giving way to the Lüneburg Heath.

In the Carolingian world, governance was exercised over peoples, as opposed to territories; accordingly, references to 'the Saxons' outnumber those to 'Saxony' by no small margin. Even on the rare occasions when contemporaries described 'Saxony' as a physical territory, they did so through recourse to ethnography: take, for example, the following description from the mid-ninth century work known as the *Translation of Saint Alexander*, which delineates the borders of the Saxons as follows:

To the south they have the Franks and part of the Thuringians ... and the channel of the Unstrut River. To the north however they have the Northmen, the most ferocious peoples. To the east there are the Abodrites, and to the west the Frisians, from whom they have protected their borders without intermission, whether by treaty or ultimately by war.[15]

Likewise within Saxony, territory appears to have been defined by human geography: thus the Eastphalians, Westphalians and Angarians lived in Eastphalia, Westphalia and Engern respectively.[16] To contemporary observers, Saxony was simply where the Saxons lived.

The Saxons and the Franks had a history of contact long before the Saxon wars of Charlemagne.[17] In fact, in the absence of writing in pre-conquest Saxony, it is precisely through these contacts that early Saxon history can be best delineated. As early as the sixth century, there is evidence for a high degree of interaction between Franks and Saxons, as recorded in a variety of sources; Fredegar depicts the Saxons as a subject people, illustrated most poignantly by their annual tribute of 500 cows offered first to the Merovingian king Clothar I (d. 561) in circa 555–557, and then to his successors up until the reign of King Dagobert (d. 639).[18]

---

[15] Rudolf and Meginhard, *Translatio sancti Alexandri*, ed. G. H. Pertz, *MGH SS* 2 (Hanover: Hahn, 1829), c. 1, p. 675: 'A meridie quidem Francos habentes et partem Thuringorum ... et alveo fluminis Unstrotae dirimuntur. A septentrione vero Nordmannos, gentes ferocissimas. Ab ortu autem solis Obodritos, et ab occasu Frisos, a quibus sine intermissione vel foedere vel concertatione necessario finium suorum spacia tuebantur.' Röckelein, *Reliquientranslationen nach Sachsen*, pp. 19–20; see also the excellent discussion of L. Leleu, 'Les sources saxones et la spatialisation du pouvoir en Saxe, IXe-XIe siècles. Première résultats', *Territorium* (2012), 1–39. See further C. Ehlers, *Die Integration Sachsens in das fränkische Reich (751–1024)* (Veröffentlichungen des Max-Planck-Instituts für Geschichte 231) (Göttingen: Vandenhoeck & Ruprecht, 2007), pp. 43–4.

[16] Cf. Springer, *Die Sachsen*, pp. 250–4.

[17] For this, see especially Flierman, *Saxon Identities*, pp. 53–87.

[18] Fredegar, *Chronicon*, ed. J. M. Wallace-Hadrill, *The Fourth Book of the Chronicle of Fredegar with Its Continuations* (London: Nelson, 1960), IV:74, pp. 62–3; cf. *Fredegarii continuationes* in *Ibid*, c. 31, p. 101; Gregory of Tours, *Libri Historiarum X*, eds. B. Krush and W. Levison, *MGH SRM* 1:1 (Hanover: Hahn, 1951), IV:14, pp. 145–7. See also Flierman, *Saxon Identities*, p. 77; Springer, *Die Sachsen*, pp. 97–9.

When the Pippinids (or early Carolingians) enter the scene in the late seventh century, they appear to have been in the process of reducing the Saxons to a similar tributary position. In 688 the *Earlier Annals of Metz* report how Pippin of Herstal, 'having worn down the Suaves and Bavarians and Saxons by frequent attacks and numerous battles, henceforth made them subject them to his power'.[19] A later entry in the annals, comprising a 'career retrospective' of sorts, celebrates Pippin's renewed subjugation of previously subject peoples including, but by no means limited to, the Saxons.[20]

At around the same time, in the closing years of the seventh century, two Anglo-Saxon missionaries, the two Ewalds (known as 'the Black' and 'the White' respectively, on account of their hair colour), ventured into Saxony; the account of their martyrdom is recorded by their near-contemporary and fellow countryman, Bede. As Bede wrote in his *Ecclesiastical History* (completed in 731), when the two missionaries arrived in Saxony,

they entered the lodging of a certain steward, and asked him to direct them to the satrap who was over him, for they had an embassy and a useful message to announce to him. For the Old Saxons did not have a king, but rather many satraps were placed above their people, who, in the event of war, cast lots equitably. In wartime they all follow and obey the leader to whom the lot falls; once the war is completed, they all become satraps of equal power again. Accordingly the steward received them and promised to direct them to the satrap who was over him, as they had asked, but he delayed them for several days.[21]

From here, the story took a downward turn. The 'barbarians' feared lest the missionaries succeed in their object, and so accordingly they took matters into their own hands: they killed the missionaries before they had an opportunity to speak to the satrap, an action which ultimately brought down the satrap's vengeance upon themselves.[22] The missionaries' tragic

---

[19] *Annales Mettenses priores*, ed. B. Simpson, *MGH SRG* 10 (Hanover: Hahn, 1905), 688, p. 4: 'Hinc Suavos et Baiowarios et Saxones crebris irruptionibus frequentibusque preliis contritos sue ditioni subiugavit.'

[20] *Ibid*, 691, p. 12; cf. Springer, *Die Sachsen*, pp. 166–7.

[21] Bede, *Historica Ecclesiastica*, ed. C. Plummer, *Venerabilis Baedae opera historica*, 2 vols. (Oxford: Clarendon, 1896), vol. I, V:10, pp. 299–300: 'intrauerunt hospitium cuiusdam uilici, petieruntque ab eo, ut transmitterentur ad satrapam, qui super eum erat, eo quod haberent aliquid legationis et causae utilis, quod deberent ad illum perferre. Non enim habent regem idem Antiqui Saxones, sed satrapas plurimos suae genti praepositos, qui ingruente belli articulo mittunt aequaliter sortes, et, quemcumque sors ostenderit, hunc tempore belli ducem omnes sequuntur, huic obtemperant; peracto autem bello, rursum aequalis potentiae omnes fiunt satrapae. Suscepit ergo eos uilicus, et promittens se mittere eos ad satrapam, qui super se erat, ut petebant, aliquot diebus secum retinuit'. See also below, pp. 135–7.

[22] Cf. I. N. Wood, 'Pagans and holy men, 600–800' in P. N. Chatháin and M. Richter (eds.), *Irland und die Christenheit* (Stuttgart: Klett-Cotta, 1987), pp. 347–61, here p. 352.

fates aside, this episode gives us our first, and only contemporary, glimpse into internal conditions in pre-conquest Saxony. Admittedly, Bede's choice of vocabulary for Saxon leaders, 'satraps', was plucked from descriptions of the Philistines in the Book of Samuel, which may be seen in itself as an implicit moral judgement of the Saxons.[23] All the same, his account captures the political disunity that would be a feature of Saxon affairs well into the eighth century, as well as the potential for effective coordination between different Saxon groups.[24] It acts moreover as a welcome intermission from the main body of evidence for pre-conquest Saxony, namely the annalistic sources, which, in addition to focusing overwhelmingly on Frankish-Saxon military relations, are non-contemporary and hence tinged with the retrospective glow of Carolingian ascendancy.

The Saxons next entered the stage in 715, when, presumably in response to the death of Pippin of Herstal in the previous year, they seized the opportunity to raid the lands of the Chatuarian Franks.[25] In 718, Charles Martel, having emerged against the odds as Pippin's successor, responded in kind: the *Earlier Annals of Metz* recount how 'he devastated Saxony with a great blow, and came as far as the Weser River, and having subjugated the entire region, he returned home a victor'.[26] Further campaigns under Charles' leadership followed in 720, 724, 728, 729 and 738.[27] Many of these endeavours are only recorded in terse entries, such as 'Charles in Saxony', but more detail is given in a couple

---

[23] I Samuel 5:11, 6:16; see also Becher, 'Die Sachsen im 7. und 8. Jahrhundert', p. 189; Becher, '*Non enim habent regem*', pp. 9–11; Flierman, *Saxon Identities*, pp. 94-7; Wood, 'Beyond satraps and ostriches', pp. 272–3.

[24] Springer, *Die Sachsen*, pp. 131–4.

[25] *Annales Mettenses priores,* ed. Simpson, 715, p. 21; *Annales Petaviani*, ed. G. H. Pertz, *MGH SS* I (Hanover: Hahn, 1826), 715, p. 7; *Annales Tiliani*, ed. G. H. Pertz, *MGH SS* I (Hanover: Hahn, 1826), 715, p. 6; *Annales sancti Amandi*, ed. G. H. Pertz, *MGH SS* I (Hanover: Hahn, 1826), 715, p. 6.

[26] *Annales Mettenses priores,* ed. Simpson, 718, p. 26: 'vastavit Saxoniam plaga magna et pervenit usque ad Viseram fluvium. Omnique illa regione subacta ad propria victor revertitur'. See also *Annales Alamannici*, ed. G. H. Pertz, *MGH SS* I (Hanover: Hahn, 1826), 718, p. 24; *Annales Laureshamenses*, ed. G. H. Pertz, *MGH SS* I (Hanover: Hahn, 1826), 718, p. 24; *Annales Mosellani*, ed. J. M. Lappenberg, *MGH SS* 16 (Hanover: Hahn, 1859), 718, p. 494; *Annales Nazariani*, ed. G. H. Pertz, *MGH SS* I (Hanover: Hahn, 1826), 718, p. 25; *Annales Petaviani*, ed. Pertz, 718, p. 7; *Annales sancti Amandi*, ed. Pertz, 718, p. 6; *Annales Sangallenses maiores*, ed. I. ab Arx, *MGH SS* I (Hanover, 1826), 718, p. 73; *Annales Tiliani*, ed. Pertz, 718, p. 6.

[27] *Annales Alamannici*, ed. Pertz, 720, 738, pp. 24, 26; *Annales Laubacenses*, ed. G. H. Pertz, *MGH SS* I (Hanover: Hahn, 1826), 720, p. 7; *Annales Laureshamenses*, ed. Pertz, 720, 738, pp. 24, 26; *Annales Mettenses priores*, ed. Simpson, 738, p. 30; *Annales Mosellani*, ed. Lappenberg, 720, 738, pp. 494–5; *Annales Nazariani*, ed. Pertz, 720, 738, pp. 25, 27; *Annales Petaviani*, ed. Pertz, 720, 728, 729, 738, pp. 7, 9; *Annales sancti Amandi*, ed. Pertz, 720, p. 6; *Annales Sangallenses maiores*, ed. ab Arx, 720, 738, pp. 73–4; *Annales Tiliani*, ed. Pertz, 720, 729, pp. 6, 8; *Fredegarii continuationes*, ed. Wallace-Hadrill, cc. 11, 19, pp. 90, 93. A further campaign in 736 campaign is attested in the

of sources. Take, for instance, the description of Charles' 724 campaign in the *Continuations of Fredegar*, which report how 'in that time the Saxons rebelled, and prince Charles attacked and vanquished them and returned home a victor'.[28] Later, in 738, the annalist provided even more detail:

The most pagan Saxons who live beyond the Rhine River rebelled again, and the vigorous man Charles, together with the Frankish host, crossed the Rhine at the place where it meets the Lippe River with a clear purpose. He laid waste the greater part of that region with very terrible slaughter, ordered that most savage people to be tributary, and accepted many hostages from them; thus, with the Lord's favour, he returned home a victor.[29]

The characterization of 'rebellion' in these reports is telling: from the vantage point of Fredegar's Continuator, writing between 768 and 786, the Saxons were perceived to have had an enduring political relationship with, and a subordinate position to, their Frankish neighbours.[30] The religious language ('most pagan', 'with the Lord's favour') in this report is also worthy of note, although it may be more indicative of priorities in the period in which it was written than of those in the period it purportedly describes.

Charles Martel died in 741. He was succeeded in his role as mayor of the palace by his sons, Pippin and Carloman, whose early rule was marked by the same separatist tendencies which Charles had himself confronted. Once again, the Saxons took advantage of the power vacuum following Charles' death. They rebelled in concert with Theudebald of Alemannia and other peoples in 741; in 743, Saxons are further attested fighting the Franks under the leadership of Duke Odilo of Bavaria.[31] In both cases, loose alliances between Saxons and other anti-Pippinid factions should be envisaged. Later in 743, and possibly as a result of Saxon participation in earlier revolts, Carloman undertook his first campaign against the Saxons; he negotiated the surrender of the

---

Earlier Annals of Metz, but this section of the text appears to be dependent upon the *Continuations of Fredegar* for 738 and is thus likely misdated. See also Flierman, *Saxon Identities*, p. 84.

[28] *Fredegarii continuationes*, ed. Wallace-Hadrill, c. 11, p. 90: 'Per idem tempus rebellantibus Saxonis eis Carlus princeps ueniens praeoccupavit ac debellauit uictorque reuertetur.'

[29] *Ibid*, c. 19, p. 93: 'Itemque rebellantibus Saxonis paganissimis qui ultra Renum fluuium consistunt, strenuus uir Carlus hoste commoto Francorum in loco ubi Lippia fluuius Renum amnen ingreditur sagace intentione transmeauit, maxima ex parte regione illa dirissima cede uastauit, gentemque illam seuissimam ex parte tributaria esse praecepit atque quam plures hospitibus ab eis accepit; sicque opitulante Domino uictor remeauit ad propria.'

[30] For this dating, see R. McKitterick, 'The illusion of royal power in Carolingian annals', *The English Historical Review*, 115(460) (2000), 1–20, here 5–7.

[31] *Annales Guelferbytani*, ed. G. H. Pertz, MGH SS 1 (Hanover: Hahn, 1826), 741, p. 27; *Annales Mettenses priores*, ed. Simpson, 743, p. 33; see also Springer, *Die Sachsen*, pp. 169–70.

Syburg, an important fortification, along with that of its leader, the so-called 'duke' of the Saxons, Theodoric.[32] It was to be the first in a long series of campaigns: over the next fifteen years, no fewer than ten campaigns were recorded, first under Carloman's own leadership and then, after his withdrawal into a monastery in 747, under that of his brother Pippin.

Near-annual campaigning in Saxony was thus a feature of Frankish politics long before 'the' Saxon wars of Charlemagne. Indeed, despite differences in the evidential base (the Saxon wars of Charlemagne are far better recorded), there appear to have been a number of similarities between the two periods of campaigning: notably, the stress laid upon Christian conversion; the literary depiction of Saxon rebellion and perfidy; the attention paid to prominent fortresses; the taking of hostages and/or captives; and the role played by alliances (in addition to the 741 and 743 episodes, the Saxons participated in the rebellion of the Pippinid Gripho in 747–748).[33] The first of these, namely, the interest in Christian conversion, is particularly noteworthy, as this marked the start of a significant trend. Saxons are recorded receiving Christian sacraments (namely baptism) upon submission to Frankish forces in 744, 747, 748 and 753; on the last of these occasions, the *Earlier Annals of Metz* report, Saxons further swore oaths to Pippin (now king of the Franks) 'that any priests who wished to go into Saxony to preach the name of the Lord and to baptize them had license to do so'.[34] The connection between political submission and Christian conversion had been established, even if the conversions themselves appear to have

---

[32] *Annales Mettenses priores*, ed. Simpson, 743, p. 35; *Annales qui dicuntur Einhardi*, ed. F. Kurze, *MGH SRG* 6 (Hanover: Hahn, 1895), 743, p. 5; *Annales Regni Francorum*, ed. F. Kurze, *MGH SRG* 6 (Hanover: Hahn, 1895), 743, p. 4; *Annales Tiliani*, ed. Pertz, 743, p. 219; see also *Annales Alamannici*, ed. Pertz, 743, p. 26; *Annales Guelferbytani*, ed. Pertz, 743, p. 27; *Annales Nazariani*, ed. Pertz, 743, p. 27. Carloman may have led an earlier campaign against the Saxons, though this is uncertain: cf. *Annales Laureshamenses*, ed. Pertz, 742, p. 26.

[33] For the vocabulary of 'rebellion' and 'perfidy', the stress laid upon Christian religion and the taking of hostages and/or captives, see *Annales Mettenses priores*, ed. Simpson, 744, 748, 753, pp. 36, 40–1, 44; *Fredegarii continuationes*, ed. Wallace-Hadrill, cc. 27, 31, 35, pp. 99, 101, 103. For Saxon involvement in the rebellion of Gripho, see *Annales Alamannici*, ed. Pertz, 748, p. 26; *Annales Fuldenses*, ed. F. Kurze, *MGH SRG* 7 (Hanover: Hahn, 1891), 748, p. 5; *Annales Guelferbytani*, ed. Pertz, 748, p. 27; *Annales Laureshamenses*, ed. Pertz, 748, p. 26; *Annales Mettenses priores*, ed. Simpson, 748, pp. 40–1; *Annales Mosellani*, ed. Lappenberg, 748, p. 495; *Annales Nazariani*, ed. Pertz, 748, p. 27; *Annales Petaviani*, ed. Pertz, 748, p. 11; *Annales qui dicuntur Einhardi*, ed. Kurze, 747, 748, p. 7; *Annales Regni Francorum*, ed. Kurze, 747, 748, p. 6; *Annales Tiliani*, ed. Pertz, 747, p. 219.

[34] *Annales Mettenses priores*, ed. Simpson, 748, 753, pp. 41, 44: 'ut quicumque de sacerdotibus in Saxoniam ire voluisset ad predicandum nomen Domini et ad baptizandum eos licentiam habuisset'; *Fredegarii continuationes*, ed. Wallace-Hadrill, cc. 27, 31, 35, pp. 99, 101, 103.

been transient. There is no evidence to suggest continuous Christian observance in Saxony from this period.

There was, however, an important difference between these campaigns and the Saxon wars to follow: the payment of tribute, specified at the rate of 300 horses each year, suggests a rather more modest objective in this earlier period.[35] Carloman and Pippin aimed to reduce the Saxons to the status of a subject people, but, crucially, did not intend to incorporate Saxony into the Frankish kingdom. Conquered Saxons were not expected to serve on Frankish campaigns, to take up offices, or to become loyal servants (*fideles*) of the Frankish king; rather, their obligations extended to the maintenance of peace and the payment of tribute, the latter of which served as a symbolic enactment of their status. The forced conversion of some Saxons does, of course, point towards the development of a more extensive political relationship. Yet Carloman and Pippin simply did not have Charlemagne's ambitions in this area: they were not fighting a war of conquest.

Pippin died in 768, bequeathing his kingdom and his title to his two sons, Charlemagne and Carloman; shortly thereafter, in 771, Carloman died, and Charlemagne extended his rule over a now unified Frankish kingdom. The next year Charlemagne led his first campaign into Saxony. Perhaps at this stage he was simply following in the footsteps of his father. Over the next couple of years, however, new goals emerged: the conquest, Christianization and full incorporation of Saxony into the Carolingian world.

HISTORY WITHOUT HISTORIES

I shall return to the history of the Saxon wars in Chapter 1. For now, I shall offer a brief overview of the sources available for Saxony in the conquest and the Carolingian periods, and shall further consider the possibilities afforded, and limitations imposed, by the extant material. The conquest period is undoubtedly the best-recorded thirty-odd years in pre-Ottonian Saxon history. The blossoming annalistic tradition provides a wealth of contemporary historiographical sources, which may be complemented by the slightly later perspective of Einhard's *Life of Charlemagne*; to this may further be added an array of legal sources,

---

[35] For references to the payment of tribute under Carloman and Pippin, see *Annales Fuldenses*, ed. Kurze, 758, p. 7; *Annales Mettenses priores*, ed. Simpson, 753, 758, pp. 44, 50; *Annales qui dicuntur Einhardi*, ed. Kurze, 758, p. 17; *Annales Regni Francorum*, ed. Kurze, 758, p. 16; *Annales Tiliani*, ed. Pertz, 758, p. 219. Contrast to *Fredegarii continuationes*, ed. Wallace-Hadrill, cc. 31, 35, pp. 101, 103: in c. 31, the continuator states that the same tribute offered under Clothar, consisting of 500 cows, would be paid henceforth.

charters, poems and letters. Yet this relative surfeit of documentation should not be contrasted too strongly with the subsequent period: although contemporary annals may have lost interest in Saxony, a variety of other sources can be used to illuminate the history of Carolingian Saxony.

Historiographical Sources

To begin with: the annalistic corpus. Of particular use when attempting to understand the Saxon wars are the detailed entries of the *Royal Frankish Annals* and their revised version, which cover the years 741–829 and 741–801 respectively.[36] It is generally accepted that these annals were associated with the Carolingian court in some manner, whether in their composition, compilation or dissemination.[37] Their respective dates, and stages of composition, are far more difficult to determine. I follow the arguments of Roger Collins, who posits that the entries in the *Royal Frankish Annals* for the years 741 to 788 were composed circa 790.[38] This is of great importance for understanding the narrative significance of Widukind's capitulation to Charlemagne in 785, which anticipates the triumphant conclusion of the text, that is, the submission of Tassilo in 788. This date further helps to explain the disparate rhetoric used to describe the conflicts of 772–785 and 793–804 respectively. The revised version, meanwhile, has been variously dated to circa 801, 814–817 or 829.[39] The precise date notwithstanding, one thing is clear: the reviser wrote, in contrast to the original author(s), with full knowledge of the renewed hostilities.

To these may be added a plethora of other 'minor' annals. Some of these are dependent upon the *Royal Frankish Annals* for the conquest period, notably the *Earlier Annals of Metz* and the *Tilian Annals*, though even here their emphases remain their own.[40] Other sources offer largely

---

[36] *Annales Regni Francorum*, ed. Kurze; *Annales qui dicuntur Einhardi*, ed. Kurze.

[37] See, for example, the comments of R. McKitterick, *History and Memory in the Carolingian World* (Cambridge: Cambridge University Press, 2004), pp. 20–2, 101–2.

[38] See especially R. Collins, 'The "reviser" revisited: another look at the alternative version of the *Annales Regni Francorum*' in A. C. Murray (ed.), *After Rome's Fall: Narrators and Sources of Early Medieval History: Essays Presented to Walter Goffart* (Toronto: University of Toronto Press, 1998), pp. 191–213, here pp. 193–4, 197, 213; see further M. Becher, *Eid und Herrschaft: Untersuchungen zum Herrscherethos Karls des Großen* (Vorträge und Herrschaft 39) (Sigmaringen: J. Thorbecke, 1993), pp. 74–7; R. McKitterick, *Charlemagne: The Formation of a European Identity* (Cambridge: Cambridge University Press, 2008), pp. 38–9, 48.

[39] For comments on this text's dating, see Collins, 'The "reviser" revisited', pp. 197–213; McKitterick, *Charlemagne*, p. 27.

[40] *Annales Mettenses priores*, ed. Simpson; *Annales Tiliani*, ed. Pertz. For the *Annales Mettenses Priores*, see further Y. Hen, 'The Annals of Metz and the Merovingian past' in Y. Hen and M. Innes

independent testimony. Particularly notable in this regard are the *Lorsch Annals*, whose detailed entries cover the years 703–803.[41] The first section of the text, comprising the entries for the years 703–785, is associated with the monastery of Lorsch; these entries bear marked similarities to other annalistic compilations, notably the *Moselle Annals*, a source dependent on the *Lorsch Annals*.[42] The second and final section is associated with the abbey of Reichenau, and is thought to have been written up in a near-contemporary fashion, although the precise mechanics of this are still disputed.[43] Other annals, or groups of annals, which offer independent accounts of the conquest period include the *Petavian Annals*; the *Annals of Saint Amand* and the associated *Laubach Annals*; the *Annals of Baluze of Saint Gall*; and the *Alemannic Annals* and an array of associated texts, comprising the *Wolfenbüttel Annals, Annals of Saint Nazarius, Reichenau Annals, Brief Annals of Saint Gall,* and *Greater Annals of Saint Gall*.[44] Although the precise dating and localization of these works, not to mention their precise relationships to each other, are difficult to establish, many of these works appear to date to the late eighth or early ninth century; at the very least, they draw on authentic early material. These 'minor' annals provide important counterpoints to those expressed in the *Royal Frankish Annals* and their revision.

These annals form the main narrative for the Saxon war; to them may be added the perspective afforded by Einhard's *Life of Charlemagne*, a work variously dated within the period circa 817–829.[45] Precisely when it is dated within this span has a bearing on its interpretation. Traditionally, the work has been dated to circa 829, that is, to the time of the first palace rebellion, and has been read as a coded critique of Louis the Pious' rule; more recently, Matthew Innes and Rosamond McKitterick

(eds.), *The Uses of the Past in the Early Middle Ages* (Cambridge: Cambridge University Press, 2000), pp. 175–90, here especially pp. 175–6; McKitterick, *History and Memory*, pp. 125–6; Collins, 'The "reviser" revisited', p. 197.

[41] *Annales Laureshamenses*, ed. Pertz.

[42] *Annales Mosellani*, ed. Lappenberg; see also R. Collins, 'Charlemagne's imperial coronation and the Annals of Lorsch' in J. Story (ed.), *Charlemagne: Empire and Society* (Manchester: Manchester University Press, 2005), pp. 52–70, here pp. 56–8.

[43] Collins, 'Charlemagne's imperial coronation', pp. 59–64; McKitterick, *History and Memory*, pp. 105–10.

[44] *Annales Petaviani*, ed. Pertz, pp. 15–18; *Annales sancti Amandi*, ed. Pertz, pp. 12, 14; *Annales Laubacenses*, ed. Pertz, pp. 12, 15; *Annales Sangallenses Baluzii*, ed. G. H. Pertz, *MGH SS* I (Hanover: Hahn, 1826), p. 63; *Annales Alamannici*, ed. Pertz, pp. 40–4, 47–8; *Annales Guelferbytani*, ed. Pertz, pp. 40–5; *Annales Nazariani*, ed. Pertz, pp. 40–4; *Annales Augienses*, ed. G. H. Pertz, *MGH SS* I (Hanover: Hahn, 1826), p. 67; *Annales Sangallenses breves*, eds. G. H. Pertz and I. ab Arx, *MGH SS* I (Hanover: Hahn, 1826), pp. 64–5; *Annales Sangallenses maiores*, ed. ab Arx, pp. 74–5. For an assessment of these texts, see further J. R. Davis, *Charlemagne's Practice of Empire* (Cambridge: Cambridge University Press, 2015), pp. 179–205.

[45] Einhard, *Vita Karoli Magni*, ed. Holder-Egger.

associated its composition with the promulgation of the *Ordinatio imperii* in 817, and suggest that it may be understood as legitimizing the new emperor's rule.[46] In either case, it was a unitary composition written with the benefit of hindsight, and therefore is in the position to discuss the wars as a unified whole, unlike many of the annals, whose constituent parts reflect different authors writing in different periods.

Following the conclusion of the Saxon war, the narrative source base dries up. An exception is the *Stellinga*, a popular movement which proved to be influential in the civil war following the death of Louis the Pious, discussed in Chapter 2, which is recorded in four contemporary sources: Nithard's *Histories*, a work commissioned by the West Frankish King Charles the Bald; the *Annals of Saint Bertin*, a set of annals composed by a certain Prudentius, soon-to-be bishop of Troyes (843/844–861), who likewise supported Charles the Bald; the *Fulda Annals*, which is largely accepted as the work of Rudolf of Fulda; and finally, the *Xanten Annals*, a work which may be attributed to Gerward of Lorsch. It should be noted that these last three texts were compilations, and the authors named were only responsible for a section of these larger works.[47] All of these works are assumed to have been written within a few years of the events in question. Otherwise, there is little, if any, discussion of contemporary Saxon affairs in Frankish historiographical works. Save for summary notices of Saxon troops serving alongside Frankish forces and a few chance entries in the *Fulda Annals* and the *Xanten Annals* marking the deaths of bishops, noting a famine in the region, and once, more entertainingly, detailing the escapades of two renegade priests, Saxony largely disappears from the Frankish narrative record.

[46] See here especially, among other contributions, M. Innes and R. McKitterick, 'The writing of history' in R. McKitterick (ed.), *Carolingian Culture: Emulation and Innovation* (Cambridge: Cambridge University Press, 1994), pp. 193–220, here pp. 203–8; McKitterick, *Charlemagne*, pp. 11–14; McKitterick, *History and Memory*, pp. 29–30; contrast to F. L. Ganshof, *The Carolingians and the Frankish Monarchy* (London: Longman, 1971), p. 4; K. H. Krüger, 'Neue Beobachtungen zur Datierung von Einhards Karlsvita', *Frühmittelalterliche Studien*, 32 (1998), 124–45; H. Löwe, 'Die Entstehungszeit der *Vita Karoli* Einhards', *DA*, 39 (1983), 85–103; S. Patzold, 'Einhards erste Leser: zu Kontext und Darstellungsabsicht der "Vita Karoli"', *Viator multilingual* 42 (2011), 33–55.

[47] Nithard, *Historiae*, eds. P. Lauer and S. Glansdorff, *Histoire des fils de Louis le Pieux* (Les classiques de l'histoire au Moyen Âge 51) (Paris: Les Belles Lettres, 2012); *Annales Bertiniani*, eds. F. Grat, J. Vielliard and S. Clémencet, *Annales de Saint-Bertin* (Paris: C. Klincksieck, 1964); *Annales Fuldenses*, ed. Kurze; *Annales Xantenses*, ed. B. Simpson, *MGH SRG* 12 (Hanover: Hahn, 1909). For Nithard's histories, see especially J. L. Nelson, 'Public and private history in the work of Nithard', *Speculum*, 60(2) (1985), 251–93; see further S. Airlie, 'The world, the text and the Carolingian: royal, aristocratic and masculine identities in Nithard's *Histories*' in P. Wormald and J. L. Nelson (eds.), *Lay Intellectuals in the Carolingian World* (Cambridge: Cambridge University Press, 2007), pp. 51–76. For the *Annales Xantenses*, see H. Löwe, 'Studien zu den Annales Xantenses', *DA*, 8 (1951), 59–99.

There are only two 'historiographical' Saxon texts from this period: the *Corvey Annals*, whose entries throughout this period are exceedingly brief, and, somewhat more helpfully, the so-called Saxon Poet's *Deeds of the Emperor Charlemagne*, a nearly 6,000-line versified epic written in the early 890s which can be localized, as I have argued elsewhere, to the bishopric of Paderborn.[48] Although the content of this latter work is dependent upon earlier sources, notably the revised version of the *Royal Frankish Annals*, Einhard's *Life of Charlemagne* and an unidentified set of minor annals, it nonetheless offers a window onto the context in which it was written, and particularly onto an ongoing tithe dispute.

There are later historiographical works which are of some relevance, however limited, to this period. Some insights may be gleaned from the mid-tenth century *Deeds of the Saxons* of Widukind of Corvey, while Adam of Bremen's late eleventh-century history, *Deeds of the Archbishops of the Church of Hamburg*, contains certain choice details of interest.[49] Yet by and large, contemporary and near-contemporary historiographical perspectives on late-eighth and ninth-century Saxon history are provided by hostile Frankish sources, which concentrate solely on two segments of Saxon history, the Saxon wars and the *Stellinga*, to the exclusion of the remainder of the period.

The extant material, then, provides ample testimony as to how the Franks represented and justified the Saxon wars to other Franks. For the historian of Carolingian Saxony, however, it poses many challenges. To declare that Frankish annals present a deeply biased, distorted and negative view of the Saxons is to state the obvious. While this bias may be tempered, it may not be overcome completely, at least not during the conquest period itself: there are no contemporary Saxon perspectives. Yet in the post-conquest period, there is a variety of Saxon responses both to its recent history and to its historiographical representation. One of these, the Saxon Poet's versified history, has already been mentioned above. Further responses are to be found in a rich corpus of Saxon hagiographical texts.

---

[48] *Annales Corbeienses*, ed. J. Prinz, *Die Corveyer Annalen, Abhandlungen zur Corveyer Geschichtsschreibung 10:7* (Münster: Aschendorff, 1982); Poeta Saxo, *Annalium de gestis Caroli magni imperatoris libri V*, ed. P. Winterfeld, *MGH Poet.* 4:1 (Berlin: Weidemann, 1899). See also I. Rembold, 'The Poeta Saxo at Paderborn: episcopal authority and Carolingian rule in late ninth-century Saxony', *EME*, 21(2) (2013), 169–96; contrast with K. H. Krüger, 'Die ältern Sachsen als Franken. Zum Besuch des Kaisers Arnulf 889 im Kloster Corvey', *WZ*, 151/152 (2001/2002), 225–44.

[49] Adam of Bremen, *Gesta Hammaburgensis ecclesiae pontificum*, ed. B. Schmeidler, *MGH SRG* 2 (Hanover: Hahn, 1917); for this text, see also T. Barnwell, 'Fragmented identities: otherness and authority in Adam of Bremen's *History of the Archbishops of Hamburg-Bremen*' in C. Gantner, R. McKitterick and S. Meeder (eds.), *The Resources of the Past in Early Medieval Europe* (Cambridge: Cambridge University Press, 2015), pp. 206–22.

Introduction

Hagiographic Sources

Ninth-century Saxony witnessed an outpouring of hagiographical writing. These texts both recorded and actively shaped the process by which newly established monasteries and bishoprics attempted to forge communities, both within and beyond the clergy and monastic brethren. They constructed local narratives of a shared past: in these works, Charlemagne's conversion of the Saxons is tethered to, and ultimately elided with, the foundation of the Christian centres described in the texts. They further contributed to the process of community formation through the introduction of powerful local patrons, whether through the recognition of a local saint or through the authentication of imported relics.

Hagiographers set out to reveal divine, rather than earthly, truths. Their works were formulaic, sometimes to the point of being positively riddled with *topoi*, and were often ahistorical; the miracle stories which they customarily contain present considerable problems of interpretation which are generally sidestepped in this rational age. These texts cannot be used to gain a clear view of the historical past they purportedly (if indirectly) describe, precisely because their aim was to present idealized images of sanctified behaviour as models for their readers, which inevitably meant that the social world which surrounded these *milites Christi* was reshaped in order to highlight the saints' exceptional sanctity and zeal. Yet, even in the absence of details which can be corroborated, they can nonetheless prove useful to the historically minded reader. The more plausible a work of hagiography was, the more effective it was, which meant that hagiographers, and especially hagiographers of recent saints or relic translations, had a stake in depicting a believable, if fictive, past. Moreover, the specific emphases in these texts provide insight into the contexts in which they were produced, and the ends to which they were employed. The results can be exceedingly illuminating.

Four overlapping genres of hagiographic material survive from Carolingian Saxony: saints' lives, miracle collections, sermons and translation narratives. The last of these, the translation narratives, tracked the movement ('translation') of relics from one location to another, and were written not only to impress upon a new audience the relics' authenticity, but also to connect the saintly patrons with their new centre, generally through the performance of miracles. These categories are by no means hard and fast: saints' lives often contained miracle collections, and even independent miracle collections could be subsequently appended to existing lives, as in the case of Anskar's *Miracles of*

16

Saint Willehad.[50] Translation narratives, meanwhile, often contained a degree of autobiographical material about a saint, and sometimes were produced in parallel with saints' lives, as in the case of the *Life* and *Translation of Saint Liborius.*[51]

Many of these works can be seen to respond to other works composed at the same centre. This is most elegantly displayed at the monastery of Werden on the Ruhr, where three versions of a saint's life were composed within a thirty-year period: Altfrid's *Life of Saint Liudger,* dated to circa 839–849; the *Second Life of Saint Liudger,* written circa 850; and the *Third Life of Saint Liudger,* thought to have been created soon after 864.[52] Over the course of the ninth century, the monastery of Werden produced at least two more works relating to this saint: the two recensions of the so-called *Werden Privilege,* purportedly a legal text, but one which was deeply indebted to the monastery's hagiographic output.[53] Based on further textual links, Werden has been suggested as the place of composition for the *Old Life of Lebuin,* a work which Matthias Springer has plausibly dated to the episcopacy of Radbod of Utrecht (899–917).[54]

Werden was not the only Christian centre to boast a rich hagiographic corpus. Another acknowledged centre for hagiographic composition was the monastery of Corvey, which produced the *Translation of Saint Vitus,* Agius' *Life and Death of Hathumoda,* and possibly the *Life of Saint Rimbert*

---

[50] For this text, and for the *vita* to which it was appended, see respectively Anskar, *Miracula sancti Willehadi,* and *Vita sancti Willehadi,* both eds. C. de Smedt, F. van Ortroy, H. Delehaye, A. Poncelet and P. Peeters, *Acta Sanctorum III Novembris* (Brussels, 1910).

[51] Anonymus Paderbrunnensis, *Vita et Translatio sancti Liborii,* ed. V. de Vry, *Liborius, Brückenbauer Europas: die mittelalterlichen Viten und Translationsberichte: mit einem Anhang der Manuscripta Liboriana* (Paderborn: Schöningh, 1997). See also Röckelein, *Reliquientranslationen nach Sachsen,* pp. 96–100; see further K. Honselmann, 'Reliquientranslationen nach Sachsen', ed. V. H. Elbern, *Das erste Jahrtausend: Kultur und Kunst im werdenden Abendland an Rhein und Ruhr,* 3 vols. (Düsseldorf: L. Schwann, 1962), vol. I: pp. 159–93, here pp. 173–5; R. Schieffer, 'Reliquientranslationen nach Sachsen' in Stiegemann and Wemhoff, *799,* vol. III: pp. 484–97, here pp. 484–6.

[52] Altfrid, *Vita sancti Liudgeri,* and *Vita tertia sancti Liudgeri,* ed. W. Diekamp, *Die vitae sancti Liudgeri* (Die Geschichtsquellen des Bisthums Münster 4) (Münster: Theissing, 1881); *Vita secunda sancti Liudgeri* in Freise, *Vita.* See also I. Rembold, 'Rewriting the founder: Werden on the Ruhr and the uses of hagiography', *Journal of Medieval History,* 41(4) (2015), 363–87.

[53] *Miracula sancti Liudgeri, Privilegium Werthinense A,* and *Privilegium Werthinense B,* ed. W. Diekamp, *Die vitae sancti Liudgeri* (Die Geschichtsquellen des Bisthums Münster 4) (Münster: Theissing, 1881).

[54] *Vita sancti Lebuini antiqua,* ed. A. Hofmeister, *MGH SS* 30:2 (Leipzig: K. W. Hiersemann, 1934). For the composition of this text in Werden, see R. Drögereit, *Werden und der Heliand: Studien zur Kulturgeschichte der Abtei Werden und zur Herkunft des Heliand* (Essen: Fredebeul & Koenen, 1951), pp. 61–4; cf. Springer, *Die Sachsen,* p. 147. For the dating of this text to Radbod's episcopacy, see M. Springer, 'Was Lebuins Lebensbeschreibung über die Verfassung Sachsens wirklich sagt oder warum man sich mit einzelnen Wörtern beschäftigen muß' in Hässler, Jarnut, and Wemhoff, *Sachsen,* pp. 223–39, here pp. 224–5.

over the course of the ninth century.[55] Admittedly, two of these texts appear to have been commissioned by other communities: the *Life and Death of Hathumoda* was written for the incipient community at Gandersheim following the death of its first abbess in 874, whereas the *Life of Saint Rimbert* was composed, either at Corvey or at the female monastery of Neuenheerse, at the close of the ninth century for the (arch)bishopric of Hamburg-Bremen.[56] Yet just as Corvey produced hagiographic works commissioned by other communities, so too did other communities produce hagiography with a bearing on Corvey's own community. Paschasius Radbertus, a monk at and, for a short period, abbot of Corvey's mother house, Corbie, produced two works with great import for its Saxon foundation: the *Life of Saint Adalhard* and the *Epitaph of Arsenius*.[57] The former was written soon after Adalhard's death in 826, and undertook not only to describe the foundation of its dedicatee, the community at Corvey, but also to personify the monastery and its mother house in its concluding poetic dialogue of love and unity, the *Eclogue*. The first book of the *Epitaph of Arsenius*, written circa 838, offers further detail concerning Corvey's beginnings, and seeks moreover to present a favourable portrait of its second abbot, Wala of Corbie, who had become a controversial figure following his role in the second palace rebellion. It was in response to this text that the *Translation of Saint Vitus* was drafted, certainly after 837, and possibly as late as between 842 and 860.[58] The latter work strove to present a picture of

---

[55] *Translatio sancti Viti*, ed. I. Schmale-Ott, *Übertragung des hl. Märtyrers Vitus* (Fontes minores 1) (Münster: Aschendorff, 1979); Agius of Corvey, *Vita et obitus Hathumodae*, ed. G. H. Pertz, *MGH SS* 4 (Hanover: Hahn, 1841); *Vita sancti Rimberti*, ed. G. Waitz, *MGH SRG* 55 (Hanover: Hahn, 1884). For the *Translatio sancti Viti*, see Honselmann, 'Reliquientranslationen', pp. 175–7; K. H. Krüger, *Studien zur Corveyer Gründungsüberlieferung* (Abhandlungen zur Corveyer Geschichtsschreibung 9) (Münster: Aschendorff, 2001), pp. 77–122; Röckelein, *Reliquientranslationen nach Sachsen*, pp. 100–8; Schieffer, 'Reliquientranslationen', pp. 488–90.

[56] For the argument that the *Life of Saint Rimbert* was composed at Neuenheerse, see I. N. Wood, *The Missionary Life: Saints and the Evangelisation of Europe, 400–1050* (Harlow: Longman, 2001), pp. 134–5. For the many debates surrounding Hamburg-Bremen, see below, p. 145, footnote 8.

[57] Paschasius Radbertus, *Vita sancti Adalhardi*, ed. J. P. Migne, *Patrologia Latina 120* (Paris, 1852); Paschasius Radbertus, *Epitaphium Arsenii*, ed. E. Dümmler, *Radbert's Epitaphium Arsenii* (Abhandlungen der Kgl. Akademie der Wissenschaft zu Berlin, Phil.-hist. Classe II) (Berlin: W. de Gruyter, 1900). For the dating of these texts, see the introductory remarks of A. Cabaniss, tr., *Charlemagne's Cousins: Contemporary Lives of Adalard and Wala* (Syracuse: Syracuse University Press, 1967), pp. 2–3; see also H. Mayr-Harting, 'Two abbots in politics: Wala of Corbie and Bernard of Clairvaux', *Transactions of the Royal Historical Society*, 40 (1990), 217–37, here p. 219. See further M. de Jong, *The Penitential State: Authority and Atonement in the Age of Louis the Pious, 814–840* (Cambridge: Cambridge University Press, 2009), pp. 103–5; Krüger, *Studien zur Corveyer Gründungsüberlieferung*, pp. 53–76.

[58] For the dating of this text, see *Translatio sancti Viti*, ed. Schmale-Ott, pp. 20–7; Röckelein, *Reliquientranslationen nach Sachsen*, p. 102.

Corvey's past that minimized its association with its rebellious abbot, and which asserted its independence from its mother house.[59]

Further evidence as to the history of Corvey is afforded by the *Translation of Saint Pusinna*, a text composed circa 862–875 at its sister house, Herford, following a relic translation in 860.[60] A lesser-known text may also be placed at the nunnery: the *Miracles of Saint Pusinna*, a brief summary of miracles.[61] This degree of documentation for Herford is relatively rich, compared with that of other Saxon nunneries. Only two other texts have survived that can be identified with female institutions in Saxony; if the *Life of Saint Rimbert*'s possible composition at Neuenheerse is included, there are three.[62] Agius' *Life and Death of Hathumoda* was composed at Corvey circa 875 for the community of Gandersheim, while the *Life of the Virgin Liutbirga* was written circa 870, presumably for the community of Wendhausen, to which the anchoress Liutbirga's cell was attached.[63] It should be noted that the founding families of these houses feature extensively in these narratives, to a far greater extent than in hagiography written for male communities.

Monasteries were not the only type of centres to engage in hagiographic compositions. The bishops of Bremen, and (later) the purported archbishops of Hamburg-Bremen, produced or commissioned three or perhaps even four hagiographic compositions over the course of the ninth century. The first of these, the *Life of Saint Willehad*, was composed circa 843 and has often been attributed to the community of Echternach.[64] More recently, James Palmer has made a convincing case

---

[59] K. H. Krüger, 'Zur Nachfolgeregelung von 826 in den Klöstern Corbie und Corvey' in N. Kamp and J. Wollasch (eds.), *Tradition als historische Kraft: interdisziplinäre Forschungen zur Geschichte des früheren Mittelalters* (Berlin: W. de Gruyter, 1982), pp. 181–96.

[60] *Translatio sanctae Pusinnae*, ed. R. Wilmans, *Die Kaiserurkunden der Provinz Westfalen, 777–1313*, 2 vols. (Münster: F. Regensberg, 1867), vol. I; see also Röckelein, *Reliquientranslationen nach Sachsen*, pp. 108–17; see further Honselmann, 'Reliquientranslationen', pp. 178–80; Schieffer, 'Reliquientranslationen', pp. 493–4.

[61] *Miracula sanctae Pusinnae*, ed. K. Honselmann, 'Berichte des 9. Jahrhunderts über Wunder am Grabe der hlg. Pusinna in Herford' in J. Bauermann (ed.), *Dona Westfalica: Georg Schreiber zum 80 Geburtstage* (Schriften der Historischen Kommission für Westfalen 4) (Münster: Aschendorff, 1963), pp. 128–36; for the dating of this text, see pp. 131–2.

[62] See above, p. 18.

[63] *Vita Liutbirgae virginis*, ed. O. Menzel, *Das Leben der Liutbirg: Eine Quelle zur Geschichte der Sachsen in karolingischer Zeit* (Deutsches Mittelalter 3) (Leipzig: K. W. Hiersemann, 1937); see also F. S. Paxton, *Anchoress and Abbess in Ninth-Century Saxony: The Lives of Liutbirga of Wendhausen and Hathumoda of Gandersheim* (Washington, DC: Catholic University of America Press, 2009), pp. 3, 19.

[64] G. Niemeyer, 'Die Herkunft der Vita Willehadi', *DA*, 12 (1956), 17–35; Wood, *The Missionary Life*, pp. 90–1.

for its composition within Bremen.[65] Bremen boasted a much deeper connection with Willehad than Echternach, where Willehad had sought refuge for a mere two years during the Saxon wars, and where his feast day was omitted in a late ninth-century sanctoral cycle.[66] Willehad was remembered as the first bishop of Bremen, and his *Vita* describes in great detail how his relics were brought from Blexen to rest in Bremen cathedral.[67] The attribution of this text to Bremen is further strengthened by the fact that, in its earliest extant manuscripts, the text circulated alongside Anskar's *Miracles of Saint Willehad*, a work which that bishop of Bremen wrote to promote Willehad's cult circa 850. Over the course of the next century, the bishopric of Bremen underwent many changes, eventually resulting in the alleged formation of the archbishopric of Hamburg-Bremen. This 'formation' was purportedly recorded, but more likely purposefully advanced, by Rimbert's *Life of Saint Anskar*, which he composed following his mentor's death in 865.[68] The notion of this dual archbishopric was further solidified by the subsequent composition of the *Life of Saint Rimbert* at either the monastery of Corvey or the female community of Neuenheerse, a work which was probably commissioned by Rimbert's successor, Bishop Adalgar.[69] These works did not simply record Bremen's history: they actively shaped it.

Near the end of the century, the bishopric of Paderborn similarly ventured into the enterprise of hagiographic production. During the episcopate of Biso (887–909), two works of hagiography were commissioned: the *Life* and the *Translation of Saint Liborius*.[70] The first of these is of limited interest to the historian of Carolingian Saxony: its description

[65] For a Bremen composition, see especially J. T. Palmer, *Anglo-Saxons in a Frankish World, 690–900* (Studies in the Early Middle Ages 19) (Turnhout: Brepols, 2009), p. 173; Palmer, 'Anskar's imagined communities', pp. 175–6; Palmer, 'Beyond Frankish authority', p. 144; see further J. Ehlers, 'Die Sachsenmission als heilsgeschichtlichen Ereignis' in F. J. Felten and N. Jaspert (eds.), *Vita religiosa im Mittelalter: Festschrift für Kaspar Elm zum 70. Geburtstag* (Berliner historische Studien 31) (Berlin: Duncker & Humblot, 1999), pp. 37–53, here pp. 37–8; L. E. von Padberg, *Heilige und Familie: Studien zur Bedeutung familiengebundener Aspekte in den Viten des Verwandten- und Schülerreises um Willibrord, Bonifatius, und Liudger* (Quellen und Abhandlungen zur mittelrheinischen Kirchengeschichte 83) (Mainz: Selbstverlag der Gesellschaft für mittelrheinische Kirchengeschichte, 1997), pp. 37–8.

[66] Palmer, *Anglo-Saxons in a Frankish World*, p. 173.

[67] *Vita sancti Willehadi*, eds. de Smedt, van Ortroy, Delehaye, Poncelet, and Peeters, cc. 8, 10, pp. 845A–846B; Palmer, *Anglo-Saxons in a Frankish World*, p. 173.

[68] For this, see above all E. Knibbs, *Ansgar, Rimbert and the Forged Foundations of Hamburg-Bremen* (Farnham: Ashgate, 2011).

[69] Rimbert, *Vita sancti Anskarii*, ed. G. Waitz, *MGH SRG 55* (Hanover: Hahn, 1884); see Knibbs, *Ansgar, Rimbert and the Forged Foundations of Hamburg-Bremen*; Palmer, 'Anskar's imagined communities', p. 180; Wood, *The Missionary Life*, pp. 134–5.

[70] Rembold, 'The Poeta Saxo at Paderborn', 180–95; Röckelein, *Reliquientranslationen nach Sachsen*, pp. 96–100.

of Liborius, a late fourth-century bishop of Le Mans, is largely dependent on other extant sources, most notably the *Acts of the Bishops Living in the City of Le Mans*, although its initial chapters may reveal some of the author's own ideas on apostolic succession. The *Translation*, likewise, is dependent on earlier works. Previous recensions of the *Translation of Saint Liborius* (labelled Avranches and Erconrad) had been circulated in the aftermath of the 836 translation. Notably, the anonymous Paderborn cleric added a significant amount of independent material, comprising some nine chapters, to the beginning of his narrative.[71] These chapters offer a local perspective on the Saxon wars and Charlemagne's conversion of the Saxons, as well as on the foundation and subsequent history of the bishopric of Paderborn. It is also worth noting that the *Life* and *Translation of Saint Liborius* were commissioned alongside the Saxon Poet's versified life, which may further be considered under the genre of hagiography: the work ends, after all, with Charlemagne numbered among the apostles, leading converted Saxon souls up to heaven. These works appear to have been written with the aim of restoring Paderborn's reputation, eminence and royal favour in an era when it was increasingly relegated to the sidelines.[72]

Other hagiographic works surviving from ninth-century Saxony include the *Translation of Saint Alexander*, commissioned by Waltbraht for his new foundation at Wildeshausen and composed by Rudolf and Meginhard of Fulda in two sections (which can be dated between 850 and 865 and between 865 and 868 respectively); the *Sermon of Saint Marsus*, a sermon which records the translation of saints' relics around 864, which Hedwig Röckelein has plausibly localized to the canonical community of Niggenkerke in Höxter; and finally the *Life of Saint Meinolf*, a late ninth-century life which Klemens Honselmann has partially reconstructed from a set of later saints' day readings.[73] The overall body of hagiographic writing, then, is surprisingly large, and proves

---

[71] For these earlier recensions, see Avranches, *Translatio sancti Liborii*, ed. F. Baethgen, *MGH SS* 30:2 (Leipzig: K. W. Hiersemann, 1934); Erconrad, *Translatio sancti Liborii*, eds. A. Cohausz, V. Mellinghoff-Bourgerie, and R. Latouche, *La Translation de Saint Liboire (836) du diacre Erconrad: Un Document de l'époque carolingienne récemment découvert et les Relations déjà connues du Transfert des Reliques* (Archives historiques du Maine 14) (Le Mans: Société historique de la province du Maine, 1967).

[72] Rembold, 'The Poeta Saxo at Paderborn', 195.

[73] Rudolf and Meginhard, *Translatio sancti Alexandri*, ed. Pertz; *Sermo sancti Marsi*, ed. K. Honselmann, 'Eine Essener Predigt zum Predigt zum Feste des hl. Marsus aus dem 9. Jahrhundert', *WZ*, 110 (1960), 199–221; *Vita sancti Meinolfi*, ed. K. Honselmann, 'Die älteste Vita Meinolfi: Brevierlesungen zu den Festen des Heiligen aus dem Ende des 9. Jahrhunderts', *WZ*, 137 (1987), 185–206; see also especially Röckelein, *Reliquientranslationen nach Sachsen*, pp. 117–34; see further Honselmann, 'Reliquientranslationen', pp. 177–8; Schieffer, 'Reliquientranslationen', pp. 490–3, cf. pp. 494–6.

extraordinarily useful as a window onto specific Christian centres in ninth-century Saxony.

Hagiographic compositions can go a long way towards explaining the dynamics of ninth-century religious centres in Saxony; they can further speak to the attempts to create communities and appeal to the support of the local laity. Yet these texts can only tell us so much about the mechanics of how the Christian message was propagated to the wider populace. To learn more, we must turn to another body of evidence: vernacular literature, and in particular, vernacular biblical poetry.

Vernacular Literature

The most famous work of vernacular literature to survive from Carolingian Saxony is, without a doubt, the *Heliand*, a gospel harmony in alliterative Old Saxon verse of which nearly 6,000 lines survive, although its extant manuscripts are incomplete.[74] While its importance is undisputed, its origins have proven far more contentious. Arguments have ranged far and wide regarding its place of composition: Münster, Paderborn, Hamburg, Utrecht, Merseburg, Halberstadt, Bremen, Magdeburg, Münsterdorf, Mainz and Normandy have all been suggested in turn.[75] More plausibly, scholars have made cases for Fulda, Werden, and Corvey, basing their arguments on palaeographical, linguistic and contextual evidence.[76] Of these, I would be inclined to favour a Fulda

---

[74] *Heliand*, eds. O. Behaghel and B. Taeger, *Heliand und Genesis* (Altdeutsche Textbibliothek 4), 9th edn (Tübingen: M. Niemeyer, 1984). I address this text at greater length in a forthcoming book chapter: I. Rembold, 'The Christian message and the laity: the Heliand in post-conquest Saxony' in N. Edwards, M. Ni Mhaonaigh and R. Flechner (eds.), *Transforming Landscapes of Belief in the Early Medieval Insular World and Beyond* (Converting the Isles 2) (Turnhout: Brepols), in press.

[75] For the list of places suggested, see Drögereit, *Werden und der Heliand*, p. 93; J. K. Bostock, K. C. King, and D. McLintock (eds.), *A Handbook on Old High German Literature* (Oxford: Clarendon, 1976), p. 179.

[76] For those who advocate a Fulda composition, see especially G. Baesecke, 'Fulda und die altsächsischen Bibelepen' in J. Eichhoff and I. Rauch (eds.), *Der Heliand* (Wege der Forschung 321) (Darmstadt: Wissenschaftliche Buchgesellschaft, 1973), pp. 54–92; see further K. Gantert, *Akkommodation und eingeschriebener Kommentar: Untersuchungen zur Übertragungsstrategie des Heliand-dichters* (ScriptOralia 111) (Tübingen: G. Narr, 1998), pp. 24–5; D. H. Green, 'Three aspects of the Old Saxon Biblical epic, the *Heliand*' in Green and Siegmund, *Saxons*, pp. 247–69, here pp. 249–50; M. B. Gillis, *Heresy and Dissent in the Carolingian Empire: the Case of Gottschalk of Orbais* (Oxford: Oxford University Press, 2017), p. 45; C. Zurla, 'Medium and message: the confluence of Saxon and Frankish values as portrayed in the Old Saxon Heliand', unpublished Ph.D. thesis, McGill University (2004), pp. 22–7. For Werden, see especially Drögereit, *Werden und der Heliand*, pp. 93–110; see further P. Augustyn, *The Semiotics of Fate, Death, and the Soul in Germanic Culture: the Christianization of Old Saxon* (Berkeley Insights in Linguistics and Semiotics 50) (New York: P. Lang, 2002), p. 1; H. J. Hummer, *Politics and Power in Early Medieval Europe: Alsace and the Frankish Realm, 600–1000* (Cambridge: Cambridge University Press, 2005), pp. 139–40; W. Krogmann, 'Die Praefatio in librum antiquum lingua Saxonica conscriptum' in

composition, as much of the evidence marshalled for Corvey and Werden is palaeographical or linguistic, and thus may reflect the location of the copyist rather than that of the original author. Fulda, on the other hand, possessed the main source which the poet employed: the *Codex Fuldensis*, Victor of Capua's Latin translation of Tatian's *Diatessaron*, which also served as the basis for an Old High German translation in the same period.[77] The idea of an alternative, and as yet unattested, Old Latin translation of the *Diatessaron* has found little favour in recent years.[78] The work's dating, meanwhile, is relatively straightforward: the *Heliand* was most probably written circa 821–840.

Far more complicated, and far less contentious, is the history of the Old Saxon *Genesis*.[79] This text was first discovered in 1875 by Eduard Sievers, who observed linguistic and narrative differences in a section of an Old English *Genesis* text dating to the late tenth century. Sievers argued that this section of the text, which describes the fall of Satan and that of man, was not only an interpolation but, furthermore, a translation from Old Saxon, a hunch which was, rather remarkably, later substantiated: parts of his hypothesized Old Saxon *Genesis* were discovered in ninth-century marginalia.[80] Here, the copyist chose to include, episodically, sections from three different parts of the poem: the fall of man; Cain

J. Eichhoff and I. Rauch (eds.), *Der Heliand* (Wege der Forschung 321) (Darmstadt: Wissenschaftliche Buchgesellschaft, 1973), pp. 20–53, here pp. 26–7; T. L. Markey, *A North Sea Germanic Reader* (Munich: Fink, 1976), p. 264; R. McKitterick, 'Werden im Spiegel seiner Handschriften (8./9. Jahrhundert)' in S. Patzold, A. Rathmann-Lutz, and V. Scior (eds.), *Geschichtsvorstellungen: Bilder, Texte, und Begriffe aus dem Mittelalter: Festschrift für Hans-Werner Goetz zum 65. Geburtstag* (Vienna: Böhlau, 2012), pp. 326–53, here pp. 334–5. Finally, for Corvey, see E. J. Goldberg, *Struggle for Empire: Kingship and Conflict under Louis the German, 817–876* (Ithaca: Cornell University Press, 2006), p. 184; see also B. Bischoff, 'Der Schriftheimat der Münchener Heliand-Handschrift', *Beiträge zur Geschichte der deutschen Sprache und Literatur*, 101(2) (1979), 161–70.

[77] Victor of Capua, *Codex Fuldensis*, ed. E. Ranke, *Codex Fuldensis: Novum Testamentum Latine interprete Hieronymo* (Marburg, 1868). The original manuscript (which I have not consulted) is Fulda, Hessische Landesbibliothek, Codex Bonifatianus 1.

[78] See, for example, G. Quispel, *Tatian and the Gospel of Thomas: Studies in the History of the Western Diatessaron* (Leiden: Brill, 1975), and J. fon Weringha, *Heliand and Diatessaron* (Studia Germanica 5) (Assen: Van Gorcum, 1965). For an historiographical assessment, see V. A. Pakis, '(Un)Desirable origins: The *Heliand* and the Gospel of Thomas' in V. A. Pakis (ed.), *Perspectives on the Old Saxon Heliand: Introductory and Critical Essays, with an Edition of the Leipzig fragment* (Medieval European Studies) 12 (Morgantown: West Virginia University Press, 2010), pp. 120–63. For a rebuttal of this line of scholarship, see B. Fischer, 'Bibelausgaben des frühen Mittelalters' in *La Bibbia nell'Alto Medioevo* (Settimane 10) (Spoleto: Il Centro, 1963), pp. 519–600, here p. 557; A. den Hollander and U. Schmid, 'The *Gospel of Barnabas*, the *Diatessaron*, and method', *Vigiliae Christianae*, 61(1) (2007), 1–20.

[79] *Genesis*, ed. A. N. Doane, *The Saxon Genesis: An Edition of the West Saxon Genesis B and the Old Saxon Vatican Genesis* (Madison: University of Wisconsin Press, 1991).

[80] E. Sievers, *Der Heliand und die angelsächsische Genesis* (Halle: M. Niemeyer, 1875), see especially pp. 5–8; for the Old English *Genesis* text, see Bodleian Library, Junius 11, which is available in a digital facsimile edition as well as a standard edition: see I. Gollancz, *The Caedmon Manuscript of*

and Enoch; and Abraham and Sodom. Unfortunately, it remains impossible to reconstruct the original extent of the work: between its two manuscript attestations, some 1,100 lines of verse have been preserved.[81] Yet it may have been comparable to the *Heliand* in both scale and intention.[82] Certainly, there appear to have been considerable similarities in the two works' content, form and reception.

To these biblical epics may be added a host of other Old Saxon compositions – a baptismal vow, a penitential, an *All Saints' Day Sermon* and fragments of a commentary on the psalms.[83] Despite the unresolved questions surrounding their composition – which have, in any case, dominated scholarship for far too long – these texts are of great use to the historian. All of these texts offer precious insight into the ways in which Christian teaching was disseminated in Carolingian Saxony, and thus into the process of Christianization.

Documentary Sources

The extant evidence from Carolingian Saxony is not all literary; there is also a sizeable corpus of documentary material, notably legal codes, cartularies and charters. The first of these, Saxony's abundant legal evidence, is well known, and has been much utilized in modern scholarship: the *Capitulary concerning the Saxon Regions* and the *Saxon Capitulary*, hereafter referred to as the *First* and *Second Saxon Capitularies*, respectively, as well as the *Law of the Saxons* all feature prominently in recent accounts of the Saxon war.[84] The *First Saxon Capitulary* has been variously dated to 782 or to circa 794/795: those who favour the first of these dates highlight Charlemagne's appointment of Saxon counts in that year, as well as the severity of actions at the so-called massacre of Verden; those who favour the second, meanwhile, emphasize the context of renewed rebellion, and point towards a handful of letters written by Alcuin of York in this period which appear to respond to provisions in

---

Anglo-Saxon Biblical Poetry, Junius XI in the Bodleian Library (Oxford: Oxford University Press, 1927); B. J. Muir, *A Digital Facsimile of Oxford, Bodleian Library, MS. Junius 11* (Bodleian Digital Texts 1) (Oxford: Bodleian Library, 2004). See also A. N. Doane, *The Saxon Genesis: An Edition of the West Saxon Genesis B and the Old Saxon Vatican Genesis* (Madison: University of Wisconsin Press, 1991), pp. ix, 9–42.

[81] Doane, *The Saxon Genesis*, pp. 13, 37.   [82] *Ibid*, pp. 109–10.

[83] *Abrenuntiatio diaboli et professio fidei*, Old Saxon Penitential, *Lectio psalmorum*, and *Sermo omnium sanctorum*, ed. E. Wadstein, *Kleinere altsächsische Sprachdenkmäler* (Niederdeutsche Denkmäler 6) (Norden: Soltau, 1899).

[84] *Capitulatio de partibus Saxoniae, Capitulare Saxonicum*, and *Lex Saxonum*, ed. C. von Schwerin, *MGH Fontes iuris* 4 (Hanover: Hahn, 1918).

the capitulary.[85] The Second Saxon Capitulary is explicitly dated to 797 in its preface, and the *Law of the Saxons* may likewise be dated with relative certainty to circa 802/3.[86] As Carolingian legal compilations, they may productively be used to illuminate the Carolingian court and its attitudes during the conquest period. What these texts certainly cannot supply is an unproblematic image of Saxon society and legal culture. The process of compilation was complex and laboured: a selection of legal customs was adapted and simplified for inclusion before being augmented by other provisions, notably regarding the roles of newly appointed officials and the introduction of Christianity. While these texts may preserve some features of previous Saxon legal customs, they can tell us far more about the contemporary Frankish attitudes and priorities.

The work of Thomas Faulkner, in particular, has gone a long way to reassessing the role of these laws in Saxon society. As he has suggested, the *First* and *Second Saxon Capitularies* may have only operated within their immediate context in the Saxon wars.[87] While the *Law of the Saxons* may have had greater pretensions, there is little evidence for its distribution, and hence use, in ninth-century Saxony. The only ninth-century Saxon manuscript which contains a significant amount of 'secular' (as opposed to canon) law consists of the *Law of the Salian Franks, the Law of the Ribuarian Franks*, the *Law of the Alemans* and a wide array of capitulary sources, including Ansegis' collection.[88] The *Law of the Saxons*, meanwhile, survives in one ninth-century copy from eastern Francia, and in one mid-tenth-century Saxon manuscript.[89] Even the latter manuscript cannot be said to support the straightforward application of the *Law of the Saxons* in a Saxon context: a title over chapter twenty-four of the *Law* identifies the text as the *Law of the Franks*, and when the *Law of the Saxons* concludes it is followed, without

---

[85] For the dating of the *Capitulatio* to 782, see especially M. Lintzel, 'De Capitulatio de partibus Saxoniae' in Lintzel, *Schriften*, pp. 380–9; see also R. Drögereit, 'Die schriftlichen Quellen zur Christianisierung der Sachsen und ihre Aussagefähigkeit' in W. Lammers (ed.), *Die Eingliederung der Sachsen in das Frankenreich* (Wege der Forschung 185) (Darmstadt: Wissenschaftliche Buchgesellschaft, 1970), pp. 451–69, here pp. 457–8; E. Schubert, 'Die Capitulatio de partibus Saxoniae' in D. Brosius, C. van der Heuvel, E. Hinrichs and H. van Lengen (eds.), *Geschichte in der Region. Zum 65. Geburtstag von Heinrich Schmidt* (Hanover: Hahn, 1993), pp. 3–28, here pp. 8–9. For the dating of the *Capitulatio* to circa 794 to 795, see Flierman, 'Defining and redefining Saxons', pp. 147–205; R. Flierman, 'Religious Saxons: paganism, infidelity and biblical punishment in the Capitulatio de partibus Saxoniae' in R. Meens, D. van Espelo, B. van den Hoven van Genderen, J. Raaijmakers, I. van Renswoude and C. van Rhijn (eds.), *Religious Franks: Religion and Power in Honour of Mayke de Jong* (Manchester: Manchester University Press, 2016), pp. 181–201; Flierman, *Saxon Identities*, pp. 111–12; cf. Y. Hen, 'Charlemagne's jihad', *Viator*, 37 (2006), 33–51, here 38–9.

[86] For the dating of the *Lex Saxonum*, see T. Faulkner, *Law and Authority in the Early Middle Ages: The Frankish Leges in the Carolingian Period* (Cambridge: Cambridge University Press, 2016), pp. 24–6, 70–3.

[87] *Ibid*, p. 49; see also Lintzel, 'De Capitulatio de partibus Saxoniae', here pp. 388–9.

[88] Faulkner, *Law and Authority*, pp. 72–3.   [89] *Ibid*, p. 72; Springer, *Die Sachsen*, pp. 233–4.

demarcation, by the *Law of the Thuringians*.[90] Faulkner therefore suggests that the *Law of the Saxons* 'did not come together in its current form until later in the ninth century, or that [it] was marginal to the body of written law' in ninth-century Saxony.[91] There is thus little evidence, save the very fact of their composition, that these laws were consulted to any significant degree, let alone enforced, in Carolingian Saxony. These legal texts, while highly revealing of Frankish 'policy' during the conquest period, should be employed only with the greatest circumspection to attempt to access contemporary Saxon society and legal practices.

Of somewhat greater relevance to the historian of Carolingian Saxony are a number of cartularies, among them the *Werden Cartulary*, the *Corvey Donations* and the *Codex Eberhardi*, of which the latter two pertain to the monasteries of Corvey and Fulda respectively.[92] Although the *Werden Cartulary*, dating from the mid-ninth century, is relatively straightforward to use, these other sources pose various challenges: for example, individual entries in the *Corvey Donations*, whose first section contains summaries of donations made to the monastery between 822 and 872, are extremely difficult to date, and often lack other details, such as the size of the donation. The *Codex Eberhardi*, a mid-twelfth-century summary of a now (mostly) lost ninth-century cartulary, is less yielding still. As in the case of the *Corvey Donations*, its donations are undated and sometimes fail to give any indication as to size. Nonetheless, these sources can help to shed light not only upon monastic patronage, but also upon kinship and patronage networks, elite and non-elite landownership and changing patterns of landownership in the Carolingian period.

Finally, there is a considerable body of charter evidence which can be used to reconstruct the role played by Carolingian rulers in Saxony.

---

[90] See Münster, Landesarchiv Nordrhein-Westfalen, Msc. VII Nr 5201, where the *Lex Saxonum* is to be found on pp. 5–10, the so-designated *Lex Francorum* on pp. 10–19, and the *Lex Thuringorum* on pp. 19–27, although the title of '*Lex Thuringorum*' is only given on p. 27. For this, see *Lex Saxonum*, eds. K. von Richthofen and K. F. von Richthofen, *MGH Leges (in Folio)* 5 (Hanover: Hahn, 1889), p. 10.

[91] Faulkner, *Law and Authority*, p. 73.

[92] *Cartularium Werthinense*, ed. D. P. Blok, 'Een diplomatisch onderzoek van de oudste particuliere oorkonden van Werden', unpublished Ph.D. thesis, University of Amsterdam (1960); *Traditiones Corbeienses*, ed. K. Honselmann, *Die alten Mönchslisten und die Traditionen von Corvey* (Abhandlungen zur Corveyer Geschichtsschreibung 6), 2 vols. (Paderborn: Bonifatius, 1982), vol. I; *Codex Eberhardi*, ed. H. Meyer zu Ermgassen, *Der Codex Eberhardi des Klosters Fulda* (Veröffentlichungen der Historischen Kommission für Hessen 58), 3 vols. (Marburg: Elwert, 1996). For the Werden Cartulary, see C. de Cazanove, 'Construire l'identité communautaire, les abbayes de Werden et Wissembourg du IXe au début Xe siècle', *Circé: Histoires, Cultures et Sociétés*, 5 (2014); R. McKitterick, 'The uses of literacy in Carolingian and post-Carolingian Europe: literate conventions of memory' in *Scrivere e leggere nell'alto medioevo* (Settimane 59:1) (Spoleto: Il Centro, 2012), pp. 179–211, here especially pp. 189–98.

As ever, various questions have been posed regarding the authenticity of some of these texts.[93] Some can be dismissed as outright forgeries, as in the case of an entertainingly implausible foundation source for the bishopric of Osnabrück which stipulates that the bishopric will henceforth be exempt from all royal service except the maintenance of a Greek school, in case the ruling dynasty ever wished to contract a Byzantine marriage alliance.[94] In other cases, however, it can be far more difficult to judge what may have been an interpolation or forged provision, such as in the case of a charter whose tithe provisions have been regarded as later interpolations, but which, as I have argued elsewhere, may indeed be genuine.[95] Further problems are posed by the uneven survival of these sources: charters granted to individuals, for example, have a far lower survival rate than grants to monastic institutions. Indeed, even these grants disproportionately survive as a result of their relevance to later monastic donations. Despite these challenges, however, these sources can be employed to delineate the extent of Carolingian rulers' influence in Saxony. They are of enormous value for our understanding of the social and political landscape in Carolingian Saxony.

This brief summary can in no way claim to be comprehensive. In addition to the historiographical, hagiographical, vernacular and documentary texts surveyed, there are many other sources with a bearing on Carolingian Saxony. Among them there are a variety of letters and letter collections (notably those of Alcuin, Egilmar, and Hrabanus),[96] poetry (*Poem Concerning the Conversion of the Saxons, King Charlemagne and Pope Leo* and Agius of Corvey's computational poems)[97] and memorial sources (*Catalogue of Abbots and Brothers of Corvey, Necrological*

---

[93] See here especially the excellent recent reassessments by T. Kölzer, 'Die Urkunden Ludwigs des Frommen für Halberstadt (BM2 535) und Visbek (BM2 702) und ein folgenreiches Mißverständnis', *AfD*, 58 (2012), 103–23; T. Kölzer, 'Zum angeblichen Immunitätsprivileg Ludwigs des Frommen für das Bistum Hildesheim', *AfD*, 59 (2013), 11–24; T. Kölzer, 'Ludwigs des Frommen "Gründungsurkunde" für das Erzbistum Hamburg', *AfD*, 60 (2014), 35–68.

[94] *D Kar. 1*, ed. E. Mühlbacher, *MGH, Die Urkunden Pippins, Karlmanns, und Karls des Grossen* (Hanover: Hahn, 1906), no. 273, pp. 403–5.

[95] *D Arn*, ed. P. Kehr, *MGH, Die Urkunden Arnolfs* (Berlin: Weidemann, 1940), no. 3, pp. 5–8; Rembold, 'The Poeta Saxo at Paderborn', 181–2.

[96] Alcuin, *Epistolae*, ed. E. Dümmler, *MGH Epp.* 4:2 (Berlin: Weidemann, 1895); Stephanus V papa, *Epistolae*, ed. G. Laehr, *MGH Epp.* 7:5 (Berlin: Weidemann, 1928), no. 3, pp. 359–63; Hrabanus Maurus, *Epistolae*, ed. E. Dümmler, *MGH Epp.* 5:3 (Berlin: Weidemann, 1899). For the authenticity of Egilmar's letter, see A. Spicker-Wendt, *Die querimonia Egilmari episcopi und die responsio Stephani papae: Studien zu den Osnabrücker Quellen der Karolingerzeit* (Studien und Vorarbeiten zur Germania pontificia 8) (Cologne: Böhlau, 1980); contrast to F. Staab, 'Die Wurzel des zisterziensischen Zehntprivilegs, zugleich zur Echtheitsfrage der "Querimonia Egilmari episcopi" und der "Responsio Stephani V papae"' *DA*, 40 (1984), 21–54.

[97] *Carmen de conversione Saxonum*, ed. E. Dümmler, *MGH Poet.* 1 (Berlin: Weidemann, 1881); *De Karolo rege et Leone papa*, ed. W. Hentze, *De Karolo rege et Leone papa: der Bericht über die*

Annales of Fulda).[98] There is also significant material evidence, whether in the form of surviving manuscripts, art-historical and architectural sources or evidence arising from archaeological investigations.[99] Post-conquest Saxony may not have been well recorded in contemporary historical writing, but it is far from inaccessible: rather, it abounds in available source material.

Despite this trove of primary material, and despite the significant realignments that Saxony underwent over the course of this period, only recently have scholars once again begun to engage with this period of Saxon history. This may be largely attributed to the indirect consequences of the politicization of Saxon history in the late nineteenth and early twentieth centuries, to which I shall now turn.[100]

FROM NATIONAL TO LOCAL HISTORY

In 1871, standing amid the opulence of the Hall of Mirrors in Versailles, Wilhelm I was proclaimed emperor of Germany. His recent victory in the Franco-Prussian war had given him the influence necessary to further his imperial designs. Yet he also sought ideological justification for what was, in essence, a political novelty – justification that was to be found in the historical creation of a previous 'German' empire. And thus the idea of successive German *Reiche* was born, beginning with Charlemagne and the Carolingian empire and eventually culminating in the Third Reich. This identification of Charlemagne as the first German emperor appears to have been, at root, based on his conquest of the Saxons. This is a point of view that becomes more easily comprehensible if one takes into account the territory that comprised the Prussian state. To write, then, that the late nineteenth and early twentieth centuries saw a revival in interest in the Saxon past would be an understatement: indeed, the Saxon wars became a central and defining (if contentious) point in German national historical consciousness.

Zusammenkunft Karls des Grossen mit Papst Leo III. in Paderborn 799 in einem Epos für Karl den Kaiser (Studien und Quellen zur westfälischen Geschichte 36) (Paderborn: Bonifatius, 1999); Agius of Corvey, *Versus computistici*, ed. K. Strecker, MGH Poet. 4:2.3 (Berlin: Weidemann, 1923); Agius of Corvey, *Versus computistici*, ed. E. Könsgen, 'Eine neue komputistische Dichtung des Agius von Corvey', *Mittellateinisches Jahrbuch*, 14 (1979), 66–75.

[98] *Catalogus abbatum et fratrum Corbeiensium*, ed. K. Honselmann, *Die alten Mönchslisten und die Traditionen von Corvey*) Abhandlungen zur Corveyer Geschichtsschreibung 6), 2 vols. (Paderborn: Bonifatius, 1982), vol. I; *Annales necrologici Fuldenses*, ed. G. Waitz, SS 13 (Hanover: Hahn, 1881).

[99] For a survey of the surviving archaeological and art-historical material, see Stiegemann and Wemhoff, 799.

[100] The following section represents a rewritten and lengthened version of a discussion in I. Rembold, 'Quasi una gens: Saxony and the Frankish world, c. 772–888', *History Compass* 15 (6) (2017).

This can be seen illustrated in the wall paintings at the imperial palace of Goslar, originally constructed in the early eleventh century and rebuilt in the period following the Prussian annexation of the kingdom of Hanover in 1866.[101] In 1878, three years after Wilhelm had graced the site with a personal visit, Hermann Wislicenus received a commission to paint the imperial hall, a commission which he fulfilled in monumental style over the next twenty years.[102] His cycle begins on the southern wall with the birth of Sleeping Beauty, a none-too-subtle metaphor for the German Reich, consigned to slumber only to reawaken.[103] The next (and first historical) painting features Charlemagne and may be taken to represent the establishment of the First Reich. Interestingly, Wislicenus did not choose to depict Charlemagne's imperial coronation: rather, he presented the felling of the Irminsul, the focal point of a Saxon shrine (here imagined as a wooden column topped with a carved face). Charlemagne sits astride his horse behind a cross-wielding monk as his men pull away the shattered column; the king surveys the heathen Saxons, who, bedecked with winged helmets, bow low to pay him homage. The subject itself may not be altogether original, for the felling of the Irminsul can be found depicted in many previous works – such as the mid-century fresco cycle in the Aachen town hall – yet its selection as the main image to encapsulate Charlemagne's reign, and thus the establishment of the first German empire, was comparatively new.[104] As Monika Arndt comments, Wislicenus presumably selected the theme in order to depict not only the unification of Germany, but also the expansion of Christianity, which served as a foundation for the German empires, both old and new.[105] So much seems clear from the short explanatory pamphlet of Helene Lichtenberger, drafted at the artist's request: 'The medieval empire had inherited from Charlemagne the lofty mission to achieve world domination for the protection of the Catholic Church.'[106]

Below the Irminsul, two smaller, grisaille paintings likewise depict scenes from the Saxon war: the reception of Moorish emissaries at the assembly of Paderborn, and the baptism of the Saxon leader Widukind.

[101] M. Arndt, *Die Goslarer Kaiserpfalz als Nationaldenkmal: eine ikonographische Untersuchung* (Hildesheim: Lax, 1976), pp. 3–5; H. A. Pohlsander, *National Monuments and Nationalism in 19th Century Germany* (New German-American Studies 31) (Oxford: P. Lang, 2008), pp. 240–1. I have relied upon both of these works in what follows.

[102] Arndt, *Die Goslarer Kaiserpfalz*, pp. 7, 13.

[103] Pohlsander, *National Monuments and Nationalism*, p. 243. For a catalogue of the paintings, see Arndt, *Die Goslarer Kaiserpfalz*, pp. 21–3.

[104] Arndt, *Die Goslarer Kaiserpfalz*, pp. 190–2.   [105] *Ibid*, p. 33.

[106] Helene Lichtenberger, Erklärungsschrift zum Bildprogramm in Arndt, *Die Goslarer Kaiserpfalz*, pp. 112–13, here p. 112: "Das mittelalterliche Kaisertum hatte von Karl dem Großen an die hohe Mission übernommen, eine Weltherrschaft zum Schutz der katholischen Kirche zu werden.'

These are the only images from the Carolingian period. The image cycle moves seamlessly to the Ottonian period, from the discovery of silver in the Harz mountains under Otto I to the foundation of Goslar by Henry II and his imperial coronation, and continues through the high points of Salian and Hohenstaufen rule before jumping ahead to Luther's appearance at the Council of Worms. In the penultimate (large) image in the cycle, directly opposite the first image of Sleeping Beauty, Friedrich Barbarossa awakes from his legendary sleep in the Kyffhäuer Mountain to restore once again the empire, staring across towards the final, central triptych, the proclamation of Wilhelm I as emperor. Barbarossa appears once more in the clouds above Wilhelm's head, designating him as the heir to the empire, an empire which stretched back continuously all the way to Charlemagne's conquest of the Saxons. Age-old precedent had been duly harnessed to legitimate Wilhelm's imperial innovation.[107]

The triumphalism which followed on the heels of the Franco-Prussian war was not to last, and with it passed this particular view of history. Following German defeat in the First World War, proponents of National Socialism rejected any historical precedent set by Charlemagne and his Frankish Christian Empire, and turned instead to his erstwhile Saxon adversary, Widukind, who was depicted as struggling to preserve his homeland and heritage against all odds, with great personal sacrifice. Widukind was a figure altogether more in keeping with contemporary pessimism. While Charlemagne was relabelled as the *Sachsenschlächter* ('the Saxon-slaughterer'), Widukind was raised as a hero of the First Reich and a model for German behaviour in the Third.[108] At the pinnacle of his 'popularity' in the early 1930s, he was commemorated in countless historical novels and plays, and even in civic architecture.[109]

---

[107] Arndt, *Die Goslarer Kaiserpfalz*, especially pp. 26–9, 53–7, 61–9; Pohlsander, *National Monuments and Nationalism*, pp. 242–3.

[108] See, for instance, the comments of W. J. Diebold, 'The early middle ages in the exhibition *Deutsche Größe* (1940–1942)' in J. T. Marquardt and A. A. Jordan (eds.), *Medieval Art and Architecture after the Middle Ages* (Newcastle upon Tyne: Cambridge Scholars, 2011), pp. 363–86, here pp. 373–5; P. Lambert, 'Duke Widukind and Charlemagne in twentieth-century Germany: myths of origin and constructs of national identity' in C. Raudvere, K. Stala, and T. S. Willert (eds.), *Rethinking the Space for Religion: New Actors in Central and Southeast Europe on Religion, Authenticity and Belonging* (Lund: Nordic Academic Press, 2012), pp. 97–125; P. Lambert, 'Widukind or Karl der Große? Perspectives on historical culture and memory in the Third Reich and post-war West Germany' in J. H. Lim, B. Walker and P. Lambert (eds.), *Mass Dictatorship and Memory as Ever Present Past* (Basingstoke: Palgrave Macmillan, 2014), pp. 139–61, here pp. 141–4; W. Zöllner, *Karl oder Widukind? Martin Lintzel und die NS-"Geschichtsdeutung" in den Anfangsjahren der faschistischen Diktatur* (Wissenschaftliche Beiträge der Martin-Luther-Universität Halle-Wittenberg 10) (Halle: Martin-Luther-Universität, 1975), here especially pp. 8–9.

[109] G. W. Gadberry, 'An "ancient German rediscovered": The Nazi Widukind plays of Forster and Kiß' in H. H. Rennert (ed.), *Essays on Twentieth Century German Drama and Theater: An American Reception, 1977–1999* (New German-American Studies 19) (New York: P. Lang, 2004), pp. 155–66; Lambert,

A residential development in Osnabrück in the late 1930s was named Widukindland in his honour: its streets bore the names of his kin (Abbioweg, Gevaweg); of significant sites of the Saxon wars (Eresburg-weg, Sigiburgweg, Brunisbergweg); of the Saxons' pre-conquest assembly (Markloweg); of early medieval Saxon groups and their allies (Engernweg, Ostfalenweg, Westfalenweg, Nordalbingerweg, Sachsen-weg, Friesenweg); and of various other patriotic leitmotifs: Kamer-adschaftweg, Vaterlandsweg ('Camaraderie Way', 'Fatherland Way'). Freundschaftsweg ('Friendship Way'), by contrast, was constructed in the postwar period.[110] Elsewhere, the Saxon wars were commemorated in a more monumental fashion. Verden on the Aller, the alleged site of Charlemagne's execution of 4,500 Saxons in 782, served as the inspiration for a 1935 monument whose erection was supervised by none other than *Reichsführer* Heinrich Himmler himself.[111] Its design was simple: 4,500 standing stones in the middle of a grove.

As the Nazi party gained power and ambition, however, their self-identification with the Saxon 'underdog' began to wear thin. In 1935, the party made a volte-face: Hitler began to model himself upon Charlemagne and sought to dispel previous treatments of the emperor as a *Sachsenschlächter.*[112] Some factions within the Nazi party continued to celebrate the 'Saxon past', as is indeed demonstrated by the construction of Widukindland a few years later. Others moved to depict Charlemagne (once again *Karl der Große*) as a great Germanic hero in a manner not altogether dissimilar to their Prussian predecessors. Both portrayals, and the debates they engendered, were to have a deep influence on contemporary historical writing.[113]

Naturally, some scholars diverged from the accepted interpretations. Karl Bauer denied the massacre at Verden altogether, attributing it to a copyist's misreading of 'delocare' (to deport) as 'decollare' (to execute).

'Duke Widukind', pp. 108–9, 115–18; P. Lambert, 'The immediacy of a remote past: the afterlife of Widukind in the Third Reich', *British Academy Review*, 22 (2013), 13–16; Lambert, 'Widukind or Karl der Große?', pp. 147–50.

[110] H. Jansing, 'Das Osnabrücker Widukindland – ein Stadtteil der ungewöhnlichen Straßennamen', *Neue Osnabrücker Zeitung* 18. September 2012. Available at www.noz.de/lokales/osnabrueck/artikel/7580/das-osnabrucker-widukindland-stadtteil-der-ungewohnlichen-strassennamen

[111] R. Linde, 'Exernsteine, Verden und Enger: Der völkische Sachsenkult in der Zeit der Nationalsozialismus' in C. Stiegemann, M. Kroker and W. Walter (eds.), *Credo: Christianisierung Europas im Mittelalter*, 2 vols. (Petersberg: M. Imhof, 2013), vol. I: pp. 475–82; see also Lambert, 'Duke Widukind', pp. 107–8; Lambert, 'Widukind or Karl der Große?', pp. 138–41, 146.

[112] Diebold, 'The early middle ages', p. 375; Lambert, 'Duke Widukind', pp. 109–13; Lambert, 'Widukind or Karl der Große?', pp. 151–2; Linde, 'Exernsteine', p. 481.

[113] See especially W. Lammers (ed.), *Die Eingliederung der Sachsen in das Frankenreich* (Wege der Forschung 185) (Darmstadt: Wissenschaftliche Buchgesellschaft, 1970), which seeks to underscore the politically motivated nature of historical discourse on this topic.

In so doing, he hoped to dispel the image of Charlemagne as a 'foreign invader' and his adversary Widukind as a 'German national hero'; his essay was capped off by the following short verse:

Amicus Widukindus.
Amicus Carolus.
Magis amica veritas.[114]

So too did Martin Lintzel, one of the most influential Saxon scholars from this period, set out various dissenting views, most notably in a public lecture on Saxon history.[115] Yet even Lintzel betrays, perhaps inescapably, some of the politics of the time: he was reacting to contemporary debates and in so doing necessarily engaged with current attitudes. His comment on the assembly at Marklo, which he characterized as the first parliament in history, is particularly striking in this regard: 'The word "parliament" appears rather disagreeable to us today. That is not necessarily the case historically. There have been bad, but also good, parliaments.'[116]

The Nazi party had claimed the Saxon past as their own national history, albeit in conflicting and contradictory ways. It is therefore unsurprising that the postwar period exhibited a sharp decline in Saxon historiography, albeit with one pronounced exception: the *Stellinga*, a so-called peasant revolt, became an extremely popular subject for East German historians.[117] Despite the two reports which linked the *Stellinga* to the Carolingian emperor Lothar (discussed further in Chapter 2), these scholars preferred to regard it as an autonomous peasant movement

---

[114] K. Bauer, 'Die Quellen für das sogenannte Blutbad von Verden' in Lammers, *Die Eingliederung der Sachsen*, pp. 109–50, here p. 150: 'artfremder Eindringling', 'germanische Nationalheros'. This view has also found some favour in more recent scholarship: see K. Hengst, 'Die Ereignisse der Jahre 777/78 und 782: Archäologie und Schriftüberlieferung' in Godman, Jarnut and Johanek, *Am Vorabend*, pp. 57–74, here pp. 66–9.

[115] Zöllner, *Karl oder Widukind?*, pp. 20–5.

[116] Lintzel, 'Karl der Große und Widukind' in Lintzel, *Schriften*, pp. 199–204, here p. 203: 'Das Wort Parlament pflegt uns heute etwas unsympathisch zu sein. Das ist historisch gesehen nicht unbedingt notwendig. Es hat schlechte, aber es hat auch gute Parlamente gegeben.'

[117] See, for instance, H. J. Bartmuss, 'Zur Frage der Bedeutung des Stellingaaufstandes', *Wissenschaftliche Zeitschrift der Martin-Luther-Universität Halle-Wittenberg*, 7(1) (1957), 113–23; H. J. Bartmuss, 'Ursachen und Triebkräfte im Entstehungsprozeß des "frühfeudalen deutschen Staates"', *ZfG*, 10(7) (1962), 1591–1625; Epperlein, 'Sachsen im frühen Mittelalter'; S. Epperlein, *Herrschaft und Volk im karolingischen Imperium: Studien über soziale Konflikte und dogmatisch-politische Kontroversen im fränkischen Reich* (Forschungen zur mittelalterlichen Geschichte 14) (Berlin: Akademie, 1969); E. Müller-Mertens, 'Vom Regnum Teutonicum zum Heiligen Römischen Reich Deutscher Nation: Reflexionen über die Entwicklung des deutschen Staates im Mittelalter', *ZfG*, 11(2) (1963), 319–46; E. Müller-Mertens, 'Der Stellingaaufstand: Seine Träger und die Frage der politischen Macht', *ZfG*, 20(7) (1972), 818–42; H. J. Schulze, 'Der Aufstand der Stellinga in Sachsen und sein Einfluß auf den Vertrag von Verdun', unpublished PhD thesis, Humboldt-Universität zu Berlin (1955).

which sought to shake off the weight of Frankish and elite oppression. Here, despite the merits of the resultant scholarship, the contemporary political climate for academic research (in this case, that of the DDR) is again all too evident.

Apart from East German interest in the *Stellinga*, however, the Saxon past became largely the preserve of local historians and archivists. This was a move away from national history towards *Landesgeschichte* ('regional history'), which was paralleled more generally in German historiography. The resultant scholarship has substantially enriched our knowledge of individual centres and texts; so too have the excellent volumes produced by the series *Germania Sacra* contributed greatly to our understanding of Saxon religious institutions.[118] In the absence of wide-scale analyses, however, such work has cumulatively contributed towards a fractured view of Saxon history. While scholarship on specific institutions abounded, there have been few thematic treatments of the period at large.

Naturally, there are a few notable exceptions: among these, Klemens Honselmann's cumulative work on the Christianization of the region, which has been widely influential; Reinhard Wenskus's work on ethnogenesis, which has arguably had more impact upon Saxon historiography than his onomatological study of the Saxon elite; and Helmut Beumann's seminal article of 1982, which argued that an array of Saxon historiographical and hagiographical texts which discuss the Saxon conquest may be seen as engaging in *Vergangenheitsbewältigung* ('coming to terms with the past').[119] This characterization was no doubt informed by Beumann's own postwar

---

[118] The relevant volumes of *Germania Sacra* are as follows: H. Goetting, *Das Bistum Hildesheim 1: Das reichsunmittelbare Kanonissenstift Gandersheim* (GSNF 7) (Berlin: W. de Gruyter, 1973); H. Goetting, *Das Bistum Hildesheim 2: Das Benediktiner(innen)kloster Brunshausen, das Benediktinerinnenkloster St. Marien vor Gandersheim, das Benediktinerkloster Clus, das Franziskanerkloster Gandersheim* (GSNF 8) (Berlin: W. de Gruyter, 1974); H. Goetting, *Das Bistum Hildesheim 3: Die Hildesheimer Bischöfe von 815 bis 1221 (1227)* (GSNF 20) (Berlin: W. de Gruyter, 1984); E. Klueting, *Das Bistum Osnabrück 1: Das Kanonissenstift und Benediktinerinnenkloster Herzebrock* (GSNF 21) (Berlin: W. de Gruyter, 1986); W. Kohl, *Das Bistum Münster 3: Das (freiweltliche) Damenstift Freckenhorst* (GSNF 10) (Berlin: W. de Gruyter, 1975); W. Kohl, *Das Bistum Münster 7: Die Diözese* (GSNF 37), 4 vols (Berlin: W. de Gruyter, 1999–2004); W. Kohl, *Das Bistum Münster 8: Das (freiweltliche) Damenstift Nottuln* (GSNF 44) (Berlin: W. de Gruyter, 2005); H. Müller, *Das Bistum Münster 5: Das Kanonissenstift und Benediktinerkloster Liesborn* (GSNF 23) (Berlin: W. de Gruyter, 1987); W. Stüwer, *Das Erzbistums Köln 3: Die Reichsabtei Werden an der Ruhr* (GSNF 12) (Berlin: W. de Gruyter, 1980).

[119] For the numerous contributions of Honselmann, see K. Honselmann, 'Die Urkunde Erzbischof Liudberts von Mainz für Corvey-Herford von 888', *WZ*, 89(2) (1932), 130–9; K. Honselmann, 'Die Annahme des Christentums durch die Sachsen im Lichte sächsischer Quellen des 9. Jahrhunderts', *WZ*, 108 (1958), 201–19; K. Honselmann, 'Eine Essener Predigt zum Predigt zum Feste des hl. Marsus aus dem 9. Jahrhundert', *WZ*, 110 (1960), 199–221; Honselmann, 'Reliquientranslationen', pp. 159–93; K. Honselmann, 'Berichte des 9. Jahrhundert über Wunder am graba der Hl. Pusinna in Herford' in J. Bauermann (ed.), *Dona Westfalica: Georg Schreiber zum 80 Geburtstage* (Schriften der Historischen Kommission für Westfalen 4) (Münster: Aschendorff, 1963), pp. 128–36; K. Honselmann, 'Der Bericht des Klerikers Ido von der Übertragung der

perspective, but is nonetheless applicable in this context. To these works may also be added Matthias Becher's 1996 monograph, *Rex, Dux, und Gens*, which examined the growth of Saxon political self-consciousness and political organization in the Carolingian and Ottonian periods.[120]

Only in the past twenty years, however, has wide thematic interest in Saxon history resurfaced. This development may be largely attributed to a major exhibition mounted at the Diocesan Museum in Paderborn in 1999 to commemorate the 1,200-year anniversary of Pope Leo III's meeting with Charlemagne at Paderborn. This exhibition commissioned an edited volume in advance of the opening, a comprehensive array of scholarly essays which were subsequently published as part of a three-volume catalogue, and an edition of *King Charlemagne and Pope Leo*, an epic poem written to celebrate the papal visit; an additional edited volume on the subject (with similar contributors, although independent from the exhibition) was published some three years later.[121] Similarly important for a reassessment of the period was a conference – the sixth in a series on 'Studies in Historical Archaeoethnology', held also in 1999 in San Marino – which undertook to examine the Saxons from an ethnographic perspective.[122]

The past twenty-odd years have seen a consolidation of this interest. Matthias Springer's monograph, which critically reexamined the early history of the Saxons and crucially dispelled any semblance of political or ethnic unity, was published in 2004; Hedwig Röckelein's extended

---

Gebeine des hl. Liborius', *WZ*, 119 (1969), 189–265; K. Honselmann, 'Die Bistumsgründungen in Sachsen unter Karl dem Großen, mit einem Ausblick auf spätere Bistumsgründungen und einem Excurs zur Übernahme der christlichen Zeitrechnung im frühmittelalterlichen Sachsen', *AfD*, 30 (1984), 1–50; K. Honselmann, 'Die Gründung der sächsischen Bistümer 799: Sachsens Anschluß an das fränkische Reich', *AfD*, 34 (1988), 1–2. For Reinhard Wenskus, meanwhile, see R. Wenskus, *Stammesbildung und Verfassung: das Werden der frühmittelalterlichen Gentes* (Cologne: Böhlau, 1961), here especially pp. 541–51; R. Wenskus, *Sächsischer Stammesadel und fränkischer Reichsadel* (Abhandlungen der Akademie der Wissenschaften in Göttingen. Philologisch-Historische Klasse 93) (Göttingen: Vandenhoeck & Ruprecht, 1976); Wenskus, Die ständische Entwicklung', pp. 587–616. Finally, for Beumann's seminal article, see H. Beumann, 'Die Hagiographie 'bewältigt': Unterwerfung und Christianisierung der Saschen durch Karl den Grossen' in *Cristianizzazione ed organizzazione ecclesiastica delle campagne nell'Alto Medioevo: espansione e resistenze: 10–16 aprile 1980* (Settimane 28:1) (Spoleto: Il Centro, 1982), pp. 129–68.

[120] Becher, *Rex, Dux und Gens*; see also M. Becher, 'Vitus von Corvey und Mauritius von Magdeburg: zwei sächsische Heilige in Konkurrenz', *WZ*, 147 (1997), 235–49; Becher, '*Non enim habent regem*', pp. 1–31; M. Becher, 'Karl der Große und Papst Leo III. Die Ereignisse der Jahre 799 und 800 aus der Sicht der Zeitgenossen' in Stiegemann and Wemhoff, *799*, vol. I: pp. 22–36; Becher, 'Die Sachsen im 7. und 8. Jahrhundert', pp. 188–94; M. Becher, 'Volksbildung und Herzogtum in Sachsen während des 9. und 10. Jahrhunderts', *Mitteilungen des Instituts für österreichische Geschichtsforschung*, 108(1) (2000), 67–84.

[121] Hässler, Jarnut and Wemhoff, *Sachsen*; Stiegemann and Wemhoff, *799*; *De Karolo rege et Leone papa*, ed. Hentze; Godman, Jarnut and Johanek, *Am Vorabend*.

[122] Green and Siegmund, *Saxons*.

study, which came out some two years earlier, expertly re-evaluated the role of relic translations and their representations in Saxon society, using both recent network theory and literary analysis to construct a rich portrait of Saxon religious life and its horizons.[123] Caspar Ehlers' 2007 book presented a comprehensive study of Saxon ecclesiastical development in the Carolingian and Ottonian periods.[124] More recently, in Anglophone scholarship, Eric Knibbs' 2011 monograph re-examined the complicated history of Hamburg-Bremen, while Robert Flierman's 2017 book analyses the construction of Saxon identities across the early medieval period.[125] These authors have all contributed greatly to a more nuanced understanding of late eighth- and ninth-century Saxon history and of its numerous connections with the wider Carolingian world.

---

[123] Röckelein, *Reliquientranslationen nach Sachsen*; Springer, *Die Sachsen*. Both scholars have further contributed to the study of the period with an extensive array of articles: see H. Röckelein, 'Miracle collections of Carolingian Saxony: literary tradition versus original creation', *Hagiographica*, 3 (1996), 267–76; H. Röckelein, 'Zur Pragmatik hagiographischer Schriften im Frühmittelalter' in H. Keller, T. Scharff and T. Behrmann (eds.), *Bene vivere in communitate: Beiträge zum italienischen und deutschen Mittelalter: Hagen Keller zum 60. Geburtstag überreicht von seinen Schülerinnen und Schülern* (Münster: Waxmann, 1997), pp. 225–38; H. Röckelein, 'Miracles and horizontal mobility in the early middle ages: some methodological reflections' in J. Hill and M. Swan (eds.), *The Community, the Family and the Saint: Patterns of Power in Early Medieval Europe: Selected Proceedings of the International Medieval Congress, University of Leeds, 4–7 July 1994, 10–13 July 1995* (Turnhout: Brepols, 1998), pp. 181–97; H. Röckelein, 'Halberstadt, Helmstedt und die Liudgeriden' in J. Gerchow (ed.), *Das Jahrtausend der Mönche: Kloster Welt Werden, 799–1803* (Cologne: Wienand, 1999), pp. 65–73; H. Röckelein, '"Pervenimus mirificum ad sancti Medardi oraculum". Der Anteil westfränkischer Zellen am Aufbau sächsischer Missionszentrum' in Godman, Jarnut and Johanek, *Am Vorabend*, pp. 145–62; H. Röckelein, 'Eliten markieren den sächsischen Raum als christlichen: Bremen, Halberstadt, und Herford (8.–11. Jahrhundert' in P. Depreux, F. Bougard and R. Le Jan (eds.), *Les élites et leurs espaces: mobilité, rayonnement, domination (du VIe au XIe siècle)* (Collection Haut Moyen Âge 5) (Turnhout: Brepols), 2007, pp. 273–98; H. Röckelein, 'Bairische, sächsische und mainfränkische Klostergründungen im Vergleich (8. Jahrhundert bis 1100)' in E. Schlotheuber, H. Flachenecker and I. Gardill (eds.), *Nonnen, Kanonissen und Mystikerinnen: religiöse Frauengemeinschaften in Süddeutschland* (SzGS 31) (Göttingen: Vandenhoeck & Ruprecht, 2008), pp. 23–55; H. Röckelein, 'Altfrid, Gründer des Stifts Essen und international agierender Kirchenmann?' in T. Schilp (ed.), *Frauen bauen Europa: Internationale Verflechtungen des Frauenstifts Essen* (Essener Forschungen zum Frauenstift 9) (Essen: Klartext, 2011), pp. 27–64; Springer, 'Lebuins Lebensbeschreibung', pp. 223–39; M. Springer, 'Geschichtsbilder, Urteile und Vorurteile: Franken und Sachsen in den Vorstellungen unserer Zeit und in der Vergangenheit' in Stiegemann and Wemhoff, *799*, vol. III: pp. 224–32; Springer, 'Location in space and time', pp. 11–36.

[124] Ehlers, *Die Integration Sachsens*; see also C. Ehlers, 'Die zweifache Integration: Sachsen zwischen Karolingern und Ottonen. Überlegungen zur Erschließung von Diözesen mit Klöstern und Stiften in Westfalen und Sachsen bis 1024' in K. Bodarwé and T. Schilp (eds.), *Herrschaft, Liturgie und Raum: Studien zur mittelalterlichen Geschichte des Frauenstifts Essen* (Essener Forschungen zum Frauenstift 1) (Essen: Klartext, 2002), pp. 24–50; C. Ehlers, 'Das Damenstift Gandersheim und die Bischöfe von Hildesheim', *Die Diözese Hildesheim in Vergangenheit und Gegenwart. Jahrbuch des Vereins für Geschichte und Kunst im Bistum Hildesheim*, 70 (2002), 1–31; C. Ehlers, 'Könige, Klöster, und der Raum. Die Entwicklung der kirchlichen Topographie Westfalens und Ostsachsens in karolingischer und ottonischer Zeit', *WZ*, 153 (2003), 189–216.

[125] Flierman, *Saxon Identities*; Knibbs, *Ansgar, Rimbert and the Forged Foundations of Hamburg-Bremen*.

Nevertheless, earlier historiography continues to affect contemporary treatments of the period. In Germany, despite this recent outpouring of excellent thematic scholarship, Carolingian Saxony continues to be considered largely on a local–historical level, thereby obscuring wider regional trends. A large-scale re-evaluation of the Christianization of the region has yet to be attempted.[126] In Anglophone scholarship, meanwhile, the relative absence of broad synthesizing treatments has caused many (but by no means all) scholars of the Carolingian world either to ignore Carolingian Saxony or to dismiss it as an anomaly. The roots of this apparent exceptionalism may be traced back, at least indirectly, to early twentieth-century German scholarship and its desire to approach 'pagan' Saxony as the antithesis of Christian Francia. The assumption that Carolingian Saxony was pagan or anti-Christian continues to shape modern historical attitudes towards the region.

★ ★ ★

This book sets out to reevaluate the process by which Saxony was incorporated into the Carolingian Empire and the Christian church following its violent conquest by Charlemagne. The long and contested nature of the conquest, set alongside the *Stellinga* revolt of 841 to 842/3, has led many to question the extent to these processes were achieved. Yet the vast majority of the extant evidence for Carolingian Saxony points towards the successful conversion and political integration of the region. Both during and increasingly following the Saxon wars, Saxons engaged productively with the structures of Carolingian governance; far from rejecting Christianity, the development of Christian infrastructure in Saxony appears to have been primarily the result of local activism and support.

The resultant structures in Carolingian Saxony did not correspond exactly to their Frankish counterparts. Rather, the particular circumstances present in Carolingian Saxony led to the emergence of a distinctive religious and political landscape, different from, but by no means inferior to, the Frankish world.

---

[126] The survey by Peter Johanek is excellent but necessarily brief: see P. Johanek, 'Der Ausbau der sächsischen Kirchenorganisation' in Stiegemann and Wemhoff, *799*, vol. II: pp. 494–506.

PART I

Politics of Conquest

Chapter 1

THE SAXON WARS

The Saxon wars were of great significance to the subsequent history of the region. The Saxons were brought inside the Carolingian empire and made subject to the Carolingian king. They were incorporated into the framework of Frankish political life and military campaigning, their laws codified and augmented, their elites endowed with offices and lands (and thus presented with further opportunities for advancement and enrichment); even their economies began to grow, their villages and towns to develop. They accepted baptism and were converted to the Christian faith, thereby leading to the introduction of Christian institutional structures and all the attendant ramifications. In short: the conquest ushered in a series of religious and socio-political changes which would fundamentally reshape Saxon society over the course of the next century. It placed Saxony on a new trajectory, with important consequences for its later development.

The Saxon wars can be roughly divided into two discrete phases: from 772 to 785, and from 792 to 804.[1] The nature of the wars changed greatly from the first period of campaigning to the second. The conflict up to 785 was waged between Franks and Saxons, albeit with some Frisian assistance on the Saxon side, and presumably (although less demonstrably)

---

[1] For this twofold division, see, among others, R. Collins, *Charlemagne* (Basingstoke: Macmillan, 1998), p. 164; Y. Hen, 'Charlemagne's jihad', *Viator*, 37 (2006), 33–51, here 33–5. Other historians have argued that the Saxon wars consisted of three discrete phases, namely 772 to 776/7, 778 to 785, and 792 to 804: for this perspective, see A. Lampen, 'Sachsenkriege, sächischer Widerstand und Kooperation' in Stiegemann and Wemhoff, *799*, pp. 264–72, here pp. 268–71; M. Springer, *Die Sachsen* (Stuttgart: W. Kohlhammer, 2004), pp. 178–95, 200–10; for a four-stage model, see C. Ehlers, *Die Integration Sachsens in das fränkische Reich (751–1024)* (Veröffentlichungen des Max-Planck-Instituts für Geschichte 231) (Göttingen: Vandenhoeck & Ruprecht, 2007), pp. 273–9. For a more detailed periodization of the initial stages of the Saxon war, see H.-D. Kahl, 'Karl der Große und die Sachsen. Stufen und Motive einer historischen "Eskalation"' in H. Ludat and R. C. Schwinges (eds.), *Politik, Gesellschaft, Geschichtsschreibung: Giessener Festgabe für František Graus zum 60. Geburtstag* (Beihefte zum Archiv für Kulturgeschichte 18) (Cologne: Böhlau, 1982), pp. 49–130.

some Saxon assistance on the Frankish side. It was conducted largely in western Saxony and centred upon the possession of certain fortresses, notably Eresburg and Syburg. The annals record the frequent transfer of hostages and place great emphasis on the submission of certain *optimates*: Hessi, Brun, Abbi and above all Widukind, whose capitulation and baptism in 785 marked the end of this stage. Throughout those years, Christian conversion appears to have been a pressing priority.

By contrast, in the conflict after 792, Saxons were pitted both against other (pro-Frankish) Saxons and the Abodrites, the Franks' Slavic allies; fighting was concentrated in the easternmost regions, which lacked prominent fortifications, at least until a spate of Frankish building work undertaken in 798. Unlike the earlier grants of largely elite hostages, Saxons were moved *en masse*, culminating in the alleged deportation of some 10,000 Saxons in 804. No leaders are named in this later stage of the conflict. No emphasis, moreover, is placed upon Christian conversion, perhaps because the Saxons were still perceived, even despite recent lapses, as Christians. Einhard's summary of a conquest 'waged for thirty-three continuous years' is seductive in its simplicity, but the majority of the extant evidence suggests a far more variegated picture.[2]

THE SAXON WARS AND THE WIDER WORLD

The Saxon conquest is often discussed as a long conflict waged between two discrete peoples, the Saxons and the Franks. Yet in practice, it was a series of conflicts waged between a variety of groups, held together, and sometimes torn apart, by networks of shifting alliances. These conflicts were bound up in the wider politics of the region, from Charlemagne's conquest of Lombard Italy to warfare between Slavic peoples, namely the Wilzi and Abodrites. The Saxon wars were moreover recorded by authors whose interests spanned this early medieval world, and whose accounts both sought to influence and were influenced by Carolingian politics writ large. In order to understand the Saxon wars, then, it is necessary to understand their wider context.

To turn first to the labels 'Saxons' and 'Franks': these are little more than terms of convenience. Scholars have largely concluded that the designation 'Saxon' was simply an umbrella term. It was a categorization applied externally, rather than a positive marker of self-asserted

---

[2] Einhard, *Vita Karoli Magni*, ed. O. Holder-Egger, *MGH SRG* 25 (Hanover: Hahn, 1911), c. 7, p. 9: 'per continuos triginta tres annos gerebatur'. For a discussion of the main sources for the Saxon war, see the Introduction to this book, pp. 12–14.

identity.[3] The *Royal Frankish Annals* uncover other, more local, forms of identity: the Eastphalians and Angarians, who submitted to Charlemagne in 775 with their respective leaders, Hessi and Brun; the Westphalians, who likewise submitted in 775, and who later rebelled and were reconquered in 779; and, perhaps most prominently, the Nordliudi, whose conversion was first reported in 780, and whose renewed rebellion in 798 earned the vituperation of the reviser.[4] While it is unclear precisely what these groupings constituted and how stable they were in practice, the significance of at least three of these groups – the Westphalians, Eastphalians, and Angarians – is hinted at by their presence in the *Second Saxon Capitulary* and the early ninth-century hostage list, by the different legal customs attributed to them in the *Law of the Saxons*, and, albeit at a greater distance, by the comments of Widukind of Corvey some two centuries later.[5]

The Franks, then, did not fight against a homogeneous socio-political or ethnic unit: rather, they fought against an array of local and regional groupings which coalesced, combined and detached depending on circumstance. These groups were represented collectively by the Franks as 'the Saxons', but it is unclear whether those who were externally labelled as 'Saxon' would have identified themselves in such a manner prior to or even during the conquest period. This is an important qualification to make, yet even this, on its own, is insufficient, for the conflict did not simply pit Franks against those they identified as Saxons; rather, both Franks and Saxons alike relied upon allies: Saxons on Frisians and, to a lesser extent, Slavs and Northmen; Franks on their Saxon allies (a point we shall return to consider below) and Slavic Abodrites.[6] The influence of such alliances would prove particularly decisive in the later stages of the conflict.

---

[3] For this, see above, pp. 4–5; see also M. Springer, 'Location in space and time' in Green and Siegmund, *Saxons*, pp. 11–36. See further M. Becher, '*Non enim habent regem idem Antiqui Saxones* ... Verfassung und Ethnogenese in Sachsen während des 8. Jahrhunderts' in Hässler, Jarnut and Wemhoff, *Sachsen*, pp. 1–31; M. Becher, 'Die Sachsen im 7. und 8. Jahrhundert' in Stiegemann and Wemhoff, *799*, vol. I: pp. 184–94, here pp. 188, 192; I. N. Wood, 'Beyond satraps and ostriches: political and social structures of the Saxons in the early Carolingian period' in Green and Siegmund, *Saxons*, pp. 271–97, here pp. 271–2.

[4] *Annales Regni Francorum*, ed. F. Kurze, *MGH SRG* 6 (Hanover: Hahn, 1895), 775, 779, 780, 798, pp. 40–2, 54, 56, 102–4. For the Nordliudi, see also Springer, *Die Sachsen*, p. 186.

[5] *Capitulare Saxonicum*, ed. C. von Schwerin, *MGH Fontes iuris* 4 (Hanover: Hahn, 1918), pp. 45–9, here prologue, p. 45; *Indiculus obsidum Saxonum Moguntiam deducendorum*, ed. A. Boretius, *MGH Cap.* 1 (Hanover: Hahn, 1883), pp. 233–4; *Lex Saxonum*, ed. C. von Schwerin, *MGH Fontes iuris* 4 (Hanover: Hahn, 1918), pp. 9–36, here cc. 47–8, pp. 29–30; Widukind of Corvey, *Res Gestae Saxonicae*, eds. P. Hirsch and H. E. Lohmann, *MGH SRG* 60 (Hanover: Hahn, 1935), I:14, pp. 23–4. See also Becher, 'Die Sachsen im 7. und 8. Jahrhundert', pp. 190–2; Becher, '*Non enim habent regem*', pp. 18–28; Springer, *Die Sachsen*, pp. 250–7; Wood, 'Beyond satraps and ostriches', pp. 275–6.

[6] See below, pp. 61–6.

Saxons and Their Allies

The Saxon wars were not waged in Saxony alone: Saxons made incursions onto Frankish soil on at least two occasions, and the conflict further spilled over into the territories of the Frisians, Slavs and Northmen. While there is no record of formal alliances between these groups and Saxons – unlike the treaty made between the Franks and a section of the Slavs, the Abodrites – parts of these groups provided support to Saxons at various points. In the case of Slavs and Northmen, such assistance appears to have been slight. A 792 entry in the *Wolfenbüttel Annals* records that the Slavs had joined the Saxons and Frisians in rebellion, a report that is confirmed by the more general remark of the *Lorsch Annals* that the Saxons had allied with 'the pagan peoples who bordered them'.[7] Scandinavia, meanwhile, appears to have served chiefly as a place of refuge: Widukind and his companions are recorded as having travelled to the Northmen to escape Frankish forces in 777 and 782.[8] These traces are suggestive, but little more.

By contrast, Frisia was embroiled to a much greater degree in the Saxon conflict. This is not surprising: all the extant material from the ninth century points to close relations between the two regions, from the Frisian elite's donations to the Saxon monastery of Werden to the transregional dioceses of Bremen and Münster.[9] As a diploma from the Emperor Lothar later included in the *Translation of Saint Alexander* stated, the Saxon and Frisian people were 'mixed together'.[10] There was no dividing line, and so the Saxon conflict spread swiftly to Frisia.

---

[7] *Annales Guelferbytani*, ed. G. H. Pertz, *MGH SS* 1 (Hanover: Hahn, 1826), pp. 23–31, 40–6, here 792, p. 45; *Annales Laureshamenses*, ed. G. H. Pertz, *MGH SS* 1 (Hanover: Hahn, 1826), pp. 22–39, here 792, p. 35: 'paganas gentes, qui in circuitu eorum erant'.

[8] *Annales Regni Francorum*, ed. Kurze, 777, 782, pp. 48, 62. For a discussion of Frankish–Danish relations, see S. Lamb, 'Francia and Scandinavia in the early Viking Age, c. 700–900', unpublished Ph.D. thesis, University of Cambridge (2009), here especially pp. 33–4; see also D. Melleno, 'Before they were Vikings: Scandinavia and the Franks up to the death of Louis the Pious', unpublished Ph.D. thesis, University of California Berkeley (2014), pp. 28–9, 35.

[9] *Cartularium Werthinense*, ed. D. P. Blok, Een diplomatisch onderzoek van de oudste particuliere oorkonden van Werden', unpublished Ph.D. thesis, University of Amsterdam (1960), nos. 4, 9–10, 16, 18, 24–5, 29–31, 41–2, 47–8, 50, 53, 59, 61–4, 66, pp. 159–60, 165–7, 173–6, 182–4, 187–9, 197–9, 202–4, 205, 207–8, 212–19. For the territory of the diocese of Bremen, see *Vita sancti Willehadi*, eds. C. de Smedt, F. van Ortroy, H. Delehaye, A. Poncelet and P. Peeters, *Acta Sanctorum III Novembris* (Brussels, 1910), pp. 842–6, here c. 8, p. 845B-C. For the territory of the diocese of Münster, see Altfrid, *Vita sancti Liudgeri*, ed. W. Diekamp, *Die vitae sancti Liudgeri* (Die Geschichtsquellen des Bisthums Münster 4) (Münster: Theissing, 1881), pp. 3–53, here I:24, p. 29.

[10] Rudolf and Meginhard, *Translatio sancti Alexandri*, ed. G. H. Pertz, *MGH SS* 2 (Hanover: Hahn, 1829), pp. 673–81, here c. 4, p. 677: 'commixta'. See further I. N. Wood, 'Before or after mission: social relations across the middle and lower Rhine the seventh and eighth centuries' in I. L. Hansen and C. Wickham (eds.), The Long Eighth Century: Production, Distribution and Demand (*The Transformation of the Roman World 11*) (Leiden: Brill, 2000), pp. 149–66, here pp. 159–62, 166.

The earliest recorded incident of Frisian involvement is preserved not in a contemporary annalistic source, but rather in a later work of hagiography: Altfrid's *Life of Saint Liudger*, written in the 840s. Altfrid reports how, both before and after the missionary Lebuin's death in circa 775, Saxons invaded and burned down the church he maintained in Deventer.[11] In the early 780s, he writes further of how 'the root of wickedness, Widukind, duke of the Saxon peoples and hitherto pagan, rose up, and, having turned the Frisians from the way of the Lord, burned churches and expelled the servants of the Lord, and he made the Frisians all the way over to the Fleo River relinquish their Christian faith'.[12] This report can be confirmed, in part, by an entry in the *Royal Frankish Annals* for 784 which describes how the Saxons rebelled, and 'with them a part of the Frisians'.[13]

Later, Altfrid would record another 'great infidelity' on the part of the eastern Frisians, 'of which evil Unno and Eilrat were the leaders'.[14] This disturbance lasted a year and, although it has not been securely dated, it may be tentatively placed in the period of 792 to 797, when the annals again record Frisian unrest. In 792, the *Alemannic Annals* and the *Wolfenbüttel Annals* state that the Frisians and Saxons were faithless; the *Moselle Annals* provides somewhat more detail, describing how 'a certain part of Charlemagne's army, which should have come by ship through the Frisians and Saxons, was deceived by those peoples and large numbers of them were destroyed'.[15] The following year, once again, the revised version of the *Royal Frankish Annals* includes a Saxon attack on a Frankish contingent in Frisia.[16] Finally, in 797 Charlemagne accepted hostages from Saxons and Frisians, a move which strongly suggests Frisian participation in the recent resistance.[17] That was not the only penalty they

---

[11] Altfrid, *Vita sancti Liudgeri*, ed. Diekamp, cc. 14–5, pp. 18–20.

[12] *Ibid*, c. 21, pp. 24–5: 'consurrexit radix sceleris Widukind, dux Saxonum eatenus gentilium, evertit Fresones a via Dei combussitque ecclesias et expulit Dei famulos et usque ad Fleo fluvium fecit Fresones Christi fidem relinquere'.

[13] *Annales regni Francorum*, ed. Kurze, 784, p. 66: 'cum eis pars aliqua Frisonum'. See also Springer, *Die Sachsen*, p. 192.

[14] Altfrid, *Vita sancti Liudgeri*, ed. Diekamp, c. 22, p. 27: 'infidelitatis magnae ... [c]uius mali Unno et Eilrat fuere principes'.

[15] *Annales Alamannici*, ed. G. H. Pertz, MGH SS 1 (Hanover: Hahn, 1826), pp. 22–30, 40–4, 47–60, here 792, p. 47; *Annales Guelferbytani*, ed. Pertz, 792, p. 45; *Annales Mosellani*, ed. J. M. Lappenberg, MGH SS 16 (Hanover: Hahn, 1859), pp. 491–9, here 791 [792], p. 498: 'quaedam pars exercitus eius, quae per Frisones et Saxones navigio venire debuit, ab eisdem decepta est gentibus et magna ex parte perempta'.

[16] *Annales qui dicuntur Einhardi*, ed. F. Kurze, MGH SRG 6 (Hanover: Hahn, 1895), here 793, p. 93.

[17] *Annales Lauresamenses*, ed. Pertz, 797, p. 37; *Chronicon Moissiacense*, ed. G. H. Pertz, MGH SS 1 (Hanover: Hahn, 1826), 797, p. 303; see also Collins, *Charlemagne*, p. 162; R. McKitterick, *History and Memory in the Carolingian World* (Cambridge: Cambridge University Press, 2004), p. 104.

suffered: the Astronomer, an anonymous biographer of Louis the Pious from the mid-ninth century, reports that Frisians, alongside their Saxon allies, had lost 'the right (*ius*) of their paternal inheritance ... on account of their perfidy'.[18] Whether this was through deportation or appropriation is unclear.

At numerous points throughout both stages of the Saxon conflict, then, fighting had spilled into Frisian territory, sometimes through purely Saxon initiative but often with Frisian collaboration, and even once at the instigation of Frisian leaders. The extent to which Frisian assistance may have aided Saxons in their conflict against the Franks, however, remains unclear. This stands in contrast to the Franks' principal allies, the Abodrites, whose role in the later stages of the conflict was essential to its outcome.

The Franks and the Abodrites

'The Abodrites have always given assistance to the Franks, since first the Franks concluded an alliance with them.'[19] So wrote the reviser of the *Royal Frankish Annals* in an entry for the year 798. Yet, to all intents and purposes, the Frankish and Abodrite alliance appears to have been a relatively recent creation.[20] The Abodrites and their leader, Witzin, first entered the historical stage in 789, when they joined Charlemagne for a campaign against a mutual enemy: the Wilzi, who, as the reviser darkly remarks, 'have always been hostile to the Franks; they hated their neighbours who were either subjected to or allied with the Franks, and often attacked them, pressing them down with war'.[21]

The Abodrites may have been more involved with the Franks behind the scenes, for their next appearance suggests a rather more complicated history. In 795, Charlemagne came to Bardowick and there awaited the arrival of the Slavs, whom he had ordered to meet him. Instead, a

---

[18] Astronomus, *Vita Hludowici imperatoris*, ed. E. Tremp, *MGH SRG* 64 (Hanover: Hahn, 1995), c. 24, p. 356: 'ius paterne hereditatis ... ob perfidiam'.

[19] *Annales qui dicuntur Einhardi*, ed. Kurze, 798, p. 105: 'Nam Abodriti auxiliares Francorum semper fuerunt, ex quo semel ab eis in societatem recepti sunt.'

[20] Contrast with L. Sobel, 'Ruler and society in early medieval Western Pomerania', *Antemurale*, 25 (1981), 19–142, here 43–4.

[21] *Annales qui dicuntur Einhardi*, ed. Kurze, 789, p. 85: 'Ea Francis semper inimica et vicinos suos, qui Francis vel subiecti vel foederati erant, odiis insectari belloque premere ac lacessire solebat.' For a summary of the Abodrites' involvement in the Saxon war, see S. Epperlein, 'Die Kämpfe zwischen Slawen, Franken und Sachsen und die fränkische Eroberungspolitik' in J. Herrmann (ed.), *Die Slawen in Deutschland: Geschichte und Kultur der slawischen Stämme westlich von Oder und Neisse vom 6. bis 12. Jahrhundert: ein Handbuch* (Veröffentlichungen des Zentralinstituts für Alte Geschichte und Archäologie der Akademie der Wissenschaften der DDR 14), new edn (Berlin: Akademie, 1985), pp. 326–33, here pp. 328–9.

messenger arrived, bearing ill news: Witzin, variously styled the duke or king of the Abodrites, and likewise a 'vassal of the lord king' Charlemagne, 'who had been coming to his aid', had been ambushed and killed by a group of Saxons while crossing the Elbe River.[22] After this, the Saxons who lived beyond the Elbe did not dare to come to Charlemagne, and rightly so: as the reviser remarks, 'this act spurred the spirit of the king to vanquish the Saxons more swiftly and aroused an even greater hatred of that perfidious people in him'.[23] Both the murder of Witzin by those Saxons and the response it solicited from the Franks suggest a higher degree of collaboration between the Franks and Abodrites than has been recorded.

Three years later, Saxons and Abodrites would again come to blows. In 798, a group of Saxons living beyond the Elbe rebelled and captured the royal envoys who had been sent to them, executing some and ransoming others.[24] Charlemagne responded quickly, raising an army and devastating the land between the Weser and Elbe. 'But', as the reviser wrote, 'the Saxons beyond the Elbe were inflated with pride, because they had been able to kill the king's legates without any consequences'.[25] They marched against the Abodrites in battle, and soon engaged with forces led by Thrasco, 'duke' of the Abodrites. The result was catastrophic for the Saxon side: according to Eburis, a Frankish envoy who had been present at the battle, thousands were slain, and those remaining sued for peace.[26] It was to be the most decisive engagement in the second stage of the conflict. The *Lorsch Annals* relate that the Abodrites were helped by 'the faith of the Christians and of the lord king'.[27] This in itself is an interesting comment on the Abodrites' lack of

---

[22] Witzin is styled as 'rex' and 'vassus domni regis' in the *Annales Laureshamenses*, ed. Pertz, 795, p. 36, and in the *Chronicon Moissiacense*, ed. Pertz, 795, p. 302; he is depicted as a 'rex' in *Annales regni Francorum*, ed. Kurze, 795, p. 96, in the *Annales qui dicuntur Einhardi*, ed. Kurze, 795, p. 97, and in the *Annales Mosellani*, ed. Lappenberg, 794 [795], p. 498; finally, he is labelled 'dux' in the *Annales Petaviani*, ed. G. H. Pertz, *MGH SS* 1 (Hanover: Hahn, 1826), pp. 7, 9, 11, 13, 15–18, here 795, p. 18 and *Annales Fuldenses*, ed. F. Kurze, *MGH SRG* 7 (Hanover: Hahn, 1891), here 795, p. 13. For the aid he offered to Charlemagne, see *Annales Mosellani*, ed. Lappenberg, 794 [795], p. 498: 'qui ad eius auxilium venerat'. For these titles, see further Sobel, 'Ruler and society', 44–6.

[23] *Annales qui dicuntur Einhardi*, ed. Kurze, 795, p. 97: 'Quod factum animo regis ad Saxones citius debellandos velut quosdam stimulos addidit et in odium perfidae gentis amplius excitavit.' See also O. M. Phelan, *The Formation of Christian Europe: The Carolingians, Baptism, and the Imperium Christianum* (Oxford: Oxford University Press, 2014), p. 68.

[24] *Annales regni Francorum*, ed. Kurze, 798, p. 102; see also Melleno, 'Before they were Vikings', 35, 41.

[25] *Annales qui dicuntur Einhardi*, ed. Kurze, 798, p. 105: 'Transalbiani autem superbia elati, eo quod regis legatos inpune occidere potuerunt.'

[26] *Ibid*, 798, p. 105; see further *Annales regni Francorum*, ed. Kurze, 798, pp. 102–4; *Chronicon Moissiacense*, ed. Pertz, 798, p. 303.

[27] *Annales Laureshamenses*, ed. Pertz, 798, p. 37: 'fides christianorum et domni regis'.

Christian profession, but it seems clear that on this occasion the victory belonged to the Abodrites themselves.

In 799, Charlemagne sent his son Charles the Younger beyond the Elbe to arrange the affairs of the Abodrites.[28] The Abodrites next appear in 804, when, perhaps on the strength of their 798 victory, they emerge as the chief beneficiaries of the Saxon deportations of 804. Early that year, Charlemagne met with the Abodrites at Holdonstat and, 'their cases having been pleaded and settled according to his judgement, he established Thrasco as their king'.[29] Charlemagne then undertook to relocate the Saxons living beyond the Elbe and in Wigmodia, and after he had finished clearing the land, he gave territory beyond the Elbe to the Abodrites.[30] Not only had Charlemagne marked out the architect of the Saxon victory with the title of king, he had also further enriched him with ample lands.

The Saxon deportations of 804 have generally been regarded by scholars, as they were by near-contemporaries, as marking the final settlement of the Saxon wars. Einhard, writing sometime during the reign of Louis the Pious, described how

When everyone who had resisted was routed and subjected to his power, he transported ten thousand men, along with their wives and children, out of those who lived on both banks of the Elbe River, and he dispersed them in various groups throughout Gaul and Germany. The war, drawn out through so many years, was concluded on the conditions proposed by the king and accepted by those ones.[31]

Yet since their 798 defeat, the Saxons had been relatively quiescent; when Charlemagne returned in 799, all those who had rebelled the previous year came and took oaths of fidelity. This fidelity was preserved during Charlemagne's long absence in Italy. In fact, there was only one attested conflict after the 798 battle: in 802, when there is a summary report of Charlemagne sending a contingent of Saxons to devastate the

---

[28] *Annales qui dicuntur Einhardi*, ed. Kurze, 799, p. 107; see further Springer, *Die Sachsen*, p. 208.

[29] *Annales Mettenses priores*, ed. B. Simpson, *MGH SRG* 10 (Hanover: Hahn, 1905), 804, p. 91: 'Quorum causis discussis et secundum arbitrium dispositis regem illis Trasiconem constituit.' See also Collins, *Charlemagne*, p. 164.

[30] *Annales regni Francorum*, ed. Kurze, 804, p. 118. Matthias Springer argues that there is no firm evidence that Charlemagne gave all (previously) Saxon lands beyond the Elbe to the Abodrites: for this, see Springer, *Die Sachsen*, p. 210; see also Lamb, 'Francia and Scandinavia', p. 35; Melleno, 'Before they were Vikings', pp. 36, 39, 41.

[31] Einhard, *Vita Karoli Magni*, ed. Holder-Egger, c. 7, p. 10: 'dum, omnibus qui resistere solebant profligatis et in suam potestatem redactis, decem milia hominum ex his qui utrasque ripas Albis fluminis incolebant cum uxoribus et parvulis sublatos transtulit et huc atque illuc per Galliam et Germaniam multimoda divisione distribuit. Eaque conditione a rege proposita et ab illis suscepta tractum per tot annos bellum constat esse finitum'.

lands of the Saxons beyond the Elbe.[32] In the absence of large-scale Saxon rebellion, the deportations of 804 can be understood as a grand, symbolic gesture, yet they can also, equally, be understood as a matter of client management. The grant of territory previously held by Saxons served to prop up Charlemagne's client king, Thrasco, whose worth as a vassal had already been amply illustrated by his faithful service in the battle of 798.

If the Frisians, Slavs and Northmen all played but a minor role in Saxon resistance, the Abodrites, by contrast, were integral actors in the second stage of the conflict. They achieved the greatest victory, and they too reaped the greatest reward.

The Saxon Wars in Context

The conclusion of the Saxon wars is thus best understood in terms of Charlemagne's relations with his Slavic clients, the Abodrites: they were, after all, the chief beneficiaries of the settlement. More generally, the conduct of the Saxon wars must be viewed in the context of late eighth-century Carolingian expansion: certainly, both Franks and Saxons planned their actions with an eye to this larger stage.

Charlemagne's first campaign into Saxony was launched in 772, the year after he assumed sole rule of Francia following the death of his brother, Carloman. He was able to achieve a swift trophy victory, with all attendant spoils; the *Royal Frankish Annals* record that he returned to Francia enriched with both gold and silver.[33] In so doing, he demonstrated his strength without making an overly aggressive bid for his dead brother's territory and, moreover, established himself as his father's successor in regard to his Saxon campaigns.

Nevertheless, Charlemagne's attention was divided, a fact of which the Saxons were all too aware. In 773, when Charlemagne launched a campaign against the Lombards in response to the request of Pope Hadrian, the Saxons took advantage of his absence to make incursions into Frankish territory. With the Carolingian army far away in Lombard Italy, the Saxons ventured deep into Hessia, committing arson and other acts of violence against the Frankish population.[34] Clearly, the Saxons were informed about Carolingian military movements. Further Saxon aggression accompanied Carolingian campaigns to Italy and Spain in 776 and 778, respectively; on the latter of these occasions, the Saxons

---

[32] *Annales regni Francorum*, ed. Kurze, 802, p. 117; *Annales Mettenses priores*, ed. Simpson, 802, p. 89.
[33] *Annales Regni Francorum*, ed. Kurze, 772, pp. 32–4.   [34] *Ibid*, 773, pp. 36–8.

raided deep into the Carolingian heartland, going as far south as Deutz (across the river from Cologne).[35] At one point, such coordination even elicited direct commentary on the part of an annalist. In 792, after seven years of peace, the *Lorsch Annals* record how 'the Saxons, reckoning that the people of the Avars should avenge themselves against the Christians, revealed most clearly what had previously been hidden in their hearts'.[36] In short, the Saxons rebelled, and incited the Avars to rebellion as well for good measure. Their rebellion coincided moreover with that of Charlemagne's eldest son, Pippin the Hunchback, which found widespread support throughout East Francia. Such timing was not coincidental.[37]

Of course, just as Charlemagne's absences afforded Saxons the opportunity to rebel, so too did his successes abroad bolster his own confidence and that of the Franks. Charlemagne's triumph over the Lombard king Desiderius may well have stoked his ambitions in Saxony: certainly, his campaign against the Saxons in 775, which led to the capitulation of two named Saxon leaders, was of a different magnitude than his 772 exploit in the region. Charlemagne had begun to fight a war of conquest. As the revised version of the *Royal Frankish Annals* records, it was at this point that 'he resolved that he would wage war against the perfidious and treaty-breaking Saxon people, and that he would continue thus until, conquered, they were made subject to Christian religion, or until they were entirely destroyed'.[38] His success in Lombard Italy had not only raised his sights in Saxony, but also given his actions a particularly Christian glint.

Likewise, at other points, Charlemagne's conduct of the Saxon wars may be seen to parallel his strategy elsewhere. Take, for instance, the public capitulations of the Saxon leader Widukind and the Bavarian duke Tassilo in 785 and 788 respectively, some three years apart.[39] These were carefully stage-managed affairs, conducted in full public view at Frankish assemblies; Charlemagne's victories abroad were recreated for audiences at home. Such occasions served as symbols of Charlemagne's assertion of power in Saxony and Bavaria, respectively; in both cases, Charlemagne

---

[35] *Ibid*, 776, 778, pp. 44–6, 52.
[36] *Annales Lareshamenses*, ed. Pertz, 792, p. 35: 'Saxones, aestimantes quod Avarorum gens se vindicare super christianos debuisset, hoc quod in corde eorum dudum iam antea latebat, manifestissime ostenderunt.'
[37] Hen, 'Charlemagne's jihad', 35, 39.
[38] *Annales qui dicuntur Einhardi*, ed. Kurze, 775, p. 41: 'consilium iniit, ut perfidam ac foedifragam Saxonum gentem bello adgrederetur et eo usque perseveraret, dum aut victi christianae religioni subicerentur aut omnino tollerentur'.
[39] *Annales Regni Francorum*, ed. Kurze, 785, 788, pp. 70, 80–2.

used the opportunity to present himself as a merciful but all-powerful king. Of course, such parallels may have been more apparent than real: annalists writing with the benefit of hindsight could tease out similarities in order better to advance their narratives. In this light, the account of Widukind's capitulation in the *Royal Frankish Annals* may be seen to anticipate their report of Tassilo's own downfall. I shall return to this point below.[40]

The Saxon wars were not waged in isolation. They were influenced by, and likewise actively influenced, conflicts elsewhere in the early medieval world; Saxons and Franks alike relied on alliances with other groups, perhaps most notably Frisians and Abodrites, but also including, in the case of the Franks, Saxons who had pledged their fidelity to Charlemagne. We will return to the issue of Saxon allegiance below: for now, let us turn to the means by which the campaigns were waged.

THE CONDUCT OF THE WARS

Battles and Massacres

The Abodrites' victory of 798 was not just remarkable for the many thousands of Saxons who lay slain. It was, in fact, the only recorded battle, and likewise the only occasion on which a substantial number of casualties were reported in the entire second half of the conflict. The war which Einhard describes as having been 'waged for thirty-three continuous years' saw only one pitched battle in its last nineteen years. This stands in marked contrast to the early years of campaigning, when such battles occurred with far greater frequency.

To be sure, Einhard himself minimizes the extent of open warfare in the early years of the conflict. As he writes:

Although this war dragged on for such a long period of time, Charlemagne only met with the enemy twice in battle, once next to the mountain which is called Osning in a place called Detmold, and a second time near the Haase River, and these took place in the same month, with only a few days' intermission between them. The enemy was so overthrown and defeated in these two battles that they did not dare to provoke Charlemagne any more or to resist his approach, unless protected by some fortification of the place.[41]

---

[40] See below, pp. 66–9.

[41] Einhard, *Vita Karoli Magni*, ed. Holder-Egger, c. 8, p. 11: 'Hoc bello, licet per multum temporis spatium traheretur, ipse non amplius cum hoste quam bis acie conflixit, semel iuxta montem qui Osneggi dicitur in loco Theotmelli nominato et iterum apud Hasa fluvium, et hoc uno mense, paucis quoque interpositis diebus. His duobus proeliis hostes adeo profligati ac devicti sunt, ut ulterius regem neque provocare neque venienti resistere, nisi aliqua loci munitione defensi,

Many scholars have followed Einhard's lead, concentrating above all upon the role of fortress sieges. Indeed, the Eresburg, a fortress in the Saxon-Frankish borderland, does appear to have served a considerable role in the first years of the Saxon wars: captured in 772, rebuilt in 775 and finally lost and recaptured in 776, it served as the base for further campaigns in 780 and 785, and may be reckoned the most important military site in the region.[42] Yet the other fortresses in Saxon territory mentioned in these years – the Syburg and a fortification built by Charlemagne above the Lippe River, which may be tentatively identified with the 'city of Charlemagne' (*urbs Karoli*) – occur only fleetingly in the sources, and most likely never held the strategic importance of the Eresburg. Focus on these fortresses and on their defence has obscured the extent to which open warfare dominated Charlemagne's early campaigns as depicted in the annalistic record, and in so doing has unwittingly created the impression that the massacre at Verden was an anomaly.

The massacre at Verden has long been regarded as an example of particular brutality. In 782, following a Saxon victory in the Süntel mountains, Charlemagne returned to Saxony with his army and marched to the mouth of the Aller, that is, to the vicinity of Verden. As the *Royal Frankish Annals* record, 'all the Saxons assembled once again, placed themselves under the rule of the aforementioned lord king, and returned all those malefactors who had been most culpable for the rebellion to be killed, four thousand five hundred in number'.[43] The widespread appearance of this mass execution in contemporary annalist reports suggests that it was highly significant to contemporaries.[44] The fact that it appears to have been carried out as a planned mass execution is both highly unusual and strikingly chilling. It was not, however, completely without parallel in the Carolingian era, or even in Carolingian Saxony. One may point to the 'judicial massacre' which Carloman appears to have carried out in 746 at Cannstatt, in the course of the Carolingian conquest of Alemannia, or indeed to the sentences meted out to the Saxon *Stellinga* in 842, when 154 leaders of the movement were executed and 'countless' other

---

auderent.' See also M. Lintzel, 'Die Unterwerfung Sachsens durch Karl den Großen und der sächsische Adel' in Lintzel, *Schriften*, pp. 95–127, here p. 107.

[42] *Annales regni Francorum*, ed. Kurze, 772, 775, 776, 780, 785, pp. 32–4, 40, 44–6, 56, 68.

[43] *Ibid*, 782, p. 62: 'omnes Saxones iterum convenientes subdiderunt se sub potestate supradicti domni regis et reddiderunt omnes malefactores illos, qui ipsud rebellium maxime terminaverunt, ad occidendum IIII D'.

[44] *Annales sancti Amandi*, ed. G. H. Pertz, *MGH SS* 1 (Hanover: Hahn, 1826), pp. 6, 8, 10, 12, 14, here 782, p. 12; *Annales Laubacenses*, ed. G. H. Pertz, *MGH SS* 1 (Hanover: Hahn, 1826), pp. 7, 9–10, 12, 15, 52–5, here 782, p. 13; *Annales Laureshamenses*, ed. Pertz, 782, p. 32; *Annales Petaviani*, ed. Pertz, 782, p. 17; *Annales qui dicuntur Einhardi*, ed. Kurze, 782, pp. 63–5; *Chronicon Moissiacense*, ed. Pertz, 782, p. 297.

members were deprived of limbs.[45] Leaving aside Verden's judicial character, moreover, the figure of the 4,500 slain proffered in the annals was not, in itself, exceptional in the early Saxon campaigns.[46] Mass bloodshed was a frequent feature of the early Saxon wars, as narrated in the annals.

In 775, the *Lorsch Annals* record that Charlemagne committed a 'great massacre' in Saxony, while the *Petavian Annals* number the dead at 'many thousands of pagans'.[47] The *Royal Frankish Annals* go further still, and record 'three massacres of Saxons' in that year.[48] In 778, the reviser tells how, following a battle, the retreating Saxon forces 'fell in such a massacre, that out of a vast multitude of those ones only a few are said to have reached home by flight'.[49] In 783, the year after the mass execution at Verden, the body count was especially high: the *Lorsch Annals* describe how 'many thousands of Saxons' fell in battle before going on to describe a second engagement, in which 'many thousands, more than before' perished.[50] The next year there was another engagement, the last in this stage of the conflict, and 'a great number of [Saxons] were killed'.[51] Casualties were not all on the Saxon side, however. Although the annals' triumphant focus often skirted over Frankish losses, these were occasionally included: both the devastation caused by Saxon incursions in 778 and the high death toll of the battle in the Süntel mountain in 782 were detailed in Frankish accounts, even if the latter was initially passed over in the *Royal Frankish Annals* and only later inserted into the revised version.[52] Further losses are reported by the so-called

---

[45] For Cannstatt, see *Annales Mettenses priores*, ed. Simpson, 746, p. 37; *Annales Petaviani*, ed. Pertz, 746, p. 11; *Fredegarii continuationes*, ed. J. M. Wallace-Hadrill, *The Fourth Book of the Chronicle of Fredegar with Its Continuations* (London: Nelson, 1960), c. 29, p. 100; see also E. Goosmann, 'Politics and penance: transformations in the Carolingian perception of the conversion of Carloman (747)' in C. Gantner, R. McKitterick and S. Meeder (eds.), *The Resources of the Past in Early Medieval Europe* (Cambridge: Cambridge University Press, 2015), pp. 51–67, here pp. 57–9. For the *Stellinga*, see here especially *Annales Bertiniani*, eds. F. Grat, J. Vielliard and S. Clémencet, *Annales de Saint-Bertin* (Paris: C. Klincksieck, 1964), 842, pp. 42–3: 'innumeros'; see also below, p. 128.

[46] See especially Lintzel, 'Die Vorgänge in Verden' in Lintzel, *Schriften*, pp. 147–74; see also Hen, 'Charlemagne's jihad', 37.

[47] *Annales Laureshamenses*, ed. Pertz, 775, p. 30: 'stragem magnam'; *Annales Petaviani*, ed. Pertz, 775, p. 16: 'multa milia paganorum'; see also *Annales Mosellani*, ed. Lappenberg, 775, p. 496.

[48] *Annales regni Francorum*, ed. Kurze, 775, p. 42: 'ter stragia Saxonum'.

[49] *Annales qui dicuntur Einhardi*, ed. Kurze, 778, p. 53: 'tanta strage ceciderunt, ut ex ingenti multitudine ipsorum vix pauci domum fugiendo pervenisse dicantur'.

[50] *Annales Laureshamenses*, ed. Pertz, 783, p. 32: 'ex parte Saxonum multa milia', 'de parte Saxonum etiam multa milia, plurima quam antea'. See also *Annales Mosellani*, ed. Lappenberg, 783, p. 497.

[51] *Annales qui dicuntur Einhardi*, ed. Kurze, 784, p. 69 'magno eorum numero interfecto'.

[52] *Annales Regni Francorum*, ed. Kurze, 778, p. 52; *Annales qui dicuntur Einhardi*, ed. Kurze, 778, 782, pp. 53, 61–3.

York Annals, a set of annals covering the years 732–802 which survive in Symeon of Durham's twelfth-century *History of Kings* and offer an unusual Northumbrian perspective. In the report on the campaign of 772, the annalist, rather than giving a triumphant account of the destruction of the Irminsul, records instead how, 'after losing many of his leading and noble men, Charlemagne took his men back'.[53] To put it bluntly, he retreated.

The numerical estimates of the deceased, such as the 'many thousands' of Saxons recorded dead in 775 and 783, appear consistent with the 4,500 allegedly slain in 782; similarly, the number of Saxons slain in the battle in 798, variously reported at 2,800, 2,901, and 4,000, is in an order of like magnitude, and reinforces the perception that the massacre at Verden was not an anomaly, at least in terms of scale.[54] The conflicting numbers from 798 need not concern us: all numbers of this size provided in contemporary texts were, at best, exceedingly rough estimates derived from imperfect knowledge, or even from the annalists' own prejudices and assumptions. Even the figure of 4,500 reported for 782 is probably invented: as Matthias Springer remarks, its complete absence from one recension of the *Royal Frankish Annals* and its placement, almost as an afterthought, at the conclusion of a sentence make it a likely later addition.[55] Such numbers were included to convey a general sense of immensity and may have had further figurative significance. As Guy Halsall writes:

In this largely non-urban period, it is not unlikely that armies represented the largest concentrations of men which anyone, from a king down to the lowliest slave, ever encountered. Whether of 1,000 or 80,000 men would not have mattered to any observer: any such figure would have far exceeded the numbers which any early medieval person used on a regular basis.[56]

The numbers provided for the Saxon campaigns were probably (but not necessarily) exaggerated: an undeveloped agricultural society with little evidence of stratification or central political organization could not long

[53] Symeon, *Historia regum*, ed. T. Arnold, *Symeonis monachi opera omnia*, 2 vols (London: Longman, 1885), vol. II, c. 47, p. 44: 'Multisque ex principibus ac nobilibus viris suis amissis, in sua se recepit.' See also J. Story, *Carolingian Connections: Anglo-Saxon England and Carolingian Francia, c. 750–870* (Aldershot: Ashgate, 2003), pp. 93–133, here pp. 99–100.

[54] *Annales Laureshamenses*, ed. Pertz, 798, p. 37; *Annales regni Francorum*, ed. Kurze, 798, p. 104; *Annales qui dicuntur Einhardi*, ed. Kurze, 798, p. 105; *Chronicon Moissiacense*, ed. Pertz, 798, p. 303; see also Lintzel, 'Die Vorgänge', p. 172.

[55] Springer, *Die Sachsen*, p. 190.

[56] G. Halsall, *Warfare and Society in the Barbarian West, 450–900* (London: Routledge, 2003), p. 122; see further Lintzel, 'Die Vorgänge', p. 173.

support armies of such a size. Saxon armies, taken broadly to encompass combatants and non-combatants alike, may well have been considerably larger than the resultant Saxon casualties.[57]

This is not to minimize the brutality of the wars: on the contrary, the first stage of the conflict up to 785 appears to have been particularly marked by large numbers of casualties on both sides. This high toll, and in particular the high *Saxon* toll, was acknowledged, and even applauded, by an array of authors in Francia. Elsewhere, Charlemagne's conduct of the war was regarded more critically. The Northumbrian author of the *York Annals*, commenting on the campaigns of 775, describes how Charlemagne, the 'most bellicose king of the Franks', 'devastated the region most gravely with huge and unspeakable battles, raging (*debacchans*) with arson and sword, because he was disturbed (*consternatus*) in spirit'.[58] Evidently, Charlemagne's bloody tactics met with some degree of disapproval, and not just by those on the receiving end.

By contrast, in the later years of the conflict, Charlemagne appears to have changed tack: after 785, reports of massacre are absent save for the battle of 798 and an 804 entry from the *Annals of Saint Amand* which notes that Charlemagne 'ordered some to be killed'.[59] Casualties may have remained high: in the absence of pitched battles, Charlemagne sent his troops into the countryside to quell resistance, and the ensuing devastation could encompass anything from arson to rapine, which in turn could lead to famine and disease. Yet it is noteworthy that Charlemagne and his forces appear to have avoided direct casualties in the later stages of the wars. Particularly interesting in this regard is an entry in the *Lorsch Annals* for 795, which reports that some Saxons came to Charlemagne after the murder of Witzin, king of the Abodrites. 'They promised to fulfill his order: and thus the lord king once again believed them, killing no one willingly, for the purpose of serving his faith.'[60] Charlemagne and his troops had come a long way since Verden.

---

[57] Contrast with B. S. Bachrach, *Charlemagne's Early Campaigns (768–777): a diplomatic and military analysis* (History of Warfare 82) (Leiden: Brill, 2013), here especially pp. 209–10, and the nuanced approach taken in É. Renard, 'La politique militaire de Charlemagne et la paysannerie franque', *Francia: Forschungen zur westeuropäischen Geschichte*, 36 (2009), 1–33, here especially p. 3.

[58] Symeon, *Historia regum*, ed. Arnold, c. 49, p. 46: 'rex. . . bellicosissimus Francorum'; 'quam magnis et inedicibilibus regionem praeliis gravissimis vastavit, igne ferroque debacchans, quia erat consternatus animo'; see also Springer, *Die Sachsen*, p. 178; Story, *Carolingian connections*, pp. 100–1.

[59] *Annales sancti Amandi*, ed. Pertz, 804, p. 14: 'aliquos iussit interficere'.

[60] *Annales Laureshamenses*, ed. Pertz, 795, p. 36: 'iussionem suam promittentes implere; et ita domnus rex iterum credens eis, nullum voluntate interficiens fidem suam servando'. See further *Chronicon Moissiacense*, ed. Pertz, 795, p. 302.

Hostages and Deportations

The lack of mass executions and massacres in the second stage of the conflict did not mean an end to reprisals: on the contrary, it was marked by the forced migration of the populations of entire regions of Saxony. This may be attributed, in part, to Charlemagne's reluctance either to meet Saxons in open battle or to deal out the capital punishments issued, for instance, at Verden in 782. The reasons for this will be explored at greater length below.[61]

The movement of Saxons was not in itself unique to the second stage of the conflict: on the contrary, the giving of hostages was an established ritual of capitulation. In 772, a group of Saxons offered twelve hostages to the king; further groups of hostages were offered in 775, 776 and 779.[62] Such hostages could serve as sureties: an entry from 776 noted that 'the Saxons rebelled and abandoned all their hostages', thereby suggesting that the threat of violence to hostages was intended to forestall later rebellion.[63] Yet not all hostages were taken from households of influence: an entry from 780 records the taking of hostages, 'freemen and half-freemen alike'.[64] Such hostages would have been of limited use as guarantees against further rebellion; Adam Kosto rightly remarks that, in such cases, hostages may have primarily served as 'markers of submission'.[65] In the years immediately following, the sources do not discuss prisoners as hostages (*obsides*) *per se*: in 782, the *Petavian Annals* state that 'many conquered Saxons were led into Francia', while in 783 the revised version of the *Royal Frankish Annals* describes how 'a great number of captives were led away'.[66] Such crowds of captives could have fulfilled a not dissimilar purpose from that of the non-elite hostages taken in 780, insofar as they served as visible reminders of Charlemagne's recent victory; on the other hand, they also bear comparison to the 'deportees'

---

[61] See below, p. 82.

[62] *Annales regni Francorum*, ed. Kurze, 772, 775, 776, 779, pp. 34, 40–2, 46–8, 54; *Annales qui dicuntur Einhardi*, ed. Kurze, 772, 775, 776, 779, pp. 35, 43, 47, 55; *Annales Maximiani*, ed. G. Waitz, *MGH SS* 13 (Hanover: Hahn, 1881), 775, p. 21; *Annales sancti Amandi*, ed. Pertz, 776, p. 12; *Annales Laubacenses*, ed. Pertz, 776, p. 13; *Annales Petaviani*, ed. Pertz, 779, p. 16; *Annales Laureshamenses*, ed. Pertz, 779, p. 31; *Annales Mosellani*, ed. Lappenberg, 779, p. 497; *Chronicon Moissiacense*, ed. Pertz, 779, p. 296.

[63] *Annales regni Francorum*, ed. Kurze, 776, p. 44; see further A. J. Kosto, 'Hostages in the Carolingian world (714–840)', *EME*, 11(2) (2002), 123–47, here 124.

[64] *Annales Laureshamenses*, ed. Pertz, 780, p. 31: 'tam ingenuos quam et lidos'; *Annales Mosellani*, ed. Lappenberg, 780, p. 497; *Chronicon Moissiacense*, ed. Pertz, 780, p. 296; see also Kosto, 'Hostages in the Carolingian world', 134; Lintzel, 'Die Unterwerfung Sachsens', pp. 103–4.

[65] Kosto, 'Hostages in the Carolingian world', 137.

[66] *Annales Petaviani*, ed. Pertz, 782, p. 17: 'multos victos Saxones adduxerunt in Francia'; *Annales qui dicuntur Einhardi*, ed. Kurze, 783, p. 65: 'captivorum quoque magnus abductus est numerus'.

characteristic of the later years of the wars. In this regard, it is worth briefly noting just how difficult it is to differentiate 'deportees' from 'hostages', in the traditional sense of sureties. While those whom we might term 'deportees' are sometimes labelled as captives (*captivi*) or simply discussed as relocated men, women and children, just as often the same vocabulary (*obsides*, or more rarely *hospes*) is used to denote both 'deportees' and 'hostages', the latter in the traditional sense of sureties: for example, the Latin term *obsides* is consistently used to describe those relocated in 795, with the sole exception of the report in the *Maximian Annals*. In the latter case, then, the historian is reduced to reliance on context clues and indications as to scale. The vocabulary used to describe such transfers remained largely the same, yet the functions of such movements were markedly different.

Up to 785, contemporary annalistic sources note that large numbers of hostages, or deportees, were taken on two occasions, in 782 and 783. This is in marked contrast to the final years of the wars, when the great numbers of hostages are emphasized with near uniformity. In 794, Charlemagne made his first foray into Saxony in nine years, and took hostages.[67] According to the *Lesser Annals of Lorsch*, 'he led away a third of their men and settled them in Francia'.[68] In the following year, the taking of hostages is noted by almost all annals. Some simply note this in a summary fashion,[69] but in others more detail is given. Just as in 780, the hostages appear to have been taken from across the social spectrum: the *Moselle Annals* describe how Charlemagne 'led out a not inconsiderable quantity of noble and ignoble people from that *gens* with him'.[70] Yet the scale of population movements had shifted dramatically. The *Maximian Annals*, echoing the language of the *Lesser Annals of Lorsch* from the year before, report that a third of the men from the region were taken abroad, while the *Lorsch Annals* describe how 'he brought such a multitude of hostages thence, far more than had ever been taken in his days, in the days of his father, or in the days of the Frankish kings'.[71] In the *Greater*

---

[67] *Annales qui dicuntur Einhardi*, ed. Kurze, 794, p. 97.

[68] *Annales Laurissenses minores*, ed. G. H. Pertz, *MGH SS* I (Hanover: Hahn, 1826) c. 26, p. 119: 'tertium de eis hominem in Franciam educens conlocavit'.

[69] *Annales Alamannici*, ed. Pertz, 795 (*Codices Modoetiens. et Veronens.*), p. 47; *Annales Guelferbytani*, ed. Pertz, 795, p. 45; *Annales regni Francorum*, ed. Kurze, 795, p. 96; *Annales qui dicuntur Einhardi*, ed. Kurze, 795, p. 97; *Annales Petaviani*, ed. Pertz, 795, p. 18.

[70] *Annales Mosellani*, ed. Lappenberg, 794 [795], p. 498: 'non modicam quantitatem nobilium atque ignobilium gentis illius secum adduxit'.

[71] *Annales Maximiani*, ed. Waitz, 795, p. 22; *Annales Laureshamenses*, ed. Pertz, 795, p. 36: 'tantam multitudinem obsidum inde tulit, quantam numquam in diebus suis aut in diebus patris sui aut in diebus regum Franchorum inde aliquando tulerunt'; see also *Chronicon Moissiacense*, ed. Pertz, 795, p. 302.

Annals of Saint Gall and in a strand of the *Alemannic Annals*, a hard (if improbable) figure is even given: 7,070 hostages were taken in that year.[72] Charlemagne had begun to deport Saxons *en masse*.

Further forced migrations are variously styled in the sources as the taking of hostages (*obsides* or *hospes*) or captives (*captivi*), or described, at greater length, as people being relocated. These are marked in 796–799 and, finally, in 804. In some years, a sense of scale, however approximate, is given. In 797, the *Lesser Annals of Lorsch* record the resettlement of a third of Saxon men.[73] Interestingly, it is the third time such a fraction is proffered. In 798, meanwhile, annals state that a 'multitude' or 'innumerable quantity' of hostages were given.[74] The reports from the latter year are particularly interesting: the *Royal Frankish Annals* note that 'the king accepted hostages, namely those whom the *primores* of the Saxons had designated to be most perfidious', while the *Annals of Saint Amand* describe how '1600 leaders were led away as hostages, and were dispersed throughout Francia'.[75] In this case, hostage-taking was intended neither to guarantee the future fidelity of their families nor to act as a symbolic display of submission: rather, it was intended to pacify the region by removing its most notorious malefactors, and may also have provided a pretext for leading Saxons to settle scores with local rivals. The *Earlier Annals of Metz* attribute a similar motivation to Charlemagne's decision in 804 to deport the Saxons living in Wigmodia and beyond the Elbe, 'who, through their frequent deceptions, had turned the Saxon populace away from the way of truth'.[76] Nor were combatants the only ones to pay the price. In 796, 799 and 804, men were transported with their wives and children.[77] Einhard writes that 10,000 families were deported in 804 alone.[78]

Such forced evacuations could effect the immediate pacification of a recalcitrant region, as in 798 and 804; they could also free up lands to reward supporters, whether domestic or foreign. The deportations of 804 resulted in a grant of territory to Charlemagne's newly created client

---

[72] *Annales Sangallenses maiores*, ed. I. ab Arx, *MGH SS* I (Hanover: Hahn, 1826), pp. 72–85, here 795, p. 75; *Annales Alamannici*, ed. Pertz, 795 (*Codices Turicens. et Sirmondianus*), p. 47.

[73] *Annales Laurissenses minores*, ed. Pertz, c. 29, p. 119.

[74] *Annales Alamannici*, ed. Pertz, 798 (*Codices Turicens. et Sirmondianus.*), p. 48; *Annales Petaviani*, ed. Pertz, 798, p. 18; *Annales Sangallenses maiores*, ed. ab Arx, 798, p. 75.

[75] *Annales regni Francorum*, ed. Kurze, 798, p. 104: 'rex acceptis obsidibus, etiam et his, quod perfidissimos primores Saxonum consignabant'; *Annales sancti Amandi*, ed. Pertz, 798, p. 14: 'hospites capitaneos 1600 inde adduxit, et per Franciam divisit'.

[76] *Annales Mettenses priores*, ed. Simpson, 804, p. 91: 'qui ... frequentibus maleficiis populum Saxonum a via veritatis averterant'.

[77] *Annales Laureshamenses*, ed. Pertz, 796, 799, pp. 37–8; *Annales Mettenses priores*, ed. Simpson, 804, p. 91; *Annales regni Francorum*, ed. Kurze, 804, p. 118; *Chronicon Moissiacense*, ed. Pertz, 796, 799, pp. 302, 304.

[78] Einhard, *Vita Karoli Magni*, ed. Holder-Egger, c. 7, p. 10.

king, Thrasco, and as such served as a crucial prop to his rule; so too could the lands reclaimed from other deported Saxons be granted out to supporters. An entry from the *Lorsch Annals* in 799 records how 'the lord king took a multitude of Saxons with their wives and children and settled them throughout the far reaches of his diverse lands, and he divided their land between his faithful men (*fideles*), that is, bishops, presbyters, counts, and other vassals'.[79]

Those deported *en masse*, unlike the small groups of elite hostages who were placed with Frankish hosts, were left largely to fend for themselves: two charters issued by Charlemagne to Saxons who had emigrated during this period suggest that deportees were given the option of reclaiming unused land in Francia, specifically, in these cases, in the forest of Buchonia.[80] Further indications may be gleaned from place names: Ernst Schubert points to the villages of 'Sachsenhausen' and Sachsenheim', as well as to place names ending in -horst, as evidence of new Saxon settlements in the area around modern-day Karlsruhe and Offenburg.[81] Perhaps a general policy for such deportations can be gleaned from the *Second Saxon Capitulary*, issued in 797 at the height of the deportations. Its chapter 10 discusses those 'malefactors, who, according to the law of the Saxons, ought to lose their lives. Everyone agreed', the chapter continues,

that if any of them appeal to royal power, it should be in the king's power either to return the malefactor to them to be killed, or to take the license, together with the consent of those ones, to settle the malefactor outside of his homeland with his wife, family, and all pertaining to him, either within his kingdom or in a march, wherever he should wish, and they may consider him as if dead.[82]

Those deported escaped execution, yet the difficulties they faced would have been considerable. A later appeal to Louis the Pious illustrates the

---

[79] *Annales Lauresheimenses*, ed. Pertz, 799, p. 38: 'domnus rex inde tulit multitudinem Saxanorum cum mulieribus et infantibus, et collocavit eos per diversas terras in finibus suis, et ipsam terram eorum divisit inter fideles suos, id est episcopos, presbyteros, comites et alios vassos suos'. For this passage, see also M. Becher, *Rex, Dux und Gens: Untersuchung zur Entstehung des sächsischen Herzogtums im 9. und 10. Jahrhundert* (Historische Studien 444) (Husum: Matthiesen, 1996), p. 113; cf. Springer, *Die Sachsen*, p. 209.

[80] *D Kar. 1*, ed. E. Mühlbacher, *MGH, Die Urkunden Pippins, Karlmanns, und Karls des Grossen* (Hanover: Hahn, 1906), nos. 213, 218, pp. 284–5, 290–2.

[81] E. Schubert, 'Die Capitulatio de partibus Saxoniae' in D. Brosius, C. van der Heuvel, E. Hinrichs and H. van Lengen (eds.), *Geschichte in der Region. Zum 65. Geburtstag von Heinrich Schmidt* (Hanover: Hahn, 1993), pp. 3–28, here p. 19.

[82] *Capitulare Saxonicum*, ed. von Schwerin, c. 10, pp. 48–9: 'De malefactoribus, qui vitae periculum secundum ewa Saxonum incurre debent, placuit omnibus ut qualiscumque ex ipsis ad regium potestatem confugium fecerit aut in illius sit potestate utrum interficiendum illis reddatur aut una cum consensu eorum habeat licentiam, ipsum malefactorem cum uxore et familia et omnia sua foris patriam infra sua regna aut in marcu ubi sua fuerit voluntas collocare et habeant ipsum quasi mortuum.'

poverty to which even elite Saxons could be reduced following dislocation.[83] The fate of non-elite deportees would likely have been even
more bleak.

In the background of such mass population movements, small-scale
transfers of elite hostages appear to have been a constant throughout the
wars. While it is often difficult to distinguish between hostages and
deportees in annalistic sources, as discussed above, the granting of elite
hostages is well illustrated in contemporary hagiography, and, even more
remarkably, in the so-called *List of Saxon Hostages to be led away from
Mainz*, which preserves the names of some thirty-seven Saxon hostages.[84] In this list, hostages are organized by their region of origin,
whether Westphalia, Eastphalia or Engern; identified by their own and
their father's names (e.g. Leodac son of Bodolonus); and finally marked
out by the name, and sometimes title, of their host (e.g. Bishop Aino,
Count Ansbertus). Of the thirty-seven named hostages, sixteen were
placed under the guardianship of twelve titled individuals, be they
counts, bishops or abbots, all of whom appear to have been based in
Alemannia; all of the hostages were placed under guardians either singly
or, less commonly, in groups of two, although in one exceptional case
three hostages were allocated together. Such details reveal that this group
of hostages were of high status, and that provision was made for them to
be fully immersed in the patterns of Frankish elite life. The comment at
the end of the list, which instructs their guardians to 'let these ones come
to Mainz in the middle of Lent', has been taken to suggest that the
hostages were to be sent back to Saxony imminently at the time the list
was compiled.[85] Janet Nelson has however argued that these Saxons
could have continued to serve as sureties (*credentiae*) in part of a larger
system of hostages as envisaged in the *Division of the Kingdoms* of 806.[86]
Whatever the case, these individuals did not merely act as guarantees

---

[83] *Epistolae variorum inde a morte Caroli Magni usque ad divisionem imperii collectae*, ed. E. Dümmler, *MGH Epp.* 5:3 (Berlin: Weidemann, 1899), no. 2, pp. 300–1.

[84] *Indiculus obsidum Saxonum Moguntiam deducendorum*, ed. Boretius, pp. 233–4; note that this is a modern title. See also Flierman, 'Pagan, pirate, subject, saint: defining and redefining Saxons, 150–900 A.D.', unpublished Ph.D. thesis, Universiteit Utrecht (2015), pp. 194–6; Kosto, 'Hostages in the Carolingian world', 142–4; A. J. Kosto, *Hostages in the Middle Ages* (Oxford: Oxford University Press, 2012), pp. 66–7; J.L. Nelson, 'Charlemagne and empire' in J. R. Davis and M. McCormick (eds.), *The Long Morning of Medieval Europe: New Directions in Early Medieval Studies* (Aldershot: Ashgate, 2008), pp. 223–34; Springer, *Die Sachsen*, pp. 211–2.

[85] *Indiculus obsidum Saxonum Moguntiam deducendorum*, ed. Boretius, p. 234: 'Isti veniant ad Mogontiam media quadragesima'; *Divisio Regnorum* in *Cap. 1*, ed. A. Boretius, *MGH Capitularia regum Francorum* 1 (Hanover: Hahn, 1883), no. 48, c. 13, p. 129.

[86] Nelson, 'Charlemagne and empire', pp. 226–7; see also Kosto, 'Hostages in the Carolingian world', 143; Springer, *Die Sachsen*, p. 213.

during the period of rebellion: the eventual return to Saxony of young, elite men raised in Frankish households and ecclesiastical institutions would ease the interrelated processes of Christianization and political integration.[87]

Although this list is unique in recording the granting of Saxon hostages to lay individuals, the placement of such hostages in Frankish ecclesiastical institutions is exceedingly well-attested. Saxon hostages are recorded at the archbishopric of Rheims; the bishoprics of Würzburg, Constance and Augsburg; and finally the monasteries of Corbie, St-Wandrille and Reichenau.[88] The *Translation of Saint Vitus* seems to suggest that their placement was undertaken in a systematic manner, and directly intended to support the Christianization of the region: as its anonymous author writes, Charlemagne 'ordered men of that people, who had been taken as hostages and captives in the time of conflicts, to be distributed throughout the monasteries of the Franks to be prepared in the sacred law and monastic discipline'.[89] In many cases, such a strategy appears to have paid off: once removed from their home environment, hostages quickly adapted to the culture and religion of their Frankish hosts. As Alcuin mused in a letter dated to 799, 'those [Saxons] who have moved abroad are the best Christians, as has been often observed'.[90] When hostages returned to their homeland, they brought their newly minted religious convictions with them. Hathumar, who was raised as a hostage at Würzburg, became the first bishop of Paderborn,

---

[87] Kosto, 'Hostages in the Carolingian world', 144–5; Nelson, 'Charlemagne and empire', p. 228.

[88] For Rheims, see Flodoard, *Historia Remensis ecclesiae*, ed. M. Stratmann, *MGH SS* 36 (Hanover: Hahn, 1998), II:18, pp. 172–3; for Würzburg, see Anonymus Paderbrunnensis, *Translatio sancti Liborii*, ed. V. de Vry, *Liborius, Brückenbauer Europas: die mittelalterlichen Viten und Translationsberichte: mit einem Anhang der Manuscripta Liboriana* (Paderborn: Schöningh, 1997), c. 7, p. 193; for Constance, Augsburg and Reichenau, see *Indiculus obsidum Saxonum Moguntiam deducendorum*, ed. Boretius, pp. 233–4; for Corbie, see *Translatio sancti Viti*, ed. I. Schmale-Ott, *Übertragung des hl. Märtyrers Vitus* (Fontes minores 1) (Münster: Aschendorff, 1979), c. 3, p. 36; for St-Wandrille, see *Miracula sancti Wandregisili*, eds. J. B. Sollerius, J. Pinius, G. Cuperus and P. Boschius, *Acta Sanctorum V Julii* (Antwerp, 1727), I:4, p. 282C–E. For these references, see especially Kosto, 'Hostages in the Carolingian world', 145; see also P. Depreux, 'L'intégration des élites aristocratiques de Bavière et de Saxe au royaume des francs – crise ou opportunité?' in F. Bougard, L. Feller and R. Le Jan (eds.), *Les élites au haut moyen âge: Crises et renouvellements* (Haut Moyen Âge 1) (Turnhout: Brepols, 2006), pp. 225–52, here p. 235; H. Röckelein, *Reliquientranslationen nach Sachsen im 9. Jahrhundert: über Kommunikation, Mobilität und Öffentlichkeit im Frühmittelalter* (Beihefte der Francia 48) (Sigmaringen: J. Thorbecke, 2002), pp. 75, 101 footnote 73; Springer, *Die Sachsen*, pp. 212–13.

[89] *Translatio sancti Viti*, ed. Schmale-Ott, c. 3, p. 36: 'illius gentis homines, quos obsides et captivos tempore conflictionis adduxerat, per monasteria Francorum distribuit, legem quoque sanctam atque monasticam disciplinam institui praecepit'. See also Kosto, *Hostages in the Middle Ages*, p. 68.

[90] Alcuin, *Epistolae*, ed. E. Dümmler, *MGH Epp.* 4:2 (Berlin: Weidemann, 1895), pp. 1–481, here no. 174, p. 289: 'Qui foras recesserunt, optimi fuerunt christiani, sicut in plurimis notum est.' See also Springer, *Die Sachsen*, p. 204.

and a group of Saxon hostages at the monastery of Corbie appear to have acted as the impetus behind the foundation of its sister-house, Corvey, in Saxony: in fact, one Saxon monk, a certain Theodradus, appears to have relinquished his inheritance to enable its initial construction at Hethis.[91]

The treatment of elite hostages thus stands in clear contrast to that of deported persons, a difference which may be largely traced back to the original contexts in which they were displaced. While deportations attempted to effect the immediate pacification of the region by the removal of offending parties, hostages served a different role. They guaranteed and reinforced existing peace settlements, and moreover contributed to the interwoven processes of socio-political and religious integration. They were given at those most crucial of turning points: when erstwhile rebels became suppliants.

RESISTANCE AND COLLABORATION

The crux of Einhard's disappointment with the Saxon wars was the fickleness of the Saxons. 'The war could indeed have been concluded more swiftly', he complains,

were it not for the perfidy of the Saxons. It is difficult to say how many times they were conquered, surrendered themselves as suppliants to the king, promised to fulfill his orders, gave the hostages which he ordered without delay, and received the legates which he sent. Several times they were so subdued and softened that they even promised to renounce the worship of devils and wished to submit themselves to the Christian religion. Yet just as they were prone sometimes to do these things, so too they always were ready to pervert their promises, with the result that one simply cannot judge which action can be said to have been easier for them: indeed, from the beginning of the war scarcely a year passed in which they did not alternate between such actions.[92]

---

[91] For Hathumar, see Anonymus Paderbrunnensis, *Translatio sancti Liborii*, ed. de Vry, c. 7, p. 193; for Theodradus' gift of his inheritance to Corvey, see *Translatio sancti Viti*, ed. Schmale-Ott, c. 3, p. 36; Paschasius Radbertus, *Epitaphium Arsenii*, ed. E. Dümmler, *Radbert's Epitaphium Arsenii* (Abhandlungen der Kgl. Akademie der Wissenschaft zu Berlin, Phil.-hist. Classe II) (Berlin: W. de Gruyter, 1900), I:13, pp. 41–2.

[92] Einhard, *Vita Karoli Magni*, ed. Holder-Egger, c. 7, pp. 9–10: 'Poterat siquidem citius finiri, si Saxonum hoc perfidia pateretur. Difficile dictu est, quoties superati ac supplices regi se dediderunt, imperata facturos polliciti sunt, obsides qui imperabantur absque dilatione dederunt, legatos qui mittebantur susceperunt, aliquoties ita domiti et emolliti, ut etiam cultum daemonum dimittere et Christianae religioni se subdere velle promitterent. Sed sicut ad haec facienda aliquoties proni, sic ad eandem pervertenda semper fuere praecipites, non sit ut satis aestimare, ad utrum horum faciliores verius dici possint: quippe cum post inchoatum cum eis bellum vix ullus annus exactus sit, quo non ab eis huiuscemodi facta sit permutatio.'

Similar charges are to be found in a wide array of contemporary annalistic writing. While the reviser of the *Royal Frankish Annals* stands out for his shrill denunciation of the Saxons' perfidy, his comments are paralleled in other works.[93]

In actuality, perceptions of Saxon 'faithlessness' may have stemmed largely from the lack of political organization. In the absence of a central political authority, ritual submissions removed only select groups of prominent 'rebels', and renewed resistance could equally coalesce around different leadership – or indeed involve different groups.[94] Here it is worth remembering that 'Saxon' was an external label: while, for example, both the Westphalians and the Nordliudi might both be classed as 'Saxons' by Frankish observers, the situation on the ground was considerably more complex. Of course, there were probably also instances of oath-breaking and reneged-upon treaties. Nevertheless, what contemporary annalists denounced as perfidy may appear to the modern observer as a rational observance of risk–benefit analysis. For all the triumphalism contained in Frankish historical writing, Charlemagne's victory was by no means inevitable, at least not in the early years of campaigning; commensurately, the fates of his Saxon followers were uncertain. Some profited from their fidelity, but others did not; while some rebels who submitted were punished capitally, others received abundant rewards upon their eventual capitulation. One course of action did not guarantee success, and a degree of opportunism was often profitable.

Partly by Wars, Partly by Gifts

When Charlemagne marched into Saxony with a large army, Saxons had two options: large-scale resistance or submission. If the former failed, only surrender, or, in the case of Widukind and his companions, exile, remained. The customary rites of submission, comprising oath-taking, baptism and the granting of hostages, were repeated at countless points throughout the wars, although it is worth noting that no baptisms are recorded in contemporary annalistic sources in the second half of the

[93] See, for example, *Annales qui dicuntur Einhardi*, ed. Kurze, 775, 776, 777, 785, 795, 797, pp. 41, 47, 49, 71, 97, 101; *Annales Laureshamenses*, ed. Pertz, 778, p. 31; *Chronicon Moissiacense*, ed. Pertz, 778, p. 296. See also Becher, '*Non enim habent regem*', pp. 29–31; R. Flierman, *Saxon Identities, AD 150–900* (London: Bloomsbury Academic, 2017), pp. 89–117; R. Flierman, '*Gens perfida* or *populus Christianus*? Saxon (in)fidelity in Frankish historical writing' in C. Gantner, R. McKitterick and S. Meeder (eds.), *The Resources of the Past in Early Medieval Europe* (Cambridge: Cambridge University Press, 2015), pp. 188–205.
[94] Flierman, *Saxon Identities*, pp. 94–100; Lampen, 'Sachsenkriege', p. 271.

conflict (after 785). This contrasts sharply with the earlier period, in which baptisms are reported on no fewer than five occasions.[95]

The decision to capitulate could be driven by a variety of different factors. Although the annals generally highlight the fear that Charlemagne inspired, an equally persuasive motivation was the concrete reward to be gained through submission.[96] A recurring motif in Saxon hagiography from this period stresses how Saxons were induced to submit through a combination of incentives or violence (or the threat thereof). Eigil, in the *Life of Saint Sturmi*, wrote of how the conquest was achieved 'partly by wars, partly by persuasions, partly even by gifts'; later, the anonymous author of the *Life of the Virgin Liutbirga* echoed his phrasing, noting that the wars were won 'partly by wars, partly by [Charlemagne's] character and by the zeal of his great wisdom, and additionally even by great gifts'.[97] Other authors preferred a binary comparison. The *Third Life of Saint Liudger* characterized the wars as having been carried out 'partly by favours, partly by destruction', while the *Translation of Saint Liborius* remarked that it had been waged 'partly by arms, partly by generosity'.[98] Even at the very end of the ninth century, the Saxon Poet remembered how Charlemagne 'first menaced [the Saxons] with war, then won them over

---

[95] *Annales Sangallenses Baluzii*, ed. G. H. Pertz, *MGH SS* 1 (Hanover: Hahn, 1826), p. 63, here 775, p. 63; *Annales Petaviani*, ed. Pertz, 776, 777, p. 16; *Annales Laureshamenses*, ed. Pertz, 776, 777, 780, 785, pp. 30–2; *Annales regni Francorum*, ed. Kurze, 776, 777, 780, 785, pp. 46, 48, 56, 70; *Annales qui dicuntur Einhardi*, ed. Kurze, 776, 777, 780, 785, pp. 47, 49, 57, 71; *Annales Maximiani*, ed. Waitz, 776, 777, 780, 785, p. 21; *Chronicon Moissiacense*, ed. Pertz, 776, 777, 780, 785, pp. 296–7.

[96] For this, see especially Lintzel, 'Die Unterwerfung Sachsens', pp. 118–19; see also Lampen, 'Sachsenkriege', pp. 266, 271; R. E. Sullivan, 'The Carolingian missionary and the pagan', *Speculum*, 28(4) (1953), 705–40, here 721–3.

[97] Eigil of Fulda, *Vita sancti Sturmi*, ed. P. Engelbert, *Die Vita Sturmi des Eigil von Fulda: literarkritisch-historische Untersuchung und Edition* (Veröffentlichungen der Historischen Kommission für Hessen und Waldeck 29) (Marburg: N. G. Elwert, 1968), c. 23, p. 158: 'partim bellis partim suasionibus partim etiam muneribus'; *Vita Liutbirgae virginis*, ed. O. Menzel, *Das Leben der Liutbirg: Eine Quelle zur Geschichte der Sachsen in karolingischer Zeit* (Deutsches Mittelalter 3) (Leipzig: K. W. Hiersemann, 1937), c. 1, p. 10: 'partim bellis, partim ingenio suo ac magnae sagacitatis industria, insuper etiam magnis muneribus'. My translations of passages from the *Life of Liutbirg* are deeply indebted to the translation of Frederick Paxton: see F. S. Paxton, tr., *Anchoress and Abbess in Ninth-Century Saxony: The Lives of Liutbirga of Wendhausen and Hathumoda of Gandersheim* (Washington, DC: Catholic University of America Press, 2009). See also Flierman, 'Religious Saxons: paganism, infidelity and biblical punishment in the Capitulatio de partibus Saxoniae' in R. Meens, D. van Espelo, B. van den Hoven van Genderen, J. Raaijmakers, I. van Renswoude and C. van Rhijn (eds.), *Religious Franks: Religion and Power in Honour of Mayke de Jong* (Manchester: Manchester University Press, 2016), pp. 181–201, here p. 183; Flierman, *Saxon Identities*, pp. 148–9.

[98] *Vita tertia sancti Liudgeri*, ed. W. Diekamp, *Die vitae sancti Liudgeri* (Die Geschichtsquellen des Bisthums Münster 4) (Münster: Theissing, 1881), pp. 85–134, here I:27, p. 103: 'partim beneficiis, partim destructione'; Anonymus Paderbrunnensis, *Translatio sancti Liborii*, ed. de Vry, c. 2, p. 189: 'partim armis, partim liberalitate'.

with gifts'.[99] Such characterizations were not simply made in retrospect: as early as 790, Alcuin wrote a letter which described how some were converted 'by gifts, others by threats'.[100]

There were many inducements to become a *fidelis* (literally, 'faithful man') of Charlemagne. When the *Lorsch Annals* reported the redistribution of land to Charlemagne's *fideles*, it is probable that some of the beneficiaries were Saxon.[101] Likewise, the *Translation of Saint Liborius*, a late ninth-century text produced at the bishopric of Paderborn, recorded that in the area surrounding Paderborn, the majority of men 'esteemed divine service far more than their own rites' in part because they were 'able to hold lands acquired by right of war under their own authority in so pleasant a territory'.[102] Additionally, Saxon *fideles* were sometimes granted lands outside of Saxony. A capitulary of 802 included a chapter 'concerning those Saxons who hold our benefices in Francia', instructing the royal officials (*missi*) to investigate 'how, and in what manner, they are cultivated'.[103] Later, the Saxon Poet described this practice with glowing praise, writing of how

Charlemagne enriched each man who had allied himself to his most excellent faith by spurning profane rites with resources and adorned him with many honours. Then the bounty of possessions which wealthy Gaul bears was claimed by the poor Saxons for the first time, when the king presented estates over there to many of them, from which they received clothes of costly material, mounds of silver, and sweet flowing wine. When all the leading men had been enticed by these gifts, he destroyed the rest by arms, making them subject to him.[104]

Evidently there were prizes to be won, and not just in Saxony.

[99] Poeta Saxo, *Annalium de gestis Caroli magni imperatoris libri V*, ed. P. Winterfeld, *MGH Poet.* 4:1 (Berlin: Weidemann, 1899), pp. 1–71, here V, line 39, p. 56: 'Nunc terrens bello, nunc donis alliciendo.'

[100] Alcuin, *Epistolae*, ed. Dümmler, no. 7, p. 32: 'alios premiis et alios minis'. See further Widukind of Corvey, *Res Gestae Saxonicae*, eds. Hirsch and Lohmann, I:15, p. 25. See also Flierman, 'Defining and redefining Saxons', p. 199; Flierman, *Saxon Identities*, p. 108.

[101] *Annales Lauresbamenses*, ed. Pertz, 799, p. 38.

[102] Anonymus Paderbrunnensis, *Translatio sancti Liborii*, ed. de Vry, c. 4, p. 191: 'quod ea, quae ex tanta locorum amoenitate iure belli adquisita, sub sua potuit tenere ditione, diuino magis seruitio quam suis deputauerit usibus'.

[103] *Cap. 1*, ed. A. Boretius, *MGH Cap.* 1 (Hanover: Hahn, 1883), no. 34, c. 11, p. 100: 'De illis Saxonibus qui beneficia nostra in Francia habent, quomodo an qualiter habent condricta.' See also *Cap. 1*, ed. Boretius, no. 35, c. 50, p. 104.

[104] Poeta Saxo, *Annalium de gestis Caroli magni imperatoris libri V*, ed. Winterfeld, IV, lines 125–34, p. 49: 'Nam se quisquis commiserat eius/Egregię fidei ritus spernendo profanos,/Hunc opibus ditans ornabat honoribus amplis./Copia pauperibus Saxonibus agnita primum/Tunc fuerat rerum, quas Gallia fert opulenta,/Praedia praestiterat cum rex compluribus illic,/Ex quibus acciperent preciosę tegmina vestis,/Argenti cumulos dulcisque fluenta Liei./His ubi primores donis illexerat omnes/(Subiectos sibimet reliquos obtriverat armis)'.

Nor was land the only benefit to be gained: Charlemagne further offered opportunities for political advancement. As early as 782, shortly before renewed Saxon rebellion and Charlemagne's brutal reprisals at Verden, Charlemagne held an assembly on the Lippe River and appointed 'counts of Saxon descent from among the most noble'.[105] Those appointed were provided with a handbook of sorts in the *First Saxon Capitulary* (whether already in 782, or later, circa 794/5), which detailed the various duties that counts should perform, as well as the privileges and protections that they might correspondingly enjoy.[106] Significantly, counts were to administer justice and hold regular courts; they could declare a *bannus*, a type of judicial fine (and, by implication, dip their hands into the profits); and they received *honores*, that is, land to be held contingent on the performance of their office.[107] Counts were further entrusted with military leadership, and while the specific role of Saxon counts (as opposed to general Saxon forces) in the course of the Saxon wars is unclear, the extent of the responsibilities, both military and diplomatic, entrusted to them soon thereafter would have enhanced their political stature.[108]

Finally, elite Saxon *fideles* stood a chance of making successful marriage alliances with their Frankish neighbours. Marriages of this type were already being contracted in the early years of the conquest: hence, for example, the union of Charlemagne's uncle Bernhard with an anonymous Saxon woman. Their children, Wala, Gundrada, Bernarius and Theodrada, rose to an exceptional level of prominence in the reigns of Charlemagne and Louis the Pious, with Wala in particular commanding great respect in Saxony due to his widely recognized origins.[109] Many more alliances between the Carolingian royal line and Saxon women would be made in the years to come.[110] It is more difficult to reconstruct

---

[105] *Annales Laureshamenses*, ed. Pertz, 782, p. 32: 'ex nobilissimis Saxones genere comites'; see also *Annales Mosellani*, ed. Lappenberg, 782, p. 497; *Chronicon Moissiacense*, ed. Pertz, p. 297. Cf. *Annales Maximiani*, ed. Waitz, 782, p. 21.

[106] For the dating of this text, see above, pp. 24–5.

[107] *Capitulatio de partibus Saxoniae*, ed. C. von Schwerin, *MGH Fontes iuris* 4 (Hanover: Hahn, 1918), pp. 37–44, here cc. 24, 28, 31, 34, pp. 41–4.

[108] See, for example, *Annales regni Francorum*, ed. Kurze, 809, 815, 828, pp. 129–30, 141–2, 175; Astronomus, *Vita Hludovici imperatoris*, ed. Tremp, cc. 25–6, 42, pp. 358–62, 446–8.

[109] For Wala's Saxon heritage, see Paschasius Radbertus, *Epitaphium Arsenii*, ed. Dümmler, I:12, I:13, pp. 40, 42; for Gundrada, Bernarius and Theodrada, see Paschasius Radbertus, *Vita sancti Adalhardi*, ed. J. P. Migne, *Patrologia Latina 120* (Paris, 1852), pp. 1507–56, here c. 33, pp. 1526C–1527A. For the dating of Bernhard's marriage and Wala's birth, see L. Weinrich, *Wala: Graf, Mönch und Rebell: Die Biographie eines Karolingers* (Historische Studien 386) (Lübeck: Matthiesen, 1963), pp. 12–13. See also Röckelein, *Reliquientranslationen nach Sachsen*, pp. 66–7.

[110] For these marriages, see Agius of Corvey, *Vita et obitus Hathumodae*, ed. G. H. Pertz, *MGH SS* 4 (Hanover: Hahn, 1841), pp. 165–89, here c. 2, p. 167; Einhard, *Vita Karoli Magni*, ed. Holder-Egger, c. 18, p. 23; Thegan, *Gesta Hludovici imperatoris*, ed. E. Tremp, *MGH SRG 64* (Hanover: Hahn, 1995), c. 26, p. 214; *Translatio sanctae Pusinnae*, ed. R. Wilmans, *Die Kaiserurkunden der*

the marriage alliances between the Saxon and Frankish elite. Yet there are signs that such marriages were regularly contracted. Alongside those of Welf and Egilwi and Liudolf and Oda, one can point to the marriage of the Saxon Ecbert and his Frankish wife Ida, the namesake of the famous 'Ecbertiner' family, as well as to that of the 'Frankish or Saxon' Syon and the Bavarian-Alemannic Gerildis, parents of Bishop Aldrich of Le Mans, whose tenure ran from 832 to 857.[111] Many additional marriages have been surmised from the *Namenforschung* ('name research') of Reinhard Wenskus. Such a positivist pursuit has its own attendant challenges, for it relies on similarities in naming patterns which remain a matter of speculation in the absence of further evidence.

A convenient summary of all these potential advantages of land, political office and marriages is provided by the Saxon leader Hessi, who managed to preserve, and even potentially to bolster, his wealth and influence following his submission in 775. Although Hessi disappears from the annalistic record following his capitulation, the later fortunes of his family are attested in the *Life of the Virgin Liutbirga*, a work composed in the period circa 870. The *Life* unfolds with the submission and conversion of Hessi, 'among the leading and most noble of that people', and goes on to tell of his eventual profession at the monastery of Fulda.[112] In the absence of male heirs, his extensive property was divided between his daughters, one of whom, Gisla, later used her patrimony, perhaps alongside that of her husband, to construct two female religious houses, one in Saxony and the other in Bavaria.[113] Even after endowing these

---

[110] *Provinz Westfalen, 777–1313*, 2 vols. (Münster: F. Regensberg, 1867), vol. I, pp. 539–46, here c. 3, p. 542; *D LJ*, ed. P. Kehr, *MGH, Die Urkunden Ludwigs des Deutschen, Karlmanns und Ludwigs der Jüngeren* (Berlin: Weidemann, 1934), no. 4, pp. 337–9, here p. 338. See also Depreux, 'L'intégration des élites aristocratiques', pp. 230, 234–5; Flierman, *Saxon Identities*, pp. 120–1; M. B. Gillis, *Heresy and Dissent in the Carolingian Empire: The Case of Gottschalk of Orbais* (Oxford: Oxford University Press, 2017), p. 37.

[111] For the marriage of Ecbert and Ida, see *Translatio sanctae Pusinnae*, ed. Wilmans, c. 2, p. 542; *Translatio sancti Viti*, ed. Schmale-Ott, c. 4, p. 44. For a later account of this marriage, see *Vita sanctae Idae*, ed. R. Wilmans, *Die Kaiserurkunden der Provinz Westfalen 777–1313*, 2 vols. (Münster: F. Regensberg, 1867), vol. I, cc. 1–5, pp. 471–4. For the marriage of Syon and Gerildis, see *Gesta Aldrici episcopi Cenomannensis*, ed. G. Waitz, *MGH SS* 15:1 (Hanover: Hahn, 1887), c. 1, p. 308. See further Depreux, 'L'intégration des élites aristocratiques', pp. 234, 251; G. Isenberg, 'Kulturwandel einer Region: Westfalen im 9. Jahrhundert' in Stiegemann and Wemhoff, *799*, vol. I: pp. 314–23, here p. 316; Röckelein, *Reliquientranslationen nach Sachsen*, pp. 60–1; R. Wenskus, *Sächsischer Stammesadel und fränkischer Reichsadel* (Abhandlungen der Akademie der Wissenschaften in Göttingen. Philologisch-Historische Klasse 93) (Göttingen: Vandenhoeck & Ruprecht, 1976), pp. 105–6, 111, 252.

[112] *Vita Liutbirgae virginis*, ed. Menzel, c. 1, p. 10: 'quendam inter primores ac nobilissimos gentis illius'. For this text and its implications, see also Flierman, *Saxon Identities*, pp. 147–50; cf. Springer, *Die Sachsen*, pp. 197–8.

[113] See here the comments of Depreux, 'L'intégration des élites aristocratiques', p. 233.

foundations, Gisla abounded in land and wealth. She travelled constantly to administer her many estates, and continued to spend her wealth on Christian projects. She 'constructed churches, diligently gave alms, and received pilgrims freely'.[114] The family retained a degree of political importance as well: Hessi served as a count; Gisla married a Frankish count; and her son, Bernhard, not only married a count's daughter, but also served as one himself.[115] The *Life* further underlines the family's political clout by name-dropping their connections to Bishops Theotgrim, Haimo of Halberstadt and Anskar of Bremen, and to various important laypeople, including Count Frederich and his wife Pia, Count Adalgar and Count Poppo (albeit the latter indirectly).[116] Finally, it has been suggested that Hessi may have enjoyed a propitious marriage to a woman from the Carolingian royal line: his daughter's name, Gisla, and that of a granddaughter, Rothild, certainly recall Carolingian naming patterns.[117] Even if this were not the case, however, the family retained a high status.

Hessi's survival and possible enrichment are certainly suggestive, but his is far from the most dramatic success story of the period. That distinction belongs to Widukind, whose well-timed capitulation allowed him to be transformed into the poster child for Charlemagne's Saxon victory.

The Rebel Widukind and His Submission

The *Royal Frankish Annals* first mention Widukind in 777, when all Saxons came to the public assembly at Paderborn 'except Widukind, who revolted along with a few others and fled along with his associates into Nordmannia'.[118] He next surfaced in 778, when he urged the Saxons to rebel,[119] and then again in 782, when he not only refused to come to the summons of the king, but also after his departure incited Saxons to rebellion. When Charlemagne inevitably returned, Widukind fled, leaving his associates to atone for the rebellion with their blood at

---

[114] *Vita Liutbirgae virginis*, ed. Menzel, c. 2, p. 11: 'ecclesias construendo, elemosinarum largitione sedula ac susceptione peregrinorum largiflua'. See also Paxton, *Anchoress and Abbess*, p. 48.

[115] *Vita Liutbirgae virginis*, ed. Menzel, cc. 1–2, 8, 12, pp. 10, 15, 17.

[116] *Ibid*, cc. 16, 25, 35, pp. 21, 28, 40, 43–4.

[117] *Ibid*, c. 2, pp. 10–11. See especially S. Krüger, *Studien zur Sächsischen Grafschaftsverfassung im 9. Jahrhundert* (Göttingen: Vandenhoeck & Ruprecht, 1950), p. 87; see further Flierman, *Saxon Identities*, p. 147; Paxton, *Anchoress and Abbess*, pp. 29–30; Wenskus, *Sächsischer Stammesadel*, p. 178.

[118] *Annales regni Francorum*, ed. Kurze, 777, p. 48: 'excepto quod Widochindis rebellis extitit cum paucis aliis: in partibus Nordmanniae confugium fecit una cum sociis suis'.

[119] *Ibid*, 778, p. 52.

the massacre of Verden.[120] Finally, in 785, Charlemagne received Widukind in Bardengau and commanded him to come to him in Francia, promising him safe conduct.[121] The final submission and baptism of Widukind are presented as the definitive conclusion to an accursed war.

One could argue, however, that the subjection of Saxony had already been achieved by Frankish force of arms earlier that same year, and that Widukind's submission at Attigny merely gave Charlemagne the opportunity to perform this subjection before a Frankish audience with appropriate ceremony. The exaggerated attention paid to Widukind in the *Royal Frankish Annals*, meanwhile, can be explained by the text's triumphant crescendo: his capitulation before a Frankish audience in 785 anticipated the submission of Tassilo in 788, the final year in this section of the annals.[122] In both episodes, Charlemagne not only emerges victorious, but is also shown extending Christian mercy to his undeserving opponents: he receives Widukind from the holy font following his baptism, and likewise commutes Tassilo's sentence of execution to monastic exile. While not a complete parallel, there are nonetheless commonalities between these reports.

This is not to deny Widukind's role, but merely to qualify it. Certainly, Widukind was involved with Saxon resistance. His association with the rebels of 782 could explain his public capitulation of 785. Nevertheless, the earlier crimes imputed to him may be little more than retrojections by the annalist writing only a few years after Widukind's capitulation. His failure to attend the 777 assembly, and his role in the uprising of 778, may not have been so significant at the time.[123] Widukind served a specific narrative role in the *Royal Frankish Annals* and their revision, and likewise in other association works,[124] but it is worth noting that this role can be contrasted to his depiction (or lack thereof) in other independent and semi-independent annals. In a series of annalistic compilations, comprising the *Petavian Annals, Annals of Baluze of Saint*

---

[120] *Ibid*, 782, pp. 58–60.   [121] *Ibid*, 785, p. 70.

[122] See here also the excellent analysis of Tassilo's treatment in the *Royal Frankish Annals* in M. Becher, *Eid und Herrschaft: Untersuchungen zum Herrscherethos Karls des Großen* (Vorträge und Forschungen 39) (Sigmaringen: J. Thorbecke, 1993), pp. 35–51.

[123] For Widukind's 778 appearance, see *Annales Fuldenses*, ed. Kurze, 778, p. 9; *Annales Mettenses priores*, ed. Simpson, 778, p. 67. For this point, see also I., Rembold, 'Quasi una gens: Saxony and the Frankish world, c. 772–888', *History Compass*, 15(6) (2017).

[124] Widukind appears before his 785 capitulation in the following annals: *Annales regni Francorum*, ed. Kurze, 777, 778, 782, 785, pp. 48, 52, 60–2, 70; *Annales qui dicuntur Einhardi*, ed. Kurze, 777, 782, 785, pp. 49, 61–5, 71; *Annales Fuldenses*, ed. Kurze, 778, 782, 785, p. 9–11; *Annales Laureshamenses*, ed. Pertz, 782, 785, p. 32; *Annales Mettenses priores*, ed. Simpson, 777, 778, 782, 785, pp. 65, 67, 69–70, 73; *Annales Mosellani*, ed. Lappenberg, 782, 785, p. 497; *Annales Lobienses*, ed. G. Waitz, *MGH SS* 13 (Hanover: Hahn, 1881), pp. 777, 779, 785, p. 229.

Gall, *Greater Annals of Salzburg, Laubach Annals* and finally the *Alemannic Annals* and their many associated annals (including the *Reichenau Annals, Wolfenbüttel Annals, Annals of Saint Nazarian, Brief Annals of Saint Gall* and *Greater Annals of Saint Gall*), Widukind is entirely absent from the narrative of Saxon conquest;[125] in the *Annals of Saint Amand, Maximian Annals* and *Chronicle of Moissac*, meanwhile, Widukind first appears with his ritual submission in 785.[126] While some of these annals appear to be later compositions or offer only summary comments, others can be dated as contemporary to these events and provide detailed entries; their collective silence on this score should not go unheeded.

Whether Widukind was the prominent arch-rebel depicted in the *Royal Frankish Annals* or merely a convenient figurehead whose submission allowed Charlemagne to enact his Saxon victory before a Frankish audience at Attigny, it is difficult to judge his pre-conquest position. His post-conquest position may be described with greater precision, thanks to the *Translation of Saint Alexander*, a text written by Rudolf and Meginhard of Fulda in circa 860–870 for Widukind's grandson, Waltbraht, which offers an abundance of evidence for the enduring wealth and status of Widukind's descendants. The text describes how Waltbraht was entrusted in his adolescence 'to the most pious lord King Lothar, then ruler of the western part, that he might serve the king at his court. The aforesaid king, following the custom of kings, received him mercifully and allowed him to be raised in good morals among other nobles and to partake in his society'.[127] Later Waltbraht established a monastery at Wildeshausen and transferred relics from Rome to his new foundation, an undertaking that was actively encouraged by Lothar. The emperor issued three letters in support of Waltbraht's enterprise, all of which are included in the *Translation*; twice, Lothar referred to Waltbraht expressly

---

[125] *Annales Alamannici*, ed. Pertz, pp. 40–1; *Annales Augienses*, ed. G. H. Pertz, *MGH SS* 1 (Hanover: Hahn, 1826), pp. 67–9, here p. 67; *Annales Guelferbytani*, ed. Pertz, pp. 40–1; *Annales Iuvavenses maximi*, ed. H. Bresslau, *MGH SS* 30:2 (Leipzig: K. W. Hiersemann, 1934), p. 734; *Annales Laubacenses*, ed. Pertz, p. 13; *Annales Petaviani*, ed. Pertz, pp. 16–7; *Annales Nazariani*, ed. G. H. Pertz, *MGH SS* 1 (Hanover: Hahn, 1826), pp. 23–31, 40–4, here pp. 40–1; *Annales Sangallenses Baluzii*, ed. Pertz, p. 63; *Annales Sangallenses breves*, eds. G. H. Pertz and I. ab Arx, *MGH SS* 1 (Hanover: Hahn, 1826), pp. 64–5, here p. 64; *Annales Sangallenses maiores*, ed. ab Arx, p. 75.

[126] *Annales sancti Amandi*, ed. Pertz, 785, p. 12; *Annales Maximiani*, ed. Waitz, 785, p. 21; *Chronicon Moissiacense*, ed. Pertz, 785, p. 297. See also Wood, 'Beyond satraps and ostriches', 276.

[127] Rudolf and Meginhard, *Translatio sancti Alexandri*, ed. Pertz, c. 4, p. 676: 'domno piisimo regi Hluthario, tunc occidentalium partium dominatori, commendavit, ut palatinorum consotius ministerium regis impleret. Quem praedictus rex secundum regium morem clementer suscipiens, ac moraliter nutritum suae familiaritatis participem inter alios proceres esse concessit.' For the post-conquest position of the family, see also Ehlers, *Die Integration Sachsens*, pp. 164–70; Flierman, *Saxon Identities*, p. 151.

as his 'fidelis'.[128] Certainly, Widukind's descendants appear to have enjoyed the advantages of *Königsnähe* ('nearness to the king'). The *Translation of Saint Alexander* does not simply illuminate Waltbraht's political connections, however, but also further offers insight into the family's landed possessions. As Hedwig Röckelein has persuasively argued, the contours of Widukinder landholding may be reconstructed from the account of the translation: as she writes, 'a series of connections, in terms of landowning, personal dependency, and familial relationships existed between the places visited, the people who were healed, and the translator Waltbraht himself. The places all belonged in the zone of influence of Waltbraht's family, the Widukinde'.[129] The itinerary of the relics traced Waltbraht's own possessions, which appear to have been extensive indeed. Widukind's capitulation, then, does not appear to have diminished the scope of his lordship: if anything, it may have buttressed his position. The *Translation of Saint Alexander* acts as a crucial witness for the continued, and probably enhanced, position of Widukind's family long after his famous 785 submission.

Uncertain Rewards

Both Widukind and Hessi clearly profited from the conquest. Some have postulated that their successes were shared more widely by the Saxon elite. Perhaps most famous in this regard is Martin Lintzel's 1934 essay 'The conquest of Saxony by Charlemagne and the Saxon elite', in which he put forward the thesis that the Saxon elite, grasping the advantages which they could gain from compliance, quickly became Charlemagne's collaborators and proceeded to wage a war against the lower classes.[130] Before the conquest, he argued, the lower classes had an equal voice in politics: the annual assembly at Marklo, as described in the *Old Life of Lebuin*, included representatives from all social backgrounds – noble, free, and half-free – in equal numbers.[131] Charlemagne proposed to alter this state of affairs. In return for the elite's participation in his war of conquest, he not only enriched the Saxon elite, as in the examples above, but also further raised their legal status, as shown by the vastly inflated wergilds in

---

[128] Rudolf and Meginhard, *Translatio sancti Alexandri*, ed. Pertz, c. 4, pp. 677–8.
[129] Röckelein, *Reliquientranslationen nach Sachsen*, p. 315: 'Zwischen den Haltepunkten, den geheilten Personen und dem Translator Waltbrecht bestanden eine Reihe grundbesitzrechtlicher, personenrechtlicher und/oder verwandtschaftlicher Beziehungen. Die Orte gehöhrten alle in den Einflußbereich der Widukinde, der Familie des Translators Waltbert.'
[130] Lintzel, 'Die Unterwerfung Sachsens', pp. 95–127.
[131] *Ibid*, pp. 125–6; see further M. Lintzel, 'Die Vita Lebuini antiqua' in Lintzel, *Schriften*, pp. 235–62.

the *Law of the Saxons*.[132] Lintzel further points to the fervent desire of the rebelling *Stellinga* to return to pre-conquest conditions, and the violence with which they attacked their social superiors, as an additional argument in support of his model.[133]

Although this thesis has been widely, if by no means universally, accepted in academic circles, it is nonetheless problematic.[134] Lintzel's image of pre-conquest political life is drawn exclusively from the *Old Life of Lebuin*, a saint's life of dubious credibility, most probably composed almost a century and a half after the events it purportedly describes.[135] His interpretation of the *Stellinga*, meanwhile, fails to account for the participation and encouragement of Lothar.[136] Both of these points will be addressed at greater length in Chapter 2. For the time being, it suffices to address Lintzel's reading of the *Law of the Saxons* and the advantages it purportedly offered to the Saxon elite.[137] This law demanded extremely stratified wergilds in the case of murder, set at 1,440 'minor' *solidi* for slain noblemen, with an additional 'ruoda' payment of 120 *solidi*; for 'maiden' noblewomen, the amount demanded in payment could be doubled, leading to a final sum of 3,000 *solidi*.[138] By comparison, the wergild payments set for half-freemen and slaves were 120 and 36 *solidi* respectively; freemen were, rather curiously, left out entirely.[139]

That a nobleman's life was valued at as much as twelve times the life of a half-freeman and forty times that of a slave is certainly striking, and has attracted much scholarly attention. Yet the inflated wergild demanded for noblemen, and, even more so, for noblewomen, was never more than an absurd abstraction. According to the conversion rate provided in the *Law of the Saxons* itself, the sum of 3,000 'minor' *solidi* stipulated as compensation for the death of a 'maiden' noblewomen was as much as three to six times that of the Saxons' annual tribute of 500 cows allegedly demanded by Clothar in the sixth century (the value of cows was itself dependent upon age, and thus variable); unfortunately, the law does not record the

---

[132] Lintzel, 'Die Unterwerfung Sachsens', pp. 121–2; see further Lintzel, 'Die Stände der deutschen Volksrechte, hauptsächlich der Lex Saxonum' in Lintzel, *Schriften*, pp. 309–79.

[133] Lintzel, 'Die Unterwerfung Sachsens', pp. 121–2.

[134] For critiques of Lintzel's model, see especially E. J. Goldberg, 'Popular revolt, dynastic politics, and aristocratic factionalism in the Early Middle Ages: the Saxon *Stellinga* reconsidered', *Speculum*, 70(3) (1995), 467–501, here 476–7, footnote 47; Springer, *Die Sachsen*, p. 207.

[135] See below, pp. 135–6.   [136] See below, pp. 116–29.

[137] See here especially Lintzel, 'Die Stände der deutschen Volksrechte', pp. 309–79; Lintzel, 'Die Entstehung der Lex Saxonum' in Lintzel, *Schriften*, pp. 390–419; see also G. Landwehr, 'Die Liten in den altsächsischen Rechtsquellen. Ein Diskussionsbeitrag zur Textgeschichte der *Lex Saxonum*' in G. Landwehr (ed.), *Studien zu den germanischen Volksrechten. Gedächtnisschrift für Wilhelm Ebel* (Rechtshistorische Reihe 1) (Frankfurt: P. Lang, 1982), pp. 117–42, here especially pp. 127–8.

[138] *Lex Saxonum*, ed. von Schwerin, cc. 14–15, p. 21.   [139] *Ibid*, cc. 16–17, p. 22.

value of horses, thus complicating a comparison between wergild payments and the annual tribute of 300 horses imposed by Pippin in 758.[140] Such a vast sum, so completely out of proportion to the tribute demanded from the Saxons, should not be taken to reflect either the status of Saxon elites or the advantages which Charlemagne offered them; rather, it may be interpreted as a rather ineffectual attempt at deterrence in the midst of continuing instability. The *Second Saxon Capitulary*, which had advocated a similar strategy some years earlier, actually states as much:

> Likewise, as it pleased the lord king, with the consent of his Frankish and Saxon *fideles*, to establish a greater *bannus* on account of peace and because of feuds and major crimes, it has been decided that he may order the 60 *solidi* to be doubled, or may order the transgressor to pay anything between 100 and 1000 *solidi* in compensation, according to the context and severity of the case.[141]

Certainly, the high payments advocated here were symptomatic of weakness, and it is in this context, and not that of the systematic advancement of the elite, that the implausibly high wergilds of the *Law of the Saxons* may be best understood. Lintzel's arguments are thus ultimately unpersuasive, and not simply for the reasons discussed above. At a more basic level, his thesis that Saxon elites profited in concrete ways from their association with Charlemagne is roundly contradicted by the surviving charter evidence.[142] Certainly, some elite Saxons, such as Widukind and Hessi, derived clear economic, social and political benefits from their association with Charlemagne. At the same time, success is generally noisier than failure, and other Saxon *fideles* faced more uncertain futures.

This is best illustrated by the remarkable survival of a handful of charters and one petition from the early ninth century.[143] In the earliest of these documents, a charter granted in 811, the petitioner, Bennit, appealed to Charlemagne to confirm his possession of an area of land in Buchonia. As the charter narrates, Bennit's father Amalungus

> preferred to remain loyal to us rather than to persist in infidelity with the others, and so he left the place of his birth, came to us and, while he was in our service, came to a village called Uuluisanger, where in that time Franks and Saxons lived

---

[140] *Ibid*, c. 66, pp. 33–4. For the annual tribute under Clothar, see Fredegar, *Chronicon*, ed. J. M. Wallace-Hadrill, *The Fourth Book of the Chronicle of Fredegar with Its Continuations* (London: Nelson, 1960), IV:74, pp. 62–3; for the annual tribute under Pippin, see *Annales Regni Francorum*, ed. Kurze, 758, p. 16.

[141] *Capitulare Saxonicum*, ed. von Schwerin, c. 9, p. 48: 'Item placuit ut quandoquidem voluit domnus rex propter pacem et propter faidam et propter maiores causas bannum fortiorem statuere una cum consensu Francorum et fidelium Saxonum secundum quod ei placuerit, iuxta quod causa exigit et oportunitas fuerit solidos LX multiplicare in duplum et solidos C sive usque ad mille conponere faciat qui eius mandatum transgressus fuerit.'

[142] Springer, *Die Sachsen*, p. 207.   [143] *Ibid*, pp. 204, 206–7.

together, but although he desired to stay there, he was not able to. Then he went on to the place called Waldesbecchi between the Weser River and the Fulda River and occupied a piece of the Buchonian forest, which, when he was dying, he bequeathed to his son Bennit.[144]

Bennit claimed that his father had remained faithful to Charlemagne under great pressure, and eventually abandoned his land and home to serve him. Thereafter, he was subjected to the uncertainties of a migrant life: unable to stay in the first place to which he had travelled, he moved on, and eventually reclaimed a piece of forest and developed the land. When he died, Bennit's inheritance of the enclosed field (*bifang*) which he had managed to carve out within the forest was so uncertain that he travelled to Charlemagne to have his possession confirmed. Such a confirmation was duly issued, but there is no mention of any additional favours, despite all his family had risked and lost.

The trajectories of Amalungus and Bennit were not simply a regrettable aberration. Their circumstances are echoed, or rather are reproduced verbatim, in another charter from 813. In this later charter, Charlemagne confirms the possessions of a certain Asig, otherwise known as Adalricus, son of Hiddi. Like Amalungus, Hiddi remained true to Charlemagne and thus left Saxony, travelling first to Uuluisanger and later on to Buchonia, where he too carved out a section of land for himself. Here, however, there was an additional wrinkle: his enclosure was belatedly claimed by a local count, and it was for this reason that Asig sought Charlemagne's confirmation, which was once again granted. In this case, as in that of Bennit, no further compensation is attested.[145]

Perhaps most dramatic, however, is a letter of petition written to Louis the Pious by an unknown Saxon, and later placed in a small formulary collection assembled at the archbishopric of Mainz (perhaps pointing to the demand for such a model).[146] It spins a dramatic tale of the difficulties

---

[144] *D Kar. 1*, ed. Mühlbacher, no. 213, pp. 284–5, here p. 285: 'praefatus Amalungus mallens fidem suam servare quam cum ceteris infidelibus perseverare, reliquens locum nativitatis suae veniens ad nos et, dum in nostro esset obsequio, venit ad villam cuius est vocabulum Uuluisanger, quam tunc temporis Franci et Saxones inhabitare videbantur, cupiens ibi cum eis manere, sed minime potuit. Tunc pergens ad locum qui dicitur Uualdesbecchi inter Uuiseraa et Fuldaa, proprisit sibi partem quendam de silva quae vocatur Bocchonia, quam moriens dereliquit filio suo Bennit'. See also Flierman, *Saxon Identities*, p. 125; Gillis, *Heresy and Dissent*, p. 36; K. Honselmann, 'Die Annahme des Christentums durch die Sachsen im Lichte sächsischer Quellen des 9. Jahrhunderts', *WZ*, 108 (1958), 201–19, here 207.

[145] *D Kar 1*, ed. Mühlbacher, no. 218, pp. 290–2; see also Gillis, *Heresy and Dissent*, p. 36.

[146] For the manuscript context of this formula, see F. Unterkircher, *Sancti Bonifacii epistolae. Codex Vindobonensis 751 der Oesterreichischen Nationalbibliothek. Faksimile-Ausg. der Wiener Handschrift der Briefe des heiligen Bonifatius* (Codices selecti phototypice impressi 24) (Graz: Akadem. Druck- und Verlagsanstalt, 1971), pp. 25, 35.

of its anonymous author and his family. This is calculated, no doubt, to produce a positive reception at court, but it is nonetheless indicative of the very real challenges that those displaced could face. The author of the letter begins by describing how his father and cousin, named Richart and Richolf respectively, both held lands in Saxony. Yet their allegiance to Charlemagne soon proved their undoing:

When they were in the service of your father, the Lord Emperor Charlemagne of blessed memory, their pagan neighbours stirred unrest because of their hatred of Christian religion and without warning pillaged their homes for all their possessions, because they understood that they wished to remain in the Christian faith and would not deny it in any way. Afterwards it came to pass that the lord emperor sent my cousin Richolf into the administrative district above the Elbe along with Count Rorih, Count Gotesscalc, Count Had, and Garih, and they were all killed there together because of their Christian allegiance. Having heard this, my father Richart proceeded to bring the news to the Lord Emperor Charlemagne. But while he was underway, my mother was apprehended by the same men who had earlier killed the aforesaid *missi*, and remained in their hands as a surety, and all of her effects, moveable and otherwise, were prised away through theft. When my father learned of this, he moved secretly and seized her stealthily, and he fled with her into the county of Marstheim to his maternal inheritance.[147]

This was, however, far from being the end of their travails. When, at the conclusion of the wars, those living in Wigmodia and beyond the Elbe were deported, so too was the author's family. Despite the faithful service and many sacrifices of his father and cousin, his family was still living in near destitution, deprived of their paternal inheritance, for almost a decade and a half after the conclusion of the wars. His eventual fate, and that of his family, are unknown.

---

[147] *Epistolae variorum inde a morte Caroli Magni*, ed. Dümmler, no. 2, p. 301: 'Dum autem in servitio patris vestri, felicis memoriae domni Caroli imperatoris, extiterunt, propinqui eorum atque pagenses, causa christianitatis furore se super eos turbantes, omnia quae in domibus propriae elaborationis habuerunt, cuncta raptim diripuerunt; eo quod in fide christianitatis velle eos persistere senserunt, et eam negare ullo modo noluerunt. Postea vero contigit, ut domnus imperator patruelem meum Richolf misit in missaticum super Elbam cum his inferius scriptis, id est Rorih comite, Gotesscalc comite, Had comite et Garih; qui omnes una ibidem fuerunt occisi propter christianitatis stabilimentum. Quo audito, perrexit pater meus Richart nuntiare hoc domno imperatori Carolo. Et dum in illa via fuit, adprehensa est ipsa mater mea ab eisdem viris, qui illos praefatos missos antea interfecerunt, et inter manus fideiussorum commendatam reliquerunt; ceteraque omnia, quae ibidem in sumptibus vel aliis quibuslibet rebus reperta sunt, secum per rapinam priserunt. Quod cum compertum fuit patri meo, transivit latenter et eam quasi furtim arripuit; fugitque cum ea in pagum, qui vocatur Marstheim, in maternam hereditatem suam.' See also Depreux, 'L'intégration des élites aristocratiques', p. 231; Flierman, *Saxon Identities*, p. 126; Gillis, *Heresy and Dissent*, p. 36; Honselmann, 'Die Annahme des Christentums', 207–8.

A comparative case suggests that the anonymous petitioner may have received some form of restitution. In 819 Louis the Pious issued a charter to three men, Ething, Hruotmor and Thancmar, who had together raised a complaint to his *missi*. These men claimed that they had remained in the faithful service of the emperor throughout the wars, but that at their conclusion their own properties were confiscated along with those of the rebels. Louis the Pious judged that they had lost their land unlawfully, and could thus reclaim their inheritance.[148] This was, needless to say, a positive outcome for the petitioners, but even so, it had been a long time coming.

The wartime experiences of all these men, from Bennit and Asig to Ething, Hruotmor and Thancmar, not to mention the anonymous petitioner, may well be exaggerated. They were almost certainly articulated in such a manner as to elicit sympathy at the Carolingian court, as exhibited, for example, in the stress laid upon the Christian fidelity of these men, in contrast to their pagan opponents. Certainly, all had the resources to appeal to the emperor: both Bennit and Asig travelled to Aachen to lodge their petitions, while the three petitioners in the last case journeyed to Ingelheim. Even the anonymous Saxon had the advantage of an education, as his elegantly phrased letter clearly attests. In the cases of Bennit and Asig, we have some indication as to their later fortunes: both Bennit and Asig (or one of his descendants) donated the above-mentioned lands in Buchonia to the monasteries of Corvey and Fulda, respectively. This accounts for the unusual preservation of their charters in the original, for charters to lay recipients generally do not survive.[149] This may attest to the continued uncertainty of their tenure. Yet other details provided in Corvey's cartulary evoke their later success. Both one of Bennit's probable descendants, Amalungus (II), and – more questionably – Asig (here, with the alternative spelling Esic) himself, appear to have formed marriage alliances with the Ecbertiners, one of the most powerful families in Carolingian Saxony.[150] This is in itself revealing of some degree of political clout; so too may Asig's/Esic's appointment as

---

[148] *D Kar.* 2, ed. T. Kölzer, *MGH, Die Urkunden Ludwigs des Frommen*, 3 vols. (Wiesbaden: Harrassowitz, 2016), vol. I, no. 162, pp. 402–4.

[149] For Bennit's donation to Fulda, see *Codex Eberhardi*, ed. H. Meyer zu Ermgassen, *Der Codex Eberhardi des Klosters Fulda* (Veröffentlichungen der Historischen Kommission für Hessen 58), 3 vols. (Marburg: Elwert, 1996), vol. II, c. 4, p. 15; Asig's donation to Corvey may be surmised from the preservation of his original charter at the monastery. For issues of lay documentary practice more generally, see especially W. C. Brown, M. Costambeys, M. Innes and A. J. Kosto (eds.), *Documentary Culture and the Laity* (Cambridge: Cambridge University Press, 2013).

[150] *Traditiones Corbeienses*, ed. K. Honselmann, *Die alten Mönchslisten und die Traditionen von Corvey* (Abhandlungen zur Corveyer Geschichtsschreibung 6), 2 vols. (Paderborn: Bonifatius, 1982), vol. I, no. 163, p. 110; *Notitiae fundationis monasterii Corbeiensis*, ed. O. Holder-Egger, *MGH SS* 15:2

count and later appearance as a *fidelis* of the Emperor Lothar be taken as evidence of continued importance. By the mid-ninth century, then, both the families of Amalung and Hiddi, as well as perhaps those of the other petitioners, had recovered a position of authority and influence in Saxony.

Such reversals could hardly have been anticipated. The prospects of these families had been injured over a considerable period, if less dramatically than these sources may claim, as a direct result of their fidelity to Charlemagne. The experiences of these men and their families, while atypical in some regards, help to illustrate the various pressures which could test even the most robust loyalty. These petitioners claim that both they and their families had remained faithful during the wars, but it is easy to imagine others who may have reneged on their oaths when threatened with the loss of their lands and possessions. Indeed, a letter sent from Pope Hadrian to Charlemagne in 786 confronts this very possibility: when asked what to do about Saxons who had reverted to paganism, he recommended that priests consider whether they had done so 'voluntarily' or if they had 'been compelled involuntarily' to observe pagan rites.[151] Clearly, it was at least conceivable to the Frankish king and the bishop of Rome that some Christian Saxons had lapsed in their observance of the faith under pressure from others. Conversely, of course, commensurate pressures seem to have led many to convert. It is in this light that we should interpret the continuous rhythm of submission and resistance, the insidious 'perfidy' that the annalists so regularly decry.

CONQUEST AND CONVERSION

The perfidy which contemporary annalists denounced, however, was not just a matter of political disloyalty. Rather, as Robert Flierman has persuasively argued, *fides* denoted 'a complex and loaded concept, that carried at once political (loyalty, fidelity) and religious (Christian faith)

(Hanover: Hahn, 1888), p. 1044. See also Krüger, *Studien zur Sächsischen Grafschaftsverfassung*, pp. 77–8, 82; Wenskus, *Sächsischer Stammesadel*, pp. 236, 248, 275–6, 345–6, 371.

[151] *Codex Carolinus*, ed. W. Gundlach, *MGH Epp.* 3:1 (Berlin: Weidemann, 1892), no. 77, p. 609: 'voluntatis'; 'extra voluntatem coacti'; see also Flierman, 'Defining and redefining Saxons', pp. 175–6; Flierman, 'Religious Saxons', pp. 189–91. Ernst Schubert interprets this letter differently, taking Pope Hadrian's comment to pertain to the voluntary or involuntary nature of Christian conversion of the Saxons in question: for this, see Schubert, 'Die Capitulatio', p. 11. I am grateful to Jinty Nelson for this reference. See further R. E. Sullivan, 'The papacy and missionary activity in the early middle ages', *Mediaeval Studies*, 17 (1955), 46–106, here 82.

overtones'.[152] The Saxon wars were not simply a matter of political incorporation: they were also wars of conversion.

These early years of the Saxon wars were characterized by religious violence: in 772, at the outset of the conflict, the Franks razed the Irminsul, a Saxon shrine, and in the years that followed Saxons would retaliate in kind, attempting to burn Boniface's church at Fritzlar in 773 and further destroying Frankish churches and monasteries in 778.[153] The religious significance of the wars was moreover amplified in Frankish representations of these conflicts. Battles especially were seen through the lens of religion: the *Petavian Annals* describe one especially grave Saxon defeat as an occasion on which 'many thousands of pagans' perished.[154] The *Royal Frankish Annals* go further still, and link Frankish victories directly to divine intervention. Nor were they alone in doing so. In 774, Pope Hadrian I wrote to congratulate Charlemagne for his recent 'immense victories, which the omnipotent Lord God, our Redeemer, deigned to concede to you through the intercession of saint Peter, prince of the apostles'.[155] Apparently the source of divine favour could be pinned down with some degree of accuracy, unsurprisingly, to Rome.

The *Royal Frankish Annals* additionally report various miracles occurring in these years, underscoring still further the role of divine agency in Frankish representations of the conflict. The first of these is recorded in 772, when Frankish troops destroyed the Irminsul, a Saxon shrine, during a major drought and after two or three days ran out of water. While the army was resting, presumably weak from dehydration, 'suddenly, by the generosity of divine grace, water flowed out in such a torrent that the entire army had enough to drink'.[156] The next year, when Saxons attempted to set alight Boniface's church at Fritzlar, which the saint had prophesied would never succumb to fire, the annalist recorded God's attendant revenge. Two youths in white appeared, visible to pagans and Christians alike, to protect the church from fire, and the Saxons, being unable to set the church aflame, took flight in fear.[157] Finally, in 776, Saxons set upon the fortress at Syburg but were repulsed by the sudden appearance of 'two shields alight with red flames, which revolved above

---

[152] Flierman, '*Gens perfida*', pp. 189–95, here especially p. 189; Flierman, *Saxon Identities*, pp. 93, 100–104, here especially p. 93.

[153] *Annales regni Francorum*, ed. Kurze, 772, 773, 778, pp. 34, 36–8, 52.

[154] *Annales Petaviani*, ed. Pertz, 775, p. 16: 'multa milia paganorum'.

[155] *Codex Carolinus*, ed. Gundlach, no. 50, pp. 569–70: 'de inmensis victoriis, quas vobis omnipotens et redemptor noster dominus Deus per intercessiones beati Petri principis apostolorum concedere dignatus est'.

[156] *Annales regni Francorum*, ed. Kurze, 772, p. 34: 'subito divina largiente gratia … in quodam torrente … aquae effusae sunt largissimae, ita ut cunctus exercitus sufficienter haberet'.

[157] *Ibid*, 773, pp. 36–8.

the church'; in their subsequent flight, they were slain down almost to a man.[158] 'How much the miracle of the Lord was performed above them for the salvation of the Christians, no one can say', the annalist conceded. 'Yet the more the Saxons were terrified, the more the Christians were comforted and praised omnipotent God, who saw worthy to reveal his power before his servants.'[159]

Meanwhile, the conversion of the Saxons was underway: baptisms are reported in 775, 776, 777, 780 and 785.[160] Such baptisms were by no means divorced from the violence which characterized the conquest: on the contrary, they were the direct result of that violence and the power which proceeded from it. A typical entry from the *Royal Frankish Annals* records how in 776, after a recent Frankish victory,

the terrified Saxons came to the source of the Lippe River, delivered their country through a pledge with all their hands, promised that they would be Christians, and placed themselves under the power of the Lord King Charlemagne and of the Franks. Then the Lord King Charlemagne, together with the Franks, rebuilt the Eresburg fort anew and constructed another fort above the Lippe, to which the Saxons came along with their wives and children, and an innumerable multitude of them were baptized.[161]

Here, Saxons were baptized in the shadow of Charlemagne's new fort, a visible symbol of Frankish domination. The next year, Charlemagne held an assembly in Paderborn, in a newly quiescent Saxony (Widukind and his associates had fled to the Northmen). 'There', as the *Royal Frankish Annals* note, 'a multitude of Saxons were baptized and, according to their custom, they agreed that if they changed back any more to their evil customs, they would forfeit all their freedom and property'; only if 'they observed Christianity in all ways and preserved the fidelity of the afore-mentioned Lord King Charlemagne and his sons and the Franks' could

---

[158] *Ibid*, 776, p. 46: 'duorum scutorum colore rubeo flammantes et agitantes supra ipsam ecclesiam'.

[159] *Ibid*, 776, p. 46: 'Et quantum super eos Dei virtus propter salutem christianorum operata est, nullus narrare potest; attamen quantum illi plus pavore perterriti fuerunt, tanto magis christiani confortati omnipotentem Deum laudaverunt, qui dignatus est suam manifestare potentiam super servos suos.'

[160] *Annales Sangallenses Baluzii*, ed. Pertz, 775, p. 63; *Annales Petaviani*, ed. Pertz, 776, 777, p. 16; *Annales Laureshamenses*, ed. Pertz, 776, 777, 780, 785, pp. 30–2; *Annales regni Francorum*, ed. Kurze, 776, 777, 780, 785, pp. 46, 48, 56, 70; *Annales qui dicuntur Einhardi*, ed. Kurze, 776, 777, 780, 785, pp. 47, 49, 57, 71; *Annales Maximiani*, ed. Waitz, 776, 777, 780, 785, p. 21; *Chronicon Moissiacense*, ed. Pertz, 776, 777, 780, 785, pp. 296–7.

[161] *Annales regni Francorum*, ed. Kurze, 776, p. 46: 'Et Saxones perterriti omnes ad locum, ubi Lippia consurgit, venientes ex omni parte et reddiderunt patriam per wadium omnes manibus eorum et spoponderunt se esse christianos et sub dicioni domni Caroli regis et Francorum subdiderunt. Et tunc domnus Carolus rex una cum Francis reaedificavit Eresburgum castrum denuo et alium castrum super Lippiam, ibique venientes Saxones una cum uxoribus et infantibus innumerabilis multitudo baptizati sunt.'

the Saxons hope to retain their rights.[162] 'If they ever changed their faith again', continued the *Earlier Annals of Metz*, 'they would be deprived of their inheritance and sent into perpetual slavery'.[163]

The connection between force and Christian profession was rendered even more stark in a poem written either for or soon after the Paderborn assembly in 777, the *Poem Concerning the Conversion of the Saxons*. In a work replete with Virgilian echoes, the anonymous poet, who has been variously identified as Lull, Paulinus or Angilbert,[164] described with evident approval the violent measures by which Charlemagne had led the Saxons to the baptismal font:

Prince Charlemagne, girded with gleaming arms,
Adorned with a plumed helmet,
Aided by the miraculous power of the eternal judge,
Conquered this people through various massacres, through a thousand
  victories,
And crushed them through bloodied shields, through bellicose spears,
Through the strength of courage, through blood-smeared arrows,
And he subjected them to himself with a glittering sword
And dragged the legions of forest-worshippers to the heavenly kingdom ...
... Afterwards, he sent the unlearned Christ-worshippers,
Wet with the dew of the salutary bath,
To the stars of heaven
In the name of the Father, the Begotten, and blessed Holy Breath,
Which is known to be the only hope of our life.
He anointed those bathed by sacred baptism with the chrism,
So that even now they might prevail to transcend the smoky flames,
And he led the new progeny of Christ into the hall.[165]

---

[162] *Ibid*, 777, p. 48: 'Ibique multitudo Saxonum baptizati sunt et secundum morem illorum omnem ingenuitatem et alodem manibus dulgtum fecerunt, si amplius inmutassent secundum malam consuetudinem eorum, nisi conservarent in omnibus christianitatem vel fidelitatem supradicti domni Caroli regis et filiorum eius vel Francorum.'

[163] *Annales Mettenses priores*, ed. Simpson, 777, p. 66: 'si amplius mutassent fidem eorum, in servitium sempiternum perdita hereditate incidissent'.

[164] For Lull, see K. Hauck, *Karolingische Taufpfalzen im Spiegel hofnaher Dichtung: Überlegungen zur Ausmalung von Pfalzkirchen, Pfalzen und Reichsklöstern* (Nachrichten der Akademie der Wissenschaften in Göttingen: I. Philologisch-Historische Klasse 1985:1) (Göttingen: Vandenhoeck & Ruprecht, 1985), pp. 56–74; for Paulinus of Aquileia, see D. Schaller, 'Der Dichter des "Carmen de conversione Saxonum"' in G. Bernt, F. Rädle and G. Silagi (eds.), *Tradition und Wertung: Festschrift für Franz Brunhölzl zum 65. Geburtstag* (Sigmaringen: J. Thorbecke, 1989), pp. 27–45; for Angilbert, see S. A. Rabe, *Faith, Art, and Politics at Saint-Riquier: The Symbolic Vision of Angilbert* (Philadelphia: University of Pennsylvania Press, 1995), pp. 54–9.

[165] *Carmen de conversione Saxonum*, ed. E. Dümmler, *MGH Poet.* 1 (Berlin: Weidemann, 1881), pp. 380–1, here lines 40–7, 56–62, pp. 380–1: 'Hanc Carolus princeps gentem fulgentibus armis/ Fortiter adcinctus, galeis cristatus acutis,/Arbitri aeterni mira virtute iuvatus,/Per varios casus domuit, per mille triumphos,/Perque cruoriferos umbos, per tela duelli,/Per vim virtutum, per spicula lita

78

In the poet's view, not only had Charlemagne triumphed decisively over the Saxons; the conversion of the Saxons had also been realized.[166] His celebratory message was not unique: a report from the *Petavian Annals* concerning the same assembly narrates how 'Saxons gathered together for catholic baptism there, and many thousands of that gentile populace were baptized ... afterwards King Charlemagne worthily rejoices with John the Baptist, who also "baptized, preaching baptism in the remission of sins"' (Mark I:4).[167] Likewise, the *Moselle Annals* on the same occasion describe how 'a very great multitude of Saxons were baptized. From the passing of Pope Gregory up to the present day there have been 172 years'.[168] The annalist's implication is clear: the conversion of the (Anglo-)Saxons, begun almost two centuries before by Pope Gregory the Great, had finally been achieved.

Such optimism would all too soon be undercut by renewed rebellion. In 778, as the *Moselle Annals* recorded, the Saxons, 'that perfidious people, feigning the faith of Christ', crossed the Rhine into Francia, leaving a wide swathe of destruction in their wake.[169] Such resistance was not merely political in nature: the *Life of Saint Sturmi* described Saxon apostasy, while the *Life of Saint Willehad* reported, even more concretely, that four missionaries had been killed in a Saxon uprising.[170] Nonetheless, the foundations of a Christian mission were being laid: missionaries continued to be appointed; mass baptisms performed. Optimism returned, and by 785, Christian triumphalism was once again in the air.

From the perspective of circa 790, when the first section of the *Royal Frankish Annals* was probably composed, the year 785 appeared to mark the final settlement of the Saxon wars.[171] As the anonymous annalist

---

cruore/Contrivit, sibimet gladio vibrante subegit;/Traxit silviculas ad caeli regna phalanges'; 'Post-que salutiferi perfusos rore lavacri,/Sub patris et geniti, sancti sub flaminis almi/Nomine, quo nostrae constat spes unica vitae,/Christocolasque rudes ad caeli sidera misit,/Chrismatibus sacro inunxit baptismate lotos,/Quo iam fumiferas valeant transcendere flammas,/Progeniemque novam Christi perduxit in aulam.' My translation is greatly indebted to that of Susan Rabe.

[166] See also Bachrach, *Charlemagne's Early Campaigns*, p. 628; Flierman, 'Gens perfida', pp. 196–7; Flierman, *Saxon Identities*, pp. 106–7; Springer, *Die Sachsen*, p. 184.

[167] *Annales Petaviani*, ed. Pertz, 777, p. 16: 'ibi convenerunt Saxones ad baptismum catholicum, et baptizata multa milia populorum gentilium ... in postmodum Karolus rex merito gaudet cum Iohanne baptista, qui et baptizavit praedicans baptismum in remissionem omnium peccatorum'. For this, see Hauck, *Karolingische Taufpfalzen*, p. 19.

[168] *Annales Mosellani*, ed. Lappenberg, 777, p. 496: 'ibi paganorum Saxonum multitudo maxima baptizata est. A Gregorii papae obitum usque ad presentum annum fiunt 172 anni'. For this, see Hauck, *Karolingische Taufpfalzen*, p. 19.

[169] *Annales Mosellani*, ed. Lappenberg, 778, p. 496: 'gens perfida, mentientes fidem Christi'.

[170] Eigil of Fulda, *Vita sancti Sturmi*, ed. Engelbert, c. 24, p. 159; *Vita sancti Willehadi*, eds. de Smedt, van Ortroy, Delehaye, Poncelet and Peeters, c. 6, p. 844D.

[171] Flierman, 'Gens perfida', pp. 198–9; Flierman, *Saxon Identities*, p. 108; Springer, *Die Sachsen*, pp. 200–1.

reported, in that year Charlemagne wintered in the fortress of Eresburg with his family, sending out detachments and occasionally himself campaigning in the surrounding Saxon countryside. 'He despoiled the rebellious Saxons, seized their fortresses, marched through their defended places, and cleared the roads.'[172] After Easter, he convened a general assembly at Paderborn, and 'thence he continued on open roads throughout the whole of Saxony, wherever he wished and without any resistance'.[173] Finally, he sent emissaries to the rebels Widukind and Abbi, commanding them to come to him in Francia. Later, when Charlemagne had returned to Francia, Widukind and Abbi came to him in Attigny and received baptism, 'and then all of Saxony was subjugated'.[174] The *Lorsch Annals* recalled verbatim the earlier report of the *Moselle Annals*: 'From the passing of Pope Gregory up to the present day, there have been a hundred and eighty years.'[175] Once again, as an effusive letter from Pope Hadrian attests, the conversion of the Saxons was perceived to have been fully accomplished.[176] In the following years, the Saxons were incorporated into the structures of Frankish political and religious life. They served on campaign in Bavaria in 787, and against the Sorbs and Avars in 789 and 791, respectively; they were further present at Tassilo's judgement at the assembly of Ingelheim in 788.[177] In short: the Saxons had been brought inside the Frankish fold, with all the Christian observance such a designation implied.[178]

When rebellion broke out again in 792, the tone changed, and this time it did not change back. Nowhere was this clearer than in the *Lorsch Annals*. 'Just like dogs who return to their vomit', the annalist scathingly wrote, recalling the famous axiom of Proverbs 26:11,

so too those who had formerly rejected paganism again left the Christian religion, deceiving both the Lord and the lord king, who had granted them so many benefits, and joined with the pagan peoples who bordered them. Sending their *missi* to the Avars, they attempted to rebel first against God, then against

---

[172] *Annales regni Francorum*, ed. Kurze, 785, p. 68: 'Saxones, qui rebelles fuerunt, depraedavit et castra cepit et loca eorum munita intervenit et vias mundavit.'

[173] *Ibid*, 785, pp. 68–70: 'inde iter peragens vias apertas nemini contradicente per totam Saxoniam, quocumque voluit'.

[174] *Ibid*, 785, p. 70: 'et tunc tota Saxonia subiugata est'.

[175] *Annales Laureshamenses*, ed. Pertz, 785, p. 32: 'A transitu Gregorii papae usque praesentem fiunt anni centum octoginta.' Contrast with *Annales Mosellani*, ed. Lappenberg, 785, p. 497. See also Flierman, '*Gens perfida*', pp. 198–9; Flierman, *Saxon Identities*, p. 108.

[176] *Codex Carolinus*, ed. Gundlach, no. 76, pp. 607–8. See also Flierman, '*Gens perfida*', p. 199; Flierman, 'Defining and redefining Saxons', p. 175; Flierman, *Saxon Identities*, p. 108; Sullivan, 'The papacy and missionary activity', 82.

[177] *Annales regni Francorum*, ed. Kurze, 787, 788, 789, 791, pp. 78, 80, 84 88.

[178] Flierman, '*Gens perfida*', p. 199; Flierman, *Saxon Identities*, pp. 108–9.

the king and Christians; they destroyed all the churches within their borders by demolition or fire, threw off the bishops and priests who had been placed over them, killed others, and returned completely to the worship of idols.[179]

It was not the only source to turn to Scripture: the *Petavian Annals* likewise drew on a pre-Vulgate version of Isaiah 26:11, 'wrath seizes the [un]learned people', thereby foreshadowing the Saxons' eventual fate; the quotation is taken from a canticle celebrating the Israelites' (and hence, Franks') eventual triumph over their enemies.[180] Nor was this the only source to allege that Saxons had committed apostasy: the closely related *Moselle Annals*, following a joint Saxon and Frisian attack on Frankish forces, reported that both peoples, 'having carried out such a slaughter, were once again made pagan'.[181] Even Alcuin was scathing in his criticism: in a series of letters from 796, the Saxons appear as a 'wretched' and 'most hard' people, who 'had lost the sacrament of baptism so many times, because they never hand the foundation of faith in their hearts'.[182] In 799, his rhetoric became even more heated: the Saxons were an 'impious (*nefando*) people', an 'accursed generation'.[183] The narrative of Christian triumphalism had been replaced by one of Saxon faithlessness.

It is unclear what prompted this shift in representation. The unexpected renewal of Saxon resistance no doubt earned the vitriol of Frankish chroniclers; additionally, Springer has posited that the Franks' alliance with the pagan Abodrites complicated the narrative of providential victories.[184] These appear, however, insufficient reasons to explain the complete absence of religious justifications. I would be more inclined to follow the view recently advanced by Flierman, that the Franks already viewed Saxons as part not only of the Frankish kingdom but also of the *populus Christianorum*, and may have largely continued

---

[179] *Annales Laureshamenses*, ed. Pertz, 792, p. 35: 'quasi canis qui revertit ad vomitum suum, sic reversi sunt ad paganismum quem pridem respuerant, iterum relinquentes christianitatem, mentientes tam Deo quam domno rege, qui eis multa beneficia prestetit, coniungentes se cum paganas gentes, qui in circuitu eorum erant. Sed et missos suos ad Avaros transmittentes conati sunt in primis rebellare contra Deum, deinde contra regem et christianos; omnes ecclesias que in finibus eorum erant, cum destructione et incendio vastabant, reiicientes episcopos et presbyteros qui super eos erant, et aliquos comprehenderunt, nec non et alios occiderunt, et plenissime se ad culturam idolorum converterunt'. See also Flierman, '*Gens perfida*', p. 201; Flierman, *Saxon Identities*, pp. 110–11; Phelan, *The Formation of Christian Europe*, pp. 67–8.

[180] *Annales Petaviani*, ed. Pertz, 792, p. 18: 'Zelus adprehendit populum [in]eruditum.'

[181] *Annales Mosellani*, ed. Lappenberg, 791 [792]: 'quique etiam caede peracta rursum pagani effecti sunt'.

[182] Alcuin, *Epistolae*, ed. Dümmler, no. 110, p. 157: 'infelicis'; no. 111, p. 161: 'durissimo'; 118, p. 164: 'toties baptismi perdidit sacramentum, quia numquam habuit in corde fidei fundamentum'.

[183] *Ibid*, no. 177, p. 293: 'populo nefando'; no. 184, p. 309: 'maledicta generatione'.

[184] Springer, *Die Sachsen*, pp. 207–8.

to do so, despite recent lapses.[185] Certainly, in contrast to the earlier period, conversion does not seem to have been an objective during later Frankish campaigns: there are no reports of mass baptisms in the entire annalistic corpus after 785, a fact which, given the frequent conflation of baptism and Christian conversion in the period, is undoubtedly significant.[186] Only once more, in 794, are Saxons depicted 'promising to be Christian'.[187] While Einhard later wrote that the peace settlement hinged on the Saxons' adoption of the Christian faith, contemporaries were silent on this score. The Saxons were already regarded as Christians, however imperfectly so.

The outbreak of renewed hostilities in 792, coterminous as it was with Pippin the Hunchback's rebellion, may thus be perceived to mark an internal rebellion, not an external war. Hence Charlemagne's reluctance to engage Saxons in open battle and his disavowal of the massacres which had characterized the early conduct on Saxon campaigns, and hence likewise the heightened rhetoric of Frankish observers. After all, as Flierman writes, 'it was Frankish impatience to claim the Saxons as insiders and *fideles*, that allowed the charge of *perfidia* to thrive as it did'.[188]

Whether or not the Saxons were perceived as Christians by contemporaries from 785 onwards, they were certainly regarded as such by the end of the conflict in 804. The verdict of ninth-century hagiographers is clear on this score: these later authors unanimously place the conversion of the Saxons squarely within the conquest period. Almost all ninth-century 'Saxon' hagiographical texts, that is, *Lives* or *Translations* about saints or relics which were active in Saxony, state this explicitly. References to the successful conversion of the Saxons under Charlemagne appear (in approximate order of composition) in the *Translation of Saint Vitus*, Altfrid's *Life of Saint Liudger* (to be later reiterated in the *Second* and *Third Lives of Saint Liudger*), the *Life of Saint Willehad*, Rudolf and Meginhard's *Translation of Saint Alexander*, the *Translation of Saint Pusinna*, Rimbert's *Life of Saint Anskar*, the *Life of the Virgin Liutbirga*, the *Translation of Saint Liborius*, the *Life of Saint Meinolf* and, finally, the *Life of Saint Rimbert*.[189] Many of these narratives ostensibly describe saints or relic

---

[185] Flierman, '*Gens perfida*', p. 199; Flierman, *Saxon Identities*, pp. 108–9.

[186] For the conflation of baptism and conversion, see below, p. 203.

[187] *Annales Laureshamenses*, ed. Pertz, 794, p. 36: 'promittentes christianitatem'; *Annales Regni Francorum*, ed. Kurze, 794, p. 96; *Chronicon Moissiacense*, ed. Pertz, 794, p. 302. See also Flierman, '*Gens perfida*', p. 200; Flierman, *Saxon Identities*, p. 110.

[188] Flierman, '*Gens perfida*', p. 205; Flierman, *Saxon Identities*, p. 117.

[189] *Translatio sancti Viti*, ed. Schmale-Ott, c. 3, pp. 34–6; Altfrid, *Vita sancti Liudgeri*, ed. Diekamp, I:23, p. 27; *Vita secunda sancti Liudgeri*, ed. E. Freise, *Die Vita sancti Liudgeri: Vollständige Faksimile-Ausgabe der Handschrift Ms. Theol. lat. fol. 323 der Staatsbibliothek Berlin – Preußischer Kulturbesitz. Text, Übersetzung und Kommentar, Forschungsbeiträge* (Graz: Akadem. Druck- und Verlagsanstalt,

translations from much later in the ninth century. It is thus all the more remarkable that they weave Charlemagne's conversion of the Saxons into their narratives in order to connect their particular saint or relics to this 'illustrious' past. The conversion of the Saxons is presented as a supreme Christian victory already achieved by Charlemagne.

This is not to say that the 'faithlessness' of the Saxons is removed entirely from later hagiographic representations. The negative wartime depiction of the Saxons in the *Royal Frankish Annals* and its revision are rehashed in a few later hagiographical texts describing this earlier period: Eigel's *Life of Saint Sturmi* and the *Life of Saint Willehad* describe the Saxons as a 'vicious and perverse people' and 'hostile people' respectively.[190] The *Translation of Saint Liborius* even depicts the Saxons as 'semi-pagan', the only time in the entire ninth-century Saxon corpus that such a gradation between Christianity and paganism is acknowledged as possible.[191] Yet with the exception of the *Life of Saint Sturmi*, which goes up only until 779, these narratives nonetheless acknowledge the eventual conversion of the Saxons under Charlemagne. In the *Life of Saint Willehad*, the conversion is described in pastoral terms: 'having been compelled, the wild neck of the Saxons then grew tame under the gentle yoke of Christ'.[192] The *Translation of Saint Liborius*, meanwhile, could not be more explicit in its depiction of Charlemagne as an apostle.[193] These sources report Saxon lapses during the conquest, but the Christian faith eventually prevails.

1999), pp. 9–24, here I:1, p. 9 (this extract only refers explicitly to the conversion of the East Saxons); *Vita tertia sancti Liudgeri*, ed. Diekamp, I:27, p. 103; *Vita sancti Willehadi*, eds. de Smedt, van Ortroy, Delehaye, Poncelet and Peeters, c. 8, p. 845A-D; Rudolf and Meginhard, *Translatio sancti Alexandri*, ed. Pertz, c. 3, p. 676; *Translatio sanctae Pusinnae*, ed. Wilmans, c. 1, p. 541; Rimbert, *Vita sancti Anskarii*, ed. G. Waitz, *MGH SRG* 55 (Hanover: Hahn, 1884), c. 12, p. 33; *Vita Liutbirgae virginis*, ed. Menzel, c. 1, p. 10; Anonymus Paderbrunnensis, *Translatio sancti Liborii*, ed. de Vry, cc. 2, 7, pp. 188–9, 193–4; *Vita sancti Meinolfi*, ed. K. Honselmann, 'Die älteste Vita Meinolfi: Brevierlesungen zu den Festen des Heiligen aus dem Ende des 9. Jahrhunderts', *WZ*, 137 (1987), 185–206, here 194 (this text refers specifically to the conversion of the Westphalians in 777); *Vita sancti Rimberti*, ed. G. Waitz, *MGH SRG* 55 (Hanover: Hahn, 1884), c. 1, p. 81. For non-hagiographic references to the conversion of Saxony, see, for example, Hrabanus Maurus, *Liber de oblatione puerorum*, ed. J. P. Migne, *Patrologia Latina 107* (Paris, 1851), col. 432A–B; Poeta Saxo, *Annalium de gestis Caroli magni imperatoris libri V*, ed. Winterfeld, V, lines 667–88, p. 71. See further Honselmann, 'Die Annahme des Christentums', 201–19.

[190] Eigil of Fulda, *Vita sancti Sturmi*, ed. Engelbert, c. 24, p. 159: 'gens prava et perversa'; *Vita sancti Willehadi*, eds. de Smedt, van Ortroy, Delehaye, Poncelet and Peeters, c. 5, p. 843F: 'illi aversi'.

[191] Anonymus Paderbrunnensis, *Translatio sancti Liborii*, ed. de Vry, c. 3, p. 189: 'semipaganae'; see also E. Shuler, 'The Saxons within Carolingian Christendom: post-conquest identity in the *translationes* of Vitus, Pusinna, and Liborius', *Journal of Medieval History*, 36(1) (2010), 39–54, here 50–1.

[192] *Vita sancti Willehadi*, eds. de Smedt, van Ortroy, Delehaye, Poncelet and Peeters, c. 8, p. 845B: 'et sub leni iugo Christi Saxonum ferocia licet coacta iam mitescerent colla'.

[193] See below, p. 239.

There are still occasional references to the post-conquest Saxons as backsliding, or even as being on the brink of lapsing following the end of the conquest. Yet in the vast majority of these hagiographical sources, the Christianity of the post-conquest Saxons is acknowledged and celebrated. All of these narratives agree on this fundamental point: the Saxons converted during the conquest period. The Saxons had become part of the Christian church.

* * *

The long-term ramifications of the Saxon wars are readily apparent. The precise effects of conquest on ninth-century Saxony, by contrast, are considerably more contentious. Traditionally, scholars have argued that the brutality of the wars precluded a full acceptance of the Christian faith; at most, the elite have been supposed to have eagerly accepted Christianity and Frankish lordship because of the advantages it offered them vis-à-vis the lower orders of Saxon society, thus leading, eventually, to the eruption of tensions in the *Stellinga*. This charge will be addressed in Chapter 2. My reassessment of the evidence, however, suggests a rather different set of outcomes.

First, the wars did not advance a pre-existing Saxon elite at the expense of the lower orders, or, at the very least, did not do so consistently. The clearest winners from the Saxon campaigns were the Abodrites, and even they were not to enjoy the fruits of their victory for long. While some elite Saxons benefitted from their association with Charlemagne, others incurred losses; the patterns of resistance and collaboration cannot be ascribed to clear divisions in Saxon society, but rather to the pragmatic opportunism with which individual actors and groups chose their positions.

Second, and even more significantly for this study, at the conclusion of the wars the Saxons were recognized to be subject both to the Carolingian king and to the Christian God, and, consequently, to be within both the Carolingian political order and the Christian church. The latter point is of particular importance: following the end of the wars, authors looking back would be clear in their categorization of the Saxons as Christian. What concerned authors after this point was not how to bring the Saxons within the Christian fold, but instead, as we shall see in Chapter 4, how to secure the full correct Christian observance of an already, if imperfectly, Christian people.

Chapter 2

THE *STELLINGA*

After the conclusion of the Saxon wars, the Saxons appear to have been model imperial subjects. In the later years of Charlemagne and throughout the reign of Louis the Pious, Saxon forces, often led by Saxon counts, and notably acting on imperial orders, waged a series of campaigns against the Slavs and developed and manned a fortified border region. At the forefront of the Carolingian push eastwards, the Saxons remained largely aloof from the rebellions which rocked Louis the Pious' reign. Instead, they meticulously maintained their fidelity to the emperor, responding to his summons in 830, 832, 834 and 839.[1] Only on the last of these occasions are any Saxon forces attested as taking part in a rebellion: Nithard reports that Saxons were to be found among the forces of the emperor's estranged son, Louis the German.[2]

As a result of these rebellions, Louis the Pious revised his sons' shares in the empire, carving up new subkingdoms and inheritances. In his original plan, laid out in the *Ordinance of the Empire* of 817, Louis had allocated Saxony, along with the greater part of the empire, to the portion to be co-ruled by himself and his firstborn son, Lothar, and to be inherited by

---

[1] *Annales Bertiniani*, eds. F. Grat, J. Vielliard and S. Clémencet, *Annales de Saint-Bertin* (Paris: C. Klincksieck, 1964), 830, 832, 834, 839, pp. 2, 6, 11, 27, 33–5; *Annales Fuldenses*, ed. F. Kurze, *MGH SRG* 7 (Hanover: Hahn, 1891), 839, p. 29. For this, and for these references, see R. Flierman, *Saxon Identities, AD 150–900* (London: Bloomsbury Academic, 2017), pp. 125–6. See also K. H. Krüger, 'Die ältern Sachsen als Franken. Zum Besuch des Kaisers Arnulf 889 im Kloster Corvey', *WZ*, 151/152 (2001/2002), 225–44, here 228–9; M. Last, 'Niedersachsen in der Merowinger- und Karolingerzeit' in H. Patze (ed.), *Geschichte Niedersachsens: Grundlagen und frühes Mittelalter* (Veröffentlichungen der Historischen Kommission für Niedersachsen und Bremen 36), 5 vols. (Hildesheim: Lax, 1977), vol. I: pp. 543–652, here pp. 601–2.

[2] Nithard, *Historiae*, eds. P. Lauer and S. Glansdorff, *Histoire des fils de Louis le Pieux* (Les classiques de l'histoire au Moyen Âge 51) (Paris: Les Belles Lettres, 2012), I:8, p. 40; see also B. S. Bachrach and D. Bachrach, 'Saxon military revolution, 912–973? Myth and reality', *EME*, 15(2) (2007), 186–222, here 208. One may also point towards Bishop Goswin of Osnabrück's participation in Louis the Pious' deposition in 833, but there are no records of broader Saxon participation in that rebellion.

the latter upon his death.[3] In 831, in response to the first rebellion, Louis reduced Lothar's portion, granting lands in East Francia, including Saxony, to the inheritance of his third son, Louis the German.[4] This arrangement proved short-lived: in 838 Louis the Pious reversed his earlier grant, and in 839 he confirmed that both Saxony and East Francia would belong to the inheritance of Lothar, with the exception of Bavaria, which remained in the hands of Louis the German.[5]

One could point towards these 'reassignments' as contributing to a sense of mixed loyalties; indeed, following the death of Louis the Pious, the Saxon elite were divided, with some supporting Lothar and others Louis the German (as we shall see at greater length below).[6] Yet prior to Louis the Pious' death in 840, there is no evidence to suggest that either Louis the German or Lothar exercised any control over Saxony, with the sole exception of the 839 episode; certainly, neither developed close ties to the region, in stark contrast to their governance in Bavaria and Italy, respectively. Louis the Pious remained in control of Saxony throughout his lifetime, and his authority, notably, was respected.

Louis the Pious' authority, while unchallenged in Saxony, was also distant. His father, Charlemagne, had travelled to Saxony twenty times in the course of his reign; by contrast, Louis the Pious visited only once, in 815, near the start of his reign.[7] Saxony was no longer a main priority. This 'devaluation' in importance is reflected in the surviving sources: indeed, the Saxons only feature in Carolingian annals, with a few exceptions, insofar as they participated in Carolingian campaigns against, and diplomacy to, the Slavs and Danes. No attention is paid to internal

---

[3] *Cap. 1*, ed. A. Boretius, *MGH Cap.* 1 (Hanover: Hahn, 1883), no. 136, prologue, cc. 1–2, pp. 270–1.

[4] *Cap. 2*, eds. A. Boretius and V. Krause, *MGH Cap.* 2 (Hanover, 1897), no. 194, c. 14, p. 24; E. J. Goldberg, *Struggle for Empire: Kingship and Conflict under Louis the German, 817–876* (Ithaca: Cornell University Press, 2006), p. 62.

[5] *Annales Bertiniani*, eds. Grat, Vielliard and Clémencet, 838, 839, pp. 24, 32; Nithard, *Historiae*, eds. Lauer and Glansdorff, I:6, p. 34; see also E. J. Goldberg, 'Popular revolt, dynastic politics, and aristocratic factionalism in the Early Middle Ages: the Saxon *Stellinga* reconsidered', *Speculum*, 70(3) (1995), 467–501, here 484–5; Goldberg, *Struggle for Empire*, pp. 87–92; J. L. Nelson, *Charles the Bald* (London: Routledge, 1992), pp. 95–6.

[6] See below, pp. 100, 119–20.

[7] For Charlemagne's visits to Saxony, see *Annales Regni Francorum*, ed. F. Kurze, *MGH SRG* 6 (Hanover: Hahn, 1895), 772, 775, 776, 777, 779, 780, 782 (when he visited twice), 783, 784, 785, 794, 795, 796, 797 (when he visited twice), 798, 799, 804, 810, pp. 32–4, 40–2, 46–8, 54–6, 58–60, 62, 64–6, 68–70, 94–6, 98–100, 102–4, 106, 118–19, 131; for Louis the Pious' visit, see *Ibid*, 815, p. 142. See also C. Ehlers, *Die Integration Sachsens in das fränkische Reich (751–1024)* (Veröffentlichungen des Max-Planck-Instituts für Geschichte 231) (Göttingen: Vandenhoeck & Ruprecht, 2007), p. 291; H. Röckelein, *Reliquientranslationen nach Sachsen im 9. Jahrhundert: über Kommunikation, Mobilität und Öffentlichkeit im Frühmittelalter* (Beihefte der Francia 48) (Sigmaringen: J. Thorbecke, 2002), p. 24.

Saxon developments until the emergence of the *Stellinga* in 841. Indeed, as far as historians were concerned, the *Stellinga* movement was 'the' main event in ninth-century Saxon history. As Eric Goldberg has noted, it elicited more contemporary reports (four) than Charlemagne's coronation as emperor (three): accounts of the *Stellinga* survive in Nithard's *Histories*, Prudentius' section of the *Annals of Saint Bertin*, Rudolf of Fulda's section of the *Fulda Annals*, and finally in the *Xanten Annals*.[8]

The basic narrative of the *Stellinga* may be summarized as follows. In 841, in the midst of the civil war between the sons of Louis the Pious, the Emperor Lothar appealed to the Saxons for their assistance. More specifically, he appealed to the *Stellinga*, a group drawn from the 'lower orders' of Saxon society, by offering them the right to observe their customary law. The *Stellinga* agreed, and over the course of the next year the movement appears to have enjoyed remarkable success, in stark contrast to Lothar's larger offensive. By 842, Lothar was seeking a negotiated peace with his brothers; the *Stellinga*, however, continued to agitate, and were put down by violent force not once but twice, first by Lothar's brother and erstwhile adversary, King Louis the German, and later by local elites.

The *Stellinga* revolt has traditionally been interpreted as an aberration. The movement has been claimed as the only example of a large-scale armed peasant revolt in early medieval Europe, and likewise as one of the few pagan reactions of a Christianized region. Its participants are credited with a vehemently anti-elite and anti-Christian agenda, and are portrayed as seeking return to the pre-conquest conditions which they had enjoyed some seventy years previously. In effect, the revolt is viewed as a response to the changes ushered in by the Saxon wars, and is consequently taken as indicative of the perceived failures of the conquest.

This chapter will seek to challenge this position. First, it will revisit the long-term effects of the conquest on Saxon society and assess the role played by continued cross-border campaigning under Louis the Pious. Having identified a rather different set of preconditions for the revolt, it will reexamine the various motivations attributed to the *Stellinga*, namely class, law and religion. It will then propose a new narrative for the *Stellinga*, with particular attention paid to their cooperation with Lothar, before finally turning to the lasting influence of the *Stellinga* on perceptions of orders and law in Saxon society. Upon reconsideration, the *Stellinga* revolt appears less remarkable, but more explicable, than has hitherto been assumed. The *Stellinga* possessed neither the exceptionalism nor the revolutionary fervour so often attributed to them; they were

---

[8] Goldberg, 'Popular revolt', 480.

certainly not seeking to unravel the changes of the previous two generations.[9] To reevaulate the *Stellinga* is to pursue the effects of the conquest in the *longue durée*. It is the contention of this chapter that the *Stellinga*, far from signalling the failure of incorporation, point towards the successful, if incomplete, integration of Saxony in the Carolingian world.[10]

FROM THE SAXON WARS TO THE *STELLINGA*

Whether or not it was recorded, or deemed worthy of attention by contemporaries, a transformation was underway. As indicated in the introduction, the Saxon wars had set great changes in motion – changes including, but not limited to, religious identity, political culture and orientation and social structure. The very phenomenon of the *Stellinga* testifies to the significance of this transformation. In what follows, I shall attempt to reconstruct the contours of these shifts, first by investigating the effects of protracted external warfare on Saxon society, then by examining the evidence for inter-elite competition in the aftermath of the Saxon wars, and finally by considering how far these developments may have had an impact on non-elite actors – the men (and potentially women) who would come to form the *Stellinga*.

Warfare after the Saxon Wars

The last years of the Saxon wars were marked by increased conflict along Saxony's eastern frontier, and, in particular, increased conflict between the Saxons north of the Elbe and the Franks' Slavic allies, the Abodrites. In 804, the traditional date assigned to the end of the Saxon wars, Charlemagne appears to have been primarily concerned with the management of this new border, and with the relations of peoples, Abodrites and Saxons, living along it. Certainly, Charlemagne had already subjugated the greater part of the Saxons well before 804, even sending out Saxon forces to deal with Saxons living beyond the Elbe in 802.[11] Those living beyond the Elbe, meanwhile, appear to have fought primarily against the Abodrites' increased strength in the area: if, in resisting the Abodrites, they were also resisting the Franks' allies, this appears to have been a secondary benefit.

It was these, and other, liminal Saxons who were deported in 804; in the same settlement, Saxon lands beyond the Elbe were transferred to the

---

[9] Cf. the similar approach recently taken to the 996 Norman peasants' revolt by B. Gowers, '966 and all that: the Norman peasants' revolt reconsidered', *EME*, 21(1) (2013), 71–98.

[10] See here also the comments of Ehlers, *Die Integration Sachsens*, p. 261.

[11] *Annales Regni Francorum*, ed. Kurze, 802, p. 117.

control of the Abodrites.[12] Thereafter, warfare continued (if no longer under the wider umbrella of 'the Saxon wars'). This is not the place to explore the complex northeastern politics of Charlemagne and his successor, Louis the Pious, which encompassed military and diplomatic relations not only with the Abodrites but also with other Slavic groups, most notably the Sorbs and Wilzi, and with the Danes.[13] It suffices to say that the eastern Saxon frontier became increasingly militarized, in particular through the construction and fortification of castles along the Elbe, and that cross-border campaigning continued, first under the leadership of Charlemagne's presumptive heir, Charles the Younger, and later under the leadership of various Frankish and, increasingly, Saxon *primores*.[14]

In the later years of Charlemagne, the Saxons played a large role in the management of the frontier; campaigns were launched beyond the Elbe in 806, 808, 809 and 811.[15] These were not small forays. A capitulary from circa 807 gave detailed instructions for the mobilization of Saxon forces. In the case of campaigns undertaken in Spain or against the Avars, one out of every six fighting men was instructed to attend; for those waged in Bohemia, the ratio rose to one out of every three. Closer to home, full participation was ordered: 'if it is necessary to defend the homeland against the Sorbs, then all should come together'.[16] Saxon men, presumably from all levels of society, were expected to serve. Yet if everyone participated in the conduct of warfare, the narrative sources focus on the leadership of a few. The *Royal Frankish Annals* report how, in 809, the Saxon Count Egbert was placed in charge of building a fortification at Itzehoe, across the Elbe, and began its construction with the help of other Saxon counts.[17] In 813, the *Annals* announce that Saxon elites were involved in negotiations with the Danes.[18]

---

[12] Cf. M. Springer, *Die Sachsen* (Stuttgart: W. Kohlhammer, 2004), p. 210.

[13] For sophisticated recent studies of these issues, see S. Lamb, 'Francia and Scandinavia in the early Viking Age, c. 700–900', unpublished Ph.D. thesis, University of Cambridge (2009), pp. 28–45, 56–61; D. Melleno, 'Before they were Vikings: Scandinavia and the Franks up to the death of Louis the Pious', unpublished Ph.D. thesis, University of California, Berkeley (2014).

[14] For the fortification of the Elbe region, see *Annales Regni Francorum*, ed. Kurze, 806, 808, 809, 811, 822, pp. 121, 127, 129–30, 135, 158.

[15] *Ibid*, 806, 808, 809, 811, pp. 121–2, 125, 127–30, 134–5. For the role of the Saxons in the management of this border, see also Bachrach and Bachrach, 'Saxon military revolution', 206–8.

[16] *Cap. 1*, ed. Boretius, no. 49, c. 2, p. 136: 'si vero circa Surabis patria defendenda necessitas fuerit, tunc omnes generaliter veniant.' See also É. Renard, 'La politique militaire de Charlemagne et la paysannerie franque', *Francia: Forschungen zur westeuropäischen Geschichte*, 36 (2009), 1–33, here 9.

[17] *Annales Regni Francorum*, ed. Kurze, 809, pp. 129–30; see also Melleno, 'Before they were Vikings', p. 48.

[18] *Annales Regni Francorum*, ed. Kurze, 813, p. 138; see also Melleno, 'Before they were Vikings', p. 38.

In 815, a year after his accession, Louis the Pious undertook to regrant confiscated lands to his Saxon and Frisian *fideles*. As the Astronomer records,

his imperial clemency restored the right of paternal inheritance to the Saxons and Frisians, which they had legally lost under his father on account of their perfidy. Some assigned this to his generosity, others to imprudence, as those peoples, accustomed to natural ferocity, ought to be restrained by such reins, lest, unbridled, they should run wantonly into rebellion. The emperor, however, was certain that he could chain them more closely to himself if he granted greater benefits to them, and he was not deceived in his hope: for afterwards those peoples were always extremely devoted to him.[19]

This was probably not a general amnesty, and it is notable in this regard that all surviving restitution charters stress the fidelity of both the petitioner and his family. Rather, it represented an opportunity for individual Saxon *fideles*, or at least those who could plausibly represent themselves as such, to regain lands in areas lost through collective perfidy. This included lands in the regions beyond the Elbe which had been granted to the Abodrites in the 804 settlement, and which had already begun to be reabsorbed into Saxon territory in 809/810, when Count Egbert received orders to construct a fortification at Itzehoe.[20] By 817 at the latest, this territory had been formally reincorporated: both the Astronomer and the *Royal Frankish Annals* refer to 'Saxony across the Elbe' (*Saxonia Transalbiana*) in this year.[21]

---

[19] Astronomus, *Vita Hludovici imperatoris*, ed. E. Tremp, *MGH SRG* 64 (Hanover: Hahn, 1995), c. 24, p. 356: 'Quo etiam tempore Saxonibus atque Frisonibus ius paterne hereditatis, quod sub patre ob perfidiam legaliter perdiderant, imperatoria restituit clementia. Quod alii liberalitati, alii adsignabant inprovidentiae, eo quod hae gentes, naturali adsuaefactę feritati, talibus deberent habenis coherceri, ne scilicet effrenes in perduellionis ferrentur procacitatem. Imperator autem eo sibi artius eos vinciri ratus, quo eis beneficia largiretur potiora, non est spe sua deceptus: nam post haec easdem gentes semper sibi devotissimas habuit.' See also P. Depreux, "L'intégration des élites aristocratiques de Bavière et de Saxe au royaume des francs – crise ou opportunité?' in F. Bougard, L. Feller and R. Le Jan (eds.), *Les élites au haut moyen âge: Crises et renouvellements* (Haut Moyen Âge 1) (Turnhout: Brepols, 2006), pp. 225–52, here pp. 231–2; Flierman, *Saxon Identities*, pp. 125–6; M. B. Gillis, *Heresy and Dissent in the Carolingian Empire: The Case of Gottschalk of Orbais* (Oxford: Oxford University Press, 2017), p. 37.

[20] A. Jenkis, 'Die Eingliederung "Nordalbingiens" in das Frankenreich' in W. Lammers (ed.), *Die Eingliederung der Sachsen in das Frankenreich* (Darmstadt: Wissenschaftliche Buchgesellschaft, 1970), pp. 29–58; B. Wavra, *Salzburg und Hamburg: Erzbistumsgründung und Missionspolitik in karolingischer Zeit* (Giessener Abhandlungen zur Agrar- und Wirtschaftsforschung des Europäischen Ostens 179) (Berlin: Duncker & Humblot, 1991), p. 239; for these references, see J. T. Palmer, 'Anskar's imagined communities' in H. Antonsson and I. H. Garipzanov (eds.), *Saints and Their Lives on the Periphery* (Cursor mundi 9) (Turnhout: Brepols, 2010), pp. 171–88, here p. 184.

[21] Astronomus, *Vita Hludovici imperatoris*, ed. Tremp, c. 29, p. 380; *Annales regni Francorum*, ed. Kurze, 817, p. 147.

Such a shift in policy created the potential for restitutions on a grand scale in reincorporated territory, and presumably resulted in a flood of petitions of the type discussed above in the previous chapter.[22] Some restitutions may have been made; it appears probable that the anonymous petitioner who requested the return of his paternal inheritance beyond the Elbe received some form of compensation.[23] Yet not all, or even most, lands were restored to their original owners. Many of those to benefit were presumably the emperor's Saxon *fideles*, particularly those who, in their capacity as office-holders, were involved in border defence. The *Imperial Formulae,* a collection of 'sample' sources compiled during the reign of Louis the Pious which provided models for the drafting of charters, contains an 'imperial donation' charter.[24] In this document, Louis announced that he had 'granted the ownership of two villas pertaining to us across the Elbe River situated in *that* pagus, which are called *this* and *that*, the Slavs having been expelled thence, to two of our *fideles* from Saxony, namely *these* counts, on account of their faithful service'.[25] This was not a restoration: it was an *ex novo* grant from the emperor's largesse, and its inclusion in such a collection points to the potential demand for such charters.

Thereafter, Louis increasingly delegated management of the now-extended Saxon frontier to the Saxon counts. Later in 815, he sent 'all the Saxon counts', along with the Abodrites, into Danish territory in an effort to restore Harald to the Danish throne; the next year, the 'Saxon counts' campaigned with the Eastern Franks against the Sorbs.[26] In 819, the *Royal Frankish Annals* refer to the 'commanders of the Saxon border and imperial legates' who brought the emperor's erstwhile ally, the Abodrite Sclaomir, before his presence.[27] These officials are alternatively

[22] See above, pp. 71–5.

[23] *Epistolae variorum inde a morte Caroli Magni usque ad divisionem imperii collectae*, ed. E. Dümmler, *MGH Epp.* 5:3 (Berlin: Weidemann, 1899), pp. 299–350, here no. 2, pp. 300–1.

[24] For this source, see A. Rio, *Legal practice and the written word in the early Middle Ages: Frankish formulae, c. 500–1000* (Cambridge: Cambridge University Press, 2009), pp. 132–7.

[25] *Formulae imperiales*, ed. K. Zeumer, MGH Formulae Merowingici et Karolini aevi 1 (Hanover: Hahn, 1886), no. 2, pp. 288–9: 'duobus fidelibus nostris de Saxonia, illo videlicet et illo comitibus, propter illorum fidele servicium duas villas iuris nostri trans Albiam fluvium in pago illo constitutas, quarum vocabula sunt illa et illa, eiectis inde Sclavis, in proprietatem concedimus'. See also Depreux, 'L'intégration des élites aristocratiques', pp. 247–8; see also S. Krüger, *Studien zur Sächsischen Grafschaftsverfassung im 9. Jahrhundert* (Göttingen: Vandenhoeck & Ruprecht, 1950), p. 51.

[26] *Annales Regni Francorum*, ed. Kurze, 815, p. 142: 'omnes Saxonici comites'; Astronomus, *Vita Hludovici imperatoris*, ed. Tremp, c. 26, p. 362: 'Saxonici comites'. See also Bachrach and Bachrach, 'Saxon military revolution', 206; Lamb, 'Francia and Scandinavia', p. 41; Melleno, 'Before they were Vikings', p. 58.

[27] *Annales Regni Francorum*, ed. Kurze, 819, p. 149: 'praefectos Saxonici limitis et legatos imperatoris'; see also Bachrach and Bachrach, 'Saxon military revolution', 207.

styled in the Astronomer as the 'dukes of the Saxons'.[28] Nine years later, 'almost all the Saxon counts and marcher lords (*markiones*)' came together to negotiate peace with the Northmen.[29] These frequent references to Saxon office-holders may be seen to contrast with the *Royal Frankish Annals'* treatment of other groups involved in cross-border campaigning and diplomacy, such as the Abodrites and Eastern Franks, who are referred to collectively, irrespective of position. Such a disparity suggests that elite Saxons played a substantial role in the organization of border defence and in the leadership of campaigns and negotiations.

The militarization of the Saxon frontier thus offered Saxon elites the opportunity to improve their status. Those who served on campaigns could develop political relationships; they could be rewarded by the grant of lands, whether in the form of gifts or restorations, or of office (generally countships). Such grants could, in turn, be used to shore up elite authority within Saxony.[30] It is to this, and to inter-elite competition more generally, that I shall now turn.

Inter-Elite Competition

Just as in the case of the Saxon wars, cross-border campaigning did not create a new 'Saxon elite', nor did it advance the interests of existing elites in a systematic manner. Rather, warfare provided advantages to certain elite individuals and families, often at the expense of other elite Saxons.[31] This could lead to tensions, even among loyal Carolingian supporters. Indeed, in the case of the Saxon wars, the Saxon legal corpus tackles a wide range of inter-elite disputes. Chapter 29 of the *First Saxon Capitulary* instructs that 'all counts are to strive to preserve peace and concord among themselves, and if by chance a dispute or discord should arise, they should not shirk our business or cares on this account'.[32] The following chapter goes on to consider even more egregious acts, decreeing that anyone who killed a count was to have his inheritance confiscated.[33] This is a provision which presupposes an inheritance, and one, moreover, worth the trouble

---

[28] Astronomus, *Vita Hludovici imperatoris*, ed. Tremp, c. 31, p. 390: 'ducibus Saxonum'.
[29] *Annales Regni Francorum*, ed. Kurze, 828, p. 175: 'pene Saxoniae comites simul cum markionibus'.
[30] See here Flierman, *Saxon Identities*, pp. 124–5.
[31] See here also the comments of Flierman, *Saxon Identities*, pp. 128–9; R. Wenskus, 'Die ständische Entwicklung in Sachsen im Gefolge der fränkischen Eroberung' in *Angli e Sassoni al di qua e al di là del mare: 26 aprile–10 maggio 1984* (Settimane 32:2) (Spoleto: Il Centro, 1986), pp. 587–616, here pp. 611–2.
[32] *Capitulatio de partibus Saxoniae*, ed. C. von Schwerin, *MGH Fontes iuris* 4 (Hanover: Hahn, 1918), pp. 37–44, here c. 29, p. 43: 'Ut universi comites pacem et concordiam ad invicem habere studeant; et si forte inter eos aliqua discordia aut conturbium ortum fuerit, aut nostrum solatium vel profectum pro hoc non demittant.'
[33] *Ibid*, c. 30, p. 43.

of confiscation. Later, in 803 or 804, the *Law of the Saxons* addressed the issue of nobles who sold other nobles across the border, instructing that full wergild should be levied in the cases where those sold as slaves could not be redeemed.[34] Clearly, the divergent interests of Saxon elites were perceived as leading to disputes – disputes which could sometimes, but by no means always, result in acts of violence.

Some disputes may have pre-existed the Saxon wars; other disputes no doubt arose in the course of the wars themselves, for privileges, whether in the form of lands or offices, offered to some elite Saxons necessarily impinged upon the interests of others. Still more may have arisen in the period following the conquest, as cross-border campaigning continued to create opportunities for advancement of certain elite individuals, and as Louis' formal reincorporation of lands beyond the Elbe privileged certain Saxons above others. Once begun, disputes were rarely settled, at least not in a manner equally acceptable to all parties; the possibility of appeal, rather than operating as a fail-safe, kept such disputes current. Those who considered themselves wronged not only maintained their claims, but even passed them along to subsequent generations: all extant restitution charters concern renewed claims from the sons of men disinherited during the wars. The accession of a new ruler could act as a flashpoint for such appeals: it is no coincidence that a significant proportion of the extant Saxon restitution charters date from early in the reign of Louis the Pious, or that Louis soon instituted a programme of grants beyond the Elbe. The appearance of multiple rival candidates for the throne, as was the case in 840, with the outbreak of the civil war, served to complicate the picture still further, as frustrated elite claimants turned to multiple sources of authority for often-contradictory judgements.

This pattern of latent disputes and renewed claims, raised upon the accession of a new ruler, was in no way unique to Saxony. In fact, it conforms to the model which Matthew Innes employed in his study of governance in Carolingian Alemannia. As Innes wrote, 'Carolingian rule in Alemannia rested, in its material and physical aspects, on expropriation'; the initial redistribution which came in the wake of Carolingian conquest 'reverberated down the subsequent century and a half'.[35] Innes pointed to continued inter-elite conflict, mediated through appeals to

---

[34] *Lex Saxonum*, ed. C. von Schwerin, *MGH Fontes iuris* 4 (Hanover: Hahn, 1918), pp. 9–36, here c. 20, p. 23; cf. E. Müller-Mertens, 'Der Stellingaaufstand: Seine Träger und die Frage der politischen Macht', *ZfG*, 20(7) (1972), 818–42, here 841.

[35] M. Innes, 'Property, politics and the problem of the Carolingian state' in W. Pohl and V. Wieser (eds.), *Der frühmittelalterliche Staat: europäische Perspektiven* (Forschungen zur Geschichte des Mittelalters 16) (Vienna: Verlag der Österreichischen Akademie der Wissenschaften, 2009), pp. 299–313, here p. 310.

Carolingian authority, particularly at the point of accession; hopes for eventual restitution encouraged continued engagement with the structures of Carolingian rule. One may further turn to the work of Warren Brown on the Carolingian conquest of Bavaria, and, in particular, to the inquest performed by Louis the Pious upon his assumption of power, in which he sought to determine whether imperial officials had wrongly prised lands from local Bavarian officials and landholders.[36]

Of course, in various ways, experiences in Alemannia, Bavaria and Saxony diverged. The Saxon wars were significantly more protracted than the Alemannian and Bavarian conquests; their effects were considerably more muddled. The *Law of the Saxons*, promulgated at the close of the conquest, presupposed a certain level of dislocation: it included a provision that 'all gifts and sales are to remain legitimately stable', as well as instructions for correct procedure in the case of contested ownership of lands.[37] On an even more basic level, it is not known whether Saxon conceptions of property ownership prior to the conquest matched up to those observed in Frankish practice. Certainly, Brown has argued that following its conquest, definitions of property rights shifted in Carolingian Bavaria, a region with extensive contacts to Francia prior to its takeover.[38] In Saxony, where there was no writing prior to the conquest, such a shift may have been greater still. Literate modes of property conveyance and legal title were a Frankish import, still closely linked to fledgling monastic and ecclesiastical institutions.[39] The manner of property conveyance, and perhaps even conditions of ownership, thus underwent a not insignificant transformation, leading to additional complications in property disputes.[40] Finally, Saxon society appears to have been less stratified than much of the Frankish world: donors to the monasteries of Corvey, Werden and Fulda appear to have been drawn from a free class which spanned the (officially codified) legal categories of nobles and freemen. Such disputes, then, would probably have reverberated across a far broader section of society in Saxony, as those who had lost out in the Saxon wars or in their aftermath attempted to recover their possessions.

---

[36] W. C. Brown, *Unjust Seizure: Conflict, Interest, and Authority in an Early Medieval Society* (Ithaca: Cornell University Press, 2001), pp. 73–101, 140–65.

[37] *Lex Saxonum*, ed. von Schwerin, cc. 61, 63, pp. 32–3: 'Traditiones et venditiones omnes legitime stabiles permaneant'.

[38] Brown, *Unjust Seizure*, especially pp. 75–83.

[39] For a comparable example of the transition to written modes of property conveyance, see M. Innes, 'Rituals, rights and relationships: some gifts and their interpretation in the Fulda cartulary, c. 827', *Studia Historica: Historia Medieval*, 31 (2013), 25–50.

[40] For changing conditions of land ownership and dependency, see especially Wenskus, 'Die ständische Entwicklung', pp. 587–616.

The Stellinga

The Practice of Justice

Appeals to Carolingian rulers were not the only way in which Saxon elites attempted to advance or consolidate their positions. They could also do so through military service (as discussed above), through recourse to local justice and/or through patronage of religious institutions. Let us turn here to the practice of justice. On a basic level, elites could turn to local justice to confirm their control over lands; if they occupied a position of legal authority, they could further enrich themselves with the profits accruing from the dispensing of justice. Some exceeded even these benefits: a number of ninth-century sources record that counts in Saxony abused their positions of authority, presumably to their own advancement. Indeed, in a letter to Bishop Badurad of Paderborn, an imperial *missus*, Louis the Pious urged him to protect Corvey's judicial and military exemptions from the incursions of counts, complaining that 'certain counts wish to break and uproot our aforementioned command, that is to say, they round up the men, freemen and half-freemen alike, who live on the land of that monastery, and compel them to go to war or wish to detain them according to judicial custom'.[41] Counts were overstepping their bounds in the dispensing of justice as well as in the marshalling of resources. Likewise, in the period following the suppression of the *Stellinga*, comital justice appears to have caused legitimate grievances; in an entry of the *Fulda Annals* in 852, Rudolf describes how Louis the German

departed for Saxony, chiefly in order to judge their suits, which had been neglected by corrupt and deceitful judges and frustrated in many ways by the delays of their law, so that, so they say, they had suffered long-lasting and grave injuries . . . Therefore he held a general assembly in Minden, where he not only justly settled the cases that had been brought to him by the people, but also received his own possessions by the decision of the judges of that *gens*. Thence he proceeded through the lands of Enger, the Harudi, the Suabians, and the Hochseegau, halting each night and, as opportunity permitted, dispensing judgement in the various suits of the people.[42]

---

[41] *D Kar.* 2, ed. T. Kölzer, *MGH, Die Urkunden Ludwigs des Frommen*, 3 vols. (Wiesbaden: Harrassowitz, 2016), vol. II, no. 330, p. 817: 'quidam comites memoratum praeceptum nostrum infringere et convellere velint, in eo videlicet quod homines tam liberos quam et latos, qui super terram eiusdem monasterii consistunt, in hostem ire conpellant et distringere iudiciario more velint'.

[42] *Annales Fuldenses*, ed. Kurze, 852, pp. 42–3: 'profectus est in Saxoniam ob eorum vel maxime causas iudicandas, qui a pravis et subdolis iudicibus neglecti et multimodis, ut dicunt, legis suae dilationibus decepti graves atque diuturnas patiebantur iniurias . . . Igitur in loco, qui appellatur Mimida . . . habito generali conventu tam causas populi ad se perlatas iusto absolvit examine quam ad se pertinentes possessiones iuridicorum gentis decreto recepit. Inde transiens per Angros, Harudos, Suabos et Hohsingos et per mansiones singulas, prout se praebuit oportunitas, causas populi diiudicans'.

This passage, in addition to providing yet another example of how a ruler's accession could act as a flashpoint for appeals, is arresting for the very fact that Louis the German was obliged to intervene in person to restore his own rights. If counts did not respect the rights and privileges of royal or ecclesiastical lands, their treatment of the possessions of their local rivals and subordinates can be assumed to have been commensurately worse.[43] A final example can be found in the *Translation of Saint Alexander*, which records how a man was blinded 'on account of the hatred of his enemies, who held the seat of lawgivers (*sedem legislatorum*)'.[44] The practice of justice was often shaped, if not outright perverted, by the interests of those in charge. In Saxony, this was the counts.

Advancement did not only come through crooked means: Saxon elites could also raise their status and socio-economic position through the patronage of monasteries. The work of Innes, in particular, has illuminated the many benefits that patrons could glean from such 'charitable' activity.[45] On a basic level, donors received social and religious capital. They kept up with the Joneses while also clearing the way to heavenly salvation: many donations were expressly given 'for the soul' (*pro anima*) of the donor and/or their family members. Patrons also could gain more tangible rewards. If lands were disputed, whether with local rivals or within extended kin groups, the very act of donation confirmed the full rights of the donor; take, for example, the donation of Theganbald, who in 796 granted land to the monastery of Werden which he had previously given to his nephew Berger.[46] Finally, donations did not necessarily entail the loss of control over donated property; in fact, many donors received back donated lands in usufruct, often in return for a nominal

---

[43] Cf. S. Epperlein, 'Sachsen im frühen Mittelalter: Diskussionsbeitrag zur Sozialstruktur Sachsens im 9. Jahrhundert und seiner politischen Stellung im frühen Mittelalter', *Jahrbuch für Wirtschaftsgeschichte*, 7(1) (1966), 189–212, here 201; S. Epperlein, *Herrschaft und Volk im karolingischen Imperium: Studien über soziale Konflikte und dogmatisch-politische Kontroversen im fränkischen Reich* (Forschungen zur mittelalterlichen Geschichte 14) (Berlin: Akademie, 1969), pp. 63–4.

[44] Rudolf and Meginhard, *Translatio sancti Alexandri*, ed. G. H. Pertz, *MGH SS* 2 (Hanover: Hahn, 1829), pp. 673–81, here c. 6, p. 679: 'propter invidiam inimicorum suorum, qui sedem legislatorum possidebant'. See also P. Depreux, 'Défense d'un statut et contestation d'un modèle de société. Conjuration, révolte et répression dans l'Occident du Haut Moyen Âge' in P. Depreux (ed.), *Revolte und Sozialstatus von der Spätantike bis zur Frühen Neuzeit* (Pariser Historische Studien 87) (Munich: Oldenbourg, 2008), pp. 93–109, here p. 106; T. Faulkner, *Law and Authority in the Early Middle Ages: The Frankish Leges in the Carolingian Period* (Cambridge: Cambridge University Press, 2016), pp. 60–1; K. Leyser, *Communications and Power in Medieval Europe: The Gregorian Revolution and Beyond* (London: Hambledon, 1994), p. 54.

[45] For this, and for what follows, see M. Innes, *State and Society in the Early Middle Ages: The Middle Rhine Valley, 400–1000* (Cambridge: Cambridge University Press, 2000), especially pp. 13–50.

[46] *Cartularium Werthinense*, ed. D. P. Blok, 'Een diplomatisch onderzoek van de oudste particuliere oorkonden van Werden', unpublished Ph.D. thesis, University of Amsterdam (1960), no. 8, p. 164.

rent. When such arrangements extended beyond one generation, patrons could stipulate who would control the lands after their own demise, thereby restricting the claims of their wider kin-group; here, the example of Helmbald, who stipulated that both himself and his son were to hold donated lands in usufruct in return for an annual payment of one *solidus*, stands as a case in point.[47] In short, patronage of monasteries allowed elites to show religious devotion, to gain saintly intercession, to enact their status, to connect themselves to wider patronage networks and to define and confirm their control over land.

The decades after the Saxon wars were full of uncertainties. Many members of the elite wished to recover from recent setbacks, while others wished to consolidate their recent gains. In either case, engagement with the regime and its various structures of authority proved the best road to advancement. Some chose to invoke their (ostensibly) unsullied fidelity in appeals to Carolingian rulers, while others proved their merits and secured favour through military service. Some used local office to enhance their local standing; others built extensive patronage relationships with local monasteries. One path did not preclude another: these were complementary strategies, best deployed in concert with one another.

Non-Elite Actors

The changes ushered in both during and following the conquest did not simply have an impact on Saxon elites: rather, they were felt across the social spectrum. So too did Saxons from all levels of society adopt strategies of self-preservation in the face of change. Here, too, levels of ambition varied: some may have sought merely to minimize any diminishment in status, while others would have attempted to preserve their current condition, or even, sometimes, to improve their station. Indeed, the strategies for advancement discussed above did not simply apply to the Saxon elites (who in any case defy clear definition): rather, they afforded Saxons from all levels of society the possibility of bettering their situation, if to varying degrees. But while some non-elite Saxons may have used the possibilities of the new political order to move up in the world, others found their position diminished, sometimes as a direct result of the elite formation discussed earlier in this chapter.[48]

Take, for instance, military service. While non-elite Saxons would not have had the same opportunities for military leadership as Saxon counts,

---

[47] *Ibid*, no. 24, pp. 182–3.
[48] See here especially Wenskus, 'Die ständische Entwicklung', pp. 596–8.

they nonetheless appear to have played a significant role in cross-border campaigning. This is clearly attested in the capitulary from 807 discussed above; such 'peasant' fighting forces may well have paved the way for the early tenth-century 'agrarian soldiers' (*agrarii milites*) discussed in Widukind of Corvey's *Deeds of the Saxons*.[49] Such service would have allowed non-elites the chance to enter into patronage networks, thus securing status and access to resources within Saxony; they enjoyed similar possibilities to the Frankish peasant Ripwin, whose modest rise in fortunes as a result of his military service has been so evocatively described by Innes.[50]

Of course, Ripwin did not rise by military service alone: he also benefited from his strategic patronage of, and long-lasting association with, his local monastery. Non-elite (free) donors to monasteries were afforded the same advantages, spiritual and temporal, as their elite counterparts. It is therefore unsurprising that in Saxony, too, we find significant numbers of donations from what appear to be well-to-do peasants, or even, on occasion, ambitious middling peasants. Naturally, it remains difficult to discern an individual's status from the size of his or her donation; even wealthy counts could be parsimonious, but when their non-titled contemporaries exhibit similar tendencies, they become indistinguishable from non-elite donors in the surviving source collections. It suffices here to say that donations to Saxon monasteries were, on average, of such a size as would be conceivable for non-elite donors.[51]

In a handful of cases, a more positive argument for non-elite donors can be advanced. For example, the monastery of Corvey received no less than sixteen donations in the village of Cogharden.[52] All of these donations were of unstated size; many were given jointly, in what appear to be groups of male kin, by a total of thirty-six named individual donors, whose relatively low status can be inferred from their lack of title and

---

[49] See above, p. 89; Widukind of Corvey, *Res Gestae Saxonicae*, eds. P. Hirsch and H. E. Lohmann, *MGH SRG* 60 (Hanover: Hahn, 1935), I:35, pp. 48–9. See further O. G. Oexle, 'Gilden als soziale Gruppen in der Karolingerzeit' in H. Jankuhn, W. Janssen, R. Schmidt-Wiegand, and H. Tiefenbach (eds.), *Das Handwerk in vor- und frühgeschichtlicher Zeit* (Abhandlungen der Akademie der Wissenschaften in Göttingen: Philologisch-Historische Klasse. Dritte Folge 122) (Göttingen: Vandenhoeck & Ruprecht, 1981), vol. I: pp. 284–354, here p. 350; O. G. Oexle, 'Peace through conspiracy' in B. Jussen (ed.), *Ordering Medieval Society: Perspectives on Intellectual and Practical Modes of Shaping Social Relations* (Philadelphia: University of Pennsylvania Press, 2001), pp. 285–322, here p. 300; Renard, 'La politique militaire', 9 footnote 46. For the *agrarii milites*, see also Bachrach and Bachrach, 'Saxon military revolution', especially 197, 199, 215–16, 218–19.

[50] For Ripwin's career and military service, see Innes, *State and Society*, pp. 147–50; contrast to G. Halsall, *Warfare and Society in the Barbarian West, 450–900* (London: Routledge, 2003), pp. 77–81.

[51] See below, pp. 177–82.

[52] *Traditiones Corbeienses*, ed. K. Honselmann, *Die alten Mönchslisten und die Traditionen von Corvey* (Abhandlungen zur Corveyer Geschichtsschreibung 6), 2 vols. (Paderborn: Bonifatius, 1982), vol. I, nos. 78, 88–95, 101, 107, 111, 132, 150, 158, 220, pp. 95, 97–100, 104, 108–9, 120.

their general absence (with a few exceptions) from the witness lists of their neighbours and co-patrons in Cogharden. These repeated dona-tions, which are largely grouped together in the *Corvey Donations*, suggest that those living in Cogharden were motivated by particular circum-stances to donate to the monastery. Perhaps Cogharden was a recently colonized settlement, and donors in the area were attempting to confirm their possession of developed and/or reclaimed land in a manner akin to what Innes has described in the region of the Haune.[53] They may have done so preemptively, or indeed under the pressure of conflicting claims, whether from the monastery, local elites or even their neighbours themselves. The surviving evidence appears to suggest the last of these: certainly, the stark division between donors and witnesses may indicate competition at a village level, and points towards donors actively seeking to enshrine their rights and privileges, sometimes at their neighbours' expense.

Finally, there was justice. Just as in the case of elite Saxons, non-elite Saxons would have experienced a great degree of upheaval both during and after the conquest, thereby increasing the potential for conflicting claims and disputes. Non-elite Saxons did not in general have recourse to kings and emperors, due to various practical considerations. Assuming they could marshal the necessary resources, they could avail themselves of local justice, whether in the form of comital courts or customary pro-cedures. The former carried the potential for abuse; it is likely, then, that many favoured customary procedures, although these too may have privileged those of more elevated social status.

Non-elite actors did not enjoy the same range of possibilities as their elite counterparts. Yet they had agency; they too could adopt strategies with the aim of staying afloat, and perhaps even flourishing, in a changing world.

★ ★ ★

The *Stellinga* did not emerge from a vacuum, but rather from the changes in Saxon society both during and following the Saxon wars. The conquest, stretched out over thirty-three years, had resulted in great upheaval; it led to significant reassignment of territories and lands, which

---

[53] M. Innes, 'Rituals, rights and relationships: some gifts and their interpretation in the Fulda cartulary, c. 827', *Studia Historica: Historia Medieval*, 31 (2013), 25–50. Note, however, that some donors allude to their inheritance in Cogharden: see *Traditiones Corbeienses*, ed. Honselmann, nos. 111, 220, pp. 100, 120.

in turn led to the confusion and contestation of property claims. Even following the conquest, Saxon society remained mobilized for war at all levels; the Carolingian military machine continued to push eastwards, resulting in restorations of territory and *ex novo* grants of land. This was not simply a matter of lands changing hands: even conceptions of property ownership may well have been transformed. New, written, forms of property conveyance were introduced by the Franks, and new strategies of property management, namely the foundation and patronage of religious institutions, were increasingly employed. When, in the midst of this confusion, disputes arose, there were new, Frankish forms of justice – comital and royal courts – to which claimants could turn; elite claimants in particular sought recourse to royal justice, especially at the point of a ruler's accession, and especially in cases of long-standing grievances. All of these changes created possibilities: possibilities for elite formation and advancement, but also, correspondingly, possibilities for diminishment in status and impoverishment. So too for those lower down the social spectrum, there existed possibilities for advancement paired with greater threat of degradation: non-elites could be, and often were, at the receiving end of elite formation.

In the years leading up to the *Stellinga*, then, there was a significant degree of uncertainty for those of lower status in Saxony. It is therefore unsurprising that some resorted to horizontal associations in an attempt to mitigate this; certainly, the work of Otto Gerhard Oexle has pointed to the formation of horizontal associations in times of upheaval, strife and military threat.[54] Add in the civil war between the sons of Louis the Pious, and the preconditions for the *Stellinga* movement become clear. When compelled to take sides, Saxon elites divided down the middle, whether because of 'campaign' promises, preexisting loyalties or inter-elite tensions and competition. Saxons of lesser status were not initially canvassed for support, but they were equipped, and indeed organized, to fight. When Lothar's fortunes in the war changed, so too did his base of support, and he began to canvass for support among the lower orders. In Saxony, a horizontal association called the *Stellinga* rallied to his side.

---

[54] Oexle, 'Gilden als soziale Gruppen', pp. 305–7; O. G. Oexle, '*Conjuratio* und Gilde im frühen Mittelalter. Ein Beitrag zum Problem der sozialgeschichtlichen Kontinuität zwischen Antike und Mittelalter' in B. Schwineköper (ed.), *Gilden und Zünfte: Kaufmännische und gewerbliche Genossenschaften im frühen und hohen Mittelalter* (Vorträge und Forschungen 29) (Sigmaringen: J. Thorbecke, 1985), pp. 151–214, here pp. 152–3. See also M. McComb, '"Each by the law of his choosing": resistance, memory, and the Saxon *Stellinga*' (2012), paper presented at the Graduate History Colloquium, Cornell University. My thanks to Max for sending me a copy of his paper.

The Stellinga

The *Stellinga* first entered the historical stage in July 841, when the Emperor Lothar appealed to the group for support. Nithard, in his *Histories*, seems to credit Lothar alone with the formation of the movement: as he writes, Lothar

sent into Saxony for the *frilingi* (freemen) and *lazzi* (half-freemen), of whom there are an innumerable multitude, promising that if they allied with him, he would permit them thereafter to keep the law which their ancestors kept in the time when they were worshippers of idols. As they desired this above all else, they established a new name for themselves, that is, the *Stellinga*.[55]

There are other indications, however, that the *Stellinga* predated Lothar's overtures. Prudentius, in the *Annals of Saint Bertin*, certainly implies that Lothar was approaching a group that had already been formed:

Lothar, turning back and coming to Aachen, strove to win over the Saxons and other nearby peoples in order to renew the fight, so much so that he permitted the Saxons who are called the *Stellinga*, of whom it is thought there is a very large number in that people, the choice of any law or the customs of the Old Saxons, whichever they preferred.[56]

Even the name of the movement suggests a horizontal association of sorts: Norbert Wagner's philological research has identified '*Stellinga*' as an Old Saxon word for comrades or companions.[57] The specificity of Lothar's concession, not to mention the very fact of his request for assistance, may indicate that he was eliciting support from an already extant group.[58]

The *Stellinga* thus appear, in all probability, to have existed before Lothar's application. They may even have borne the name of *Stellinga*, though this is uncertain. While the *Annals of Saint Bertin* seem to suggest as much, Nithard clearly states that the group only chose the name

---

[55] Nithard, *Historiae*, eds. Lauer and Glansdorff, IV:2, p. 132: 'etiam in Saxoniam misit frilingis lazzibusque, quorum infinita multitudo est, promittens, si secum sentirent, ut legem, quam antecessores sui tempore quo idolorum cultores erant habuerant, eandem illis deinceps habendam concederet. Qua supra modum cupidi, nomen novum sibi, id est Stellinga, imposuerunt'.

[56] *Annales Bertiniani*, eds. Grat, Vieilliard and Clémencet, 841, pp. 38–9: 'Hlotharius terga uertens et Aquasgranii perueniens, Saxones ceterosque confines restaurandi praelii gratia sibi conciliare studet, in tantum ut Saxonibus qui Stellingi appellantur, quorum multiplicior numerus in eorum gente habetur, optionem cuiuscumque legis uel antiquorum Saxonum consuetudinis, utram earum mallent, concesserit.'

[57] N. Wagner, 'Der Name der Stellinga', *Beiträge zur Namenforschung*, 15(2) (1980), 128–33, here 133. See also McComb, 'Each by the law of his choosing'.

[58] Depreux, 'Défense d'un statut', p. 105; cf. H. J. Schulze, 'Der Aufstand der Stellinga in Sachsen und sein Einfluß auf den Vertrag von Verdun', unpublished Ph.D. thesis, Humboldt-Universität zu Berlin (1955), p. 63.

Stellinga after Lothar's canvassing for support.[59] Yet at this early stage, the *Stellinga* might be better approached not as participants in a revolt, but rather as members of a guild (*gilda*) or *coniuratio*, terms used to designate horizontal associations.[60] Prior to Lothar's involvement, they left no trace in the historical record and probably had only limited ambitions. They were presumably tolerated by local elites, as were many other such horizontal associations, which continued to exist on a local level and to cater to the needs of their members.

Class and Community

The men who made up the *Stellinga* were drawn from the lower rungs of Saxon society, prompting many to argue that it ought to be approached first and foremost as a class-based movement which sought to undermine the newly won privileges of the elite. Some have argued that the men formed a class of dependent farmers in a proto-feudal environment;[61] others have opted for a more fluid group encompassing individuals of diverse social and tenurial standing.[62] Of the two, the latter is a far more tenable position. The sources describing the *Stellinga* defy any attempts at rigid categorization, using a mixture of tenurial, social and legal language to describe the participants.[63] The *Fulda Annals* portray the participants as

---

[59] *Annales Bertiniani*, eds. Grat, Vielliard and Clémencet, 841, p. 38; Nithard, *Historiae*, eds. Lauer and Glansdorff, IV.2, p. 132. The *Xanten Annals* likewise report that they only adopted the name 'Stellinga' in the course of 841: see *Annales Xantenses*, ed. B. Simpson, MGH SRG 12 (Hanover: Hahn, 1909), 841, p. 12.

[60] For the use of the term 'guild', see Oexle, 'Gilden als soziale Gruppen', p. 287; see here also R. McKitterick, *Perceptions of the Past in the Early Middle Ages* (Notre Dame: University of Notre Dame Press, 2006), p. 71.

[61] H. J. Bartmuss, 'Zur Frage der Bedeutung des Stellingaaufstandes', *Wissenschaftliche Zeitschrift der Martin-Luther-Universität Halle-Wittenberg*, 7(1) (1957), 113–23, here 113–14; H. J. Bartmuss, 'Ursachen und Triebkräfte im Entstehungsprozeß des "frühfeudalen deutschen Staates"', *ZfG*, 10(7) (1962), 1591–1625, here 1592–6; J. Herrmann, 'Sozialökonomische Grundlagen und gesellschaftliche Triebkräfte für die Herausbildung des deutschen Feudalstaates', *ZfG*, 19(6) (1971), 752–89, here 771–2.

[62] See especially Epperlein, 'Sachsen im frühen Mittelalter', 190–1; Epperlein, *Herrschaft und Volk im karolingischen Imperium*, p. 59; E. Müller-Mertens, 'Vom Regnum Teutonicum zum Heiligen Römischen Reich Deutscher Nation: Reflexionen über die Entwicklung des deutschen Staates im Mittelalter', *ZfG*, 11(2) (1963), 319–46, here 327; Müller-Mertens, 'Der Stellingaaufstand', 826–35. For a historiographical discussion, see Goldberg, 'Popular revolt', 468–9, footnote 7.

[63] W. Eggert, 'Rebelliones servorum. Bewaffnete Klassenkämpfe im Früh- und frühen Hochmittelalter und ihre Darstellung in zeitgenössischen erzählenden Quellen', *ZfG*, 23(10) (1975), 1147–64, here 1155–8; Ehlers, *Die Integration Sachsens*, pp. 261–3; Goldberg, 'Popular revolt', 482–3; Müller-Mertens, 'Der Stellingaaufstand', 826. For a comparative perspective on the ambiguity of these categories, see A. Rio, '"Half-free" categories in the early middle ages: fine status distinctions before professional lawyers' in P. Dresch and J. Scheele (eds.), *Legalism: Rules and Categories* (Oxford: Oxford University Press, 2015), pp. 129–52.

former slaves, or *liberti* (freedmen), whereas the *Xanten Annals*, in a passage reminiscent of I Samuel 25:10, characterize the ensuing conflict as being waged between slaves and masters, terms which, when deployed together, could indicate a range of relationships as well as legal categories.[64] Nithard, who offers a detailed description of Saxon society, relates that the *Stellinga* were composed of *frilingi* (freemen) and *lazzi* (half-freemen), which he translates into Latin as *ingenuiles* and *serviles*, employing adjectives generally used to denote types of landed tenure.[65] A further complication is to be found in the various types of punishment which Louis the German used to finally suppress the *Stellinga*: Gerd Althoff has argued that these differences may reflect the differing legal categories of the participants.[66] The image the sources give, then, is one of heterogeneity.

This is entirely in keeping with what we know of other horizontal associations, which, while sub-elite, generally encompassed a range of legal, socio-economic or tenurial categories.[67] It is therefore reductionist to approach such associations as primarily based around class, and not simply because they transcended these boundaries in status. On a more basic level, the Carolingians simply had no clear concept of 'class', at least not in the modern sense.[68] As recent work has elucidated, the vocabulary describing what we might term 'class' had considerably more complex dimensions in the Carolingian period. The term *nobilis*, for instance, was endowed with various moral, social, economic and legal attributes;[69] similarly, on the other end of the spectrum, *servus* was a term used to describe a relationship, whether that existing between a slave and his master, or between a vassal and his king.[70]

---

[64] *Annales Fuldenses*, ed. Kurze, 842, p. 33; *Annales Xantenses*, ed. Simpson, 841, p. 12; for the reference to I Samuel, see Eggert, 'Rebelliones servorum', 1156. For slavery and unfreedom in the early Middle Ages, see especially the important contributions of Alice Rio: A. Rio, 'Freedom and unfreedom in early medieval Francia: the evidence of the legal formulae', *Past & Present*, 193 (2006), 7–40; A. Rio, 'High and low: ties of dependence in the Frankish kingdoms', *Transactions of the Royal Historical Society*, 18 (2008), 43–68; A. Rio, 'Self-sale and voluntary entry into unfreedom', *Journal of Social History*, 45(3) (2012), 661–85; A. Rio, *Slavery after Rome, 500–1100* (Oxford: Oxford University Press, 2017).

[65] Nithard, *Historiae*, eds. Lauer and Glansdorff, IV:2, pp. 130–2; see also Springer, *Die Sachsen*, pp. 266–7.

[66] G. Althoff, *Family, Friends and Followers: Political and Social Bonds in Early Medieval Europe* (Cambridge: Cambridge University Press, 2004), p. 98; see also the comments of Depreux, 'Défense d'un statut', pp. 96–8.

[67] Oexle, 'Gilden als soziale Gruppen', p. 332.

[68] See here the insightful comments of Flierman, *Saxon Identities*, pp. 128–30.

[69] R. Stone, *Morality and Masculinity in the Carolingian Empire* (Cambridge: Cambridge University Press, 2011), pp. 21–5.

[70] See, for example, Rio, *Legal Practice and the Written Word in the Early Middle Ages*, pp. 227–8.

Even more fundamentally, categories such as 'freemen' and 'half-freemen' are not the same things as groups: those who experience similar conditions do not *ipso facto* form a community.[71] Communities do not exist merely on the basis of geographic proximity, nor of similar economic circumstances. Rather, they are created entities, brought together by shared interaction, shared functions and shared goals, and capable of collective action. In order to account for the formation of the *Stellinga*, then, it is necessary to explore not only the shared experiences and conditions which may have underwritten their collective action, but also the contexts in which such collective action was possible.

As Susan Reynolds has argued more generally, one of the main ways in which rural societies came together to form a community was through the dispensing of justice and the settlement of disputes according to customary practice.[72] One may point to the example of Brittany, as explored in the work of Wendy Davies, or indeed to conquest-era Saxony itself.[73] Such local means of conflict resolution were largely tolerated and sometimes encouraged by Carolingian authorities.[74] The *Second Saxon Capitulary* of 797 not only set lower judicial fines for conflicts resolved locally 'according to their [the Saxons'] customary practice', but also gave local communities the right to form judicial assemblies and, if consensus could be established, even to commit arson in order to compel otherwise intransigent neighbours to come to judgement.[75] Furthermore, it allowed men to be condemned to death according to 'the law of the Saxons', although here the right of appeal to royal justice is stressed.[76] These three provisions, alongside scattered references in various hagiographical sources,[77] point towards the

---

[71] See the excellent study of R. Brubaker, 'Ethnicity without groups', *European Journal of Sociology*, 43(2) (2002), 163–89; see also the comments of O. G. Oexle, 'Kulturwissenschaftliche Reflexionen über soziale Gruppen in der mittelalterlichen Gesellschaft: Tönnies, Simmel, Durkheim und Max Weber', *Historische Zeitschrift. Beihefte*, 17 (1994), 115–59, here 159.

[72] S. Reynolds, *Kingdoms and Communities in Western Europe, 900–1300* (Oxford: Clarendon, 1997), pp. 113–4. For a comparative perspective, see W. Davies, 'People and places in dispute in ninth-century Brittany' in W. Davies and P. Fouracre (eds.), *The Settlement of Disputes in Early Medieval Europe* (Cambridge: Cambridge University Press, 1986), pp. 65–84; W. Davies, *Small Worlds: The Village Community in Early Medieval Brittany* (London: Duckworth, 1988), p. 64.

[73] Davies, *Small Worlds*, pp. 146–52.   [74] Reynolds, *Kingdoms and Communities*, p. 114.

[75] *Capitulare Saxonicum*, ed. C. von Schwerin, *MGH Fontes iuris* 4 (Hanover: Hahn, 1918), pp. 45–9, here cc. 4, 8, pp. 46–8: 'iuxta consuetudinem eorum'. See also Faulkner, *Law and Authority*, p. 52.

[76] *Capitulare Saxonicum*, ed. von Schwerin, c. 10, p. 48: 'secundum ewa Saxonum'.

[77] *Vita secunda sancti Liudgeri*, ed. E. Freise, *Die Vita sancti Liudgeri: Vollständige Faksimile-Ausgabe der Handschrift Ms. Theol. lat. fol. 323 der Staatsbibliothek Berlin – Preußischer Kulturbesitz. Text, Übersetzung und Kommentar, Forschungsbeiträge* (Graz: Akadem. Druck- und Verlagsanstalt, 1999), pp. 9–24, here c. 28, p. 15; such assemblies may also be suggested in Anonymus Paderbrunnensis, *Translatio sancti Liborii*, ed. V. de Vry, *Liborius, Brückenbauer Europas: die mittelalterlichen Viten und Translationsberichte: mit einem Anhang der Manuscripta Liboriana* (Paderborn: Schöningh, 1997), c. 2,

continuation of local conflict-resolution mechanisms, including local judicial assemblies, under the Carolingians.

The men who dispensed customary justice came together to form legal communities: they undertook collective action together, and may have sworn oaths together as well. Yet while such groups may have existed chiefly for the resolution of local disputes, they also had the inherent potential for wider political action.[78] As Reynolds writes, '[s]worn communes and *conjurationes* ['conspiracies'] constituted the extension to new purposes of habits and procedures long familiar in the practice of law'.[79] Hence, she contends, the eleventh-century Peace of God movement was successful, at least in part, because it was predicated upon a tradition of oath-taking and collective dispute settlement.[80] Similarly, as the recent work of Bernard Gowers has demonstrated, the origins of the 996 Norman peasant revolt are to be found in local assemblies.[81] These are later examples, but the principle they illustrate is applicable. The practice of collective justice not only played a decisive role in the formation of rural communities, but also provided the framework for the formation of guilds, *coniurationes* and other associative bodies capable of political action.

Oexle has repeatedly highlighted the 'total' nature of associative groups.[82] These groups were often constructed within, rather than in opposition to, existing social networks: they could operate through legal communities, groups of tenants, networks of craftsmen or tradesmen or even parish communities (and it is notable in this regard that some of the

---

p. 189. For the use of 'frequens/frequentia' to denote assembly sites, see T. Reuter, 'Assembly politics in Western Europe from the eighth century to the twelfth' in P. Linehan and J. L. Nelson (eds.), *The Medieval World* (London: Routledge, 2001), pp. 432–50, here p. 436.

[78] Reuter, 'Assembly politics', especially pp. 442–3; see further the remarks of McKitterick, *Perceptions of the Past*, pp. 71–3.

[79] Reynolds, *Kingdoms and Communities*, p. 33.

[80] *Ibid*, p. 34; for more on the Peace of God movement and its connection to *placita*, see C. Wickham, 'Public court practice: the eighth and twelfth centuries compared' in S. Esders (ed.), *Rechtsverständnis und Konfliktbewältigung: gerichtliche und aussergerichtliche Strategien im Mittelalter* (Cologne: Böhlau, 2007), pp. 17–30, here especially pp. 29–30.

[81] Gowers, '966 and all that', 71–98; C. Wickham, 'Consensus and assemblies in the Romano-Germanic kingdoms: a comparative approach' in V. Epp and C. H. F. Meyer (eds.), *Recht und Konsens im frühen Mittelalter* (Vorträge und Forschungen 82) (Ostfildern: J. Thorbecke, 2017), pp. 389–426.

[82] O.G. Oexle, 'Die mittelalterlichen Gilden: ihre Selbstbedeutung und ihr Beitrag zur Formung sozialer Strukturen' in A. Zimmerman (ed.), *Soziale Ordnungen im Selbstverständnis des Mittelalters* (Miscellanea Mediaevalia 12) (Berlin: W. de Gruyter, 1979), vol. I: pp. 203–26, here especially pp. 205–6. For *coniurationes* and the *Stellinga*, see also Althoff, *Family, Friends and Followers*, p. 98; Epperlein, 'Sachsen im frühen Mittelalter', 204–5; Epperlein, *Herrschaft und Volk im karolingischen Imperium*, pp. 55–8, 68; Goldberg, 'Popular revolt', 470; McComb, 'Each by the law of his choosing'.

first attested guilds were associations of priests).[83] They served as a context in which social bonds could be created or confirmed, notably through the practice of communal eating, which was accompanied by traditional entertainments, often leading to clerical condemnation of the 'pagan' (read: secular) nature of such groups.[84] The resulting social bonds could be deployed in the form of mutual aid in the event of natural disaster, or even mutual defence in the event of external threat: for instance, we observe the latter in the case of the peasants between the Seine and Loire, who joined together in 859 to defend against a group of Danes.[85] Finally, guilds were self-regulating, insofar as they maintained the peace 'from below', in particular through communal judgement.[86] This could lead to the accusation that they followed their own, arbitrary law, as Oexle notes; hence the comments of Alpert of Metz, who, in the early eleventh century, described a merchant guild as 'pronouncing judgements not according to the law, but according to their will'.[87] Similar accusations, relating both to the law and to paganism, surface in the case of the *Stellinga*.

Such a perspective suggests that, circa July 841, the *Stellinga* existed as in the form of a guild, or horizontal association. As such, they were

---

[83] See especially Oexle, 'Gilden als soziale Gruppen', pp. 331–3; Oexle, 'Conjuratio und Gilde', p. 156. I am also grateful here for the comments of Robert Flierman and Bernard Gowers in personal correspondence. Flierman rightly remarked that rural societies could also come together as parish (or local church) communities, and it is possible that the local communities which formed the *Stellinga* were bound by parish ties. Likewise, as Gowers suggested, tenurial obligations – notably transport services – could have helped to enable horizontal ties spanning local communities: for a comparative example of this in practice, see Y. Morimoto, 'Aspects of the early medieval peasant economy as revealed in the polyptych of Prüm' in P. Linehan and J. L. Nelson (eds.), *The Medieval World* (London: Routledge, 2001), pp. 605–20, here pp. 615–8.

[84] For communal eating and its importance, see Althoff, *Family, Friends and Followers*, p. 97; Oexle, 'Die mittelalterlichen Gilden', p. 204; for accusations of paganism and an evaluation of their (in)validity, see Oexle, 'Gilden als soziale Gruppen', pp. 309–25; Oexle, 'Conjuratio und Gilde', p. 164.

[85] *Annales Bertiniani*, eds. Grat, Vielliard and Clémencet, 859, p. 80. See also Depreux, 'Défense d'un statut', p. 109; Eggert, 'Rebelliones servorum', 1152; Goldberg, 'Popular revolt', 500; Oexle, 'Gilden als soziale Gruppen', p. 307; Oexle, 'Conjuratio und Gilde', p. 153; C. Wickham, 'Space and society in early medieval peasant conflicts' in *Uomo e spazio nell'alto medioevo* (Settimane 50:1) (Spoleto: Il Centro, 2003), pp. 551–85, here pp. 567–8.

[86] Oexle, 'Peace through conspiracy', pp. 285–322.

[87] Alpertus, *De diversitate temporum*, eds. H. van Rij and A. S. Abulafia, *Alpertus van Metz, Gebeurtenissen van deze tijd en Een fragment over bisschop Diederik I van Metz* (Amsterdam: Verloren, 1980), II:20, p. 80: 'iudicia non secundum legem sed secundum voluntatem decernentes'. For this reference, see Oexle, 'Die mittelalterlichen Gilden', p. 210; Oexle, 'Kulturwissenschaftliche Reflexionen', 149–50; O. G. Oexle, 'Die Kultur der Rebellion: Schwureinungen und Verschwörung im früh- und hochmittelalterlichen Okzident' in M. T. Fögen (ed.), *Ordnung und Aufruhr im Mittelalter: historische und juristische Studien zur Rebellion* (Studien zur Europäischen Rechtsgeschichte 70) (Frankfurt: V. Klostermann, 1995), pp. 119–37, here p. 133; Oexle, 'Peace through conspiracy', pp. 304–5.

presumably tolerated, at least on a local level; while Carolingian capitularies condemned such groups, Oexle argues that local powerbrokers,
from masters to clergy, appear to have largely accepted these types of
associations.[88] At this stage, the *Stellinga* had not engaged in any recorded
acts of violence; it is unclear whether they had leaders, or whether these
first emerged in the course of their conflict against Louis the German and
his supporters.[89] The *Stellinga* only took up arms in response to Lothar's
petition, and even then they appear to have coordinated their efforts
with Lothar and his leading men. In fact, they appear to have operated
within the framework of Carolingian politics until their violation of
Lothar's truce in summer 842. The origins of the *Stellinga* are to be found
not in revolt, but rather in the tradition of early medieval guilds.

Law, Custom, and Religion

The argument that the *Stellinga* originated as a guild is significantly
strengthened by the specific content of Lothar's concession to the *Stellinga*: the right to observe their customary laws. Prudentius, in the *Annals
of Saint Bertin*, records how Lothar offered the *Stellinga* 'the choice of any
law or the customs of the Old Saxons, whichever they preferred', noting
that they reverted to their ancestral laws.[90] Nithard, similarly, writes that
Lothar permitted *Stellinga* to observe their ancient law, further describing
how 'each lived by ancient custom, according to whichever law he
wished'.[91] Many scholars, assuming a strict division between written
law and custom, have cast Old Saxon customs as a foil to the
Carolingian-codified Saxon capitularies and law code, that is, the *First
Saxon Capitulary* of 782 or circa 794/5, the *Second Saxon Capitulary* of 797

---

[88] There was ample Carolingian legislation prohibiting or restricting horizontal associations: see, for
example, *Cap. 1*, ed. Boretius, no. 20, c. 16, p. 51; no. 28, c. 31, p. 77; and no. 44, c. 10, p. 124; for
these references, see Epperlein, *Herrschaft und Volk im karolingischen Imperium*, pp. 42–50; Oexle,
'Conjuratio und Gilde', pp. 151–4. For the general toleration of horizontal associations by local
powerbrokers, see Oexle, 'Gilden als soziale Gruppen', pp. 306, 330. Of course, toleration was
not guaranteed: in the case of the 859 episode discussed above, p. 106, the horizontal association
was put down by force by the local elite. For the ways in which such groups were sometimes
restricted and other times tolerated, see Althoff, *Family, Friends and Followers*, pp. 96–7; Gowers,
'966 and all that', 85–6.

[89] Certainly, by the time of Louis the German's violent suppression of the *Stellinga*, Frankish authors
described the movement as having leaders ('auctores'): see *Annales Bertiniani*, eds. Grat, Vielliard
and Clémencet, 842, pp. 42–3; *Annales Fuldenses*, ed. Kurze, 842, p. 33. For this, see Epperlein,
Herrschaft und Volk im karolingischen Imperium.

[90] *Annales Bertiniani*, eds. Grat, Vielliard and Clémencet, 841, p. 39: 'optionem cuiuscumque legis
uel antiquorum Saxonum consuetidinis, utram earum mallent'.

[91] Nithard, *Historiae*, eds. Lauer and Glansdorff, IV:2, p. 132: 'more antiquo qua quisque volebat lege
vivebat'.

and the *Law of the Saxons* of circa 802/3.[92] Some have even gone further still, and have accepted at face value the insinuations of Prudentius and, to a certain degree, Nithard, which elide Old Saxon custom and pagan observance.[93] Thus, Lothar's concession to the *Stellinga* has been interpreted, effectively, as unravelling the changes brought about by the Saxon conquest, whether the imposition of Carolingian control or even the conversion of the Saxons.

There are, however, many problems with such interpretations. First and foremost, the *Stellinga*'s observance of their ancestral laws did not constitute an anti-Christian reaction. Particularly revealing in this regard is a passage from Notker's *Deeds of Charlemagne*, which some, following the initial suggestion of Woldemar Wenck, have taken to refer to the *Stellinga*. Notker wrote as follows:

He [Louis the German] never sullied his word in judgement or his hands in the shedding of Christian blood except once, in dire necessity. I do not dare to describe it until I see some little Louis or Charles standing beside you. After that massacre, he could not be brought by any means to condemn anyone to death. He was accustomed to punish those charged with infidelity or treachery with this penalty, that, having deprived them of their honours, he would never, on any occasion or after any length of time, soften and permit them to return to their former position.[94]

---

[92] See, for example, Goldberg, 'Popular revolt', 476–80; Lintzel, 'Die Unterwerfung Sachsens durch Karl den Großen und der sächsische Adel' in Lintzel, *Schriften*, pp. 95–127, here pp. 121–2; Müller-Mertens, 'Der Stellingaaufstand', 838–9. See the excellent recent rebuttal of this position in Faulkner, *Law and Authority*, p. 49.

[93] For the classification of the *Stellinga* as a 'pagan' movement, see Goldberg, 'Popular revolt', 480, 482, 494–5; Goldberg, *Struggle for Empire*, pp. 109–12; H. W. Goetz, *Life in the Middle Ages: From the Seventh to the Thirteenth Century* (Notre Dame: University of Notre Dame Press, 1993), p. 118; W. Haubrichs, *Die Anfänge: Versuche volkssprachiger Schriftlichkeit im frühen Mittelalter, (ca. 700–1050/60)* (Geschichte der deutschen Literatur von den Anfängen bis zum Beginn der Neuzeit 1:1) (Frankfurt: Athenäum, 1988), p. 331; Lintzel, 'Die Unterwerfung Sachsens', p. 117; Müller-Mertens, 'Der Stellingaaufstand', 840; H. Patze, 'Mission und Kirchenorganisation in karolingischer Zeit' in H. Patze (ed.), *Geschichte Niedersachsens: Grundlagen und frühes Mittelalter* (Veröffentlichungen der Historischen Kommission für Niedersachsen und Bremen 36), 5 vols. (Hildesheim: Lax, 1977), vol. I: pp. 653–712, here p. 701; F. S. Paxton, *Anchoress and Abbess in Ninth-Century Saxony: The Lives of Liutbirga of Wendhausen and Hathumoda of Gandersheim* (Washington, DC: Catholic University of America Press, 2009), p. 42; T. Reuter, 'Charlemagne and the world beyond the Rhine' in J. Story (ed.), *Charlemagne: Empire and Society* (Manchester: Manchester University Press, 2005), pp. 183–94, here p. 188; H. Schmidt, 'Über Christianisierung und gesellschaftliches Verhalten in Sachsen und Friesland', *NJ*, 49 (1977), 1–44, here 39; J. W. Thompson, *Feudal Germany* (Chicago: University of Chicago Press, 1928), p. 175; Wenskus, 'Die ständische Entwicklung', pp. 590–1. Some scholars, however, have argued against, or openly voiced doubts concerning, the paganism of the *Stellinga*: see, for example, Bartmuss, 'Zur Frage der Bedeutung', 114–16; Springer, *Die Sachsen*, p. 268; Schulze, 'Der Aufstand der Stellinga', pp. 62, 77–82, 95.

[94] Notker Babulus, *De Carolo Magno*, ed. H. F. Haefele, MGH SRG Nova series 12 (Berlin: Weidemann, 1959), II:11, p. 68: 'qui numquam linguam suam iudicio aut manus suas effusione sanguinis christiani commacularet praeter ultimam necessitatem. Quam prius enarrare non audeo

The judicial context of this passage makes it clear that the one massacre in which Louis shed blood was not a battle but rather a judicial sentence, handed down on account of infidelity; the only attested mass execution from his reign was performed in the context of the *Stellinga*. If Notker is discussing the *Stellinga* here, as I believe he is, it is indeed noteworthy that he identifies them as Christian.

Even without Notker's testimony, however, there is little evidence to suggest that the *Stellinga* identified themselves as pagans. Neither the *Annals of Saint Bertin* nor Nithard's *Histories* describe the *Stellinga* committing any aggressive 'pagan' acts, such as plundering or burning churches – events that would surely be recorded if they had transpired.[95] Even more striking is the fact that the *Stellinga's* purported 'reversion' to paganism is omitted completely in Gerward's *Xanten Annals* and Rudolf's *Fulda Annals*. Admittedly, both of these sources also pass over the involvement of Lothar and the *Stellinga's* return to ancient custom. Nevertheless, the absence of paganism in these reports speaks volumes, particularly as Rudolf had elsewhere, in the *Translation of Saint Alexander*, showered considerable attention upon pre-conquest Saxon paganism.[96] Surely if the *Stellinga* were known to be pagan, it would be decried widely, loudly and directly.

Certainly, both Nithard and Prudentius play with the implication of paganism, but in the end even they fall short of directly ascribing paganism to the *Stellinga*. Indeed, Nithard's account of the *Stellinga* begins by describing how Charlemagne, 'just as is well known to everyone in Europe ... converted the Saxons from the empty worship of idols to the true Christian religion of God through many and diverse labours'.[97]

---

quam aliquem parvulum Ludowiculum vel Carolastrum vobis astantem video. Post quam tamen cedem nullo unquam modo compelli potuit, ut quempiam condempnaret ad mortem. Sed tamen hac districtione infidelitatis vel insidiarum insimulatos coercere solebat, ut honoribus privatos nulla umquam occasione vel temporis longitudine mollitus ad pristinum gradum conscendere pateretur'. See also W. B. Wenck, *Das fränkische Reich nach dem Vertrage von Verdun (843–861)* (Leipzig: G. Wigand, 1851), p. 353, footnote 1; see further Schulze, 'Der Aufstand der Stellinga', p. 74.

[95] For the moral judgement that accompanied the desecration of churches during Lothar's Aquitanian campaign, see *Annales Bertiniani*, eds. Grat, Vielliard and Clémencet, 841, p. 40; likewise, for the anger directed at Nominoë for his alleged desecration of churches, see *Conc. 3*, ed. W. Hartmann, *MGH, Die Konzilien der karolingischen Teilreiche 843–859* (Hanover: Hahn, 1984), no. 20, pp. 203–6, here especially p. 204. I am grateful to Robert Flierman and Rachel Stone for these comments and references.

[96] *Annales Fuldenses*, ed. Kurze, 842, pp. 33–4; *Annales Xantenses*, ed. Simpson, 841–2, pp. 12–3; Rudolf and Meginhard, *Translatio sancti Alexandri*, ed. Pertz, cc. 2–3, pp. 675–6; see also Bartmuss, 'Zur Frage der Bedeutung', 114; Schulze, 'Der Aufstand der Stellinga', p. 78.

[97] Nithard, *Historiae*, eds. Lauer and Glansdorff, IV:2, p. 130: 'Saxones quidem, sicut universis Europam degentibus patet, Karolus, magnus imperator ab universis nationibus non inmerito

His later statement that the *Stellinga* observed the law that 'their ancestors kept in the time when they were worshippers of idols' likewise intimates that the Saxons were no longer perceived to be pagan.[98] In the *Annals of Saint Bertin*, when the *Stellinga* adopted customary law, they merely 'chose to imitate the rites of the pagans'.[99] The *Annals* later allege that the *Stellinga* 'almost left the Christian faith', yet here the qualifier 'almost' is key: these men were still viewed as Christians.[100] Both authors employed the insinuation of paganism, but the failure of these reports openly to attribute paganism to the *Stellinga*, placed alongside the silence of the two other annalistic reports which describe the *Stellinga*, renders it unlikely that the *Stellinga* were pagan.

The insinuation of paganism served a specific end in these reports: it further delegimitized Lothar, who had supported the *Stellinga*.[101] Both Nithard and Prudentius supported the West Frankish king Charles the Bald, who was in alliance with Louis the German; both wrote during or soon after the civil war against Lothar, and portrayed him in a highly negative light throughout. In Nithard's account, Lothar's greed propelled him to commit increasingly grave crimes, among which oath-breaking, the persecution of the Church and sowing discord among the Christian *populus* are named.[102] In the Battle of Fontenoy, God was revealed to favour the cause of Charles and Louis, but Lothar continued on undeterred.[103] A month later he approached the *Stellinga* and offered them the option of customary law. Nor did Lothar stop there in his abandonment of Christian principles: he 'also brought in the Northmen for the sake of their aid and placed a part of the Christians under their rule'.[104] The latter especially worried Louis, who 'feared lest the Northmen and the Slavs, because of their affinity to the Saxons who are called

vocatus, ab idolorum vana cultura multo ac diverso labore ad veram Dei christianamque religionem convertit.'

[98] *Ibid*, IV:2, p. 132: 'antecessores sui tempore quo idolorum cultores erant habuerant'.

[99] *Annales Bertiniani*, eds. Grat, Vielliard and Clémencet, 841, p. 39: 'ritum paganorum imitari ... delegerunt.'

[100] *Ibid*, 842, p. 42: 'christianam fidem pene reliquerant'. See also Schulze, 'Der Aufstand der Stellinga', p. 78.

[101] I should like to thank Robert Flierman for this comment; for this point, see Flierman, *Saxon Identities*, p. 128. Cf. Bartmuss, 'Zur Frage der Bedeutung', 114–16. Bartmuss not only argues that these texts were intended to delegitimize Lothar, but also asserts that the very association of Lothar with the *Stellinga* is erroneous.

[102] E. Screen, 'The importance of the emperor: Lothar I and the Frankish civil war, 840–843', *EME*, 12(1) (2003), 25–51, here 27–31.

[103] Nithard, *Historiae*, eds. Lauer and Glansdorff, II:10, pp. 86–8; see also Nelson, 'Public and private history', 262–5.

[104] Nithard, *Historiae*, eds. Lauer and Glansdorff, IV:2, p. 132: 'Insuper autem Lodharius Nortmannos causa subsidii introduxerat partemque christianorum illis subdiderat.'

the *Stellinga*, might join together, invade the realm to vindicate themselves, and obliterate Christian religion in those parts'.[105] These were the elements, Nithard intoned, with whom Lothar associated: 'every reader . . . may examine, infer, and judge, whether he acted justly'.[106]

Similarly, in the *Annals of Saint Bertin*, Lothar's coalition with the *Stellinga* is directly followed by his alliance with Harald the Northman, which the author does not allow to pass without comment: 'this was truly a wholly abominable crime, that those people, who had inflicted such calamity on Christians, were offered up the Christian *populus*, their lands, and the churches of Christ, so that the persecutors of the Christian faith became the masters of Christians, and the Christian *populus* served the worshippers of demons'.[107] Nor did Lothar's disregard for Christian religion end there, according to the annalist: he soon proceeded to Le Mans with acts of 'plunder, conflagration, rape and sacrilege', sacking churches and even extracting oaths from nuns.[108] As Elina Screen has written, Lothar emerges from such reports as 'the antithesis of the ideal ruler'.[109] Much can be attributed to exaggeration. Despite Prudentius' insinuations to the contrary, the Harald with whom Lothar allied appears to have been baptized, whether or not he can be equated with King Harald, who was baptized in 826.[110] The *Stellinga* were presumably also depicted in such a manner in order to fit into the wider framework of his alleged irreligious conduct.

The attribution of paganism to the *Stellinga* rests upon the conflation of concepts: whether of secular fidelity and religious fidelity, or of law and religion. The first is neatly illustrated in the *Annals of Saint Bertin* when Louis the German comes in 842 to crush the *Stellinga*: Prudentius

---

[105] *Ibid*, IV:2, p. 134: 'Igitur metuens Lodhuvicus ne idem Nortmanni nec non et Sclavi, propter affinitatem, Saxonibus qui se Stellinga nominaverant conjugerent regnumque sibi vindicaturi invaderent et christianam religionem his in partibus annullarent.' See also below, p. 201.

[106] Nithard, *Historiae*, eds. Lauer and Glansdorff, II: prologue, p. 42: 'quique lector . . . decernat, colligat et si juste egerit cognoscat'.

[107] *Annales Bertiniani*, eds. Grat, Vielliard, and Clémencet, 841, p. 39: 'dignum sane omni detestatione facinus, ut qui mala christianis intulerant, idem christianorum terris et populis Christique ecclesiis praeferrentur, ut persecutores fidei christianae domini christianorum existerent et daemonum cultoribus christiani populi deseruirent!'; see also Bartmuss, 'Zur Frage der Bedeutung', 115; S. Coupland, 'From poachers to gamekeepers: Scandinavian warlords and Carolingian kings', *EME*, 7(1) (1998), 85–114, here 90–3.

[108] *Annales Bertiniani*, eds. Grat, Vielliard and Clémencet, 841, p. 40, 'rapinis, incendiis, stupris, sacrilegiis'.

[109] Screen, 'Lothar I and the Frankish civil war', 30; see further S. Airlie, 'The world, the text and the Carolingian: royal, aristocratic and masculine identities in Nithard's *Histories*' in P. Wormald and J. L. Nelson (eds.), *Lay Intellectuals in the Carolingian World* (Cambridge: Cambridge University Press, 2007), pp. 51–76, here p. 67.

[110] Coupland, 'From poachers to gamekeepers', 92.

described how the *Stellinga* 'had almost left the Christian faith and had resisted Louis and his *fideles* so fervently'.[111] The political crime of rebelling against Louis the German and the rebels' near-desertion of the Christian faith are so intertwined that they cannot be separated. This depiction may, in fact, draw on earlier reports of the Saxons during the conquest period. Less than forty years had passed since the conclusion of the conquest, and it is hardly surprising that the annalist turned to the developed rhetoric of Saxon perfidy established, above all, by the revised version of the *Royal Frankish Annals*.[112] What is unexpected is that he was alone in doing so. After all, accusations of (political and religious) perfidy abounded elsewhere in the Carolingian world, most notably in (Christian) Brittany. The poet Ermoldus Nigellus wrote of how the Breton *gens*

preserved only the Christian name, and that in a perfidious manner, for their faith, worship, and works were very far off. No care remained for orphans, widows, and churches. One brother slept with his sister, another seized his brother's wife; everyone lived in incest and committed unspeakable acts. They lived in the briars and placed their beds in the wilds; they were glad to live for rapine in a savage manner.[113]

Later in the same work, Ermoldus depicted Louis the Pious offering terms for peace: 'let him', Louis declaims, referring to the Breton leader Murman, 'be yoked to the Christian herd in peace and faith; let him, miserable, leave the arms of demons through the love of God'.[114] Clearly, Ermoldus did not shy away from accusations of paganism, despite the centuries of Christian observance in Brittany; given the relative novelty of Christianity in Saxony, one would expect worse.

In both the *Annals of Saint Bertin* and in Nithard's *Histories*, the attribution of paganism to the *Stellinga* is predicated upon the elision of

---

[111] *Annales Bertiniani*, eds. Grat, Vielliard and Clémencet, 842, pp. 42–3: 'qui et christianam fidem pene reliquerant et sibi suisque fidelibus tantopere obstiterant'; Goldberg, 'Popular revolt', 494.

[112] My thanks to Robert Flierman for this suggestion.

[113] Ermoldus Nigellus, *In honorem Hludowici*, ed. E. Faral, *Poème sur Louis le Pieux et épitres au Roi Pépin* (Les classiques de l'histoire de France au moyen age 14), 2nd edn (Paris: Société d'Édition "Les Belles Lettres", 1964) III: 1298–1305, p. 102: 'Christocolum retinet tantum modo perfida nomen,/Namque opera et cultus sunt procul atque fides./Cura pupillorum, viduae, sive ecclesiarum/Nulla manet; coeunt frater et ipsa soror./Uxorem fratris frater rapit alter et omnes/ Incestu vivunt atque nefanda gerunt./In dumis habitant lustrisque cubilia condunt,/Et gaudent raptu degere more ferae.' I am grateful to Rachel Stone for these comparisons. See also I. N. Wood, 'Ideas of mission in the Carolingian world' in W. Fałkowski and Y. Sassier (eds.), *Le monde carolingien: bilan, perspectives, champs de recherches: actes du colloque international de Poitiers, Centre d'études supérieures de civilisation médiévale, 18–20 novembre 2004* (Culture et société médiévales 18) (Turnhout: Brepols, 2009), pp. 183–98, here p. 196.

[114] Ermoldus Nigellus, *In Honorem Hludowici*, ed. Faral, III: 1574–5, p. 120: 'Christicoloque gregi jugatur pace fideque,/Linquat amore Dei daemonis arma miser.' See also Stone, *Morality and Masculinity*, p. 75.

law and religion. The *Stellinga* are depicted rallying behind the old customary law, which, as Nithard writes, 'their ancestors kept in the time when they were worshippers of idols'.[115] In the *Annals of Saint Bertin*, the *Stellinga* are given the choice between any law or the customs of the Old Saxons in exchange for their support. 'As they were always prone to evil', the report continues, 'they chose to imitate the rites of the pagans rather than to preserve the sacraments of the Christian faith'.[116] Certainly, both authors were employing the Christian concept of *lex*, which encompassed not only secular legislation but also divine law.[117]

There are, however, other indications that the observance of pre-Christian law was not perceived to be inimical to the new faith. The Saxon Poet, writing at the end of the ninth century, certainly did not see any opposition between the two: in the fictional conditions he lays out for the so-called 'Peace of Salz', thought to mark the end of the Saxon wars, he depicts Charlemagne granting the Saxons the right to follow their 'paternal laws'.[118] Even more arresting is Rudolf of Fulda's depiction of Old Saxon law in the *Translation of Saint Alexander*, written before 865: the Old Saxons 'used the best laws for vengeance against criminals, and they strove to observe the most advantageous and worthy probity of customs, following the law of nature, by which they would have been able to achieve true beatitude, if they had not been ignorant of their creator'.[119] This is one of the few instances in which Rudolf is independent from his source, Tacitus' *Germania*, and he chose to depict Old Saxon law as virtuous.[120] Finally, the abbot of Corvey was loath to refuse a donation of land that was bequeathed 'according to the custom of Saxon law, with a mound of earth and the green branch of a tree'.[121]

---

[115] Nithard, *Historiae*, eds. Lauer and Glansdorff, IV:2, p. 132: 'quam antecessores sui tempore quo idolorum cultores erant habuerant'.

[116] *Annales Bertiniani*, eds. Grat, Vielliard and Clémencet, 841, p. 39: 'Qui semper ad mala procliues magis ritum paganorum imitari quam christianae fidei sacramenta tenere delegerunt'.

[117] For this, see Springer, *Die Sachsen*, p. 268; see also M. de Jong, *In Samuel's Image: Child Oblation in the Early Medieval West* (Brill's Studies in Intellectual History 12) (Leiden: Brill, 1996), pp. 8–12. My thanks to Robert Flierman for this comment. See here also the comments of R. M. Karras, 'Pagan survivals and syncretism in the conversion of Saxony', *The Catholic Historical Review*, 72(4) (1986), 553–72, here 558.

[118] Poeta Saxo, *Annalium de gestis Caroli magni imperatoris libri V*, ed. P. Winterfeld, *MGH Poet.* 4:1 (Berlin: Weidemann, 1899), pp. 1–71, here IV, lines 110–111, p. 48: 'legibus . . . patriis'; see also Faulkner, *Law and Authority*, p. 61; Leyser, *Communications and Power: The Gregorian Revolution*, p. 53.

[119] Rudolf and Meginhard, *Translatio sancti Alexandri*, ed. Pertz, c. 2, p. 675: 'Legibus etiam ad vindictam malefactorum optimis utebantur. Et multa utilia atque secundum legem naturae honesta in morum probitate habere studuerunt, quae eis ad veram beatitudinem promerendam proficere potuissent, si ignorantiam creatoris sui non haberent.'

[120] Faulkner, *Law and Authority*, pp. 57–60.

[121] *Traditiones Corbeienses*, ed. Honselmann, no. 153, p. 108: 'secundum morem saxonice legis cum terre cespite et viridi ramo arboris'.

The scribe who recorded this transaction was presumably describing a customary procedure (not altogether so dissimilar from its Frankish counterparts) which would have been amply familiar to his readers; at the very least, his abbot does not seem to have a problem with it.

There is thus little reason to approach the *Stellinga* as a 'pagan movement' on the basis of their interest in customary law. Nithard and Prudentius play with the implication of paganism, but do so to a clear narrative end; meanwhile, other sources confirm that the observance of Old Saxon customs was not seen to be inherently 'anti-Christian'. Similarly, the *Stellinga*'s observance of ancient custom does not mean that they rejected Carolingian authority, as both Nithard and Prudentius implied: on the contrary, local collective justice was tolerated, and sometimes even encouraged, by the Carolingian authorities.

Recent scholarship has fundamentally reassessed early medieval justice and dispute settlement, stressing its variety, plurality and flexibility.[122] There was no innate opposition between written and customary law,[123] nor was there only one legitimate source for legal authority: as Innes writes, 'Carolingian legal practice can be characterized as a system of "substantive legalism": participants advanced legal arguments from a variety of sources (not only the *leges* ['laws'] and the capitularies but also local practice, Biblical and canonical texts and Roman law), but with no definitive single repository of "formal law"'.[124] Parties to a dispute could, in the first instance, attempt to reach their own settlement or to submit to a process of arbitration. If they chose to seek legal redress, participants had a multiplicity of mutually compatible legal frameworks to which they could turn, and in which there was ample room for negotiation. Even written laws may simply represent, in the words of Alice Rio, 'the upper limit of what could be expected from a person by whom one had been wronged'.[125] The practice of law was thus more variegated than the surviving legal sources allow.

---

[122] See here especially W. Davies and P. Fouracre (eds.), *The Settlement of Disputes in Early Medieval Europe* (Cambridge: Cambridge University Press, 1986); *La giustizia nell'alto Medioevo (secoli v-viii)* (Settimane 42) (Spoleto: Il Centro, 1995); and *La giustizia nell'alto Medioevo (secoli ix-xi)* (Settimane 44) (Spoleto: Il Centro, 1997).

[123] See especially R. McKitterick, *The Carolingians and the Written Word* (Cambridge: Cambridge University Press, 1989), pp. 37–8; see further the comments of L. Roach, 'Law codes and legal norms in later Anglo-Saxon England', *Historical Research*, 86(233) (2013), 465–86, here especially 484–5.

[124] M. Innes, 'Charlemagne, justice and written law' in A. Rio (ed.), *Law, Custom, and Justice in Late Antiquity and the Early Middle Ages: Proceedings of the 2008 Byzantine Colloquium* (London: Centre for Hellenic Studies, 2011), pp. 155–203, here pp. 171–2.

[125] Rio, *Legal Practice and the Written Word in the Early Middle Ages*, p. 209.

These issues have been addressed at length in Brown's excellent study of dispute resolution in Carolingian Bavaria.[126] A comparable study is not possible in Saxony, but its surviving material nevertheless corroborates this image of legal complexity. Alongside the *Law of the Saxons*, whose problematic features have been discussed above, there appear to have been alternative sources of law, whether in the form of unwritten or written laws or customs.[127] Indeed, no single literary reference to the enactment of justice in early medieval Saxony appears to correlate with the *Law of the Saxons*. The judicial blindings that are mentioned in the *Translation of Saint Alexander* are without basis in the *Law*;[128] likewise, when Gottschalk refers to his oblation being invalid under Saxon law, because the witnesses were Franks rather than Saxons, there is no corresponding Saxon legal statute extant.[129] Even the donation to Corvey mentioned above, which was made 'with an earthen mound and the green branch of a tree', seems inexplicable in the light of the *Law*.[130] In Widukind's *Deeds of the Saxons*, an allusion is made to the variety of old, pre-conquest Saxon law, though 'it is not for this book to unpick it, for the law of the Saxons can be found, diligently described, in many places'.[131] Yet in the form that the *Law of the Saxons* has been transmitted, as Faulkner observes, there is only one instance in which separate legal customs for the different regions of Saxony have been preserved.[132] The legal realities were more complex in Carolingian Saxony than is presented by the surviving normative sources.

The *Stellinga*'s observance of ancient custom, then, was not necessarily an anti-Carolingian reaction: rather, it can be seen as fitting within the

---

[126] Brown, *Unjust Seizure*.   [127] See above, pp. 25–6.

[128] Rudolf and Meginhard, *Translatio sancti Alexandri*, ed. Pertz, cc. 6, 9, p. 679; see also Faulkner, *Law and Authority*, pp. 60–1; Leyser, *Communications and Power: The Gregorian Revolution*, p. 54.

[129] Hrabanus Maurus, *Liber de oblatione puerorum*, ed. J. P. Migne, *Patrologia Latina 107* (Paris, 1851), pp. 419–40, here col. 431; for this, see Faulkner, *Law and Authority*, pp. 64–6; M. B. Gillis, 'Noble and Saxon: the meaning of Gottschalk of Orbais' ethnicity at the Synod of Mainz, 829' in R. Corradini, M. B. Gillis, R. McKitterick and I. van Renswoude (eds.), *Ego Trouble: Authors and Their Identities in the Early Middle Ages* (Forschungen zur Geschichte des Mittelalters 15) (Vienna: Verlag der Österreichischen Akademie der Wissenschaften, 2010), pp. 197–210, here especially pp. 200–1; Gillis, *Heresy and Dissent*, p. 29. Matthew Gillis observes, however, that there was a 'passage of Carolingian – not specifically Saxon – legislation' which established the principle of swearing oaths with witnesses of the same ethnicity; for this, see Gillis, *Heresy and Dissent*, p. 38.

[130] *Traditiones Corbeienses*, ed. Honselmann, no. 153, p. 108: 'cum terre cespite et viridi ramo arboris'.

[131] Widukind of Corvey, *Res Gestae Saxonicae*, eds. Hirsch and Lohmann, I:14, p. 24: 'non est in hoc libello disserere, cum apud plures inveniatur lex Saxonica diligenter descripta'.

[132] *Lex Saxonum*, ed. von Schwerin, cc. 47–8, pp. 29–30; see also Faulkner, *Law and Authority*, pp. 76–7. See further M. Becher, 'Die Sachsen im 7. und 8. Jahrhundert' in Stiegemann and Wemhoff, *799*, vol. I: pp. 184–94, here p. 192; I. N. Wood, 'Beyond satraps and ostriches: political and social structures of the Saxons in the early Carolingian period' in Green and Siegmund, *Saxons*, pp. 271–97, here p. 285.

framework of Carolingian 'substantive legalism'. Local communities, formed to ensure the maintenance of local order, were widely accepted in the Carolingian world, and indeed such communities were accepted and promoted in Saxony during the conquest period. There are signs that the promotion of comital courts may have impinged upon the traditional prerogatives of such collective groups. Charles West, in his recent study of the region between the Marne and Moselle, found substantial evidence that the *mallum* court, traditionally used to refer to bottom-up judicial meetings and assemblies, took on a much more technical meaning over the course of the ninth century:

> the *mallum* underwent a redefinition, moving from indicating a kind of 'bottom-up' traditional meeting of free Franks to a more specific, almost technical label for a meeting held under the aegis of the count or his representative ... There was no room in this understanding of the *mallum* court for the kind of autonomous community justice that the word seems initially to have indicated.[133]

There are some indications, as discussed above, that a similar process was underway in Saxony.[134] It is in this context that we should place the *Stellinga*'s wish to obtain Lothar's concession, with its explicit permission to live according to customary law.

The *Stellinga* were not attempting to revert to paganism, nor were they seeking to unravel the changes which had followed Carolingian conquest and incorporation. They were not even a class-based movement which rallied around the destruction of elite privilege. Rather, they are better understood as a guild or horizontal association, which – in addition to a myriad of other functions – participated in the dispensing of customary justice. As such, they were accepted and tolerated in local Saxon society.

Such an interpretation is not only useful insofar as it 'normalizes' the *Stellinga* – that is, interprets the group as a phenomenon born of its time, rather than as an aberration – but further helps to explain the interactions between the *Stellinga* and Carolingian politics at large, and, specifically, their alliance with, and fidelity to, the Emperor Lothar.

THE EMPEROR AND THE *STELLINGA*

The connection of the *Stellinga* to Carolingian politics has been the subject of some debate. Its first thorough treatment dates to 1955, when

---

[133] C. West, *Reframing the Feudal Revolution: Political and Social Transformation between Marne and Moselle, c. 800 to c. 1100* (Cambridge: Cambridge University Press, 2013), p. 25.
[134] See above, pp. 95–6.

Heinz-Joachim Schulze submitted his dissertation to the Humboldt University in East Berlin. Schulze argued that Lothar's support crumbled following his decisive defeat at the battle of Fontenoy in June 841. When his brothers, inflated by their success, proposed to divide the Carolingian lands north of the Alps between themselves, he was driven in desperation to seek allies from unexpected sources, most notably the *Stellinga*, a popular movement which, in Schulze's account, violently opposed the newly enriched Saxon elite and strove for the return of pre-conquest conditions, although notably not the return of paganism.[135] Lothar's support of the *Stellinga* created a crisis in the Eastern regions, and eventually forced his brothers to consent to a threefold division. This was later enshrined in the Treaty of Verdun, which resulted in the formation of the East Frankish, Middle and West Frankish kingdoms.[136] While Lothar's alliance with the *Stellinga* may have won him the Middle Kingdom, it arguably had more lasting consequences further east. The experience of the *Stellinga* united the nobility of East Francia firmly behind his brother Louis the German, and so caused the awakening of the first 'German' political community.[137]

In the early days of the DDR, such an interpretation would have been on-message politically, to say the least. Not only were the contours of modern Germany the result of a peasant uprising, but so too was the awakening of German political consciousness to be found in the conservative reaction to the *Stellinga*. A popular uprising in Saxony was thus granted the pivotal role in the emergence of a new world order. Down in Halle, however, Hans-Joachim Bartmuss was having none of it. Only two years later, he published an article which argued vociferously against Schulze's interpretation.[138]

Leaving to one side the many other considerations that lay behind the Treaty of Verdun, not to mention the persisting divisions in the East Frankish elite, Bartmuss challenged the very core of Schulze's argument: the connection of Lothar to the *Stellinga*. As he pointed out, only two of the four contemporary sources on the *Stellinga*, namely Nithard's *Histories* and the *Annals of Saint Bertin*, connect Lothar to the movement in any way. Both of these sources were West Frankish and betray a deep-seated bias against Lothar: hence their exaggerated and distorted representation of his dealings with Harald the Northman, for instance.[139] Lothar, Bartmuss continued, would have no reason to ally with the *Stellinga*: their agenda threatened to undermine the elites upon whose support his

---

[135] Schulze, 'Der Aufstand der Stellinga', pp. 50–3.   [136] *Ibid*, pp. 96–130.
[137] *Ibid*, pp. 131–48.   [138] Bartmuss, 'Zur Frage der Bedeutung', 113–19.   [139] *Ibid*, 114–16.

own rule depended.[140] Lothar never went into Saxony, and thus cannot be seen as offering any practical support to the movement. Bartmuss thus consigns Lothar's alliance with the *Stellinga* to the realm of fiction, leaving open the question of whether it was the conscious invention of Nithard, the earlier of these two sources, or a more general West Frankish rumour.[141] In either case, the purpose was clear: to tarnish Lothar through association.

Bartmuss' interpretation has been rightly rejected,[142] but it still exposes an important problem with contemporary reports about the *Stellinga*. In the manner that it has been presented, Lothar's support of the *Stellinga* appears unfathomable. Why would he risk alienating his *fideles* for an alliance with some Saxon peasants? An appeal to rumour would be an elegant solution to this problem, especially since rumours played a large role in the civil war. Nithard recounts how, in the immediate aftermath of Fontenoy, Lothar's supporters spread a rumour that Charles had been killed and Louis gravely wounded, thus undermining their victory.[143] Yet this does not seem a convincing manner to account for Nithard's report, which is possibly the earliest of the four accounts: his connection of the *Stellinga* to Lothar is, after all, corroborated in the *Annals of Saint-Bertin*. Both works admittedly shaped their material to somewhat tendentious ends: indeed, Nithard's *Histories* and the *Annals of Saint Bertin*, both of which play with the implication of paganism in their accounts of the *Stellinga*, do not offer sufficient evidence to class the *Stellinga* as 'pagan'. The elision of religious and earthly fidelity has a long history of its own, particularly in the case of the Saxons, and neither report explicitly says that the *Stellinga* were pagan. The connection to Lothar, on the other hand, is utterly unprecedented, and made explicit in both of these independent reports. There is no reason, other than its sheer incomprehensibility, to discredit the connection between Lothar and the *Stellinga* that is depicted in both sources.

Subsequent analyses of the *Stellinga* have eschewed both of these interpretations; indeed, scholars have largely sidelined the political situation, focusing instead on the changing socio-economic situation in Carolingian Saxony. An exception is the article by Eric Goldberg, who rightly argued that the division of the Saxon elite largely precipitated the *Stellinga* revolt.[144] In this account, Lothar appealed to the *Stellinga* in a

---

[140] *Ibid*, 116.   [141] *Ibid*, 116, 119.
[142] See, for example, Eggert, 'Rebelliones servorum', 1158; Epperlein, *Herrschaft und Volk im karolingischen Imperium*, p. 65.
[143] Nithard, *Historiae*, eds. Lauer and Glansdorff, III:2, pp. 96–8.
[144] Goldberg, 'Popular revolt', 484–93.

moment of political desperation, thereby alienating the East Frankish nobility.[145] The basic question that Bartmuss implicitly raised – 'how could Lothar possibly think that supporting the *Stellinga* was worthwhile?' – remains unanswered.

If, however, the *Stellinga* were not violently anti-elite and anti-Christian as they have often been depicted, as I have argued above, then Lothar's alliance with the *Stellinga* may appear somewhat more explicable.[146] Indeed, Lothar's involvement with the *Stellinga* was neither the gross miscalculation of a desperate man, nor did it result in the complete alienation of his East Frankish allies. Instead, Lothar's support of the *Stellinga* can be understood to a far greater degree within the framework of Carolingian politics.

Lothar first appealed to the *Stellinga* in July 841, shortly after the Battle of Fontenoy. He had suffered a defeat, but it was not a decisive one: Lothar retained significant support, while his brothers struggled to turn their victory into political capital. Charles the Bald in particular appears to have floundered following the battle: rumours of his defeat had spread across the countryside, and potential recruits 'regarded the paucity of his supporters scornfully ... and with a variety of excuses delayed their submission to him at the present time'.[147] Yet while Fontenoy did not in itself determine the outcome of the war, it nevertheless marked a change in Lothar's position. There was probably not a flood of defections from his cause, despite Nithard's allegations to the contrary.[148] All the same, Lothar recognized that it was time to start courting peoples whom he had previously neglected, such as the Saxons.

If Lothar had attempted to win Saxon support before, few traces remain of such an appeal. Certainly, early in 841, Lothar granted confirmations to the monastery of Prüm, which held some lands in Saxony.[149] Further, at the behest of Adalbert of Metz, he attempted to elicit support from beyond the Rhine.[150] Neither of these, however, can be seen as a particular appeal to Saxon forces. Despite this benign neglect, Lothar nevertheless maintained a degree of Saxon support: as Nithard writes, at the start of the war, the elite were 'divided into two factions in the dissension between Lothar and his brothers, one of which followed

---

[145] *Ibid*, 494–7.   [146] See also Springer, *Die Sachsen*, p. 268.

[147] Nithard, *Historiae*, eds. Lauer and Glansdorff, III:2, p. 98: 'eandem paucitatem ... spernentes, variis fictionibus illi se per praesens subdere distulerunt'.

[148] *Ibid*, IV:2, p. 132.

[149] *D Lo I*, ed. T. Schieffer, *MGH, Die Urkunden Lothars I. und Lothars II* (Berlin: Weidemann, 1966), nos. 56–7, pp. 159–62.

[150] Nithard, *Historiae*, eds. Lauer and Glansdorff, II:7, pp. 68–70.

Lothar, the other one, Louis'.[151] By contrast, Louis the German regarded Saxon support as essential to his claim from the outset of the civil war. Almost immediately following his father's death in June 840, Louis the German hurried to Saxony to marshal support.[152] Only a few months later, in December, he returned once again, appointing a faithful supporter to the bishopric of Halberstadt,[153] and issuing a total of four charters to the important monastery of Corvey.[154] This was a remarkable number, given that only two other charters granted by Louis survive from the civil war. The favour he showered on Corvey came at the expense of Lothar's supporters: one of his grants to Corvey features some twenty *mansi* (a unit of assessment roughly equivalent to the land that could be exploited by one household) previously held in benefice by Count Banzleib, one of Lothar's *fideles*. Likewise, Louis appears to have enriched Corvey with the revenues of the diocese of Osnabrück, whose bishop had presumably supported Lothar in the rebellions against Louis the Pious.[155] This bait-and-switch strategy appears to have worked: Louis the German enjoyed significant, if not unified, Saxon support in the early stages of the war.

Thus, in July 841, eager to elicit aid from a territory where his brother had largely commanded support, and presumably eager to reassert the claims of his *fideles,* Lothar dispatched messengers to the *Stellinga* to entice them to his side. The messengers he sent were probably men familiar with Saxony, perhaps even elite Saxon *fideles* such as Waltbraht, the grandson of Widukind, who would have provided the information and background for Lothar's Saxon strategy.[156] Through such men, Lothar conceded to the *Stellinga* the right to observe whatever law or custom they chose in return for their support. In so doing, Lothar was not offering a return to paganism, or the unravelling of changes which had followed Carolingian conquest and incorporation. On the contrary, he

---

[151] *Ibid*, IV:2, pp. 130–2: 'pars illorum quę nobilis inter illos habetur in duabus partibus in dissensione Lodharii ac fratrum suorum divisa unaque eorum Lodharium, altera vero Lodhuvicum secuta est'.

[152] *Ibid*, II:1, p. 46; see also Goldberg, 'Popular revolt', 487, note 98.

[153] Goldberg, *Struggle for Empire*, p. 97.

[154] *D LD*, ed. P. Kehr, *MGH, Die Urkunden Ludwigs des Deutschen, Karlmanns und Ludwigs der Jüngeren* (Berlin: Weidemann, 1934), nos. 26–9, pp. 31–6; see also B. Bigott, *Ludwig der Deutsche und die Reichskirche im Ostfränkischen Reich (826–876)* (Historische Studien 470) (Husum: Matthiesen, 2002), pp. 85–7; Goldberg, 'Popular revolt', 485, 487–8; K. H. Krüger, *Studien zur Corveyer Gründungsüberlieferung* (Abhandlungen zur Corveyer Geschichtsschreibung 9) (Münster: Aschendorff, 2001), p. 39; Röckelein, *Reliquientranslationen nach Sachsen*, pp. 55–6; Schulze, 'Der Aufstand der Stellinga', p. 66.

[155] Stephanus V papa, *Epistolae*, ed. G. Laehr, MGH Epp. 7:5 (Berlin: Weidemann, 1928), pp. 354–65, no. 3, p. 360. For the authenticity of this source, see above, p. 27, footnote 96.

[156] I am grateful to Robert Flierman for this suggestion. For Waltbraht's connection to Lothar, see Rudolf and Meginhard, *Translatio sancti Alexandri*, ed. Pertz, c. 4, pp. 676–8.

was operating well within the bounds of Carolingian governance, which had long allowed the observance of local custom. Even the very act of granting such a privilege in return for military assistance had Carolingian precedent: indeed, as Müller-Mertens observed, Louis the Pious had earlier offered the Christians in Merida the freedom to observe their law in an attempt to elicit support there.[157]

Although Saxon freemen and half-freemen had long fought as part of Carolingian forces, it was, admittedly, somewhat novel for a Carolingian ruler to appeal directly to such men as autonomous actors. Yet it was by no means an unknown strategy. Even Louis the German called upon non-elite assistance in the past: an 832 entry in the *Annals of Saint Bertin* records how in that year Louis revolted against his father 'with all the Bavarians, freemen and slaves, and Slavs'.[158] In Saxony, moreover, there was considerable precedent for the lower orders of society being involved in armed conflict, whether on their lord's behalf or indeed on their own initiative. The *Law of the Saxons* devotes no fewer than three chapters to the question of lords' liability for crimes, including murder, committed by half-freemen and slaves at their behest.[159] More significantly, both freemen and half-freemen played a decisive role in the Saxon wars: hence the deportations, and hence as well the occasions on which such men were taken as hostages in their own right – for example in 780, when the *Lorsch Annals* record that both *ingenui* (freemen) and *liti* (half-freemen) were taken as hostages.[160] On this occasion, it is unclear whether *ingenui* are to be equated with Nithard's *frilingi/ ingenuiles* or rather with the Frankish *ingenui*, that is, the highest class recognized in the *Salian Law*: nevertheless, the inclusion of half-freemen among the hostages is telling.[161] Following the wars' conclusion, the lower orders may have continued to be involved in military endeavours. The capitulary from circa 807, with its provisions for how Saxon men were to band together to support those who went on campaign, appears

[157] Einhard, *Epistolae*, ed. K. Hampe, *MGH Epp.* 5:3 (Berlin: Weidemann, 1899), no. 12, pp. 115–6; see also Faulkner, *Law and Authority*, pp. 50–1; Müller-Mertens, 'Der Stellingaaufstand', 836. For a wider perspective on this grant, see J. Conant, 'Louis the Pious and the contours of empire', *EME*, 22(3) (2014), 336–60.

[158] *Annales Bertiniani*, eds. Grat, Vielliard and Clémencet, 832, p. 5: 'cum omnibus Baioariis, liberis et seruis, et Sclauis'.

[159] *Lex Saxonum*, ed. von Schwerin, cc. 18, 50, 52, pp. 22–3, 30–1.

[160] *Annales Laureshamenses*, ed. G. H. Pertz, *MGH SS* 1 (Hanover: Hahn, 1826), pp. 22–39, here 780, p. 31; see also Wenskus, 'Die ständische Entwicklung', p. 609.

[161] See further the pertinent remarks of G. Landwehr, 'Die Liten in den altsächsischen Rechtsquellen. Ein Diskussionsbeitrag zur Textgeschichte der *Lex Saxonum*' in G. Landwehr (ed.), *Studien zu den germanischen Volksrechten. Gedächtnisschrift für Wilhelm Ebel* (Rechtshistorische Reihe 1) (Frankfurt: P. Lang, 1982), pp. 117–42, here p. 122. See also above, p. 54.

to envisage a broad base of potential military recruits.[162] Freemen and half-freemen may even have fought in the civil war before Lothar's overtures: as Goldberg rightly suggests, some of the men who later joined the *Stellinga* may have been armed and trained to serve under their lords on the side of Louis the German.[163]

Lothar was not just seeking support among the lower orders in Saxony. Around the same time as he approached the *Stellinga*, he confirmed the privileges of the monastery of Fulda, which, while based in Hesse, was also a significant landowner in Saxony in its own right. A month later, at Mainz, the *Fulda Annals* record that he sent emissaries to the Saxons, requesting that they bring his son, Lothar II, with them to meet him at Speyer.[164] While it is uncertain exactly when Lothar may have sent his son to Saxony, and to whom he might have entrusted him – whether to the Saxon elite faction which supported him or even to the *Stellinga* themselves – the report is nevertheless remarkable. As Goldberg remarked, this may well mean that the young Lothar, at the tender age of six years, had been sent to the Saxons as a subking, or at the very least as a symbol of Lothar's commitment to rule in Saxony.[165]

Certainly, Lothar's appeal for Saxon support appears to have worked. The *Stellinga* rallied to his side and, crucially, do not appear to have jeopardized his relations with the East Frankish, or even Saxon, elite. In September 841 Lothar marched towards Paris with a sizeable contingent of Saxons as part of his army; some members of the *Stellinga* may even have numbered among his troops.[166] The Saxons are further glimpsed fighting in cooperation with Lothar's ally, Pippin II of Aquitaine, albeit in a late, and ultimately confused, account of the war in Benedict of Saint Andrea's *Chronicle*.[167]

It was, however, to be a winter of setbacks and defeats. To be sure, his alliance with the *Stellinga* bore some fruit: the *Xanten Annals* describe the successes of the *Stellinga* at the expense of their masters (*domini*), presumably the *fideles* of Louis the German.[168] But elsewhere, Lothar met with disappointment. His initial push to Paris was frustrated by the forces of his brother, Charles, and the rising waters of the Seine River; so too were his

---

[162] See above, p. 89.   [163] Goldberg, 'Popular revolt', 492–3.

[164] *Annales Fuldenses*, ed. Kurze, 841, p. 32.

[165] Goldberg, 'Popular revolt', 495; see also M. Becher, *Rex, Dux und Gens: Untersuchungen zur Entstehung des sächsischen Herzogtums im 9. Und 10. Jahrhundert* (Historische Studien 444) (Husum: Matthiesen, 1996), p. 124; Ehlers, *Die Integration Sachsens*, p. 297; Schulze, 'Der Aufstand der Stellinga', pp. 106–7; Screen, 'Lothar I and the Frankish civil war', 48.

[166] Nithard, *Historiae*, eds. Lauer and Glansdorff, III:3, p. 102.

[167] Benedict, *Chronicon*, ed. G. H. Pertz, *MGH SS* 3 (Hanover: Hahn, 1839), c. 25, p. 712.

[168] *Annales Xantenses*, ed. Simpson, 841, p. 12.

later attempts to engage Charles abortive, and he failed in his efforts to gain the support of the Breton duke Nominoë.[169] In the East, the forces of his *fidelis*, Otgar of Mainz, were forced into retreat.[170] The Battle of Fontenoy may not, on its own, have been decisive, but Lothar's failure to gain any significant traction in the following months was.

Soon after Otgar's retreat, in February 842, Louis sent Count Bardo into Saxony.[171] He soon returned and 'announced the Saxons had spurned the orders of Lothar, and were willing to do anything that Louis and Charles might command them willingly'.[172] According to Goldberg, Louis the German now commanded the support of a unified Saxon elite, who had returned from campaign 'empty-handed' only to behold, as Goldberg writes, 'the destruction that the pagan *frilingi* (freemen) and *lazzi* (half-freemen) had wrought with Lothar's consent since they had left home over four months earlier'.[173] Yet, while Louis may well have won some supporters in Saxony at Lothar's expense, such desertions can be easily explained without taking the *Stellinga* into account. Lothar had passed an inconclusive winter following his defeat at Fontenoy, and his main East Frankish ally had been put to flight.

In any case, Louis was far from winning the unified support of the Saxon elite. Lothar still counted among his followers a number of Saxon *fideles* who were evidently untroubled by his support of the *Stellinga*, and some of whom may have even served as messengers to the group. He retained the support of some Saxon *fideles* long after the conclusion of the civil war. Count Esic was still Lothar's *fidelis* as late as 843, when he was granted a benefice by the ruler;[174] Waltbraht appears to have still been loyal to Lothar almost a decade later, when Lothar drafted three letters on his behalf.[175] Given the paucity of information about individual allegiances in Saxony in this period, such indications are telling. Even more strikingly, Lothar's support of the *Stellinga* does not appear to have alienated ecclesiastical landowners in Saxony. He retained supporters in

---

[169] Nithard, *Historiae*, eds. Lauer and Glansdorff, III:3–4, pp. 102–10. [170] *Ibid*, III:4, p. 110.

[171] *Ibid*, III:5, 7, pp. 120–2.

[172] *Ibid*, III:7, p. 122: 'nuntians quod Saxones mandata Lodharii sprevissent et, quicquid Lodhuvicus et Karolus illis praeciperent, libenter id facere vellent'.

[173] Goldberg, 'Popular revolt', 497.

[174] *D Lo I*, ed. Schieffer, no. 70, pp. 184–5; see also E. M. Screen, 'The reign of Lothar I (795–855), emperor of the Franks, through the charter evidence', unpublished Ph.D. thesis, University of Cambridge (1998), p. 220; Schulze, 'Der Aufstand der Stellinga', p. 67.

[175] Rudolf and Meginhard, *Translatio sancti Alexandri*, ed. Pertz, c. 4, pp. 677–8. See also H. Röckelein, 'Heilige als Medien der Christianisierung. Das Fallbeispiel des hl. Alexander', paper presented at 'Christianisierungsgeschichte der Region Oldenburger Münsterland, Cloppenburg, on 22 November 2014. My thanks to Hedwig Röckelein for providing me with a transcript of her lecture. Contrast with Schulze, 'Der Aufstand der Stellinga', p. 67.

the monasteries of Fulda and Prüm, both of which owned substantial tracts of land in Saxony. The notaries of the monastery of Werden, meanwhile, continued to date their charters with reference to Lothar's regnal years up until January 845, despite the fact that the monastery fell squarely within Louis' kingdom.[176]

If the *Stellinga* really had been a violently anti-Christian and anti-elite movement, such continued support would be difficult to fathom. Yet, as I have suggested above, such characterizations are probably false. Lothar, certainly, did not see his support of the *Stellinga* as conflicting with the image of himself that he wished to promote. As Screen has observed, Lothar continued 'to present himself in terms very similar to those that Nithard was anxious to discredit: as the legitimate heir of Louis the Pious; as one concerned with the cost of fraternal conflict and anxious to make suitable amends for it; and as the religious ruler, in a right relationship with God'.[177] Indeed, about a decade after the conclusion of the *Stellinga*, Lothar depicted himself as a champion for Christianity among the Saxons in the letters he wrote in support of Waltbraht's relic translation.[178] His support of the *Stellinga* did not interfere with his role as a Christian ruler.

Nor does it appear to have affected his relations with his followers. The *Stellinga* did, as part of their service to Lothar, take up arms against their 'social superiors', a fact that was widely observed by contemporaries: the *Fulda Annals* characterized the *Stellinga* as 'a most powerful conspiracy of freedmen who endeavoured to overthrow their legitimate masters', while the *Xanten Annals*, after noting that 'the power of the slaves grew rapidly above their masters', described how 'the nobles of that region were greatly weakened and humbled.'[179] Even Nithard recorded how the *Stellinga* 'almost expelled the masters from the realm'.[180] This action may well have been coordinated with Lothar's men specifically against the *fideles* of Louis the German: Prudentius' description of the *Stellinga* as those men 'who had resisted Louis and his *fideles* so fervently' seems to suggest as much.[181] Even more telling in this regard is a passage from Nithard's *Histories*.

Nithard's main account of the *Stellinga* comes near the start of book four. 'Because I consider the deeds of the Saxons to be very important', he

---

[176] *Cartularium Werthinense*, ed. Blok, nos. 58–62, pp. 211–5.

[177] Screen, 'Lothar I and the Frankish civil war', 45.

[178] Rudolf and Meginhard, *Translatio sancti Alexandri*, ed. Pertz, c. 4, pp. 677–8; contrast to Goldberg, *Struggle for Empire*, p. 155.

[179] *Annales Fuldenses*, ed. Kurze, 842, p. 33: 'validissimam conspirationem libertorum legitimos dominos opprimere conantium'; *Annales Xantenses*, ed. Simpson, 841, p. 12: 'potestas servorum valde excreverat super dominos suos,' 'nobiles illius patriae a servis valde afflicti et humiliati sunt'.

[180] Nithard, *Historiae*, eds. Lauer and Glansdorff, IV:2, p. 132: 'dominis e regno poene pulsis'.

[181] *Annales Bertiniani*, eds. Grat, Vielliard, and Clémencet, 842, pp. 42–3: 'qui. . .sibi suisque fidelibus tantopere obstiterant'.

wrote, 'I think that they ought not to be omitted'.[182] Nithard then goes on to give a detailed account of Charlemagne's conversion of the Saxons, the ordering of Saxon society and the division of the Saxon elite in the ensuing civil war. He describes Lothar's involvement with the *Stellinga* and with Harald the Northman, and concludes by voicing Louis' fears that the *Stellinga* might join with the Northmen and Slavs. Historians have largely treated this passage as a digression. All the events Nithard describes, including Lothar's application to the *Stellinga*, are significantly out of sequence with Nithard's chronological narration. Bartmuss thus suggests that this account may have been inserted at this juncture to vilify Lothar further, and thus to justify the putative two-way division of the empire discussed by Charles and Louis in the previous chapter.[183] Crucially, however, Nithard's account of the *Stellinga* was not a digression: he marks out his reasons for including these details at this specific juncture. Immediately before turning to discuss the conversion of the Saxons, Nithard recounts that 'Louis proceeded to Cologne on account of the Saxons'.[184] Similarly, after describing Louis' fears regarding the *Stellinga*, Nithard brings us back to the present day: 'it was for this reason most of all,' he wrote, 'as we have told above, that Louis went to . . .'.[185] At this juncture, however, the copyist breaks off, leaving most of the column-width blank before the final verb, 'adiit'.[186] As only this single manuscript of the text survives, it is difficult to reconstruct the reason behind this omission.[187] Perhaps the scribe wished to signal that the manuscript he was consulting was itself defective at this point; perhaps, as August Gfrörers has suggested, this lacuna (which is one of a handful in the manuscript) represents a deliberate gap on the part of the copyist.[188]

---

[182] Nithard, *Historiae*, eds. Lauer and Glansdorff, IV:2, p. 130: 'Quorum casus, quoniam maximos esse perspicio, praetereundos minime puto.'

[183] Bartmuss, 'Zur Frage der Bedeutung', 115–16.

[184] Nithard, *Historiae*, eds. Lauer and Glansdorff, IV:2, p. 130: 'Lodhuvicus vero Saxonum causa Coloniam petiit.' See also Schulze, 'Der Aufstand der Stellinga', pp. 55, 70–2, 108; Springer, *Die Sachsen*, pp. 264–5.

[185] Nithard, *Historiae*, eds. Lauer and Glansdorff, IV:2, p. 134: 'quamobrem, uti praetulimus, praemaxime . . . adiit'.

[186] Paris, Bibliothèque nationale de France, Lat. 9768, fol 15r. This manuscript is available to consult online.

[187] For the circulation of this text, see J. L. Nelson, 'History-writing at the courts of Louis the Pious and Charles the Bald' in A. Scharer and G. Scheibelreiter (eds.), *Historiographie im frühen Mittelalter* (Veröffentlichungen des Instituts für Österreichische Geschichtsforschung 32) (Vienna: Oldenbourg, 1994), pp. 435–42, here p. 440.

[188] A. F. Gfrörer, *Geschichte der ost- und westfränkischen Carolinger vom Tode Ludwigs des Frommen bis zum Ende Conrads I. (840–918)* (Freiburg: Herder, 1848), p. 63; for this reference, see Schulze, 'Der Aufstand der Stellinga', pp. 71–2.

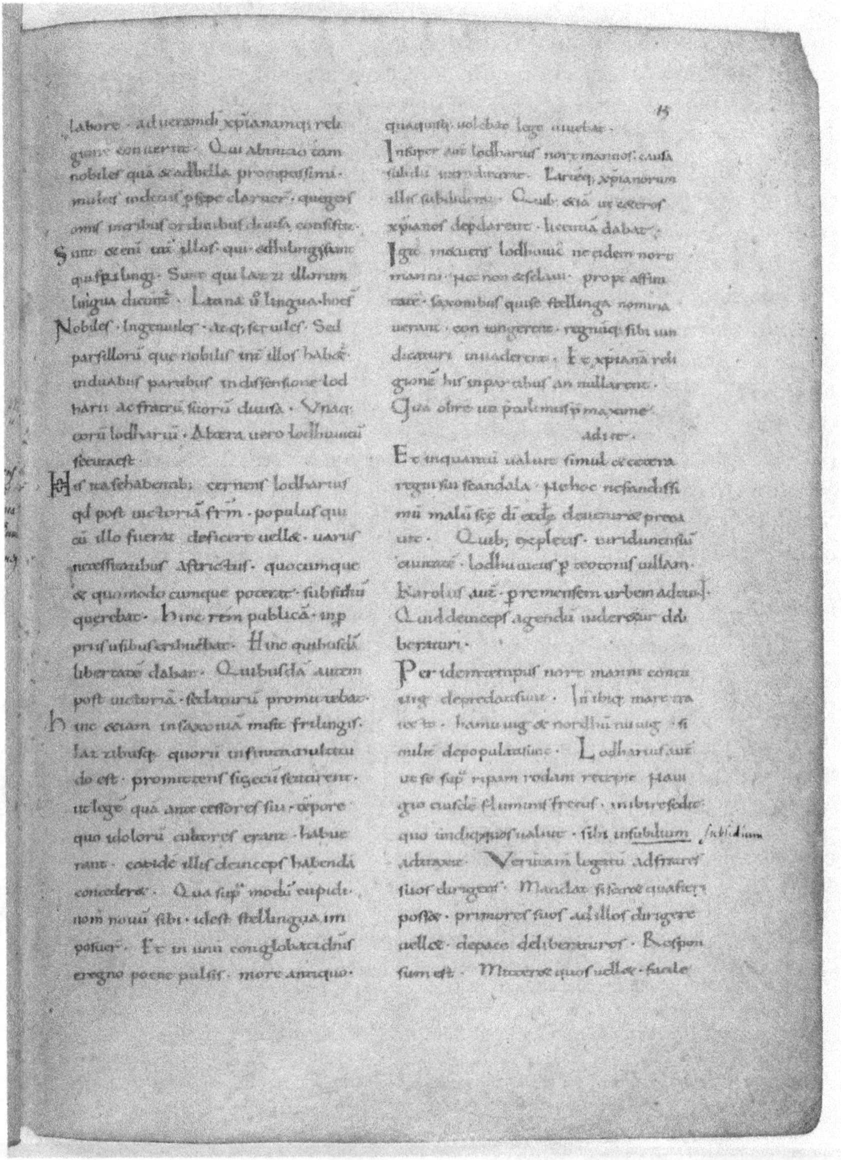

Figure 2.1.   Nithard, *Histories*, in MS Paris, Bibliothèque nationale de France, Lat. 9768, folio 15 recto

Such a lacuna is regrettable. Nevertheless, even in the absence of further detail, it seems clear that Nithard included his description of the *Stellinga* to a specific end, for it was at this juncture that Louis the German first addressed the issue. It is worth noting that Louis' initial response to the *Stellinga* was not to proceed into Saxony and violently quell the movement. He may well have had the opportunity to do so: indeed, Charles returned west 'in order to deal with the affairs of his kingdom' around the same time.[189] Instead, Louis proceeded to Cologne, a city in which Lothar commanded significant support, in order to deal with the *Stellinga*. Unfortunately, it is at this point that the lacuna interrupts Nithard's narration: we do not hear what Louis intended to accomplish vis-à-vis the *Stellinga* in Cologne. One can, however, deduce that there were people in Cologne, perhaps Lothar's leading men, who Louis believed could still influence the *Stellinga*, and that Louis wished to avail himself of all potential aid from such channels before resorting to armed conflict.[190] This is, in itself, telling: it indicates that Lothar's subordinates still wielded, or were perceived as wielding, a substantial degree of control over the actions of the *Stellinga* as late as spring 842. Still more significant is the fact that Louis appears to have seen the *Stellinga* as a group to be dealt with, at least initially, through diplomacy.

Soon after Louis' visit to Cologne, the brothers began, through emissaries, to discuss the terms for a negotiated peace. In June 842 the three brothers met together and a truce was declared, pending a proposal for the equitable division of kingdoms. A little over a year later, the precise terms of such a division were agreed upon and formalized with the Treaty of Verdun, thereby creating the East, Middle and West Frankish kingdoms.

In the meantime, however, not everyone was satisfied with the truce. Pippin II of Aquitaine, who realized that his interests had been disregarded by his erstwhile ally Lothar, sent men to attack one of Charles' followers, Egfrid, Count of Toulouse.[191] Likewise in Saxony, the *Stellinga* continued to agitate, although their reasons for doing so are unknown.[192] Perhaps they were emboldened by their previous success and wished to remain on the land they had claimed from Louis' *fideles*, or perhaps they feared that their wartime actions against Louis' *fideles* would be avenged regardless of their subsequent conduct. Their actions bear

---

[189] Nithard, *Historiae*, eds. Lauer and Glansdorff, IV:2, p. 130: 'regnum suum ordinaturus'.
[190] See also Gfrörer, *Geschichte der ost- und westfränkischen Carolinger*, p. 40. On a similar note, it might also be observed that immediately before Louis proceeded to Saxony in order to dispense justice in 852, he held talks with some of Lothar's leading men in Cologne: see *Annales Fuldenses*, ed. Kurze, 852, p. 42.
[191] Nithard, *Historiae*, eds. Lauer and Glansdorff, IV:4, p. 142.   [192] *Ibid*, IV:4, p. 142.

productive comparison to the eleventh-century peasants described in Lampert of Hersfeld, who, following peace negotiations in 1074, took it into their own hands to destroy the royal Harzburg because they feared the king's eventual reprisals.[193]

The temerity of the *Stellinga*, like that of the later Saxon peasants, was swiftly avenged. After holding an assembly in Salz that August, Louis proceeded to Saxony, where, according to Nithard, he 'nobly curbed the mutineers who called themselves *Stellinga*, as has been said above, with lawful massacre'.[194] The more thorough account of his actions at this stage is provided by the *Annals of Saint Bertin*, which record how

Louis, having scoured all of Saxony, subjugated with violence and terror all those who had hitherto opposed him, so that, having seized all the leaders of such a great impiety, who had almost left the Christian faith, and who had resisted Louis and his *fideles* so fervently. He punished 140 with beheading, hanged fourteen, crippled countless others by chopping off their limbs, and left no one opposing him in any way.[195]

Louis' actions, however punitive, did not have the desired effect. Later, in the winter of 842/3, Nithard describes how the *Stellinga* 'rebelled again in Saxony against their masters but, having joined in battle, were struck down with great slaughter'.[196] This is the last time that the *Stellinga* appear on the historical record. The reasons behind their continued agitation are unknown.

The *Stellinga* may have originated as a guild which came together in the practice of customary judgement; during the early stages of the civil war, they may have coordinated their efforts with Lothar and his leading men. But by the end of summer 842, matters had changed. Through their violation of the truce, and without the legitimation provided by

---

[193] Lampert, *Annales*, ed. O. Holder-Egger, *MGH SRG* 38 (Hanover: Hahn, 1894), 1074, pp. 183–5. For this comparison, cf. Depreux, 'Défense d'un statut', p. 107; Eggert, 'Rebelliones servorum', 1162–3; Goldberg, 'Popular revolt', 499; Leyser, *Communications and Power: The Gregorian Revolution*, p. 55; Müller-Mertens, 'Der Stellingaaufstand', 820.

[194] Nithard, *Historiae*, eds. Lauer and Glansdorff, IV:4, p. 142: 'seditiosos, qui se, uti praefatum est, Stellinga nominaverunt, nobiliter, legali tamen cede, compescuit.'

[195] *Annales Bertiniani*, eds. Grat, Vielliard, and Clémencet, 842, pp. 42–3: 'Hlodouuicus, peragrata omni Saxonia, cunctos sibi eatenus obsistentes ui atque terrore ita perdomuit ut, comprehensis omnibus auctoribus tantae impietatis qui et christianam fidem pene reliquerant et sibi suisque fidelibus tantopere obsisterant, centum quadraginta capitis amputatione plecteret, quatuordecim patibulo suspenderet, innumeros membrorum praecisione debiles redderet nullumque sibi ulla-tenus refragantem relinqueret.' See also above, p. 103, for the suggestion that these different punishments may relate to different legal categories; see further McComb, 'Each by the law of his choosing'.

[196] Nithard, *Historiae*, eds. Lauer and Glansdorff, IV:6, pp. 152–4: 'Stellinga in Saxonia contra dominos suos iterum rebellarunt, sed praelio commisso nimia cede prostrati sunt'.

Lothar's support, the *Stellinga* had transgressed the acceptable limits of Carolingian social norms. They were in open revolt. This violation not only prompted Louis the German's violent crackdown; it also decisively shaped the memory, and subsequent historiographical depiction, of the *Stellinga*. It is to this, the historiographical afterlife of the *Stellinga*, that I shall now turn.

AFTER THE *STELLINGA*

The surviving accounts of the *Stellinga* are uniformly negative. Contemporaries went out of their way to paint the *Stellinga* as a group of illegitimate, subversive actors: in the words of Nithard, the participants were 'mutineers', who were eventually quelled 'with lawful massacre'.[197] When they dared to rise again, they were massacred, 'and thus', Nithard remarked, 'they who presumed to rise without authority perish by that authority'.[198] Both Nithard and Prudentius heavily implied that the *Stellinga* were tainted by pagan observance. This was an accusation intended to tarnish the movement and, by association, Lothar. Even the *Fulda Annals* and the *Xanten Annals*, both of which are largely favourable to Lothar in this period, are absolute in their condemnation of the *Stellinga*. The *Fulda Annals* described the *Stellinga* as a 'most powerful conspiracy', whereas the *Xanten Annals* recounted how the participants 'seized the name *Stellinga* for themselves, and committed many irrational acts'.[199] Louis' actions are presented in a highly positive light: according to the annalist, he 'nobly overthrew the *servi* (slaves) of the Saxons, who had been arrogantly raised up, and restored them to their proper condition'.[200] He was right to reestablish the proper order of society.

These accounts may be near-contemporary, but they were all presumably written with the benefit of hindsight. The fourth book of Nithard's *Histories*, in which his accounts of the *Stellinga* are to be found, goes up to March 843: if indeed, as seems most likely, the fourth book was framed as a cohesive whole, then Nithard must have written about the *Stellinga*

---

[197] *Ibid*, IV:4, p. 142: 'seditiosos', 'legali tamen cede'. See also the perceptive comments of McComb, 'Each by the law of his choosing'.

[198] Nithard, *Historiae*, eds. Lauer and Glansdorff, IV:6, p. 154: 'ac sic auctoritate interiit, quod sine auctoritate surgere praesumpsit.'

[199] *Annales Fuldenses*, ed. Kurze, 842, p. 33: 'validissimam conspirationem'; *Annales Xantenses*, ed. Simpson, 841, p. 12: 'nomen sibi usurpaverunt Stellingas et multa inrationabilia conmiserunt.'

[200] *Annales Xantenses*, ed. Simpson, 842, p. 13: 'servos Saxonum superbe elatos nobiliter afflixit et ad propriam naturam restituit.' See further McComb, 'Each by the law of his choosing'.

well after the final uprising. Recent work on annalistic writing has argued that authors did not necessarily, or even usually, record events on an annual basis.[201] One cannot assume that an entry describing a particular year was written in that same year. Especially when there was unrest – as there was, most notably, during the civil war – annalists might pause, resuming their narration only when it had become eminently clear in which direction the wind was blowing. The overtly negative depictions of the *Stellinga* can thus be explained by the conclusion of the movement, for, after the truce in June 842, the *Stellinga* went into open revolt. They were remembered accordingly.

After this flush of near-contemporary writing on the *Stellinga*, the source base dries up. No further references are made to the *Stellinga* by name in the entirety of the early Middle Ages; seemingly no effort is made to employ their memory, a fact which may further add to the conventional image of the *Stellinga* as a fleeting aberration. Frankish authors directed their attention elsewhere. So too did Carolingian kings. Following the surprisingly prominent role which Saxony played in the civil war, the region once again dropped off the map, at least as far as central politics were concerned. Following his father's example, Louis the German only visited Saxony three times in the course of his thirty-six-year reign: in 842, when he suppressed the *Stellinga*; in 845, when he convened a general assembly in Saxony; and finally in 852, when he settled a number of lawsuits.[202]

While Louis the German appears to have been less personally involved in Saxon affairs later in his life, the same cannot be said of his second son, Louis the Younger, who was made heir to his father's kingship in parts of East Francia, Saxony and Thuringia in the Division of Frankfurt in 865.[203] The extent of his authority during his father's lifetime is debatable; while he probably did not exercise complete control, the frequent appearance of paired Saxon and Thuringian forces in the annals, placed alongside Louis the Younger's own appeal to Saxon and Thuringian forces in his attempted rebellion of 866, suggests that he wielded a position of military authority in the area.[204] His marriage to the Saxon

---

[201] See here the comments of McKitterick, *History and Memory*, p. 102.

[202] For his actions in 842, see above, p. 128; for the 845 assembly, see *Annales Fuldenses*, ed. Kurze, 845, p. 35; for the 852 episode, see above, pp. 95–6. See also Ehlers, *Die Integration Sachsens*, p. 304. For Louis' role in Saxony more generally, see K. H. Krüger, 'Die ältern Sachsen als Franken. Zum Besuch des Kaisers Arnulf 889 im Kloster Corvey', *WZ*, 151/152 (2001/2002), 225–44, here 230–2.

[203] Goldberg, *Struggle for Empire*, pp. 275–6.

[204] For Louis the Younger's appeal, see *Annales Fuldenses*, ed. Kurze, 866, p. 64; for the further references to Saxon and Thuringian forces, see *Annales Bertiniani*, eds. Grat, Vielliard and Clémencet, 867, p. 136; *Annales Fuldenses*, ed. Kurze, 869, 872, pp. 68, 75. See also Bachrach

Liutgard – who was a member of the elite Liudolfinger family, a branch of which would later rise to power as the Ottonian dynasty – further points towards his attempts to shore up support in the area during his time as subking.[205] Following Louis the German's death in 876, Louis the Younger acceded as king of the Franks and Saxons. The significance of this development has been much heralded: Matthias Becher in particular has granted it a decisive role in Saxon political development.[206] Yet, as Sören Kaschke cautioned, the evidence for such development under Louis the Younger is lacking.[207] Louis did not long survive his father: he died following an unspecified illness in 882. He was succeeded by his brother, Charles the Fat, who would, in 884, be left as sole emperor over all Carolingian territory. Despite his wider dominion, Charles appears to have forged close relationships with Saxon religious institutions, some of which remained loyal to the emperor right up until his 887 deposition: his last two (dated) charters were granted to Saxon recipients.[208] Charles' own successor – his illegitimate nephew, Arnulf – likewise pursued a relationship with select Saxon institutions, and in particular with the monastery of Corvey.[209]

In the background of these high political realignments, Saxon society continued to develop along much the same lines as those laid out earlier in the chapter. The civil wars and, in particular, the *Stellinga* created the same possibilities for advancement and degradation as had been the case both during and after the Saxon wars; it is in this context of these continuing conflicting claims that we should interpret Louis the German's 852 trip to Saxony, on which he settled the cases and lawsuits

---

and Bachrach, 'Saxon military revolution', 205–6; Becher, *Rex, Dux und Gens*, pp. 136–41; Goldberg, *Struggle for Empire*, pp. 276–9.

[205] For the marriage to Liutgard, see *D LJ*, ed. P. Kehr, *MGH, Die Urkunden Ludwigs des Deutschen, Karlmanns und Ludwigs der Jüngeren* (Berlin: Weidemann, 1934) no. 4, p. 338; see also Becher, *Rex, Dux und Gens*, pp. 45–6, 141; Ehlers, *Die Integration Sachsens*, pp. 159, 310; Goldberg, *Struggle for Empire*, p. 278.

[206] For this, see especially Becher, *Rex, Dux und Gens*, pp. 110, 136–58. See also J. Semmler, 'Francia Saxoniaque oder Die ostfränkische Reichsteilung von 865/76 und die Folgen', *DA*, 46(2) (1990), 337–74; contrast to W. Eggert, '"Franken und Sachsen" bei Notker, Widukind und anderen. Zu einem Aufsatz von Josef Semmler' in A. Scharer and G. Scheibelreiter (eds.), *Historiographie im frühen Mittelalter* (Veröffentlichungen des Instituts für Österreichische Geschichtsforschung 32) (Vienna: Oldenbourg, 1994), pp. 514–30.

[207] S. Kaschke, 'Sachsen, Franken und die Nachfolgeregelung Ludwigs des Deutschen: *unus cum eis populus efficerentur*?', *NJ*, 79 (2007), 147–86; see also Krüger, 'Die ältern Sachsen als Franken', 233; W. Metz, *Das karolingische Reichsgut: eine verfassungs- und verwaltungsgeschichtliche Untersuchung* (Berlin: W. de Gruyter, 1960), p. 127.

[208] *D Karl*, ed. P. Kehr, *MGH, Die Urkunden Karls III* (Berlin: Weidemann, 1937), nos. 168–9, pp. 271–4.

[209] *D Arn*, ed. P. Kehr, *MGH, Die Urkunden Arnolfs* (Berlin: Weidemann, 1940), nos. 3, 28, 60, 155, pp. 5–8, 41–2, 87–8, 235–6.

which had been brought to his attention.[210] Perhaps unsurprisingly, it was in this period, following the suppression of the *Stellinga*, that elite formation appears to have gathered pace. Elites began not only to patronize but also, in ever greater numbers, to found an array of Saxon religious institutions, and particularly female monasteries. Saxon elites are further attested as forming advantageous marriage alliances with Frankish elites and similarly, perhaps partly as a result of such alliances, serving an array of rival Carolingian kings. Here, Cobbo's service to Charles the Bald and Waltbraht's service to Lothar come particularly to mind.[211]

Following the civil war, Carolingian kings may have treated Saxony as a peripheral concern. Yet by all indications, Saxons, and especially elite Saxons, were deeply invested in Carolingian rule. Saxon hagiography from this period portrayed elite Saxons and Saxon institutions specifically in terms of their extremely positive (and often ahistorical) connections to Charlemagne and later Carolingian kings. Saxon loyalty to, and enthusiasm for, Carolingian kingship would continue well into the Carolingians' final years. While the deposition and death of Charles the Fat in 887/8 marked the end of the Carolingian hegemony, it is notable that his successor, Arnulf, was the first and only contemporary Carolingian ruler to receive panegyrical treatment from a Saxon author, the so-called Saxon Poet.[212] The Saxons were, and continued to be, model Carolingian subjects. They persevered in their fidelity long after 888.

In Chapter 4 I shall explore at greater length how, in this period, Saxon authors and those writing works commissioned for, or by, Saxon institutions revised and rewrote a narrative of Saxon history, with particular attention paid to Saxon relations with Carolingian rulers.[213] Here, and for the remainder of this chapter, I should like to consider the effects of the *Stellinga* on such texts. As discussed above, there are no later reports of the *Stellinga*: following our four near-contemporary witnesses, silence prevails. There are, however, indications that the

---

[210] See above, pp. 95–6.

[211] For Cobbo's service to Charles the Bald, see *Translatio sanctae Pusinnae*, ed. R. Wilmans, *Die Kaiserurkunden der Provinz Westfalen, 777–1313*, 2 vols. (Münster: F. Regensberg, 1867), vol. I, pp. 539–46, here c. 3, p. 542. For Waltbraht's service to Lothar, see Rudolf and Meginhard, *Translatio sancti Alexandri*, ed. Pertz, c. 4, pp. 676–8; see also above, pp. 68–9, 120, 123.

[212] For the Saxon Poet's treatment of Arnulf, see Poeta Saxo, *Annalium de gestis Caroli magni imperatoris libri V*, ed. Winterfeld, V, lines 123–48, 415–24, pp. 58–9, 65; see also I. Rembold, 'The Poeta Saxo at Paderborn: episcopal authority and Carolingian rule in late ninth-century Saxony', *EME*, 21(2) (2013), 169–96.

[213] See below, pp. 235–42.

Stellinga left a legacy. Following the *Stellinga*, a number of sources can be seen to reflect on the nature of the 'orders' in Saxon society and on the importance of paternal laws and Saxon freedom. Such references speak to ways in which Saxon society developed following the *Stellinga*, both in terms of the perception of that society and also in terms of actual shifts, such as the gathering pace of elite formation, although the latter is more difficult to demonstrate in practice.

Let us turn quickly to Saxon laws and freedoms. The *Stellinga* may have been personally disavowed, and their activism, as members of the 'lower orders', condemned; however, the ancestral laws for which they fought did not suffer the same historical ignominy. As Faulkner has recently observed, references to Saxon laws, here taken to refer to more than simply the surviving written laws, feature heavily in narrative sources composed in, or about, Saxony from the mid-ninth century onwards.[214] Interestingly, with the exception of reports on the *Stellinga*, such references to Saxon and often Old Saxon, pre-Christian laws appear to be uniformly positive.

Many of these references have been discussed above, such as the central role which law-giving and judgement played at the ahistorical Marklo assembly, as described in the *Old Life of Lebuin*; Rudolf's laudatory description of Old Saxon laws ('the best laws . . . the most advantageous and worthy probity of customs'); and finally the treatment accorded to Old Saxon law included in the Saxon Poet's similarly ahistorical 'Peace of Salz'.[215] The last of these is worth quoting at greater length: as the Poet wrote, under the conditions of the peace, 'the Saxons were permitted to enjoy their own legates, their paternal laws, and the honour of liberty, under judges whom the king would assign to them'.[216] The Poet, then, accepted that Charlemagne had conceded to the Saxons the right to observe their own laws, and moreover connected such laws to the liberty (*libertas*) of the Saxons. As Karl Leyser noted, both concepts had a long afterlife in later historiography, resurfacing in particular in accounts of the eleventh-century Saxon Rebellion.[217] The laws and liberty for which the *Stellinga* fought remained a rallying cry long after the suppression of the movement.

---

[214] Faulkner, *Law and Authority*, pp. 46–50.

[215] Rudolf and Meginhard, *Translatio sancti Alexandri*, ed. Pertz, c. 2, p. 675: 'Legibus . . . optimis utebantur . . . multa utilia atque . . . honesta in morum probitate'. See also above, p. 113.

[216] Poeta Saxo, *Annalium de gestis Caroli magni imperatoris libri V*, ed. Winterfeld, IV, lines 109–11, p. 48: 'Tum sub iudicibus, quos rex inponeret ipsis / Legatisque suis permissi legibus uti / Saxones patriis et libertatis honore'.

[217] Leyser, *Communications and Power: The Gregorian Revolution*, pp. 51–67, here especially p. 53.

The 'Ordering' of Saxon Society

The degree of attention paid to the 'ordering' of Saxon society in the aftermath of the *Stellinga* is less frequently discussed. Here, it is important to note that prior to the *Stellinga* there was no clear conception of Saxony as an order-based society.[218] To be sure, the Carolingian-codified Saxon capitularies and law code contained legal categories, which were roughly similar despite some differences in terminology: all three texts used the labels *nobiles/nobiliores* (nobles), *ingenui/liberi* (freemen) and *liti* (half-freemen).[219] References to legal and tenurial categories also surface in various cartularies connected to Saxony in the period leading up to the *Stellinga*. Yet there is little evidence that society was perceived as being structured primarily in reference to these legal categories: the effect of these normative texts appears to have been rather limited, and the sheer variety of language used and relationships described in the wider body of evidences belies a homogeneous Saxon order-based system. Even in the reports describing the *Stellinga*, there is no sense of a society predominately organized by order or legal status. The *Xanten Annals* describe the *Stellinga* in terms of their relationship to the men they fought: they were *servi* (slaves) who rose against their *domini* (masters).[220] Similarly, Rudolf of Fulda, in the *Fulda Annals*, depicts *liberti* (freedmen) who fought their masters.[221] Prudentius does not even mention the status of the participants.

Instead, it is Nithard who first suggests that Saxon society was organized around a threefold division of the populace: 'the *gens* is divided into three orders: and indeed they are called among those ones *edhilingui*, *frilingi*, and *lazzi*, that is, in Latin, *nobiles, ingenuiles,* and *serviles*'.[222] It is uncertain how widely Nithard's *Histories* circulated: as noted earlier, only one early medieval manuscript survives, although there is reason to suppose that the work was more widely available.[223] The Saxon evidence could be seen to corroborate a wider diffusion, for in the decades after the *Stellinga*, Saxon society is repeatedly depicted as being divided into three or − if slaves are included − four orders, in terms somewhat

---

[218] Contrast to Goldberg, 'Popular revolt', 470–1.

[219] *Capitulatio de partibus Saxoniae*, ed. von Schwerin, cc. 15, 19–21, pp. 39–41; *Capitulare Saxonicum*, ed. von Schwerin, cc. 3, 5, pp. 46–7; *Lex Saxonum*, ed. von Schwerin, cc. 1, 14, 16–18, 20, 36, 64–5 pp. 17, 21–3, 26–7, 33.

[220] *Annales Xantenses*, ed. Simpson, 841, p. 12.   [221] *Annales Fuldenses*, ed. Kurze, 842, p. 33.

[222] Nithard, *Historiae*, eds. Lauer and Glansdorff, IV:2, p. 130: 'Que gens omnis in tribus ordinibus divisa constitit: sunt etenim inter illos qui edhilingi, sunt qui frilingi, sunt qui lazzi illorum lingua dicuntur, latina vero lingua hoc sunt nobiles, ingenuiles, atque serviles'; cf. Wood, 'Beyond satraps and ostriches', p. 277.

[223] Nelson, 'History-writing', p. 440. See also above, p. 125.

reminiscent of Nithard's description. Such descriptions are to be found in the *Translation of Saint Alexander*, the *Old Life of Lebuin*, the *Second Life of Lebuin*, and finally in Widukind of Corvey's *Deeds of the Saxons*. These literary depictions of 'ordered' Saxon society may thus be seen, in part, as a result of the *Stellinga*.[224]

Such an interpretation turns conventional wisdom on its head, particularly with regard to the *Old Life of Lebuin*. Scholars have largely viewed this text as a window onto Old Saxon society, and thus have used it to elucidate the causes of the *Stellinga*. This *Life* reports how all of the non-servile orders of Saxon society – nobles, freemen and half-freemen – came together at the Marklo assembly each year, where all decisions were made for the following years. According to this interpretation, once Charlemagne outlawed the assembly, the lower orders lost their political voice; Martin Lintzel further argued that the elite actually sided with Charlemagne during the conquest in order to increase their political dominance.[225] The lower orders, then, were subjected to deteriorating conditions until they rallied together to form the *Stellinga*, largely in order to restore the Marklo assembly and thus their political autonomy.[226]

This explanation has, however, been convincingly undercut by Matthias Springer's repeated arguments against the use of the *Old Life of Lebuin* to describe pre-conquest conditions. He considered the *Old Life of Lebuin* to have been composed after 840, and most likely in the period of 899 to 917; it was therefore written at least seventy years, and more plausibly a century and half, after the events it purportedly describes.[227] The author appears to have been ill-informed about Lebuin and was consequently reliant upon Liudger's *Life of Gregory*, the *Second Life of Saint Liudger* and, most of all, Bede's description of the two late seventh-century missionaries to Saxony, the 'Two Ewalds', in his *Ecclesiastical History*.[228] Any independent material in the *Life* is most likely

---

[224] I have benefited from a very helpful discussion with Robert Flierman on this subject. See further Faulkner, *Law and Authority*, pp. 56–8; Springer, *Die Sachsen*, p. 249.

[225] Lintzel, 'Die Unterwerfung Sachsens', pp. 95–127.

[226] For the general contours of this interpretation, see especially Goldberg, 'Popular revolt', 470–80.

[227] Springer, 'Lebuins Lebensbeschreibung', pp. 223–39; see further Springer, *Die Sachsen*, pp. 134–51; cf. Wood, 'Beyond satraps and ostriches', pp. 277–8; contrast to Lintzel, 'Die Vita Lebuini antiqua', pp. 235–62. See also above, pp. 69–71.

[228] Liudger, *Vita sancti Gregorii*, ed. O. Holder-Egger, *MGH SS* 15:1 (Hanover: Hahn, 1887); *Vita secunda sancti Liudgeri*, ed. Freise; Bede, *Historica Ecclesiastica*, ed. C. Plummer, *Venerabilis Baedae opera historica*, 2 vols. (Oxford: Clarendon, 1896), vol. I, V:10, pp. 299–301. See also Faulkner, *Law and Authority*, p. 55. It is possible that the author of the *Vita Lebuini anitqua* drew directly from Altfrid's *Vita sancti Liudgeri*, and that the *Vita secunda sancti Liudgeri* drew upon both Altfrid's *Vita* and the *Vita Lebuini antiqua*, but it is more straightforward to argue that the author of the

invented, and this includes its account of the 'general Saxon assembly' at Marklo, which, although prefaced by a borrowing from Bede, is otherwise unattested. Springer's critique is extremely persuasive on its own terms, but there is yet another wrinkle to be added: namely, the *Old Life of Lebuin* can be seen as a self-conscious attempt to explain retrospectively the causes behind the *Stellinga*, and as such, testifies to the memory of *Stellinga*.[229] So too may the other sources which discuss the 'ordered' nature of Saxon society, all of which post-date the *Stellinga*, be used as evidence for the effects of the *Stellinga*.

The first author after Nithard to put forward an 'ordered' vision of society was Rudolf of Fulda, who composed his sections of the *Translation of Saint Alexander* for Waltbraht, the loyal *fidelis* of Lothar, sometime before 865.[230] He describes how in the period before the conquest, 'that *gens* consists of four different groups, namely *nobiles* (nobles), *liberi* (freemen), *liberti* (freedmen), and *servi* (slaves). It is established in the laws', he continued, 'that no person may transcend the boundaries of their group in marriage, but that a nobleman may marry a noblewoman; a freeman, a freewoman; a freedman, a freedwoman, and a slave, a slave-girl. If indeed anyone marries a woman who is ill-matched in the excellence of her birth, he may compensate her family with the forfeiture of his life'.[231] Many have interpreted this passage as having been drawn from Tacitus' *Germania*, which Rudolf drew upon extensively in his work. Certainly, his vocabulary appears to have been influenced by Tacitus, who uses the terms *servi*, *liberti*, *ingenui* and *nobiles* in a chapter discussing slavery.[232] Even if Rudolf derived his vocabulary from Tacitus,[233] however, his fundamental conception of Saxon society as being divided into well-defined orders is not to be found in his exemplar. His characterization of

---

Vita Lebuini antiqua simply consulted the *Vita secunda sancti Liudgeri*. For the dating of the text, see Springer, 'Lebuins Lebensbeschreibung', pp. 224–5.

[229] See especially Landwehr, 'Die Liten in den altsächsischen Rechtsquellen', here p. 123; cf. Faulkner, *Law and Authority*, pp. 56–7; Wenskus, 'Die ständische Entwicklung', p. 609.

[230] See also the comments of Goldberg, *Struggle for Empire*, pp. 178–9; Leyser, *Communications and Power: The Gregorian Revolution*, p. 55; see also Last, 'Niedersachsen', 605–6.

[231] Rudolf and Meginhard, *Translatio sancti Alexandri*, ed. Pertz, c. 1, p. 675: 'Quatuor igitur differentiis gens illa constitit, nobilium scilicet et liberorum, libertorum atque servorum. Et id legibus firmatum, ut nulla pars in copulandis coniugiis propriae sortis terminos transferat, sed nobilis nobilem ducat uxorem, et liber liberam, libertus coniungatur libertae, et servus ancillae. Si vero quispiam horum sibi non congruentem et genere prestantiorem duxerit uxorem, cum vitae suae damno componat.' For this passage see also Becher, *Rex, Dux und Gens*, p. 34; Wood, 'Beyond satraps and ostriches', p. 281.

[232] Tacitus Cornelius, *Germania*, ed. A. Önnerfors, *De origine et situ Germanorum liber* (Stuttgart: Teubner, 1983), c. 25, p. 17.

[233] Bartmuss, 'Zur Frage der Bedeutung', 114; Epperlein, 'Sachsen im frühen Mittelalter', 193.

marriage laws, meanwhile, reinforced the rigid nature of these divisions.[234] Such divisions were of newfound relevance: in the words of Eric Goldberg, Rudolf 'defended the lineage, valor, and Christian faith of the Saxon nobility and attempted to free them from any association with the Stellinga rebellion'.[235] The 'ordering' of people had become, at least to Rudolf, essential to the understanding of Saxon society.

The next iteration of Saxony's tripartite division came in the *Old Life of Lebuin*. Its anonymous author also strove to describe Old Saxon society: in a passage that has been amply used by modern historians, he wrote that

'The Old Saxons did not have a king, but' appointed 'satraps' over each *pagus*, and it was their custom to convene one general assembly each year in the middle of Saxony next to the Weser in a place called Marklo. There all the satraps came together, along with twelve *nobiles* (nobles) chosen from each *pagus* and an equal number of *liberi* (freemen) and *lati* (half-freemen). There they renewed their laws, judged particular cases, and decided by common counsel what would be done that year, whether in war or in peace.[236]

Here, as Thomas Faulkner has noted, the emphasis is different from that found in Rudolf's account: the author includes these categories not in order to delineate their separation, but rather in order to reflect upon on their cooperation and joint political agency at the Marklo assembly.[237] I am inclined to see this as an ahistorical attempt to rationalize the *Stellinga* and their motivations. Here, these motivations were cast as the desire to recover their political agency, and specifically their role in law-giving and justice, which had been lost in the conquest. Certainly, the *Second Life of Lebuin*, composed by Hucbald of St-Amand sometime

---

[234] Rudolf appears to have been somewhat unique in his description of marriage laws. There is, to be sure, a chapter in the *Capitulatio de partibus Saxoniae* which imposes different fines, according to legal status, for illegal marriages, but this may also be interpreted as a prohibition of consanguineous marriage: see *Capitulatio de partibus Saxoniae*, ed. von Schwerin, c. 20, pp. 40–1. See also Faulkner, *Law and Authority*, p. 58; Last, 'Niedersachsen', pp. 605–6.

[235] Goldberg, *Struggle for Empire*, p. 179.

[236] *Vita sancti Lebuini antiqua*, ed. Hofmeister, c. 4, p. 793: '"Regem antiqui Saxones non habebant, sed" per pagos "satrapas" constitutos: morisque erat, ut semel in anno generale consilium agerent in media Saxonia iuxta fluvium Wisuram ad locum qui dicitur Marklo. Solebant ibi omnes in unum satrapae convenire, ex pagis quoque singulis duodecim electi nobiles totidemque liberi totidemque lati. Renovabant ibi leges, praecipuas causas adiudicabant et, quid per annum essent acturi sive in bello sive in pace, communi consilio statuebant.' The author's borrowings from Bede have been set within quotation marks: compare with Bede, *Historica Ecclesiastica*, ed. Plummer, vol. I, V:10, pp. 299–300. See also Wood, 'Beyond satraps and ostriches', pp. 277–8.

[237] Faulkner, *Law and Authority*, pp. 54–8.

between 917/8 and 930, places it explicitly in this context. Notably, Hucbald expanded this passage, adding an additional explanation of Saxon society plucked directly from Nithard's account of the *Stellinga*: 'that *gens* was, and remains even up to this day, divided into three orders. Indeed, these orders are called *edhilingui*, *frilingi*, and *lazzi* in their language, which in Latin can be expressed as *nobiles*, *ingenuiles*, and *serviles*'.[238] Hucbald uses precisely the same vocabulary, both in Old Saxon and in Latin, that Nithard had employed nearly a century earlier.[239] The significance of this borrowing should not be understated: Hucbald saw Nithard's extended explanation of the *Stellinga* as relevant to the Marklo assembly, and vice versa.

The final reference to the 'ordering' of Saxon society can be found in Widukind of Corvey's *Deeds of the Saxons*, written in the mid-tenth century. Widukind recounted a legendary war between the Saxons and the Thuringians in which the Saxons emerged triumphant and in control of the territory that would become 'Saxony'. As a result of this war, he wrote, 'a part of the land was given to their friends and freed allies, and the rest of that driven-out people was condemned to tribute. Consequently up to today the Saxon people is divided threefold by birth and by law, besides a servile condition'.[240] Like Rudolf, Widukind sought to accentuate, and moreover to explain historically, divisions between the different orders of Saxon society.

In the century after Nithard's composition, therefore, the tripartite (or, on one occasion, quadripartite) division of Saxon society recurs as a central motif in four different texts. These references could be dismissed as reflecting little more than a popular literary trope. Yet only one of these texts, namely Hucbald's *Second Life of Lebuin*, appears to have been directly dependent upon Nithard's work, and the variety displayed in all of these reports suggests a certain degree of independence. These references are better interpreted as explanations of, and responses to, the *Stellinga*, or, at the very least, as reflections of shifts in the perception of

---

[238] Hucbald, *Vita secunda sancti Lebuini*, ed. G. H. Pertz, *MGH SS* 2 (Hanover: Hahn, 1829), p. 361: 'erat gens ipsa, sicuti nunc usque consistit, ordine tripartito divisa. Sunt denique ibi, qui illorum lingua edlingi, sunt qui frilingi, sunt qui lassi dicuntur, quod in latina sonat lingua, nobiles, ingenuiles, atque serviles'.

[239] Springer, *Die Sachsen*, p. 147.

[240] Widukind of Corvey, *Res Gestae Saxonicae*, eds. Hirsch and Lohmann, I:14, p. 23: 'Parte quoque agrorum cum amicis auxiliariis vel manumissis distributa, reliquias pulsae gentis tributis condempnaverunt. Unde usque hodie gens Saxonica triformi genere ac lege preter conditionem servilem dividitur.' For this passage, see also Lintzel, 'Die Stände der deutschen Volksrechte', p. 370; Wenskus, 'Die ständische Entwicklung', pp. 600–2; Wood, 'Beyond satraps and ostriches', pp. 284–5.

Saxon society which followed the revolt. These texts construct memories of Old Saxony in which the orders of society played a key role, whether they cooperated and undertook joint political action, as in the case of the two *Lives* of Lebuin, or if they were strictly delineated and separate throughout Saxon history, as in the case of Rudolf and Widukind. Such constructed memories were presumably intended to reflect and explain not only the *Stellinga* but also contemporary circumstances: indeed, both Hucbald and Widukind state that these divisions continued to have effect in their respective periods.

Literary characterizations of orders thus sought both to reflect and to shape conceptions of Saxon society following the *Stellinga* more broadly. In the period following the suppression of the *Stellinga*, as clearer distinctions emerged between elite and sub-elite actors, the presence, or historical absence, of social and legal hierarchy became an integral part of the depiction of Saxon society.

★ ★ ★

The *Stellinga* movement was not simply a revolt which took advantage of the dissension provided by the civil war between the sons of Louis the Pious: on the contrary, it was intimately involved in these struggles. Before the outbreak of the civil war, the *Stellinga* may be best understood as a guild whose participants were involved in the practice of customary law. The *Stellinga* took up arms in response to an appeal by Lothar, who in return granted the Saxons a reasonable and achievable concession. Crucially, this was not the return to pagan observance which Nithard and Prudentius imply; the group's participants, although drawn from the lower orders, were recognized as legitimate military actors. Thereafter, the *Stellinga* coordinated their efforts with Lothar and his *fideles*, among whom were numbered many members of the Saxon elite. All of this changed, however, when Lothar began to discuss terms of peace with his brothers in June 842. While hostilities elsewhere ceased, the *Stellinga*, emboldened by their success, continued to agitate in Saxony. The *Stellinga*'s continued resistance provoked Louis' reaction in August of that same year, and when they rebelled again, either in late 842 or early 843, they were put down easily, without royal assistance.

Just as the *Stellinga*'s goals were more modest than has previously been supposed, so too were their effects less pronounced. They did not result in the creation of a unified East Frankish elite: on the contrary, Lothar was able to retain the support of East Frankish and even Saxon *fideles* long after the conclusion of the civil war. Yet the *Stellinga* did leave some trace. After the conclusion of the revolt, there are signs that Saxon society became increasingly stratified, and literary sources betray a much clearer demarcation of the orders of Saxony, previously only visible in Carolingian-codified legal sources. The revolt, as reflected in Saxon hagiographical and historical writing, exerted a lasting influence on social attitudes.

PART II

Conversion and Christianization

Chapter 3

FOUNDERS AND PATRONS

'In the year of the Lord's incarnation DCCC[...........], the aforementioned caesar [Charlemagne], in order to gild his reputation for virtue and good works, in one day founded eight bishoprics in Saxony, now surrendered to Christ, and arranged ecclesiastical districts for them.'[1] So wrote Thietmar of Merseburg in his own hand, pausing over the precise date of foundation. Preferring to leave his options open, he left room for twelve additional letters before continuing with his narration. His caution, while commendable, was misplaced. Regardless of which date he chose, the crux of his report was erroneous: Charlemagne did not found eight bishoprics at all, let alone in a sweeping act. Yet his account does attest to the lively interest in the origins of Saxon bishoprics which had developed by the eleventh century, an interest that is reflected in a broad range of contemporary sources.

Thietmar was not alone in attributing the formation of Saxon bishoprics to a single act of Charlemagne. Later in the eleventh century, Adam of Bremen described how eight dioceses were established in Saxony upon the capitulation of the rebel Widukind in 788 [sic] before including a forged diploma, perhaps custom-made for this purpose, in which Charlemagne established the precise diocesan boundaries of Bremen.[2] Thietmar's near-contemporary, the author of the *Quedlinburg Annals*, was somewhat more plausible in her report, which placed the foundations in 781 in terms recalling a 780 entry in the *Lorsch*

---

[1] Thietmar of Merseburg, *Chronicon*, ed. R. Holtzmann, *MGH SRG NS* 9 (Berlin: Weidemann, 1935), VII:75, p. 490: 'Anno dominicae incarn. DCCC ... predictus cesar ad suae virtutis et bonae operacionis deauracionem in una die VIII episcopatus in Saxonia Christo subdita, dispositis singularibus parochiis, constituit.'

[2] Adam of Bremen, *Gesta Hammaburgensis ecclesiae pontificum*, ed. B. Schmeidler, *MGH SRG* 2 (Hanover: Hahn, 1917), I:11–12, pp. 13–17.

Annals.[3] Yet even she ventured into anachronism in stating that Charlemagne 'arranged the diocesan boundaries' at this time, and her ensuing description of the creation of Halberstadt's diocesan boundaries can be dismissed as an invention of the *Deeds of the Bishops of Halberstadt*, a lost source which she is known to have consulted.[4]

The desire to cast the foundations of Saxon bishoprics as the culmination of a conscious strategy pursued by Charlemagne is by no means a purely medieval phenomenon. As recently as 1984, Klemens Honselmann published an article in which he argued strenuously that Charlemagne had founded six bishoprics – Paderborn, Osnabrück, Bremen, Minden, Verden and Münster – in one fell swoop as part of a single plan effected in 799, a position that he later reasserted in 1988.[5] In the absence of conclusive evidence, however, Honselmann's views have found little favour.[6] Instead, scholars assert, and rightly so, that the available documentation paints a more complicated picture, and have offered various dates of foundation for Saxon bishoprics. Yet even to assign a date of foundation is misleading; the process, and not action, by which Saxon bishoprics were established was gradual and shaped by

[3] *Annales Quedlinburgenses*, ed. M. Giese, *MGH SRG* 72 (Hanover: Hahn, 2004), 781, p. 429; *Annales Laureshamenses*, G. H. Pertz, *MGH SS* I (Hanover: Hahn, 1826), pp. 22–39, here 780, p. 31.

[4] *Annales Quedlinburgenses*, ed. Giese, 781, pp. 429–30, here p. 429: 'terminos episcopis constituit'; see further H. Büttner, 'Mission und Kirchenorganisation des Frankenreiches bis zum Tode Karls des Großen' in H. Beumann (ed.), *Karl der Grosse: Lebenswerk und Nachleben: Persönlichkeit und Geschichte*, 5 vols. (Düsseldorf: L. Schwann, 1965), vol. I, pp. 454–87, here p. 474.

[5] K. Honselmann, 'Die Bistumsgründungen in Sachsen unter Karl dem Großen, mit einem Ausblick auf spätere Bistumsgründungen und einem Excurs zur Übernahme der christlichen Zeitrechnung im frühmittelalterlichen Sachsen', *AfD*, 30 (1984), 1–50, here 1–23; K. Honselmann, 'Die Gründung der sächsischen Bistümer 799: Sachsens Anschluß an das fränkische Reich', *AfD*, 34 (1988), 1–2.

[6] See here especially the rebuttal of V. de Vry, 'Die Gründung des Bistums Paderborn im Spiegel der Berichte über die Translatio des Bischofs Liborius von Le Mans' in H. Mordek, T. M. Buck and J. Herrmann (eds.), Quellen, Kritik, Interpretation: Festgabe zum 60. Geburtstag von Hubert Mordek (Frankfurt: P. Lang, 1999), pp. 117–26, here especially pp. 123–6; see also the important recent revisions of T. Kölzer, 'Die Urkunden Ludwigs des Frommen für Halberstadt (BM2 535) und Visbek (BM2 702) und ein folgenreiches Mißverständnis', *AfD*, 58 (2012), 103–23; T. Kölzer, 'Zum angeblichen Immunitätsprivileg Ludwigs des Frommen für das Bistum Hildesheim', *AfD*, 59 (2013), 11–24; T. Kölzer, 'Ludwigs des Frommen "Gründungsurkunde" für das Erzbistum Hamburg', *AfD*, 60 (2014), 35–68. See further C. J. Carroll, 'The bishoprics of Saxony in the first century after Christianization', *EME*, 8(1) (1999), 219–46, here 222; C. Carroll, 'The archbishops and church provinces of Mainz and Cologne during the Carolingian period, 751–911', unpublished Ph.D thesis, University of Cambridge (1999), p. 35; H. Röckelein, '"Pervenimus mirificum ad sancti Medardi oraculum". Der Anteil westfränkischer Zellen am Aufbau sächsischer Missionszentrum', in Godman, Jarnut and Johanek, *Am Vorabend*, pp. 145–62; R. Schieffer, *Die Entstehung von Domkapiteln in Deutschland* (Bonner historische Forschungen 43) (Bonn: Röhrscheid, 1976), pp. 206–31; R. Schieffer, 'Die Anfänge der westfälischen Domstifte', *WZ*, 138 (1988), pp. 175–91, here p. 179; E. Schubert, Geschichte Niedersachsens: Politik, Verfassung, Wirtschaft vom 9. bis zum ausgehenden 15. Jahrhundert (Veröffentlichungen der historischen Kommission für Niedersachsen und Bremen 36), 5 vols. (Hanover: Hahn, 1997), vol. II.1, pp. 58–9.

reactive pragmatism rather than by conscious policy.[7] The Saxon bishoprics of the eleventh century, with their fixed seats, bishops and clergy; defined diocesan boundaries; dependent churches and monasteries; and large endowments, were not the product of a single 'foundation', but were rather the eventual result of gradual evolution, as the debates about the origins of Hamburg-Bremen and Verden so clearly reveal.[8]

Nevertheless, much recent work on Saxon ecclesiastical structures has been grounded in the assumption that foundations were discrete acts. This approach can be seen in the work of Caspar Ehlers, whose 2007 monograph systematically presents the date of foundation, founders and type of institution of all monasteries and bishoprics in Carolingian and Ottonian Saxony.[9] Not only does this telescope the process of foundation; also, it further does not acknowledge the multiplicity of actors in these foundations. In particular, Ehlers' designation of Carolingian rulers and their kin-group as founders of a wide array of Saxon religious institutions, whether bishoprics, cathedral chapters or monasteries, overrates their involvement in these foundations. More recently, Theo Kölzer and Thomas Vogtherr have suggested that the *Einstaatung* (roughly translated as 'state-ification') of Saxon bishoprics should be dated to the reign of Louis the German.[10] Kölzer's work has served as an important corrective to previous scholarship which placed great

---

[7] See, for example, Schieffer, *Die Entstehung von Domkapiteln*, p. 207; Schubert, *Geschichte Niedersachsens*, pp. 58–9.

[8] For the debate about Hamburg-Bremen, see especially E. Knibbs, *Ansgar, Rimbert and the Forged Foundations of Hamburg-Bremen* (Farnham: Ashgate, 2011) and Kölzer, '"Gründungsurkunde"', 35–68; see further, among (many) others, R. Drögereit, 'Erzbistum Hamburg, Hamburg-Bremen oder Erzbistum Bremen? Studien zur Hamburg-Bremer Frühgeschichte. Friedrich Prüser (1892–1974) zum Gedächtnis. Erster Teil', *AfD*, 21 (1975), 136–230; B. Wavra, *Salzburg und Hamburg: Erzbistumsgründung und Missionspolitik in karolingischer Zeit* (Giessener Abhandlungen zur Agrar- und Wirtschaftsforschung des Europäischen Ostens 179) (Berlin: Duncker & Humblot, 1991). For the debate surrounding the foundation of Verden, see especially M. Last, 'Die Bedeutung des Klosters Amorbach für Mission und Kirchenorganisation im sächsischen Stammesgebiet' in F. Oswald and W. Störmer (eds.), *Die Abtei Amorbach im Odenwald: neue Beiträge zur Geschichte und Kultur des Klosters und seines Herrschaftsgebietes* (Sigmaringen: J. Thorbecke, 1984), pp. 33–53, here pp. 40–4.

[9] C. Ehlers, *Die Integration Sachsens in das fränkische Reich (751–1024)* (Veröffentlichungen des Max-Planck-Instituts für Geschichte 231) (Göttingen: Vandenhoeck & Ruprecht, 2007); see further C. Ehlers, 'Könige, Klöster, und der Raum. Die Entwicklung der kirchlichen Topographie Westfalens und Ostsachsens in karolingischer und ottonischer Zeit', *WZ*, 153 (2003), 189–216; C. Ehlers, 'Die zweifache Integration: Sachsen zwischen Karolingern und Ottonen. Überlegungen zur Erschließung von Diözesen mit Klöstern und Stiften in Westfalen und Sachsen bis 1024' in K. Bodarwé and T. Schilp (eds.), *Herrschaft, Liturgie und Raum: Studien zur mittelalterlichen Geschichte des Frauenstifts Essen* (Essener Forschungen zum Frauenstift 1) (Essen: Klartext, 2002), pp. 24–50.

[10] See here especially Kölzer, 'Zum angeblichen Immunitätsprivileg', 20–1; T. Vogtherr, 'Visbek, Münster, Halberstadt: neue Überlegungen zu Kirchenorganisation im karolingischen Sachsen', *AfD*, 58 (2012), 125–45, here 141.

emphasis upon the 'early' and, in Kölzer's analysis, largely forged charters of Louis the Pious for Saxon bishoprics.[11] Yet the emphasis he places upon the granting of royal immunity as a 'fixed point' may overstate its significance, and likewise that of Carolingian rulers, in the longer, diachronic process of foundation.

Carolingian force of arms and Frankish mission had indeed brought the Saxons to Christian observance: this much is clear. Yet whether either Carolingian kings or Frankish religious institutions can be credited with the creation of more lasting Christian infrastructure in Saxony is rather more doubtful. While Charlemagne and Frankish religious institutions had provided manpower and support for the mission, the significance of their contributions to the resultant institutions' endowments is more difficult to gauge. At most, Carolingian kings granted privileges, far-flung monastic cells and relics to incipient Saxon foundations; grants of fiscal land, meanwhile, were restricted to a small number of high-status recipients, most notably the monasteries of Corvey and Herford. This chapter undertakes to examine how, in the apparent absence of such external patronage, Saxon religious institutions were supported. The conclusions drawn from such an investigation are of import to our understanding not only of Saxon ecclesiastical development, but also of the extent and nature of Carolingian intervention in post-conquest Saxony.

FRANKISH MISSION, FRANKISH CHURCH?

Frankish Mission

In order that he [Charlemagne] might reveal this hard assault to be more for the sake of Christian religion than for the expansion of his kingdom, he constructed churches throughout the region with all the speed that he could muster, so that the populace, who were still unlearned in the faith, could be taught to assemble and could begin to receive the divine sacraments. He also outlined, with careful prudence, the boundaries of dioceses which must be preserved, and because cities, where the seats of bishops have been established according to ancient custom, were entirely lacking in this province, he chose those places which seemed more suitable than the others both in terms of their natural excellence and the number of people. He had not yet discovered to what a barbaric and semi-pagan people he had appointed prelates. Now and then, they relapsed into perfidy, and none of the clerics seemed to be safe living among them: the

---

[11] Kölzer, 'Die Urkunden', 103–23; Kölzer, 'Zum angeblichen Immunitätsprivileg', 11–24; Kölzer, '"Gründungsurkunde"', 35–68. See also the important reassessment of Vogtherr. 'Visbek, Münster, Halberstadt'.

ecclesiastical office, and all that pertained to divine worship, was not only absent, but truly unknown in every way. Therefore he commended each of the aforementioned pontifical seats with their dioceses to prelates of churches in his kingdom, so that they themselves, whenever they were able, might proceed to instruct and confirm that people in sacred religion, and so that commendable persons from their clergy of whatever grade, with diverse training in ecclesiastical matters, might arrange to abide there continuously for a long time, until with God's favour, the doctrines of faith and salvation might grow strong there and thus the rites of the divine mystery might flourish, and then each bishop could remain worthily and boldly in his own parish.[12]

So wrote the anonymous author of the *Translation of Saint Liborius*. His words have often been quoted in historical accounts: this short passage constitutes the most programmatic description of Saxon ecclesiastical development. Even from his vantage point almost a century later, the hagiographer manages to capture the uncertainty of mission, and the challenges and reversals that Charlemagne had faced.

As early as the mid-770s, Charlemagne had already begun to assign missionary sponsors to different regions.[13] Eigil of Fulda, writing some forty years later, described how Charlemagne 'divided the entire province into episcopal parishes and gave it to the servants of the Lord in order that they might teach and baptize', further adding that Fulda's former abbot, Sturmi, received a particularly large missionary area.[14]

---

[12] Anonymus Paderbrunnensis, *Translatio sancti Liborii*, ed. V. de Vry, *Liborius, Brückenbauer Europas: die mittelalterlichen Viten und Translationsberichte: mit einem Anhang der Manuscripta Liboriana* (Paderborn: Schöningh, 1997), cc. 2–3, pp. 189–90: 'Et ut se magis christianae religionis, quam regni sui dilatandi causa, tantae rei difficultatem aggressum ostenderet, aecclesias per omnem regionem illam, ad quas rudis in fide populus confluere doceretur, et sacramentis caelestibus initiari consuesceret, sub quanta potuit celeritate construi fecit: atque parrochias diligenti ratione suis quasque terminis seruandas designans, quia ciuitates, in quibus more antiquo sedes episcopales constituerentur, illi paenitus prouinciae deerant, loca tamen ad hoc, quae et naturali quadam excellentia et populi frequentia prae caeteris oportuna uidebantur, elegit. Tum uero uix repperiebantur, qui barbarae et semipaganae nationi praesules ordinarentur. Cuius interdum ad perfidiam relabentis cohabitatio nulli clericorum tuta uidebantur, cui aecclesiasticum officium, et quicquid ad rerum diuinarum pertinet cultum, non solum deerat, uerum ignotum omnimodis erat. Quocirca unamquamque praedictarum pontificalium sedium cum sua diocesi singulis aliarum regni sui aecclesarium praesulibus commendauit, qui et ipsi, quotiens sibi uacaret, ad instruendam confirmandamque in sacra religione plebem, eo pergerent, et ex clero suo personas probabiles cuiuscumque ordinis, cum diuerso rerum aecclesiasticarum apparatu, ibidem mansuros iugiter destinarent, et hoc tamdiu, donec annuente Domino salutaris illic fidei doctrina conualesceret et ita diuini usus mynisterii proueheretur, ut proprii quoque in singulis parrochiis digne et fiducialiter possent manere pontifices.'

[13] For a discussion of this stage of the Frankish mission, see H. Büttner and I. Dietrich, 'Weserland und Hessen im Kräftespiel der karolingischen und frühen ottonischen Politik', *Westfalen*, 30(3) (1952), 133–49, here 135–7.

[14] Eigil of Fulda, *Vita sancti Sturmi*, ed. P. Engelbert, *Die Vita Sturmi des Eigil von Fulda: literarkritisch-historische Untersuchung und Edition* (Veröffentlichungen der Historischen Kommission für Hessen und Waldeck 29) (Marburg: N. G. Elwert, 1968), c. 23, p. 158: 'totam provinciam illam in

Over the next couple of years, Sturmi and his subordinates preached and built churches among the Saxons, until 778, when rebellion was renewed, and Sturmi and his men took flight. When, in the following year, Charlemagne attempted to quell dissent, Sturmi once again participated in his campaign, but soon fell ill and returned to Fulda, where he died later that same year.

If Charlemagne had already designated ecclesiastical districts in Saxony, they were far from lasting. In 780, a year after Sturmi's death, a reorganization was in the works: the *Lorsch Annals* record that Charlemagne 'divided the country between bishops, presbyters, and abbots'.[15] It may have been around this time that the area around Minden was entrusted to Erkambert, previously a monk of Fulda, and the area around Paderborn to the bishopric of Würzburg.[16] Yet this plan, like the last, was provisional rather than definitive. The following year, Charlemagne sent Willehad to Wigmodia, and when Widukind capitulated in 785, further missionary territory was carved out for a certain abbot Bernrad, who has been tentatively identified as Beornrad of Echternach.[17] Appointments

---

parochias episcopales divisit et servis Domini ad docendum et baptizandum potestatem dedit'. For the dating of this work, see J. Raaijmakers, The Making of the Monastic Community of Fulda, c.744–c.900 (Cambridge: Cambridge University Press, 2012), pp. 150–1. For a discussion of Sturmi's activity in the region, see E. Freise, 'Die Sachsenmission Karls des Großen und die Anfänge des Bistums Minden', in *An Weser und Wiehen: Beiträge zur Geschichte und Kultur einer Landschaft. Festschrift für Wilhelm Brepohl* (Mindener Beiträge 20) (Minden: Mindener Geschichtsverein, 1983), pp. 57–100, here pp. 58–60; see further Büttner, 'Mission und Kirchenorganisation', p. 473; P. Johanek, 'Der Ausbau der sächsischen Kirchenorganisation' in Stiegemann and Wemhoff, *799*, vol. II, pp. 496–7.

[15] *Annales Laureshamenses*, ed. Pertz, 780, p. 31: 'divisitque ipsam patriam inter episcopos et presbyteros seu et abbates'. See also *Annales Mosellani*, ed. J. M. Lappenberg, MGH SS 16 (Hanover: Hahn, 1859), pp. 491–9, here 780, p. 497.

[16] For Minden, see E. Müller, *Die Entstehungsgeschichte der sächsischen Bistümer unter Karl dem Grossen* (Quellen und Darstellungen zur Geschichte Niedersachsens 47) (Hildesheim: Lax, 1938), pp. 43–51; Schieffer, *Die Entstehung von Domkapiteln*, pp. 219–21; for the donations of Erkambert to Fulda, see also below, p. 181. For Paderborn, see Anonymus Paderbrunnensis, *Translatio sancti Liborii*, ed. de Vry, c. 6, p. 192; see further Müller, *Die Entstehungsgeschichte*, pp. 51–9; Schieffer, *Die Entstehung von Domkapiteln*, pp. 221–4; Schieffer, 'Die Anfänge', 182–3.

[17] *Vita sancti Willehadi*, eds. C. de Smedt, F. van Ortroy, H. Delehaye, A. Poncelet and P. Peeters, *Acta Sanctorum III Novembris* (Brussels, 1910), pp. 842–6, here c. 5, p. 844A; *Vita secunda sancti Liudgeri*, ed. E. Freise, *Die Vita sancti Liudgeri: Vollständige Faksimile-Ausgabe der Handschrift Ms. Theol. lat. fol. 323 der Staatsbibliothek Berlin – Preußischer Kulturbesitz. Text, Übersetzung und Kommentar, Forschungsbeiträge* (Graz: Akadem. Druck- und Verlagsanstalt, 1999), pp. 9–24, here I:18, p. 12; see further E. Balzer, 'Frühe Mission, adelige Stifter und die Anfänge des Bischofssitzes in Münster', *WZ*, 160 and 161 (2010–11), pp. 9–50, 9–59, here part 1, 14–38; Büttner, 'Mission und Kirchenorganisation', pp. 469–71; Johanek, 'Der Ausbau', p. 500; E. Freise, 'Vom vorchristlichen Mimigernaford zum *honestum monasterium* Liudgers' in F. J. Jakobi (ed.), *Geschichte der Stadt Münster*, 3 vols. (Münster: Aschendorff, 1993), vol. I: pp. 1–53, here pp. 26–7; Müller, *Die Entstehungsgeschichte*, pp. 21–9; I. N. Wood, 'An absence of saints? The evidence for the Christianization of Saxony' in Godman, Jarnut and Johanek, *Am Vorabend*, pp. 335–52, here pp. 338–9, 347.

probably continued as opportunity permitted. In the early 790s, Charlemagne appointed the Frisian Liudger to the area around Münster; in the later years of Charlemagne's reign, the bishopric of Liège appears to have acted as a missionary sponsor for Osnabrück, and likewise the monastery of Amorbach for Verden, a role which it continued to fulfil up to the mid-ninth century.[18] Here, 'missionary sponsor' is a catch-all term used to denote the various (and often difficult to reconstruct) roles which institutions, whether monasteries or bishoprics, played in the recruitment and provisioning of missionaries. Later still, during the reign of Louis the Pious, the incipient bishoprics of Halberstadt and Hildesheim were entrusted to Bishop Hildigrim of Châlons and the archbishopric of Rheims, respectively.[19] Corbie appears to have served a similar role for the monastic foundations of Corvey and, more questionably, Herford.[20]

It is clear, then, that Charlemagne undertook the organization of the mission in a top-down fashion. Yet his arrangements do not evince any conscious design or forward planning: rather, they constitute a rather haphazard series of reactions to opportunities and setbacks. Men of disparate rank and status within the church were appointed to lead the mission, seemingly indiscriminately: archbishops, bishops, chorbishops,

---

[18] Carroll, 'The archbishops and church provinces of Mainz and Cologne', pp. 33–4. For the appointment of Liudger to Münster, see Altfrid, *Vita sancti Liudgeri*, ed. W. Diekamp, *Die vitae sancti Liudgeri* (Die Geschichtsquellen des Bisthums Münster 4) (Münster: Theissing, 1881), pp. 3–53, here I:23, pp. 27–9. For the early history of Münster, see especially Freise, 'Vom vorchristlichen Mimigernaford', pp. 1–53; Schieffer, *Die Entstehung von Domkapiteln*, pp. 207–10. For the involvement of Liège, see Johanek, 'Der Ausbau', p. 502; Müller, *Die Entstehungsgeschichte*, p. 72; Schieffer, *Die Entstehung von Domkapiteln*, p. 212; for the involvement of Amorbach, see Last, 'Die Bedeutung des Klosters Amorbach', pp. 33–53; see further Büttner, 'Mission und Kirchenorganisation', p. 473; Johanek, 'Der Ausbau', pp. 500–1; Müller, *Die Entstehungsgeschichte*, pp. 33–4; Schieffer, *Die Entstehung von Domkapiteln*, pp. 217–19.

[19] For the involvement of Châlons-sur-Marne, see Müller, *Die Entstehungsgeschichte*, pp. 86–7; Schieffer, *Die Entstehung von Domkapiteln*, pp. 227–9; contrast with Kölzer, 'Die Urkunden', 107–8; Vogtherr, 'Visbek', 142–3. In contrast to Kölzer's arguments, I believe that Hildigrim's appointment in Châlons did not preclude him undertaking missionary work in Saxony: one may point to the activism of Archbishop Ebo of Rheims in Hildesheim. Moreover, Hildigrim has a familial connection to the Saxon mission: he was Liudger's brother and took a role in the governance of the monastery of Werden. For the predominance of familial connections among missionaries, see L. E. von Padberg, *Mission und Christianisierung: Formen und Folgen bei Angelsachsen und Franken im 7. und 8. Jahrhundert* (Stuttgart: F. Steiner, 1995), pp. 86–95. For Rheims' involvement in Hildesheim, meanwhile, see *Chronicon Hildesheimense*, ed. G. H. Pertz, *MGH SS* 7 (Hanover: Hahn, 1846), p. 848; see also H. Goetting, *Das Bistum Hildesheim 3: Die Hildesheimer Bischöfe von 815 bis 1221 (1227)* (GSNF 20) (Berlin: W. de Gruyter, 1984), p. 39; Schieffer, *Die Entstehung von Domkapiteln*, pp. 224–7.

[20] For the role of Corbie at Herford, see Paschasius Radbertus, *Epitaphium Arsenii*, ed. E. Dümmler, *Radbert's Epitaphium Arsenii* (Abhandlungen der Kgl. Akademie der Wissenschaft zu Berlin, Phil.-hist. Classe II) (Berlin: W. de Gruyter, 1900), I:15, pp. 43–4; see further J. Semmler, 'Corvey und Herford in der benediktinischen Reformbewegung des 9. Jahrhunderts', *Frühmittelalterliche Studien*, 4 (1970), 289–319.

priests and abbots were all selected at various points.[21] Sometimes they were appointed in a purely personal capacity, as in the case of Hildigrim of Châlons, who generously contributed his own resources, but seemingly not those of his West Frankish bishopric, to the foundation of an episcopal see at Halberstadt. At other points, more institutional support was proffered: the *Translation of Saint Liborius* credited the mission around Paderborn to the church of Würzburg, while the evidence from Verden suggests the continued involvement of Amorbach over a period of some fifty years, far beyond the time-span of an individual appointment.[22] Yet such consistent support was uncommon. The missionary map was constantly changing, with ill-defined territories growing and shrinking to accommodate the ever-changing supply of manpower. When a missionary died, willing replacement candidates were often lacking. The *Second Life of Saint Liudger* recorded that 'it could be difficult to find someone in the Frankish kingdom who would voluntarily go among the barbarians for the sake of preaching'.[23] After Willehad's death in 787, there is no evidence of missionary activity in Wigmodia until the consecration of Willerich as bishop of Bremen in 804/5.[24] Other missionary stations may have been permanently abandoned.

By the end of Charlemagne's reign, certain fixed Christian centres, if not fixed dioceses, had emerged. It is difficult, however, to judge precisely what role Frankish missionary sponsors played at these sites. The prelates charged with conducting the mission were often absent as they attended to other duties elsewhere: the practice of appointing prominent Frankish archbishops, bishops and abbots inevitably resulted in a certain intermittence of service. The abbots of Amorbach, for instance, who simultaneously served as bishops of Verden until 838, had to divide their time between two Christian centres with more than 250 miles between them.[25] Such double tenure was far from unusual. The first bishop of Halberstadt was also the bishop of the West Frankish see of Châlons-sur-Marne, and even after the missionary period, the first

---

[21] Schieffer, *Die Entstehung von Domkapiteln*, p. 207. For the argument that Liudger and Willehad were chorbishops, see Knibbs, *Ansgar, Rimbert and the forged foundations of Hamburg-Bremen*, pp. 33–4, 39–41, 46, 58. See further the comments of R. E. Sullivan, 'The Carolingian missionary and the pagan', *Speculum*, 28(4) (1953), 705–40, here 711.

[22] For Würzburg's involvement at Paderborn, see Anonymus Paderbrunnensis, *Translatio sancti Liborii*, ed. de Vry, c. 6, p. 192; for the continued involvement of Amorbach at Verden, see Last, 'Die Bedeutung des Klosters Amorbach', p. 39.

[23] *Vita secunda sancti Liudgeri*, ed. Freise, I:18, p. 12: 'difficile in regno Francorum potuit inveniri, qui libenter ad praedicandum inter barbaros iret'. See also Freise, 'Vom vorchristlichen Mimigernaford', p. 27.

[24] Cf. Müller, *Die Entstehungsgeschichte*, p. 27.

[25] Last, 'Die Bedeutung des Klosters Amorbach', p. 39.

two abbots of Corvey were also abbots of far-distant Corbie.[26] The *Translation of Saint Liborius*, reflecting back on the origins of Paderborn, described the difficulties inherent in such distant management: when the mission around Paderborn was entrusted to the bishopric of Würzburg, the author wrote,

Under the governance of those ones, very little was able to be accomplished, since the places were separated from each other by a very long distance, and only rarely did their occupation permit or opportunity allow the aforementioned prelates to visit this new church. They did not lack in business there. They persevered with those things which must be attended to, and the length of the journey did not lessen the effort of coming here. There the well-ordered, necessary business suffices; here, it must be dealt with delicately and with difficulty for the first time.[27]

Eventually, the anonymous author writes, the advantages of appointing a prelate 'who, present here, and not being occupied elsewhere, might sweat to accomplish many things' became apparent, and Paderborn received its first bishop.[28]

If missionary leaders themselves were often absent, their subordinates, who were often drawn from the schools and clergy of the missionary sponsors, remained in Saxony. Incipient Christian centres appear to have been organized around the principle of communal clerical life. The first attested forms of clerical organization at the later bishoprics of Paderborn and Münster were *monasteria*.[29] This term should not be translated

---

[26] For the argument that Wala succeeded Adalhard as abbot of Corvey, see K. H. Krüger, 'Zur Nachfolgeregelung von 826 in den Klöstern Corbie und Corvey' in N. Kamp and J. Wollasch (eds.), *Tradition als historische Kraft: interdisziplinäre Forschungen zur Geschichte des früheren Mittelalters* (Berlin: W. de Gruyter, 1982), pp. 181–96.

[27] Anonymus Paderbrunnensis, *Translatio sancti Liborii*, ed. de Vry, c. 6, pp. 192–3: 'Sub quorum regimine status rerum ipsius parum proficere potuit: quippe cum loca ipsa longa inter se terrarum intercapedine distarent, et praefatos praesules raro hanc nouellam aecclesiam inuisere uel occupatio permitteret uel commoditas suaderet. Neque enim ibi deerant negocia, quibus procurandis insisterent, neque huc pergendi laborem paruum faciebat itineris longitudo. Ibi res necessariae sufficientes et ordinatae, hic et tenues et cum difficultate nouiter ordinandae.'

[28] *Ibid*, c. 7, p. 193: 'qui non alibi occupatus hic tantum agendis rebus praesens insudaret'. See further Johanek, 'Der Ausbau', p. 503.

[29] For Paderborn, see Erconrad, *Translatio sancti Liborii*, eds. A. Cohausz, V. Mellinghoff-Bourgerie and R. Latouche, *La Translation de Saint Liboire (836) du diacre Erconrad: Un Document de l'époque carolingienne récemment découvert et les Relations déjà connues du Transfert des Reliques* (Archives historiques du Maine 14) (Le Mans: Société historique de la province du Maine, 1967), c. 16, p. 88; see also H. A. Erhard, *Regesta historiae Westfaliae: accedit codex diplomaticus*, 2 vols. (Münster: F. Regensberg, 1847), vol. I, Urkundenbuch zur Geschichte Westfalens, no. 20, p. 16. For Münster, see Altfrid, *Vita sancti Liudgeri*, ed. Diekamp, I:23, p. 28. See also Schieffer, 'Die Anfänge', 175–9; Schieffer, *Die Entstehung von Domkapiteln*, pp. 207–10, 221–4; cf. Freise, 'Vom vorchristlichen Mimigernaford', p. 5; W. Kohl, 'Honestum monasterium in loco Mimigernaefor: Zur Frühgeschichte des Doms in Münster' in N. Kamp and J. Wollasch (eds.), *Tradition als*

directly as 'monasteries', with all of the tenth-century baggage that implies: Rudolf Schieffer is right to warn us that *monasterium* could be used to represent a variety of different forms which were only subsequently clearly defined.[30] In some places, such as in the bishoprics of Osnabrück, Verden and Minden, where *monasteria* are attested in ninth- and tenth-century sources, such communities may have later assumed the function of cathedral chapters, in a manner not altogether dissimilar from Anglo-Saxon minsters.[31] In other places, such as in Meppen and Visbeck, such communities were joined to a larger monastery (Corvey) and adopted Benedictine observance.[32]

These early communities, and the prelates who sometimes presided over them, appear to have fulfilled three chief functions: prayer, preaching and church-building. So a wide variety of hagiographic literature relates: the *Life of Saint Sturmi* reports that Sturmi passed his days preaching and building churches, and Willehad is likewise reputed to have baptized pagans, built and restored churches and preached in rotation throughout his territory.[33] Altfrid, in his *Life of Saint Liudger*, similarly describes how Liudger built churches, ordained presbyters and preached widely in the area of his eventual see before his consecration as bishop.[34] While such descriptions are generic, they are probably also an accurate reflection of priorities. Yet how, and how far, these functions were fulfilled in practice remains unclear. The act of preaching, for instance, was complicated by a very real language barrier: while Old Saxon may only have been a dialect of Old High German, there were still significant

---

historische Kraft: interdisziplinäre Forschungen zur Geschichte des früheren Mittelalters (Berlin: W. de Gruyter, 1982), pp. 156–80.

[30] Schieffer, 'Die Anfänge', 176–8, 191; see also von Padberg, *Mission und Christianisierung*, p. 103.

[31] For Osnabrück, see Rudolf and Meginhard, *Translatio sancti Alexandri*, ed. G. H. Pertz, *MGH SS* 2 (Hanover: Hahn, 1829), pp. 673–81, here c. 6, p. 679; for Verden, see *D Arn*, ed. P. Kehr, *MGH, Die Urkunden Arnolfs* (Berlin: Weidemann, 1940), no. 78, p. 117; and finally, for Minden, see *D O I*, ed. T. Sickel, *MGH, Die Urkunden Konrad I., Heinrich I. und Otto I.* (Hanover: Hahn, 1884), no. 227, p. 312. See also Schieffer, 'Die Anfänge', 176. For minsters and the role that they assumed in Anglo-Saxon society, see especially J. Blair, 'Debate: ecclesiastical organization and pastoral care in Anglo-Saxon England', *EME*, 4(2) (1995), 193–212; J. Blair, *The Church in Anglo-Saxon Society* (Oxford: Oxford University Press, 2005); contrast to E. Cambridge and D. Rollason, 'Debate: the pastoral organization of the Anglo-Saxon church: a review of the 'minster hypothesis'', *EME*, 4(1) (1995), 87–104.

[32] For Meppen, see *D Kar. 2*, ed. T. Kölzer, *MGH, Die Urkunden Ludwigs des Frommen*, 3 vols. (Wiesbaden: Harrassowitz, 2016), vol. II, no. 346, p. 865; for Visbeck, see *D LD*, ed. P. Kehr, *MGH, Die Urkunden Ludwigs des Deutschen, Karlmanns und Ludwigs der Jüngeren* (Berlin: Weidemann, 1934), no. 73, pp. 102–4. See also Schieffer, 'Die Anfänge', 179; contrast to Kölzer, 'Die Urkunden', 114; Vogtherr, 'Visbek', 127–32.

[33] Eigil of Fulda, *Vita sancti Sturmi*, ed. Engelbert, cc. 23–4, p. 159; *Vita sancti Willehadi*, eds. de Smedt, van Ortroy, Delehaye, Poncelet, and Peeters, cc. 5, 8, pp. 844A, 845B.

[34] Altfrid, *Vita sancti Liudgeri*, ed. Diekamp, I:23, p. 28.

differences.[35] While larger-scale vernacular works survive from the mid-ninth century, only an abbreviated baptismal formula survives from the missionary period.[36] I shall discuss this issue at greater length in Chapter 4.

Similarly vexing is the question of how the churches built during the Frankish mission were endowed. There is little evidence of missionary sponsors bringing their own resources to finance such constructions. The only visible material support offered in this regard, save for clerical manpower, was the provision of relics on the part of some sponsors. This in itself was a great boon, and one which was highly valued by contemporaries, but hardly an extensive material endowment.[37] Later, in the mid-820s, the West Frankish monastery of Corbie would offer material support to its foundation of New-Corbie, or Corvey, as it came to be called. Paschasius later wrote of how 'they built the foundations of those sites and constructed those houses which might never age; they constructed workshops, and raised roofs which might never topple'.[38] Corbie further appears to have transferred its Saxon lands, the extent of which is unknown, to Corvey's ownership.[39] Yet this was evidently seen as a radical departure from precedent, and was still controversial within Corbie's own community some decades later: Paschasius notes how many complained that Wala, a founder of Corvey, had 'plundered all the possessions of our monastery in order that he might enrich those places at our cost'.[40] His reply to this critique, and his long enumeration of the reasons why Corbie had decided to bear the cost of this foundation, point to the unusual nature of such an arrangement.

It is unclear whether missionary sponsors provided economic support for the missionaries and clerics they sent into Saxony, let alone for the foundation and endowment of incipient Saxon institutions. Once again, it is only in the case of Corbie and its first attempted foundation at Hethis that any such support is attested. The *Translation of Saint Vitus* records that

---

[35] For a more general discussion of missionaries and the vernacular, see von Padberg, *Mission und Christianisierung*, pp. 140–6.

[36] For vernacular texts from later periods, see below, pp. 208–18; see also Sullivan, 'The Carolingian missionary', 714–15.

[37] See, for example, the case of Münster: Balzer, 'Frühe Mission', 26–38.

[38] Paschasius Radbertus, *Epitaphium Arsenii*, ed. Dümmler, I:15, p. 44: 'isti locorum fundamenta et domorum structuram ponebant, quae numquam veteresceret; ędificabant officinas, et culmina erigebant, quae numquam corruerent'.

[39] D Kar. 2, ed. Kölzer, vol. I, no. 226, p. 561.

[40] Paschasius Radbertus, *Epitaphium Arsenii*, ed. Dümmler, I:14, p. 42: 'bona monasterii nostri cuncta diriperet, tantum ut loca illa nostris ditaret sumptibus'. See also K. H. Krüger, *Studien zur Corveyer Gründungsüberlieferung* (Abhandlungen zur Corveyer Geschichtsschreibung 9) (Münster: Aschendorff, 2001), pp. 26, 35–7.

the monks at Hethis were dependent on their mother-house for both food and clothing; when Adalhard I was restored to his abbacy at Corbie and discovered the poverty in which the brothers were living, he immediately 'sent and ordered with all haste, paying whatever price, that if laden wagons should be found anywhere, they should be sent quickly to aid the want of the labourers with as many supplies as the cows could bear'.[41] Such interventions were not only unusual, but also clearly unsustainable: a distance of almost 600 kilometres separated Corbie from its new foundation. It is perhaps unsurprising that Adalhard's next move was to find a new site where the monks could attain self-sufficiency.

All of this suggests that the most tangible resources offered by missionary sponsors were the occasional provision of relics and the missionaries themselves. These were no mean commodities: relics were prized commodities with a high trading value, and missionaries were likewise highly educated and trained individuals.[42] Yet it is nonetheless striking that, save in the case of Corbie, no Frankish institutions or missionary sponsors are attested contributing substantially towards the endowment of religious institutions.

Somewhat more can be said in regard to the patronage of Carolingian rulers. A small number of churches appear to have been financed by Charlemagne himself, notably two stone churches that were constructed in his showcase Saxon village, Paderborn.[43] To this may putatively be added the churches later evidenced in the possession of his successors at Eresburg, Reni, Wateringas and Stocheim.[44] These churches were all presumably endowed with lands or revenues: the grant concerning the churches at Reni, Wateringas and Stocheim specifies that they are to be transferred with all their appurtenances, that is, with their tithes, properties and unfree labourers.[45] Carolingian rulers further appear in possession of monastic cells at Meppen and Visbeck, both of which were respectively endowed with basilicas; whether these were

---

[41] *Translatio sancti Viti*, ed. I. Schmale-Ott, *Übertragung des hl. Märtyrers Vitus* (Fontes minores 1) (Münster: Aschendorff, 1979), c. 3, p. 42: 'cum omni festinatione misit dans pretium iussitque, ut sicubi invenirentur carra onusta, et tam annonam quam boves compararent et cum festinatione fame laborantibus subvenirent'.

[42] K. Honselmann, 'Reliquientranslationen nach Sachsen' in V. H. Elbern (ed.), *Das erste Jahrtausend: Kultur und Kunst im werdenden Abendland an Rhein und Ruhr*, 3 vols. (Düsseldorf: L. Schwann, 1962), vol. I: pp. 159–93, here pp. 159–60; H. Röckelein, *Reliquientranslationen nach Sachsen im 9. Jahrhundert: über Kommunikation, Mobilität und Öffentlichkeit im Frühmittelalter* (Beihefte der Francia 48) (Sigmaringen: J. Thorbecke, 2002), pp. 140–54.

[43] *Annales Petaviani*, ed. G. H. Pertz, *MGH SS* 1 (Hanover: Hahn, 1826), pp. 7, 9, 11, 13, 15–8, here 777, p. 16; *Annales Laureshamenses*, ed. Pertz, 799, p. 38.

[44] *D Kar.* 2, ed. Kölzer, vol. II, nos. 255, 383, pp. 638, 955.   [45] *Ibid*, vol. II, no. 383, p. 955.

monastic or non-monastic is not stated.[46] Their role in these foundations can be deduced, however tentatively, from their later power of disposition over them.

The foundation of two monastic cells and a handful of churches, and the construction, if not endowment, of the churches in Paderborn, may thus be cautiously ascribed to Carolingian rulers. Remarkably, these ill-attested churches and cells appear to have constituted the full extent of royal foundations in Carolingian Saxony. Carolingian rulers do not appear to have proffered landed endowments to episcopal or monastic foundations: at most, they granted monastic cells in far-distant Francia, which appear to have been mainly used to provide clerical manpower. This is similar to the case of missionary sponsors. Carolingian rulers occasionally extended further patronage in the form of fiscal lands, and to this may be added the granting of fiscal privileges and donation of relics. Yet the significance of these grants, and consequently of Carolingian initiative in Saxon religious foundations more generally, appears remarkably slight.

Monastic Cells and Religious Patronage

As a recent article by Hedwig Röckelein has demonstrated, there is a noticeable pattern of Carolingian kings granting Frankish monastic cells to fledgling Saxon institutions.[47] Charlemagne appears to have granted such cells to at least three Saxon foundations: the missionary centres, and later bishoprics, of Bremen, Münster and Paderborn.[48] His successor, Louis the Pious, likewise granted a Frankish cell to Anskar's Hamburg-based northern mission, and further granted Meppen, one of the Saxon cells discussed above, to the monastery of Corvey.[49] This was an act of patronage which prefigured Louis the German's later grant of Visbeck to the same institution.[50]

---

[46] *Ibid*, vol. II, no. 346, p. 865; *D LD*, ed. Kehr, no. 73, pp. 102–4; see also Ehlers, *Die Integration Sachsens*, p. 193.

[47] Röckelein, "'Pervenimus mirificum ad sancti Medardi oraculum'", pp. 145–62; see further Röckelein, *Reliquientranslationen nach Sachsen*, pp. 74–5.

[48] Erconrad, *Translatio sancti Liborii*, eds. Cohausz, Mellinghoff-Bourgerie and Latouche, c. 16, pp. 86–90; *Vita sancti Willehadi*, eds. de Smedt, van Ortroy, Delehaye, Poncelet and Peeters, c. 8, p. 845A–B; Altfrid, *Vita sancti Liudgeri*, ed. Diekamp, I:24, p. 29.

[49] *Praeceptum diui Ludeuvici imperatoris*, ed. P. Caesar, *Triapostolatus septemtrionis: vita et gesta S. Willehadi, S. Ansgarii, S. Rimberti* (Cologne: Metternich, 1642), pp. 177–8; *D Kar. 2*, ed. Kölzer, vol. II, no. 346, p. 865. See also W. Metz, *Das karolingische Reichsgut: eine verfassungs- und verwaltungsgeschichtliche Untersuchung* (Berlin: W. de Gruyter, 1960), p. 167.

[50] *D LD*, ed. Kehr, no. 73, pp. 102–4.

Their grants do not appear, however, to have constituted a compre-hensive policy. While the grants of Frankish cells were made in the context of missionary work, whether in Saxony or further north, the Saxon cells of Meppen and Visbeck were granted to the already wealthy monastery of Corvey long after the introduction of Christianity to the region, and can be associated with a wider Carolingian tradition of patronage at this monastery. Perhaps unsurprisingly, scholars have shown more interest in the granting of Frankish monastic cells. These grants have been connected to the establishment of Saxon bishoprics.

It is unclear precisely what type of material support these Frankish monastic cells may have provided. Richly endowed monastic cells were, by and large, sought-after commodities, yet the majority of Frankish cells granted to Saxon institutions are all but unknown. Monastic cells such as the *oraculum sancti Medardi*, the *cella Justina* and the *cella Lothusa*, which were granted, respectively, to Paderborn, Bremen, and Münster, have only been localized with great difficulty and a not inconsiderable level of uncertainty, raising questions about their size and resources.[51] Even if cells were well endowed, there was the matter of distance: if the *oraculum sancti Medardi* is to be found in modern-day Saint-Mars-la-Brière, as is currently believed, it stood almost 800 kilometres distant from Paderborn. Naturally, economic support could be provided across long distances, especially in times of great strain, as in the case of Corbie sending off laden carts to its Saxon foundation.[52] This degree of support, however, appears to have been exceptional.

The economic significance of these grants appears at best doubtful. Yet at least two contemporaries, the missionary Anskar and his successor, Rimbert, vociferously asserted the importance of such a grant. In the aftermath of Charles the Bald's confiscation of the monastic cell at Turholt, which Louis the Pious had granted to Anskar and the northern mission some ten years earlier, Anskar lost no time in preparing his case. He immediately petitioned Charles to return the cell at Turholt, as well as exhorting others to petition on his behalf. According to the *Life of Saint Anskar*, a work written soon after Anskar's death by his protégé and successor, Rimbert, even Lothar and Louis the German were induced to intervene, albeit unsuccessfully, with Charles.[53]

---

[51] Röckelein, '"Pervenimus mirificum ad sancti Medardi oraculum"', pp. 150, 152–3, 157–8. For the *cella Lothusa*, see also I. Rembold, 'Rewriting the founder: Werden on the Ruhr and the uses of hagiography', *Journal of Medieval History*, 41(4) (2015), 363–87, here 371–3.

[52] See above, pp. 153–4.

[53] Rimbert, *Vita sancti Anskarii*, ed. G. Waitz, MGH SRG 55 (Hanover: Hahn, 1884), c. 21, p. 46. Eric Knibbs has argued that Anskar also assembled a dossier of documents to support his efforts: for this, see Knibbs, *Ansgar, Rimbert and the Forged Foundations of Hamburg-Bremen*, pp. 71–3.

Upon Anskar's death, Rimbert once more renewed the claim. In the *Life of Saint Anskar*, the loss of Turholt is repeatedly bewailed: the number of times (five) that Turholt is mentioned in the course of the narrative clearly underlines its importance to the author.[54] Rimbert begins his discussion of Turholt by rehearsing the reasons why Turholt was granted to the perpetual use of Anskar and his successors and elucidating the ways in which Turholt supported Hamburg: most notably by acting as a clerical training-ground for Danish and Slavic boys redeemed from slavery, and by supplying funds and provisions more generally. Later in the narrative, Rimbert goes into greater depth, describing how,

after the death of Louis the Pious, when there was a great disturbance concerning the division of the kingdom, so too our pastor's mission began to be undermined in various ways. For when the aforementioned cell of Turholt fell to the possession of the honoured King Charles, he withdrew it from the service which his father had arranged, and gave it to Raginarius.[55]

According to Rimbert, the loss of Turholt fundamentally jeopardized the future of the mission: Anskar 'began to be worn away by various needs and wants', and many of the men who had previously participated in the mission departed 'on account of poverty'.[56] A few chapters later, in a summary of a privilege purportedly given by Nicholas I, Rimbert once again underscores the unfortunate results of Turholt's alienation:

After the death of his father, the Emperor Louis of pious memory, King Charles, the brother of the abovementioned Louis, after the death of his father, the Emperor Louis of pious memory, obtained the monastery which is called Turholt, from the aforementioned place called Hamburg, which his father had given to provide supplies and food for the clerics and bishops there. For after the partition between his brothers, it appeared to lie in his kingdom, situated in West Francia. Because of this, all those who had served at the altars there began to depart. When the necessary funds had been exhausted, they retreated from

More recently, however, Theo Kölzer has postulated a later date for the forgery of one of these documents: see *Praeceptum diui Ludevvici imperatoris*, ed. Caesar, pp. 173–9; Kölzer, '"Gründung-surkunde"', 35–68.

[54] Rimbert, *Vita sancti Anskarii*, ed. Waitz, cc. 12, 15, 21, 23, 36, pp. 34, 37, 46, 50, 71.

[55] *Ibid*, c. 21, p. 46: 'Post cuius obitum cum de regni divisione magna fieret perturbatio, pastoris quoque nostri aliquo modo labefactari coepit legatio. Nam cum cella supradicta Turholt in partem cessisset venerandi regis Karoli, ipse eam a servitio, quod pater suus disposuerat, amovit et ... dedit Raginario.'

[56] *Ibid*, c. 21, pp. 46–7: 'atteri coepit necessitatibus et indigentiis'; 'causa paupertatis'. See also Knibbs, *Ansgar, Rimbert and the Forged Foundations of Hamburg-Bremen*, pp. 119, 127. I have relied greatly upon Knibbs in what follows.

those *gentes* (peoples), and in this manner the mission to the *gentes* ceased. Even the city of Hamburg was mostly deserted.[57]

In Rimbert's summary it was this, placed alongside the recent vacancy at Bremen and the 'savagery of the barbarians', that purportedly led to the creation of a dual see at Hamburg-Bremen.[58]

Yet herein lies a crucial complication: Rimbert appears to have emphasized the importance of Turholt to a specific end. For when Anskar died in 865, his protégée, Rimbert, was appointed not as bishop of Bremen, but rather as bishop of Hamburg.[59] Bereft of resources in Hamburg, Rimbert looked to the more prosperous neighbouring see of Bremen, where he had no doubt expected to succeed his mentor. Soon after his consecration, as Eric Knibbs has argued, Rimbert picked up his pen to compose the *Life of Saint Anskar,* in which he asserted that Anskar had ruled over the dual, and as yet fictional, see of Hamburg-Bremen.[60] Over the course of the next century, his claim was amplified, gradually leading to the lasting configuration of the dual archbishopric. The effects of Rimbert's campaign were felt even within his own lifetime, for there are some indications that he began to act in the capacity of the bishop of Bremen.[61] Rimbert's justification for Anskar's dual archdiocese was carefully constructed. It relied upon the 'destruction' of Hamburg by the Northmen. This was an event which he must have exaggerated, for it left almost no trace on the archaeological record.[62] Rimbert also stressed the small size of the diocese of Hamburg, to which only four baptismal churches pertained.[63] Finally, and perhaps most importantly, Rimbert based his argument for the unification of Hamburg-Bremen upon the loss of Hamburg's monastic cell in Turholt and its consequent financial straits.

The depiction of the loss of Turholt is intimately connected to the layers of possible forgery and self-promotion that accompanied the

---

[57] Rimbert, *Vita sancti Anskarii,* ed. Waitz, c. 23, p. 50: 'quia Karolus rex, frater saepedicti regis Hludowici, post dicessum imperatoris patris sui piae memoriae Hludowici abstulit a praenominato loco, qui dicitur Hammaburg, monasterium quod appellatur Turholt, utpote quod post partitionem inter fratres suos in regno suo coniacere videbatur, situm in occidentali Francia, quod illic genitor suus ad supplementum et victum episcopo et clericis eius dederat, coepere, sicut fertur, omnes ministri altaris recedere. Deficientibus quippe necessariis sumptibus, ab ipsis recesserunt gentibus, et eadem ad gentes legatio per huiusmodi factum defecit. Ipsa quoque metropolis Hammaburg pene deserta facta est'.

[58] *Ibid,* c. 23, p. 50: 'barbarorum saevitiam'.

[59] Knibbs, *Ansgar, Rimbert and the Forged Foundations of Hamburg-Bremen,* pp. 179–80.

[60] *Ibid,* pp. 45, 183–206; cf. I. N. Wood, *The Missionary Life: Saints and the Evangelisation of Europe, 400–1050* (Harlow: Longman, 2001), pp. 126–7; contrast with J. T. Palmer, 'Rimbert's *Vita Anskarii* and Scandinavian mission in the ninth century', *Journal of Ecclesiastical History,* 55(2) (2004), 235–56, here 239–40.

[61] Knibbs, *Ansgar, Rimbert and the Forged Foundations of Hamburg-Bremen,* p. 207.   [62] *Ibid,* p. 128.

[63] Rimbert, *Vita sancti Anskarii,* ed. Waitz, c. 22, p. 47.

formation of Hamburg-Bremen, and as such must be treated with caution.[64] The depredations experienced as a result of the loss of Turholt may well have been somewhat exaggerated in Rimbert's narrative. Yet even if the confiscation of Turholt did not reduce Anskar to abject poverty, its loss may nonetheless have been a difficult blow. The comparative perspective afforded by Lupus of Ferrières' efforts to reclaim the monastic cell of St-Josse reveals the range of supplies that even small monastic cells could offer: clothing, wheat, meat, fish, cheese, vegetables and wax are all mentioned explicitly.[65] St-Josse also provided funds for the monks at Ferrières, as indicated by Lupus' efforts to erect a lead roof over the church at Ferrières immediately following St-Josse's restoration.[66] Turholt lay more than 600 kilometres distant from Hamburg; there was no connecting water route, save the North Sea. It was therefore unlikely to have provided perishable commodities to Anskar and his associates, but its functions as a source of income and as a training ground for clergy should not be underestimated. On a personal level, meanwhile, the loss of Turholt may have deeply affected Rimbert: according to the *Vita sancti Rimberti*, an anonymous work undertaken soon after its protagonist's death in 888, Rimbert was himself first discovered by Anskar at Turholt and was subsequently trained there.[67]

Nevertheless, it seems unlikely that either Turholt or any of the other monastic cells granted to Saxon institutions would have formed a substantial part of the latter's endowments. Rather, it appears that these Frankish cells performed much the same functions as those performed by missionary sponsors, namely the provision of clergy and the possibility of occasional material assistance.[68] Indeed, Rimbert relates that the *cella Turholt* functioned as a place to train young boys for the Church.[69] Likewise, the role of these monasteries as a training-ground for the Saxon clergy can be found in the *Second Life of Saint Liudger*, which depicts an audience between Charlemagne and Liudger. Charlemagne offers Liudger a choice of monasteries to support him in his missionary efforts: he can either choose a large (and by implication rich) nunnery or a small

---

[64] Here, as above, see Knibbs, *Ansgar, Rimbert and the Forged Foundations of Hamburg-Bremen*.

[65] Lupus, *Epistolae*, ed. P. K. Marshall, *Servati Lupi Epistulae* (Leipzig: Teubner, 1984), especially nos. 45, 71, pp. 57–8, 74–5, but also, among others, nos. 11, 32, 42, 55, 83, 88, 92, pp. 20, 42–4, 54–5, 63–4, 82, 87, 90. For this list, see T. F. X. Noble, 'Lupus of Ferrières in his Carolingian context' in A. C. Murray (ed.), *After Rome's Fall: Narrators and Sources of Early Medieval History: Essays Presented to Walter Goffart* (Toronto: University of Toronto Press, 1998), pp. 232–50, here pp. 238–9.

[66] Lupus, *Epistolae*, ed. Marshall, nos. 13–4, pp. 21–3.

[67] *Vita sancti Rimberti*, ed. Waitz, cc. 3, 5, pp. 82–4; see further Palmer, 'Rimbert's *Vita Anskarii*', 237.

[68] Röckelein, 'Pervenimus mirificum ad sancti Medardi oraculum', p. 150.

[69] Rimbert, *Vita sancti Anskarii*, ed. Waitz, cc. 15, 36, pp. 36–7, 71.

male canonical house. Liudger's choice – the male house – reflects his desire for trained clergy over material resources.[70]

In the light of this function, it is worth noting that three of the four institutions to receive a Frankish monastic cell lacked a prominent missionary sponsor (generally a Frankish bishopric or monastery which could provide missionary manpower). As Knibbs has surmised, the missionaries Liudger and Willehad, who worked in the areas around Münster and Bremen, respectively, may conceivably have begun their missionary careers as chorbishops of Utrecht, that is, as rural bishops who were still subject to diocesan authority.[71] Yet they do not appear to have drawn upon the resources of Utrecht after their appointment to the Saxon mission, and the grants of Frankish monastic cells could have made up for the absence of institutional backing. Likewise, the grant of Turholt to Anskar followed less than a year after the archbishopric of Rheims had withdrawn its support for the Northern mission. The grant of these monastic cells, then, appears to have served a specific end: the provision of clerical manpower for the early mission. Unfortunately, this must remain at the level of conjecture, as it is largely impossible to identify individual clerics.

Following the division of the empire in 843, these cells appear to have been alienated.[72] Saxon institutions would put forward claims to their ownership, but to no avail: Carolingian rulers, even those who were faced with persistent petitions, could afford to stand firm. These monastic cells had been granted to meet a temporary shortage of clerical personnel. By the mid-ninth century, this need had been met through local recruitment. The Saxon mission had concluded, and the Northern mission had been put on hold. Frankish cells were to be turned to the more pressing agenda of the day, namely the rewarding of secular followers who had risked all during the civil war.

Fiscal Lands and Religious Patronage

In contrast to the relatively well-attested Carolingian grants of Frankish monastic cells to Saxon religious institutions, the evidence for grants of fiscal lands to these institutions is comparatively slight. In fact, there is extraordinarily little evidence for fiscal lands in Saxony in general.[73]

---

[70] *Vita secunda sancti Liudgeri*, ed. Freise, I:16, p. 12.
[71] Knibbs, *Ansgar, Rimbert and the Forged Foundations of Hamburg-Bremen*, pp. 33–4, 39–41, 46, 58.
[72] Röckelein, "'Pervenimus mirificum ad sancti Medardi oraculum'", p. 161.
[73] For some of the problems with the term 'fiscus', see below, p. 165. For discussions of fiscal lands in Saxony, see especially W. Metz, 'Probleme der fränkischen Reichsgutforschung im sächsischen Stammesgebiet', *NJ*, 31 (1959), 77–126; see further M. Balzer, 'Paderborn – Zentralort der

Presumably, Charlemagne had amassed lands in Saxony during the course of the Saxon war: individual defections would have provided pretexts for such confiscations, and the wide-scale deportations which marked the later stage of the war would have freed up even more substantial landed resources. Yet, notably, Charlemagne does not appear to have retained ownership of these lands. Confiscated lands were swiftly alienated as grants to local supporters, whether to Franks or Saxons: hence the recurring theme in Saxon hagiography of how the Saxons were induced to convert 'partly by wars, partly by persuasions, partly even by gifts'.[74] This rapid redistribution of these lands is further attested, as we have seen in Chapter 1 above, in the remarks of the *Translation of Saint Liborius*, which describes how those who had won land 'by the right of war' eagerly accepted Christian religion; similarly, a 799 entry from the *Lorsch Annals* describes how, following a mass deportation, the lands of those deported were divided between Charlemagne's supporters (*fideles*), whether bishops, priests, counts or other vassals.[75] While Honselmann has taken this passage to be evidence for Charlemagne's foundation of bishoprics in this year, such an interpretation seems unlikely.[76] The bishops and priests referred to here could simply be those who had participated in the mission.

The considerable, if indirect, evidence for confiscated land being distributed as a reward for faithful service reveals much about the nature of royal power in Saxony. Instead of seeking directly to enhance his own power, Charlemagne chose to consolidate that of his subordinates, granting confiscated land in benefice or even in full ownership to his supporters. The result was that, following the conclusion of the Saxon wars, neither Charlemagne nor his successors had much in the way of resources in Saxony; hence the rarity of royal visits to Saxony.[77] Even Louis the Younger, who was formally appointed subking, and later king, of Saxony, Thuringia and Franconia, appears to have spent his time

Karolinger in Sachsen des späten 8. und frühen 9. Jahrhunderts' in Stiegemann and Wemhoff, *799*, vol. I: pp. 116–23, here p. 118; Büttner, 'Mission und Kirchenorganisation', p. 471; Carroll, 'The bishoprics of Saxony', 229–30; Carroll, 'The archbishops and church provinces of Mainz and Cologne', pp. 283–5; M. Lintzel, 'Die Unterwerfung Sachsens durch Karl den Großen und der sächsische Adel' in Lintzel, *Schriften*, pp. 95–127, here pp. 111–12; Metz, *Das karolingische Reichsgut*, pp. 127, 139–41; Schubert, *Geschichte Niedersachsens*, pp. 28–9.

[74] Eigil of Fulda, *Vita sancti Sturmi*, ed. Engelbert, c. 23, p. 158: 'partim bellis partim suasionibus partim etiam muneribus'. See also above, pp. 62–3; Carroll, 'The bishoprics of Saxony', 230.

[75] Anonymus Paderbrunnensis, *Translatio sancti Liborii*, ed. de Vry, c. 4, p. 191: 'iure belli'; *Annales Laureshamenses*, ed. Pertz, 799, p. 38. See also above, p. 63.

[76] Honselmann, 'Die Gründung der sächsischen Bistümer', 1–2.

[77] Cf. R. McKitterick, *Charlemagne: The Formation of a European Identity* (Cambridge: Cambridge University Press, 2008), p. 177.

elsewhere.[78] Royal power in any given region was predicated on royal resources; in Saxony, the Carolingians were poor.

Carolingian rulers may have retained the rights of ownership to properties granted in benefice, as indeed a number of later ninth-century charters concerning land previously held in benefice attest. Yet, as Jane Martindale has rightly highlighted, the extent of royal control over fiscal lands granted in benefice is difficult to gauge.[79] It is important to note that many of these charters were requested by the men holding the lands in benefice; they were implicitly confirmatory in nature, endorsing an arrangement already in place. Certainly, rulers seeking to uphold their right of ownership over fiscal lands could run into considerable difficulties. In 852, as we have seen above, Louis the German travelled to Saxony and convoked an assembly at Minden, at which he not only heard local judicial suits, but also sought to reclaim his own hereditary lands which had been prised away by 'unjust usurpers'.[80] Louis did not simply reassert his rights: rather, he arranged for his cases to be adjudged, and only took possession of the lands once a verdict had been reached. His situation clearly testifies to the precarious nature of the fiscal landholding in Carolingian Saxony.

This re-granting of confiscated lands may have contributed substantially to the consolidation of Frankish control over the region, but it was to have serious consequences for Saxon ecclesiastical structures, whose foundations lagged behind the confiscations, and the necessary pacification such confiscations entailed, by a considerable distance. Episcopal and monastic foundations were thus largely unable to draw upon such royal resources in Saxony. There is only one attested case in which fiscal lands may have been granted as part of the process of foundation: circa 822, upon the request of his cousin Adalhard, Louis the Pious granted the *villa regia* ('royal villa') of Höxter to the newly formed monastery of Corvey.[81] Some scholars have argued that the bishopric of Bremen was likewise built on fiscal land, thanks to a twelfth-century reference to the town as a *villa publica* ('public villa'), but such a reference is inconclusive, even discounting its late date.[82] In the absence of comparable evidence, then,

---

[78] Metz, 'Probleme der fränkischen Reichsgutforschung', 84. For the role of Louis the Younger in Saxony, see above, pp. 130–1.

[79] J. Martindale, 'The kingdom of Aquitaine and the "dissolution of the Carolingian fisc"', *Francia*, 11 (1983), 131–91, here especially 147–52.

[80] *Annales Fuldenses*, ed. F. Kurze, MGH SRG 7 (Hanover: Hahn, 1891), 852, pp. 42–3, here p. 42: 'iniquis pervasoribus'. For the full quotation, see above, pp. 95–6.

[81] *D Kar. 2*, ed. Kölzer, vol. I, no. 226, pp. 561–2; see further Semmler, 'Corvey und Herford', 296–7; cf. B. Kasten, *Adalhard von Corbie: die Biographie eines karolingischen Politikers und Klostervorstehers* (Studia humaniora 3) (Düsseldorf: Droste, 1986), pp. 146–9.

[82] Adam of Bremen, *Gesta Hammaburgensis ecclesiae pontificum*, ed. Schmeidler, I:18, p. 25; for the suggestion that the bishopric was built on fiscal land, see F. Wilschewski, *Die karolingischen Bischofssitze*

Louis the Pious' endowment of Corvey stands apart as an exceptional instance of imperial generosity and clemency, best understood in the context of his reconciliation with, and restoration of, his kinsman Adalhard.

While Carolingian kings do not appear, as a rule, to have granted fiscal resources in Saxony to new foundations, they did extend their generosity to select institutions as opportunity permitted. Yet these gifts should not be understood as propping up a fledgling church: rather, they were made to the most prominent and well-endowed institutions, often to associate themselves with such institutions' prestige, and sometimes to elicit necessary support in times of crisis. The latter motivation stands behind a series of royal gifts to the monastery of Corvey. Shortly before his deposition in 833, Louis the Pious granted Corvey a salt-work on the Weser; upon his restoration to the throne less than a year later, he further presented the monastery with the villages of Sülbeck and Hemeln, perhaps out of gratitude for its unstinting support even after the defection of its mother-house.[83] His son, Louis the German, likewise courted Corvey's support in the civil war of 840 to 843, (re-)granting the monastery eleven *mansi* in the village of Hemeln and, even more impressively, a manor with twenty dependent *mansi* in Empelde.[84] Here, the term *mansus* denotes a unit of assessment correspondingly roughly to the lands worked by a single household.[85] Later in his reign, with his position assured, Louis the German offered one further donation to the monastery: the *villa* of Litzig, with its associated vineyards and labourers, in the middle-Rhine valley.[86] His brother Lothar would allow a *fidelis* to donate fiscal lands formerly held in benefice to the monastery, and his successors would give further gifts: Charles the Fat donated fourteen *mansi* and other lands in return for increased military service, while Arnulf granted the monastery twenty-five *hobae* (a unit akin to the Latin *mansus*).[87]

---

des sächsischen Stammesgebietes bis 1200 (Studien der internationalen Architektur- und Kunstgeschichte 46) (Petersberg: M. Imhof, 2007), p. 20; see further the helpful comments on terminology in C. Wickham, 'Consensus and assemblies in the Romano-Germanic kingdoms: a comparative approach' in V. Epp and C. H. F. Meyer (eds.), *Recht und Konsens im frühen Mittelalter* (Vorträge und Forschungen 82) (Ostfildern: J. Thorbecke, 2017), pp. 389–426, here especially pp. 394–6.

[83] D Kar. 2, ed. Kölzer, vol. II, no. 337, p. 833.

[84] D LD, ed. Kehr, nos. 28–9, pp. 34–6. See further the comments of B. Bigott, *Ludwig der Deutsche und die Reichskirche im Ostfränkischen Reich (826–876)* (Historische Studien 470) (Husum: Matthiesen, 2002), pp. 85–7.

[85] See here D. Herlihy, 'The Carolingian mansus', *The Economic History Review*, 13(1) (1960), 79–89; A. Verhulst, *The Carolingian Economy* (Cambridge: Cambridge University Press, 2002), pp. 43–5.

[86] D LD, ed. Kehr, no. 132, pp. 183–4.

[87] D Lo I, ed. T. Schieffer, MGH, *Die Urkunden Lothars I. und Lothars II* (Berlin: Weidemann, 1966), no. 112, pp. 261–2; D Karl, ed. P. Kehr, MGH, *Die Urkunden Karls III* (Berlin: Weidemann, 1937), no. 158, pp. 255–7; D Arn, ed. Kehr, no. 60, pp. 87–8.

Corvey was not the only institution to benefit from such generosity: its sister-house, Herford, was the recipient of many rich grants under Louis the German. In 851, it received demesne land in Kilver, along with ten *mansi* in Laer and Erpen; in 858, it acquired two manors with a combined thirty dependent *mansi* in the towns of Selm and Stockum, followed the very next year by an additional fourteen *mansi* in Westfalen.[88] Lastly, in 868, Louis the German donated a further two manors with thirty dependent *mansi* in Engersgau, which was, as in the case of Litzig above, outside Saxony.[89] Occasionally, other monasteries also enjoyed such patronage, if less lavishly: Louis the Younger granted the monastery of Gandersheim, a foundation of his wife's family, some Thuringian possessions, while in 887, Charles the Fat allowed lands previously held in benefice to be given in full ownership to the monastery of Neuenheerse.[90] Finally, a later charter of Zwetinbold attests to a former grant of fiscal land in Lotharingia to the Saxon monastery of Werden.[91]

There is also some evidence, however slight, of fiscal lands being granted to Saxon bishoprics.[92] A passage in Adam of Bremen's *Deeds of the Archbishops of the Church of Hamburg* describes how, shortly before Willerich of Bremen's death in 837, 'Charles presented a hundred *mansi* to the church of the Saviour at Bremen'.[93] This Charles can be tentatively identified as Charles the Bald, who had been granted Frisia as a subkingdom in 837 and could have donated lands from inside the diocese of Bremen's Frisian territory. Grants of land within Saxony were, of necessity, more modest. In 876, Louis the Younger bestowed some twelve *mansi* upon the church of Verden, while in 889, Arnulf granted Wolhelm of Münster various properties in the counties of Gifaron and Reinidi.[94] To these may be added two further instances of bishops holding fiscal lands in benefice. Bishop Biso held some ten *mansi* in benefice before donating them to the monastery of Neuenheerse in 887, and in 890 Bishop Wigbert of Verden received a lifetime grant of lands previously held in benefice.[95] In the cases of Biso and Wolfhelm,

---

[88] *D LD*, ed. Kehr, nos. 61, 93, 95, pp. 83–4, 134–5, 137–8.   [89] *Ibid*, no. 128, pp. 178–9.

[90] *D LJ*, ed. P. Kehr, *MGH, Die Urkunden Ludwigs des Deutschen, Karlmanns und Ludwigs der Jüngeren* (Berlin: Weidemann, 1934), no. 4, pp. 337–9; *D Karl*, ed. Kehr, no. 169, pp. 273–4.

[91] *D Zw*, ed. T. Schieffer, *MGH, Die Urkunden Zwetibolds und Ludwigs des Kindes* (Berlin: Weidemann, 1960), no. 19, pp. 51–3; see also Metz, *Das karolingische Reichsgut*, pp. 71–2.

[92] Carroll, 'The bishoprics of Saxony', 222–3. I have relied upon this in what follows.

[93] Adam of Bremen, *Gesta Hammaburgensis ecclesiae pontificum*, ed. Schmeidler, I:18, p. 25: 'Karolus elemosinam optulit Salvatori ad Bremensem ecclesiam C mansos.' For this, see Knibbs, *Ansgar, Rimbert and the Forged Foundations of Hamburg-Bremen*, p. 50.

[94] *D LJ*, ed. Kehr, no. 1, pp. 333–4; *D Arn*, ed. Kehr, no. 54, pp. 77–8.

[95] *D Karl*, ed. Kehr, no. 169, pp. 273–4; *D Arn*, ed. Kehr, no. 78, pp. 116–8.

it is unclear whether such grants had been made for their own uses or for that of their bishoprics, but Wigbert's example gives occasion to suspect the latter: the charter states that the properties will revert to the bishopric after Wigbert's death, with the proceeds from the lands going to the canons at Verden.

These examples, however, constitute the only concrete evidence for the granting of fiscal land to Saxon religious institutions. Christopher Carroll, following Paul Kehr's 1934 edition of Louis the German's charters, has argued for one further donation of fiscal land to a Saxon bishopric: a grant of all *fiscus* ('fiscal lands') within the boundaries of the diocese of Hildesheim, purportedly given by Louis the Pious and later confirmed by his son.[96] Yet only the confirmation survives, preserved in an abbreviated form in a fifteenth-century copy-book, and this appears to have been at the very least interpolated: Theo Kölzer has recently drawn attention to its anachronistic use of diocesan boundaries.[97] Even if the reference to diocesan boundaries is accepted as a later addition to a genuine document, the confirmation appears to be little more than a grant of immunity. *Fiscus*, after all, had multiple meanings: it could denote royal land, but it could equally refer to royal revenue, for example that generated by judicial fines. The granting of revenue from fines was a common feature of immunities from this period: indeed, Louis the Pious issued an immunity for the bishopric of Paderborn in 822 in which he granted such revenues to be used for 'stipends for paupers and for the lighting of lamps'.[98] Certainly, the remainder of the fifteenth-century text, which stipulates that no men from the church's estates, whatsoever their condition, may be detained, brought to court or pressed into military or royal service, recalls the earlier grant to Paderborn.

It is certainly possible that further donations of fiscal land were made. A 902 charter of Louis the Child for the diocese of Halberstadt grants immunity to 'whatever had been granted to the church of Halberstadt by the royal munificence of our predecessors or by other faithful men'.[99] This is a statement which implies some previous royal or imperial munificence. Yet such comments verge on speculation. Moreover, the extant evidence suggests that fiscal lands were scarce in Saxony. Wolfgang Metz has noted the complete absence of donations of

---

[96] *D LD*, ed. Kehr, no. 143, p. 200; Carroll, 'The bishoprics of Saxony', 222.

[97] Kölzer, 'Zum angeblichen Immunitätsprivileg', 24.

[98] *D Kar. 2*, ed. Kölzer, vol. I, no. 207, p. 512: 'ad stipendia pauperum et luminaria concinnanda'.

[99] *D LK*, ed. T. Schieffer, *MGH, Die Urkunden Zwetibolds und Ludwigs des Kindes* (Berlin: Weidemann, 1960), no. 15, p. 118: 'quae memoratae Halberstetensi ecclesiae a progenitoribus nostris regia munificentia sive aliorum fidelium collatione'. See also Carroll, 'The bishoprics of Saxony', 223–4.

conlaboratus, that is, the levy of a ninth, and sometimes tenth, part of proceeds from fiscal lands. Such grants were often made to ecclesiastical institutions in other parts of the empire; their absence here, as Metz argues, points towards the absence of large-scale Carolingian landholding in the region.[100] His argument is corroborated by an examination of extant Carolingian grants. A significant proportion of the fiscal lands granted to Saxon institutions, comprising slightly more than a quarter of all grants to Saxon religious institutions, lay outside Saxony.[101] Over half of the Saxon 'fiscal' lands that were granted to religious institutions were referred to as having been recently held in benefice, whether by a bishop (on two occasions) or, more commonly, by a secular *fidelis*.[102] This raises the question of whether such gifts should be attributed to rulers, to whom the land legally belonged, or to the magnates, lay or religious, who had enjoyed *de facto* ownership of the benefices, and who appear to have acted as the prime moving force behind such donations. Only a small minority of 'royal' donations came from lands in Saxony held directly by the king.[103]

Such an apparent scarcity of fiscal land may explain the selectivity with which rulers bestowed patronage: indeed, the vast majority of royal grants went to a mere two prominent monasteries, Corvey and Herford.[104] This does not appear to have been merely a matter of chance survival: on the contrary, institutions throughout Saxony actively commemorated their often tenuous links to the Carolingians in hagiography and liturgy. Instead, the Carolingians' patronage of these houses must be understood as a conscious choice. These institutions were the wealthiest and most prominent religious houses in the whole of Saxony, and rulers stood much to gain from such acts of patronage: grants of fiscal land served to reinforce rulers' connections to the monastery as well as to the wider community of monastic patrons. These relationships could be capitalized upon in times of crisis, as they were during the civil war of 840 to 843.[105]

---

[100] Metz, 'Probleme der fränkischen Reichsgutforschung', 84–5.

[101] For lands granted outside of Saxony, see Adam of Bremen, *Gesta Hammaburgensis ecclesiae pontificum*, ed. Schmeidler, I:18, p. 25; *D Lo I*, ed. Schieffer, no. 112, pp. 261–2; *D LD*, ed. Kehr, nos. 128, 132, pp. 178–9, 183–4; *D LJ*, ed. Kehr, no. 4, pp. 337–9; *D Zw*, ed. Schieffer, no. 19, pp. 51–3. See further Carroll, 'The bishoprics of Saxony', 231.

[102] For grants of land recently held in benefice, see *D LD*, ed. Kehr, nos. 29, 61, 95, pp. 35–6, 83–4, 137–8; *D Lo I*, ed. Schieffer, no. 112, pp. 261–2; *D Karl*, ed. Kehr, nos. 158, 169, pp. 255–7, 273–4; *D Arn*, ed. Kehr, nos. 3, 54, 60, 78, pp. 5–8, 77–8, 87–8, 116–8.

[103] For lands in Saxony held directly by the king, see *D Kar. 2*, ed. Kölzer, vols. I–II, nos. 226, 329, 337, pp. 561–2, 814–15, 833; *D LD*, ed. Kehr, nos. 28, 93, pp. 34–5, 134–5.

[104] Carroll, 'The archbishops and church provinces of Mainz and Cologne', p. 284; see also Metz, *Das karolingische Reichsgut*, pp. 139–40.

[105] Bigott, *Ludwig der Deutsche*, pp. 85–7.

They were equally important, however, in times of peace. Rulers' influence depended, as Matthew Innes has so ably demonstrated, on their ability to insinuate themselves into extant local networks.[106] By granting lands to these institutions, Carolingian rulers may well have been extending their reach into Saxon politics.

Nonetheless, the absence of Carolingian contributions to Saxon religious endowments is striking. The occasional patronage proffered, in the form of grants of monastic cells, fiscal lands, fiscal exemptions and relics, is far less systematic than we might expect in a region where Christian conversion had been forcibly imposed from on high. There are two potential explanations for this, the first of which is that Carolingian rulers may not have placed high value upon the establishment of religious institutions in Saxony. Patronage reflects priorities, and the fact that fiscal lands were not used to support the establishment of Christian infrastructure in Saxony speaks volumes. The second, and by no means mutually irreconcilable, explanation is that Carolingian rulers simply may not have had the resources available in Saxony to endow religious institutions.[107] Certainly, Carolingian interventions in post-conquest Saxony were few and far between. Their influence may have been significantly curtailed.

Yet, crucially, religious institutions were established in Saxony. By the mid-ninth century, although there were still deficiencies in church provision and clergy, the region boasted a reasonably developed religious landscape, complete with bishoprics, local churches and monasteries of all types. In the apparent absence of Carolingian and Frankish patronage, it appears that these institutions had been founded on the back of local patrons and local exactions. It is to the latter, and specifically, to the role of tithe, that I shall now turn.

TITHES AND THE ESTABLISHMENT OF SAXON RELIGIOUS INSTITUTIONS

'Similarly, following the mandate of God, we order that everyone – nobles, freemen, and half-freemen – shall give a tithe of their possessions and labour to the churches and priests; just as God has given to each Christian, let them return a part to God.'[108] So reads chapter 17 of the

---

[106] M. Innes, *State and Society in the Early Middle Ages: The Middle Rhine Valley, 400–1000* (Cambridge: Cambridge University Press, 2000), especially pp. 180–8.

[107] Carroll, 'The bishoprics of Saxony', 231.

[108] *Capitulatio de partibus Saxoniae*, ed. C. von Schwerin, *MGH Fontes iuris* 4 (Hanover: Hahn, 1918), pp. 37–44, here c. 17, p, 40: 'Similiter secundum dei mandatum precipimus, ut omnes decimam partem substantiae et laboris suis ecclesiis et sacerdotibus donent tam nobiles quam ingenui similiter et liti iuxta quod deus unicuique dederit christiano, partem deo reddant.'

First Saxon Capitulary. The means by which it proposes to finance local churches are essentially home-grown: land and servants would be provided by parishioners, the latter in proportion to the size of the parish, and tithes would be rendered not only from one's income and property, but also from judicial fines.

Relatively little attention has been paid to these chapters.[109] Modern scholarship on this capitulary has tended to focus on its earlier provisions, which levy capital sentences for a broad range of crimes and infractions, from killing a priest and human cannibalism to breaking the Lenten feast. Yet the element of the text which excited the most controversy among contemporaries, or at least among one very prominent contemporary, was not the draconian penalties which have caused modern commentators to label it the 'Terror Capitulary', but rather these very chapters on ecclesiastical endowments, and more specifically on tithe.

Alcuin on the Imposition of Tithe

In 796, Alcuin wrote a series of letters in which he criticized the levying of tithe in missionary territories, and specifically in Saxony.[110] These letters have been placed largely within the context not of the Saxon wars, but rather of the campaigns against the Avars, and indeed, Alcuin did apply the lessons of Saxon missionary experience to the Avar mission in a letter addressed to Archbishop Arn of Salzburg.[111] Such an interpretation derives from the traditional dating of the *First Saxon Capitulary* to 782, against which both Yitzhak Hen and Robert Flierman have recently argued.[112] The date of 794/5 which they propose for the composition of this text allows Alcuin's comments to be understood as a topical contribution to a current debate around ecclesiastical policy in Saxony.

The crux of Alcuin's critique was that tithes, and other monetary burdens, could hinder acceptance of the Christian faith.[113] As he wrote

---

[109] For the significance of the ecclesiastical provisions in this text, see especially E. Schubert, 'Die Capitulatio de partibus Saxoniae' in D. Brosius, C. van der Heuvel, E. Hinrichs and H. van Lengen (eds.), *Geschichte in der Region. Zum 65. Geburtstag von Heinrich Schmidt* (Hanover: Hahn, 1993), pp. 3–28, here pp. 11–18.

[110] For discussions of Alcuin's views on mission, see, among others Johanek, 'Der Ausbau', p. 499; Wood, 'An absence of saints?', pp. 339, 345–8; for his views on tithe, see, among others, O. M. Phelan, *The Formation of Christian Europe: The Carolingians, Baptism, and the Imperium Christianum* (Oxford: Oxford University Press, 2014), pp. 100–1; von Padberg, *Mission und Christianisierung*, pp. 206–7.

[111] Alcuin, *Epistolae*, ed. E. Dümmler, *MGH Epp.* 4:2 (Berlin: Weidemann, 1895), pp. 1–481, here no. 107, pp. 153–4.

[112] See above, pp. 24–5.

[113] For an excellent discussion of Alcuin's views on Christian formation more generally, see Phelan, *The Formation of Christian Europe*, pp. 94–146.

to the royal treasurer, Megenfrid, 'if the light yoke and sweet burden of Christ were preached to the most hard populace of the Saxons with as much urgency as tithes were collected or legal penalties for the smallest crimes were enforced, then perhaps they might not shrink from the sacraments of baptism'.[114] In a letter to Charlemagne, meanwhile, Alcuin presented his arguments against the imposition of tithe through biblical exegesis. He offers a passage from 1 Corinthians 3, explaining that 'new converts to the faith must be taught more gently, just as babies must be nourished with milk, lest bitter lessons cause fragile minds to vomit that which they drank', before moving on to Matthew 9:17, in which Jesus declares that new wine should not be placed in old bottles, 'otherwise the bottles break, the wine pours out, and the bottles are ruined'.[115] Here, Alcuin favours the exegetical explanation proffered by Jerome: 'for the pure souls of virgins who have never been polluted by the contagion of vice are different from those who have been exposed to filth and great wantonness'.[116] 'Having reflected on these things', Alcuin continues,

may your most blessed piety with wise counsel consider whether it is better to impose the yoke of tithes on this unlearned people, new to the faith, in order that a full levy may be taken from each home ... Even we who have been raised and instructed in the catholic faith only with difficulty agree to pay full tithe on our property: their tender faith, infant souls, and minds, greedy for that bounty, are much more resistant.[117]

Correct tithing practice was, in Alcuin's mind, a secondary issue when placed alongside the *desiderata* of conversion and baptism.

Alcuin's objections to the extraction of tithes, alongside his more general remarks about the futility of dictating faith through compulsion, have been much seized upon by modern commentators as the lone voice

---

[114] Alcuin, *Epistolae*, ed. Dümmler, no. 111, p. 161: 'Si tanta instantia leve Christi iugum et onus suave durissimo Saxonum populo praedicaretur, quanta decimarum redditio vel legalis pro parvissimis quibuslibet culpis edicti necessitas exigebatur, forte baptismatis sacramenta non abhorrerent.'

[115] *Ibid*, no. 110, pp. 157–8: 'nova populorum ad fidem conversio mollioribus praeceptis quasi infantilis aetas lacte esset nutrienda; ne per austeriora praecepta fragilis mens evomat, quod bibit'; 'alioquin utres rumpuntur et vinum effundetur et utres peribunt'. See further Phelan, *The Formation of Christian Europe*, pp. 102–6; R. E. Sullivan, 'Carolingian missionary theories', *The Catholic Historical Review*, 42(3) (1956), 273–95, here 281.

[116] Alcuin, *Epistolae*, ed. Dümmler, no. 110, p. 158: '"Alia est enim" ... "puritas virginalis animae et nulla prioris vitii contagione pollutae, et alia eius, quae sordibus et multorum libidini subiacuerit."'

[117] *Ibid*, no. 110, p. 158: 'His ita consideratis, vestra sanctissima pietas sapienti consilio praevideat: si melius sit, rudibus populis in principio fidei iugum inponere decimarum, ut plena fiat per singulas domus exactio illarum ... Nos vero, in fide catholica nati nutriti et edocti, vix consentimus substantiam nostram pleniter decimare: quanto magis tenera fides et infantilis animus et avara mens illarum largitati non consentit.'

of dissent against an unrelenting campaign of forcible conversion. Yet we should pause before imputing modern sensibilities to the cleric and scholar, whose view of the Saxons was not markedly different from those of other contemporary detractors. In his last (preserved) statement on the subject, a letter written to Charlemagne in 799, Alcuin reminded his king that

I once spoke to your most blessed piety concerning the levying of tithes, because it may perhaps be better to remit this public obligation for a period, until the faith takes root in their hearts, if this land is worthy of divine favour. Those who have moved abroad were the best Christians, as has been much noted. Those who remain in the region, remain in the filth of their sin. For Babylon is thought to be the home of demons because of the sins of its people, as is read in the prophets.[118]

Alcuin's characterization of Saxony as Babylon suggests implicit approval of Charlemagne's military exploits in the region.[119] His critique of both compulsory conversion and the imposition of tithes was thus primarily pragmatic in nature. Unfortunately for Alcuin's cause, so too was Charlemagne's reason for levying tithe in Saxony: the relative absence of resources for religious institutions in early ninth-century Saxony.[120]

Given the apparent scarcity of both fiscal lands and, consequently, royal endowments in Carolingian Saxony, it appears that tithes provided a vital source of income for episcopal, monastic and local churches alike, thereby paralleling East Frankish practice more broadly in this period. The conciliar minutes of east Frankish synods reveal that east Frankish bishops were far more concerned with the distribution of tithes than their better-endowed west Frankish counterparts, and indeed it was in the East that the practice of quadripartition first became widespread. According to this practice, a quarter of tithe was devoted to the bishops, a quarter to local priests, a quarter to the upkeep of church structures and the remaining quarter to alms. In this regard, as Carroll has argued, Saxony may present the culmination of a more general east Frankish trend.[121]

---

[118] *Ibid*, no. 174, p. 289: 'Olim vestrae sanctissime pietati de exactione decimarum dixi: quia forte melius est, vel aliquanto spatio ut remittatur publica necessitas, donec fides cordibus radicitus inolescat; si tamen illa patria Dei electione digna habetur. Qui foras recesserunt, optimi fuerunt christiani, sicut in plurimus notum est. Et qui remanserunt patria, in faecibus malitiae permanserunt. Nam Babylon propter peccata populi daemoniorum deputata est habitio, ut in prophetis legitur.'

[119] See further Sullivan, 'Carolingian missionary theories', 278. Contrast with D. F. Appleby, 'Spiritual progress in Carolingian Saxony: a case from ninth-century Corvey', *The Catholic Historical Review*, 82(4) (1996), 599–613, here 603.

[120] Büttner, 'Mission und Kirchenorganisation', p. 471.

[121] Carroll, 'The archbishops and church provinces of Mainz and Cologne', pp. 187–90; G. Constable, *Monastic Tithes: From Their Origins to the Twelfth Century* (Cambridge: Cambridge University Press, 1964), pp. 52–3; R. McKitterick, *The Frankish Church and the Carolingian*

Nowhere was the importance of tithe more emphasized, however, than in Carolingian Saxony. Looking back from the late ninth century, Bishop Egilmar of Osnabrück would declare that Charlemagne had 'erected bishoprics for each province out of the stipend of tithes, because the pastors and bishops there lacked other donations'.[122] This may well be an accurate reading of Charlemagne's calculations at the close of the missionary period. His comments must be read, however, within their immediate context: the growth of monastic tithe, and in particular the tithe dispute between, on the one side, the bishoprics of Osnabrück and Paderborn and, on the other, the monasteries of Corvey and Herford.

Monastic Tithe, and the View from the End of the Century

Although the principle of quadripartition only allowed the bishop to benefit directly from a quarter of all tithe revenue, he nonetheless exercised control over all tithes in his diocese. From the last third of the ninth century, however, bishops began to endow monasteries within their dioceses with tithes from certain parishes in return for the right of lordship and a nominal annual rent.[123] This is attested in an array of genuine charters for the period. In 871, Louis the German confirmed such arrangements for the nunnery of Neuenheerse, which received a second confirmation from Charles the Fat some sixteen years later; his successor, Arnulf, issued similar confirmations for the nunneries of Ridigippi and Möllenbeck.[124] These arrangements allowed bishops – or, in the case of Möllenbeck, a prominent parishioner – to found religious houses drawing only on their own relatively modest holdings: the landed endowment of the monastery of Neuenheerse, for instance, appears initially to have consisted of a mere ten *mansi*, but this was supplemented by the tithe income from four villages.[125]

Reforms, 789–895 (London: Royal Historical Society, 1977), pp. 76–8; J. M. Wallace-Hadrill, *The Frankish Church* (Oxford: Oxford University Press, 1983), pp. 288–9.

[122] Stephanus V papa, *Epistolae*, ed. G. Laehr, *MGH Epp.* 7:5 (Berlin: Weidemann, 1928), pp. 354–65, here no. 3, p. 360: 'singulos eiusdem provinciae episcopatus ex decimarum stipendiis constituisset, quia aliis ibi pastores et episcopi donariis carebant'. For the authenticity of this letter, see above, p. 27, footnote 96.

[123] For this section, see also the arguments presented in I. Rembold, 'The Poeta Saxo at Paderborn: episcopal authority and Carolingian rule in late ninth-century Saxony', *EME*, 21(2) (2013), 169–96, here 180–6. For the growth of monastic tithe across this period more generally, see Constable, *Monastic Tithes*, pp. 57–83.

[124] *D LD*, ed. Kehr, nos. 137, pp. 190–2; *D Karl*, ed. Kehr, no. 169, pp. 273–4; *D Arn*, ed. Kehr, nos. 41, 147, pp. 59–60, 223–5.

[125] *D LD*, ed. Kehr, no. 137, pp. 190–2.

Sometimes, however, such arrangements were made by other parties at the bishops' expense. In 838, Louis the Pious granted a number of churches with their tithes to the monastery of Herford, seemingly without the consent of the relevant bishops; likewise, in 888, Arnulf issued a (now interpolated) charter for the monastery of Werden in which he granted it the right to retain tithe revenues from its demesne lands.[126] Here again, this was without the involvement of the archbishop of Cologne, in whose see the monastery lay. Similarly, and far more controversially, the monastery of Corvey claimed the right to tithe revenue both from its own properties and from other subject districts. This can be seen from a number of charters which were forged and/or interpolated in the late ninth and tenth centuries: a forged (tenth-century) immunity charter purportedly given by Louis the Pious to the monastic cell of Visbeck, which listed among its appurtenances 'subjected churches in Lerigau, and the tithes from the forest of Ammeri and Ponteburg and other churches in Hesingau and Fenkigau, except one church in Saxlinga';[127] the gift of the cell at Visbeck 'with its tithes' to the monastery of Corvey;[128] and the further grant of the chapel at Eresburg 'with the tithes pertaining to it'.[129] Finally, there is the late ninth-century forgery of a charter purportedly given by Louis the German in 873, in which Corvey received the right to retain tithe revenue from its demesne land.[130] In 887, this forgery was presumably presented to, and accepted by, Arnulf, who issued a charter to Corvey and Herford confirming their right to retain such revenues.[131]

Corvey's campaign to secure tithe privileges through forgeries and falsifications appears to be a development of the late 880s, though it would continue well into, and beyond, the tenth century. Yet according to at least one disgruntled contemporary, Bishop Egilmar of Osnabrück, both Corvey and its sister-house, Herford, had arrogated such rights some forty years before against all canonical procedure. As Egilmar relates in a papal appeal, it was during the long absence of Bishop Goswin, who had sought refuge at Fulda following his prominent role in Louis the Pious' deposition, that trouble began to brew. Count Cobbo, a

---

[126] *D Kar. 2*, ed. Kölzer, vol. II, no. 383, pp. 955–6; *D Am*, ed. Kehr, no. 36, pp. 52–4.
[127] *D Kar. 2*, ed. Kölzer, vol. I, no. 198, p. 491: 'cum subiectis aecclesiis in eodem pago Leriga et cum decima de silva Ammeri et Ponteburg et ceteris ecclesiis in Hesiga et Fenkiga, excepta una ecclesia in Saxlinga'. For an recent re-assessment of this charter, see Kölzer, 'Die Urkunden', 111–14.
[128] *D LD*, ed. Kehr, no. 73, pp. 102–4: 'cum ... <decimis>'.
[129] *D Kar. 2*, ed. Kölzer, vol. II, no. 255, p. 638: 'cum ... <decimis> ad eam pertinentibus'.
[130] *D LD*, ed. Kehr, no. 184, pp. 265–7.
[131] *D Am*, ed. Kehr, no. 3, pp. 5–8. For this, and for the dating of the forged Louis the German charter, see also Rembold, 'The Poeta Saxo at Paderborn', 181–2.

prominent *fidelis* of Louis the German, arranged for the tithes from the bishopric to be channelled to the monasteries of Corvey and Herford, where his brother and sister served, respectively, as abbot and abbess. Goswin's eventual successor, Gauzbert, had been translated from his missionary see in Sweden. This was a canonical irregularity which, as Egilmar averred, prevented him from seeking redress on this issue. Egilmar's predecessor, Egilbert, had attempted to seek resolution, but had not been able to bring the matter to conclusion.[132]

When Egilmar himself attempted to recover the tithe revenues from these monasteries' substantial holdings in the diocese, 'the aforesaid monks and nuns carried an accusation to the ears of prince Arnulf against the sacred canons, referring to the order, so they said, established by King Louis and Hrabanus of Mainz, the bishop of another diocese, but adapted by witnesses of unreliable honesty, because it is said to have been forged fraudulently by these ones'.[133] The matter was judged in due course by a synod of nine bishops, including Willibert of Cologne, Egilmar's actual metropolitan, in the presence of Arnulf. Yet Egilmar claimed that the assembled bishops, 'knowing the will of the prince and of certain counts, and being resistant lest they offend them, did not presume to respond to the matter brought before them'.[134] Canonical justice had been denied him. The result, he wrote, was the continued impoverishment and pastoral neglect of the diocese of Osnabrück.

Corvey and Herford did not merely hold lands in the diocese of Osnabrück, however: both monasteries lay within, and held substantial lands in, the diocese of Paderborn. Bishop Biso of Paderborn had participated in the synod which Arnulf had convened, but it is probable that he regretted the decision that he felt compelled to make. A confirmation of the synod's decisions issued by Archbishop Liudbert of Mainz appears specifically aimed to forestall any protestations that Biso himself may offer. This synodal decree proclaims that the bishop of Paderborn, mentioned twice explicitly in contrast to other bishops who remain unnamed, must respect Corvey's and Herford's immunities, and it further confirms the rights of these institutions to retain the tithes from their widespread possessions. The decree specifies that such

---

[132] Stephanus V papa, *Epistolae*, ed. Laehr, no. 3, pp. 360–1. See also Carroll, 'The bishoprics of Saxony', 231–2.

[133] Stephanus V papa, *Epistolae*, ed. Laehr, no. 3, p. 361: 'praediciti monachi et puellae ad aures principis Arnulfi accusationem contra canonica sancita detulerunt, deferentes praeceptum ut aiunt a Hludowico rege et Rabano Magontiacense alterius pontifice diocesis statutum, sed non certis testificantionibus fidei accommodatum, quia fraudulenter dicitur ab ipsis fictum'.

[134] *Ibid*, no. 3, p. 361: 'scientes voluntatem principis et quorundam comitum et, ne eum offenderent, renitentes, nil de causa prolata respondere praesumpserunt'.

confirmation is offered because of troubles brought about by 'certain recently-ordained bishops'.[135] The plural noun is revealing. This was not simply about putting Egilmar of Osnabrück in his place. After all, Liudbert of Mainz had no authority over the bishopric of Osnabrück, which was a suffragan of the archdiocese of Cologne. Yet he was the metropolitan of the see of Paderborn, where Biso had been consecrated only a year before. Biso's name is notably absent from the list of signatories at the bottom of the decree.[136]

Biso did not put forward any blunt petitions, in contrast to his episcopal colleague in Osnabrück. Yet he did commission an array of works, both hagiographical and historiographical, with the aim of restoring Paderborn's prestige and hence its *Königsnähe*.[137] The Saxon Poet's verse life of Charlemagne, for example, contains an interesting commentary on the importance of tithe not altogether dissimilar from Egilmar's statement that Charlemagne had granted tithe to the Saxon bishoprics as the basis of their endowments. At the conclusion of the Saxon wars, which are presented as the main driving force of the narrative, the poet included the terms and provisions of the Peace of Salz, which he asserted marked the end of the Saxon war. While some of the provisions he offered derive from Einhard's account of the war's conclusion, others are unique, most notably his declaration that 'it was decided by unanimous opinion that the Saxons ought not to pay any tax or tribute to the kings of the Franks, but they would offer only the tithes established by divine law, and they would strive to obey their bishops and clergy, who would teach sacred dogma and the faith and life that is pleasing to the Lord'.[138] The peace settlement is unknown in other contemporary narratives, and its provisions may be assumed to be an invention of the anonymous poet. It is nonetheless telling that the poet depicts the peace as predicated upon the payment of tithes and the profession of obedience to the Saxon episcopate.

These perspectives from the close of the ninth century may tentatively be used to complement the contemporary evidence from the conquest period. The *First Saxon Capitulary* states that local churches should be

---

[135] *Concilium Magontiacensis*, ed. M. Stimming, *Mainzer Urkundenbuch: Die Urkunden bis zum Tode Erzbischof Adalberts I (1137)*, 2 vols. (Darmstadt: Hessische Historische Kommission, 1972), vol. I, no. 167, pp. 99–103, here p. 103: 'per quosdam episcopos recenter ordinatos'.

[136] *Ibid*, no. 167, p. 103.   [137] Rembold, 'The Poeta Saxo at Paderborn', 187–95.

[138] Poeta Saxo, *Annalium de gestis Caroli magni imperatoris libri V*, ed. P. Winterfeld, *MGH Poet*. 4:1 (Berlin: Weidemann, 1899), pp. 1–71, here IV, lines 102–8, p. 48: 'At vero censum Francorum regibus ullum/Solvere ne penitus deberent atque tributum,/Cunctorum pariter statuit sententia concors,/Sed tantum decimas divina lege statutas/Offerrent ac presulibus parere studerent/Ipsorumque simul clero, qui dogmata sacra/Quique fidem domino placitam vitamque doceret.' See also Rembold, 'The Poeta Saxo at Paderborn', 192–4.

supported by tithe revenues alongside small tracts of lands furnished by local parishioners; Alcuin protested that tithes were being extracted with excessive zeal, thereby risking the alienation of recent converts. The conclusion drawn from both sources, namely that tithes were levied and perhaps over-enthusiastically enforced to support the incipient structures of the Saxon church, is borne out by the later ninth-century evidence. The fact that bishops allocated tithe income, alongside small tracts of land, to their own monastic foundations indicates that this was the main source of revenue upon which they could draw. More eloquent, however, are the statements of Bishops Egilmar and Biso. Whether or not Charlemagne had expressly planned that such revenue should serve as the basis of episcopal endowments, Egilmar could claim it had been the sole endowment granted to his predecessors; his colleague, meanwhile, cast the payment of tithe as a condition for peace following the Saxon war. The emphasis placed by both upon tithe revenue underscores not only the centrality of this source of income, but also the noticeable absence of Carolingian or Frankish patronage.

LOCAL RELIGIOUS PATRONAGE IN CAROLINGIAN SAXONY

There is one further source of patronage that has been largely underrated in recent scholarship: that of the local populace. Local residents appear to have played a considerable role in the foundation and endowment of Saxon religious institutions. This is most visible in the array of female monastic foundations in the mid- and late ninth century which are widely acknowledged to be the work of the local Saxon elite. Yet, as I shall suggest below, local donors appear to have contributed substantially to all foundations in Carolingian Saxony, thereby undercutting the putative division made in many secondary works between 'local' and 'outside' foundations. The monasteries Corvey and Werden, whose foundation has long been ascribed to Frankish and Frisian churchmen, derived considerable material support from a wide swathe of local donors; so too do Fulda's dependent cells in Saxony appear to have been maintained largely through local patronage. This robust body of evidence stands in clear contrast to the dearth of information on Carolingian and Frankish patronage in Saxony, and suggests that that the current model of a church structure imposed by the Franks is deeply in need of revision.

The View from Corvey, Werden and Fulda

The foundation of Corvey has traditionally been attributed to the Carolingian half-brothers Adalhard and Wala. Indeed, both Adalhard and

Wala, alongside Louis the Pious, the rest of the community at Corbie and its temporary abbot, Adalhard II, were instrumental in Corvey's foundation. Yet the land on which the initial foundation was constructed (at Hethis) was provided by a Saxon monk who had come to Corbie as a hostage: as the *Epitaph of Arsenius* records, he 'gave us his own properties where a monastery might be built'.[139] What Corbie offered was, by contrast, comparatively modest: Wala persuaded Adalhard II 'to supply labour and to bear the costs' of the new construction.[140] Considerably more detail is offered by the *Translation of Saint Vitus*. According to this text, the initial impetus for a Saxon foundation had come from the Saxon hostages, who 'began to question whether it would be possible to find a place in their country where a monastery of monks could reasonably be constructed'.[141] One Saxon monk, a certain Theodradus, volunteered his own inheritance for the foundation, and Adalhard proceeded to forge the necessary consensus among Theodradus' kin-group. A monastery was duly founded at Hethis.

When it became necessary to move the foundation to a new location, that is, to the so-called *villa regia* of Höxter, the *Translation of Saint Vitus* reports how Adalhard consulted further 'with bishops and counts and the most noble men of that people', who presumably had interests in the region.[142] Only after this did he approach Louis the Pious, who, in addition to granting the *villa regia* of Höxter, confirmed the 'property and possessions which were collected inside Saxony by Saxons, loving and fearing God, in order to establish and support this work'.[143] The foundation at Corvey was far from simply being the product of imperial and Frankish support; it was also the result of local patronage and consensus. Indeed, even the site at Höxter does not appear to have been entirely under imperial control: even Paschasius alludes, albeit in a

---

[139] Paschasius Radbertus, *Epitaphium Arsenii*, ed. Dümmler, I:13, p. 42: 'de rebus suis nobis tradiderunt, quo locus edificaretur coenobii'. For an in-depth treatment of the foundation legends at Corvey, see Krüger, *Studien zur Corveyer Gründungsüberlieferung*, here especially pp. 70–1; see also Kasten, *Adalhard von Corbie*, p. 145.

[140] Paschasius Radbertus, *Epitaphium Arsenii*, ed. Dümmler, I:13, p. 42: 'ut laborem impenderet et sumptus preberet'.

[141] *Translatio sancti Viti*, ed. Schmale-Ott, c. 3, p. 36: 'sciscitari cepit, si posset illa in patria inveniri locus, ubi monachorum monasterium construi rationabiliter posset'. See also Krüger, *Studien zur Corveyer Gründungsüberlieferung*, pp. 97–103. For the dating of this text, see above, p. 18.

[142] *Translatio sancti Viti*, ed. Schmale-Ott, c. 3, p. 42: 'cum episcopis et comitibus et cum nobilissimus viris eiusdem gentis'.

[143] *D Kar. 2*, ed. Kölzer, vol. I, no. 226, p. 561: 'res seu possessiones, quae a deo timentibus vel deum diligentibus Saxonibus infra ipsam Saxoniam ad hoc opus inchoandum vel adiutorium praestandum conlatae sunt'. See also K. Honselmann (ed.), *Die alten Mönchslisten und die Traditionen von Corvey* (Abhandlungen zur Corveyer Geschichtsschreibung 6), 2 vols. (Paderborn: Bonifatius, 1982), vol. I, p. 75, footnote 41.

frustratingly oblique manner, to the man on whose inheritance Corvey had been constructed. This man has been tentatively identified as Count Bernhard, based on evidence from a twelfth- or thirteenth-century source, the *Notices of the Foundation of the Monastery of Corvey*.[144]

Long after its initial foundation, Corvey continued to receive local patronage, both from those who entered the community and from those who remained outside it. These donations are recorded, however imperfectly, in the *Corvey Donations*, which survives in two sections dating from 822 to 872 and from 963 to 1037 respectively. The first section, which contains some 288 donations, records donations in a very summary manner: the principal elements include the name of the donor, the name of the village and occasionally the county where property is donated, a description or quantification of what is donated (although this is often reduced to 'quidquid habuit') and the names of witnesses. Substantial variations can be made to this template, however: the donor can stipulate that the gift is made for the soul of a relative or name the saint to which it is directed.[145] The type of transaction, meanwhile, ranges from simple donations to trades of property and renewals of earlier donations.[146] Lastly, while donations consisted chiefly of arable land (stated in *mansi* or *iurnales*),[147] they could also be made in other forms. These included different types of land or property (forests, salt works, *bifangi, gangi*)[148] or people (*servi, mancipia, homines, coloni, liti*).[149] It is unfortunately impossible to date individual entries, and the size of donations is often unspecified. Despite these limitations, this source provides much insight into the patterns of patronage in Carolingian Saxony.

The donations made to Corvey were often small in scale, with average gifts ranging from a half-*mansus* to two *mansi*. Even the few donors who were identified with titles appear to have given relatively small tracts of land.[150] Some fourteen donors are referred to as counts, while another is referred to as a marshal. While titled individuals occasionally gave larger

---

[144] Paschasius Radbertus, *Epitaphium Arsenii*, ed. Dümmler, I:16, p. 45; *Notitiae fundationis monasterii Corbeiensis*, ed. O. Holder-Egger, *MGH SS* 15:2 (Hanover: Hahn, 1888), pp. 1043–5; see also Kasten, *Adalhard von Corbie*, pp. 145–9.

[145] For donations which are made for the soul of a deceased relative, see, for example, *Traditiones Corbeienses*, ed. Honselmann, nos. 10, 12, 21, pp. 84–6; for donations which name the saint, see, for example, *Ibid*, no. 3, p. 83.

[146] For trades and renewals of donations, see, for example, *Ibid*, nos. 98, 116, pp. 98, 102.

[147] For gifts of land expressed in *mansi* and *iurnales*, see, for example, *Ibid*, nos. 4, 14, pp. 83, 85.

[148] For gifts of *gangi*, salt works, *bifangi* and forests, see, for example, *Ibid*, nos. 7, 67, 73, 175, pp. 84, 93–4, 113.

[149] For gifts of *mancipia, homines, liti, servi* and *coloni*, see, for example, *Ibid*, nos. 11–12, 30, 41, 134, pp. 85, 88–9, 104.

[150] *Ibid*, nos. 4–5, 18, 20, 22–3, 29–30, 49, 54, 72, 103, 121, 127, 140, 147, 154, 198–9, 202, 236, 250, pp. 83–8, 90–1, 94, 99, 103–4, 106–8, 116–17, 122, 125.

gifts – such as Count Withmannus, who is recorded as having donated ten *mansi* – others presumably had fewer resources at their disposal, such as Count Buto, who gave a mere *mansus*.[151] These gifts appear to be roughly similar in size to the donations received by the Breton monastery of Redon, whose donors Wendy Davies has described as being drawn from the free peasantry.[152] This comparison may have broader implications for the degree of social stratification present in post-conquest Saxon society.

While donations were small, they were also numerous. As mentioned above, Corvey received 288 donations in the first fifty years of its existence; the cumulative effect of such donations would have been large indeed. Perhaps unsurprisingly, donations were geographically concentrated around the monastery of Corvey itself, and likewise around its various monastic cells of Visbeck and Meppen, as well as around the chapel of Eresburg.[153] Even in areas where there was no obvious pastoral presence, one donation could trigger numerous other donations: hence the numerous donations within the village of Cogharden.[154] While it is possible that the monastery's presence encouraged patronage in these areas, these concentrations may have been the result of a conscious strategy of acquisition on the part of the monastery. Paschasius, looking back on Corvey's early history, claimed that donations had not been actively solicited: in fact, his *Life of Saint Adalhard* records that Adalhard had expressly instructed the monks that 'they should not be willing to accept anything by which others might be burdened, and if they were heirs of a generous donor, they should consider carefully, lest perchance those to whom the inheritance had been designated might afterwards become indigent'.[155] Yet despite his stated scruples, donations continued to flow in. Those who made a monastic profession at Corvey brought lands with them to the monastery; others gave in order to associate themselves with the monastery and its powerful network of patrons,

---

[151] *Ibid*, nos. 4, 23, pp. 83, 86.

[152] W. Davies, *Small Worlds: The Village Community in Early Medieval Brittany* (London: Duckworth, 1988), pp. 46–7.

[153] Metz, 'Probleme der fränkischen Reichsgutforschung', 121–5; W. Rösener, 'Zur Struktur und Entwicklung der Grundherrschaft in Sachsen in karolingischer und ottonischer Zeit' in A. Verhulst (ed.), *Le grand domaine aux époques mérovingienne et carolingienne* (Ghent: Belgisch Centrum voor Landelijke Geschiedenis, 1985), pp. 173–207, here pp. 196–8.

[154] *Traditiones Corbeienses*, ed. Honselmann, nos. 78, 88–95, 101, 107, 111, 132, 150, 158, 220, pp. 95, 97–100, 104, 108–9, 120.

[155] Paschasius Radbertus, *Vita sancti Adalhardi*, ed. J. P. Migne, *Patrologia Latina* 120 (Paris, 1852), pp. 1507–56, here c. 68, p. 1542C: 'neque quidquam vellent accipere unde alii gravarentur; et si haeredes essent rerum largitoris, caute considerarent, ne forte ipsi, quorum erat haereditas, postmodum inopes fierent'.

to enact their status and compete with other patrons, to secure masses and prayers for themselves and their kin and/or to demonstrate their religious devotion.[156]

Similar patterns, if not quite so large an outpouring of public support, are evidenced at the monastery of Werden on the Ruhr.[157] Here, too, the foundation has generally been ascribed to an 'outside' missionary, the Frisian Liudger. The extent to which the Frisian Liudger counts as an 'outside' figure is in itself debatable, when taken in the context of the porous Frisian–Saxon border. Yet while Liudger traded some of his inheritance to provide the land for the monastery's foundation, the endowment of the monastery was the result of engagement with the local community.[158] The monastery's cartulary, which includes full transcriptions of some sixty-six charters from the years 793–848, reveals a clustering of lands around churches which Werden maintained.[159] Numerous tracts of land were donated or acquired around the monastery at Werden itself and around churches in Wichmond and Tinaarlo.[160] If the donations to Corvey had been modest, these donations were more modest still, sometimes only constituting a single *iurnalis*.[161] This is a far smaller increment than the Frankish *mansus*. With the exception of a vast donation of lands in Frisia made in 855, recorded in a later polyptych, there is little evidence of social stratification.[162] The scale of the gifts and the absence of official titles point towards a largely undifferentiated local society. Only one donor is expressly referred to as a count, although another donor is subsequently referred to as such.[163]

---

[156] See also above, pp. 96–9.

[157] For a discussion of Werden's holdings, see further W. Stüwer, *Das Erzbistums Köln 3: Die Reichsabtei Werden an der Ruhr* (GSNF 12) (Berlin: W. de Gruyter, 1980), pp. 242–3.

[158] For Liudger's land trade, see *Cartularium Werthinense*, ed. D. P. Blok, 'Een diplomatisch onderzoek van de oudste particuliere oorkonden van Werden', unpublished Ph.D. thesis, University of Amsterdam (1960), nos. 14–15, pp. 170–3. See also Rembold, 'Rewriting the founder', 373–5.

[159] For more on this cartulary, see especially R. McKitterick, 'The uses of literacy in Carolingian and post-Carolingian Europe: literate conventions of memory' in *Scrivere e leggere nell'alto medioevo* (Settimane 59:1) (Spoleto: Il Centro, 2012), pp. 179–211, here pp. 189–98.

[160] For donations in the vicinity (specifically, within fifteen kilometers) of Werden, see *Cartularium Werthinense*, ed. Blok, nos. 7–8, 13–5, 19, 39, 49, 51, 56, 65, pp. 162–4, 169–73, 177–8, 196, 204–7, 210, 217–18; for donations in the vicinity of Wichmond, see *Ibid*, nos. 4, 10, 16, 18, 24, 29, pp. 158–9, 166–7, 173–7, 182–3, 187; for donations in the vicinity of Tinaarlo, see *Ibid*, nos. 41–3, 47–8, 50, 53, 59, 61, 66, pp. 197–200, 202–5, 207–8, 212–14, 218–19. For a map of the lands listed in the Werden Urbare, see further A. Angenendt, *Liudger: Missionar – Abt – Bischof im frühen Mittelalter* (Münster: Aschendorff, 2005), p. 118.

[161] See, for example, *Cartularium Werthinense*, ed. Blok, nos. 52, 57, 64, pp. 207, 211, 216–17.

[162] *Urbare Werthinense*, ed. R. Kötzschke, *Die Urbare der Abtei Werden a.d. Ruhr: Die Urbare vom 9.-13. Jahrhundert* (Rheinische Urbare: Sammlung von Urbaren und anderen Quellen zur Rheinischen Wirtschaftsgeschichte 2) (Bonn: H. Behrendt, 1906), no. 2, pp. 8–15.

[163] *Cartularium Werthinense*, ed. Blok, nos. 18, 45, pp. 175–7, 201. There are also some official titles in the witness lists: see McKitterick, 'Literate conventions of memory', pp. 195–6.

In the case of Werden, however, it is clear that its rectors pursued an active strategy of acquisition: what the summary notices in the *Corvey Donations* may obscure, the full record of charters at Werden makes plain. The cartulary contains some forty-six donations, sixteen sales and three exchanges, and while both of the latter categories had at least an element of patronage, in that the sums paid for sales were often only nominal, nonetheless it can be suggested that such transactions were made at the behest of the monastic community and its rectors.[164] Even donations appear at times to have been actively requested. As a scribe notes in a donation charter from the year 800, in which three heirs grant a portion of their patrimony to the monastery, the donation had been proffered following the request of Liudger himself.[165] In this case, it appears that the land abutted a previous donation; in another donation from the same year, a boundary clause reveals that its land, too, bordered on previously donated land.[166] Such consolidation of holdings presumably simplified the monastery's management of its endowment.

Yet not all lands were donated in response to such negotiations: alongside the community's active acquisitions, local residents continued to donate lands for a variety of personal reasons. Here, it is possible to be more specific than the summary entries from Corvey allow. Some donors appear to have given land in the face of conflicting claims. One man, who had previously given land – albeit informally – to his nephew, donated the same land, perhaps in order to regain control over it; similarly, the donation of Oodhelmus, which stipulated that he and his wife would retain usufruct for the remainder of their lives, could be seen to ensure his wife's control of that land following his own death.[167] Other donations were made on the donor's deathbed to ensure their salvation or, more frequently, were given for the souls of deceased relatives. Particularly remarkable in this regard is a donation of 802, in which the lands and possessions of a murderer were given to the monastery by the victim's family, for their own souls and that of their deceased relative.[168]

---

[164] For sales, see *Cartularium Werthinense*, ed. Blok, nos. 2, 11–12, 23, 28, 32–4, 36–7, 49, 54, 66, pp. 157, 168–9, 181–2, 186, 189–94, 204–5, 208–9, 218–19; for trades, see *Ibid*, nos. 14–15, 51, 58, pp. 170–3, 206–7, 211–12. See further T. Faulkner, *Law and Authority in the Early Middle Ages: The Frankish Leges in the Carolingian Period* (Cambridge: Cambridge University Press, 2016), pp. 42–3.

[165] *Cartularium Werthinense*, ed. Blok, no. 19, pp. 177–8.   [166] *Ibid*, no. 18, pp. 175–7.

[167] *Ibid*, nos. 8, 16, pp. 164, 173–5; see also the previous donation of Oodhelmus, no. 10, pp. 166–7.

[168] *Ibid*, no. 27, p. 185. For this donation, see also Faulkner, *Law and Authority*, pp. 43–4; for a comparative example of families of feud victims donating land, see W. C. Brown, *Unjust Seizure: Conflict, Interest, and Authority in an Early Medieval Society* (Ithaca: Cornell University Press, 2001), pp. 30–2.

The sources for both Corvey and Werden, then, paint a picture of extensive local engagement. Donations were actively sought and were willingly given for a variety of intersecting motives; the resultant consolidated holdings of both institutions provided a sound economic base from which large communities of monks could be maintained. While these monasteries may have been founded 'from the outside', they depended upon the communities in which they were located.

To this picture may be tentatively added an additional wrinkle: the evidence, however late, surviving from the Hessian monastery of Fulda, which maintained the two monastic cells of Hameln and Brunshausen in Saxony.[169] Unfortunately, the vast majority of Fulda's original ninth-century cartulary, compiled during the abbacy of Hrabanus Maurus (822–842), has been lost, but one may gain a sense of its diverse holdings from a summary of Hrabanus' cartulary produced some three centuries later, the *Codex Eberhardi*. Despite the various problems of interpretation presented by such a source, some general remarks may be ventured.

The chapter dedicated to Saxon and Frisian possessions contains around a hundred donations within Saxony.[170] Some of these donations, to be sure, came from missionaries operating in the region. See, for instance, the immense donation of 170 *hubae* on the part of Erkambert, a monk of Fulda and the first bishop of Minden.[171] Most of the donations, however, can be assumed to have been given by more long-standing local residents, most of whom appear without titles.[172] On the occasions where some indication is given as to size, these donations

---

[169] For Brunshausen and its connection to Fulda, see especially H. Goetting, *Das Bistum Hildesheim 2: Das Benediner(innen)kloster Brunshausen, das Benediktinerinnenkloster St. Marien vor Gandersheim, das Benediktinerkloster Clus, das Franziskanerkloster Gandersheim* (GSNF 8) (Berlin: W. de Gruyter, 1974), pp. 22–6; see also M. M. Hildebrandt, *The External School in Carolingian Society* (Education and Society in the Middle Ages and Renaissance 1) (Leiden: Brill, 1992), pp. 121–5; M. Last, 'Zur Einrichtung geistlicher Konvente in Sachsen während des frühen Mittelalters (Ein Diskussionsbeitrag)', *Frühmittelalterliche Studien*, 4 (1970), 341–7, here 341; H. Patze, 'Mission und Kirchenorganisation in karolingischer Zeit' in H. Patze (ed.), *Geschichte Niedersachsens: Grundlagen und frühes Mittelalter* (Veröffentlichungen des Historischen Kommission für Niedersachsen und Bremen 36, 5 vols.) (Hildesheim: Lax, 1977), vol. I: pp. 653–712, here p. 697; contrast to K. Naß, 'Fulda und Brunshausen: Zur Problematik der Missionsklöster in Sachsen', *NJ*, 59 (1987), 1–62. For Hameln, see Freise, 'Die Sachsenmission Karls des Großen', pp. 65, 68.

[170] *Codex Eberhardi*, ed. H. Meyer zu Ermgassen, *Der Codex Eberhardi des Klosters Fulda* (Veröffentlichungen der Historischen Kommission für Hessen 58), 3 vols. (Marburg: Elwert, 1996), vol. II, nos. 1–115, pp. 184–97; see also M. B. Gillis, *Heresy and Dissent in the Carolingian Empire: The Case of Gottschalk of Orbais* (Oxford: Oxford University Press, 2017), p. 42.

[171] *Codex Eberhardi*, ed. Meyer zu Ermgassen, vol. II, no. 31, p. 187; see also Freise, 'Die Sachsenmission Karls des Großen', pp. 71–5.

[172] Only eight donors are titled: for counts, see *Codex Eberhardi*, ed. Meyer zu Ermgassen, vol. II, nos. 14, 32, 60, 70, 83, 110, pp. 185, 187, 190–2, 195; for bishops, see *Ibid*, nos. 9–13, 31, 78, 81, pp. 185, 187, 192; for presbyters, see *Ibid*, no. 98, p. 194; for dukes, see *Ibid*, no. 115, pp. 196–7.

appear to be on a somewhat larger scale than those offered to Corvey and Werden. Alongside more modest gifts, such as that of a *huba* with a house and family, some individuals donated sizeable tracts of land.[173] 'Adolf de Saxonia' donated some fifteen *mansi* in the region of Gandersheim (one of several gifts), while another Regino gave thirty *hubae* across Saxony and Thuringia.[174] The size of other landed donations, meanwhile, can be reconstructed from the number of dependent workers who were given at the same time: eight donations were large enough to support groups of dependent workers numbering some thirty to eighty people.[175]

It is clear, then, that Fulda held a wide array of lands within Saxony, and particularly in those regions where Fulda maintained dependent cells. Patrons in Carolingian Saxony were eager to associate themselves with the nearby monastery and its local outposts. In fact, the very origin of Fulda's Saxon cells may derive from local support: it has been suggested that Count Bernhard donated the lands for the foundation of Hameln.[176] The initial foundation of Brunshausen, meanwhile, may have been at the hands of the 'Adolf' mentioned above. He was almost certainly a relative of Liudolf, a pre-eminent figure of the Saxon elite (who was himself later to join the community at Fulda). Notably, his donation in the vicinity of Gandersheim (and thus also in the vicinity of Brunshausen) included a *specialis domus* ('special home/building'), possibly to be identified with the community of Brunshausen.[177] His descendants appear to have maintained some interest in Brunshausen: Liutwart is noted as 'magister' at the cell some decades later, when Fulda's necrology was being compiled.[178]

The survival of cartularies at both Corvey, Werden and, albeit to a lesser extent, Fulda allows us privileged access to the landholding patterns of these institutions. These monasteries cannot, of course, be taken as representative of Saxon religious institutions more broadly. They were

---

[173] *Ibid*, vol. II, no. 41, pp. 188.

[174] *Ibid*, vol. II, nos. 17, 64, pp. 186, 190. For Adolf's other gifts, see *Ibid*, nos. 2, 29, 67, 69, pp. 184, 187, 190–1; see also Goetting, *Das Benediktiner(innen)kloster Brunshausen*, p. 24.

[175] *Codex Eberhardi*, ed. Meyer zu Ermgassen, vol. II, nos. 14–15, 22, 26, 43, 64, 78, 88, 99, pp. 185–6, 188, 190, 192–4.

[176] Freise, 'Die Sachsenmission Karls des Großen', p. 68; Patze, 'Mission und Kirchenorganisation', pp. 665, 694. See further P. Depreux, 'L'intégration des élites aristocratiques de Bavière et de Saxe au royaume des francs – crise ou opportunité?' in F. Bougard, L. Feller and R. Le Jan (eds.), *Les élites au haut moyen âge: Crises et renouvellements* (Haut Moyen Âge 1) (Turnhout: Brepols, 2006), pp. 225–52, here p. 236.

[177] Goetting, *Das Benediktiner(innen)kloster Brunshausen*, p. 24; contrast to Naß, 'Fulda und Brunshausen', 27.

[178] Goetting, *Das Benediktiner(innen)kloster Brunshausen*, pp. 25–6; contrast to Naß, 'Fulda und Brunshausen', 36.

large, male institutions in – or, in the case of Fulda, nearby – a landscape dominated by small, female houses. Yet the broad range of local support for these institutions is, at the very least, evocative of wider patterns. Placed alongside the evidence of female foundations and the revealing traces of late ninth-century episcopal landholding, it suggests that local patronage played a far more central role in the establishment of Saxon ecclesiastical structures than has generally been acknowledged.[179]

Local Patronage in Carolingian Saxony

Over the course of the ninth century, some twenty-seven Saxon religious houses appear to have been founded, in addition to nine bishoprics and four monastic dependencies.[180] All of these foundations relied upon local support, albeit in varying degrees: there can be, then, no clear polarization between local or 'indigenous' and 'outside' or 'foreign' foundations, as demonstrated by the monasteries of Corvey and Werden, not to mention the Saxon cells of Fulda. Such detailed land records do not exist for any other Saxon institution in this period. Nonetheless, similar patterns can be observed for other institutions sometimes labelled as 'outside' foundations. The female monastery at Herford, for example, may have been established with Corbie's aid as Paschasius Radbertus implies, but, at least according to its later foundation legend, its original endowment was provided by the Saxon Waltger; the community at Helmstedt may have been established by Liudger's brother Hildgrim, bishop of Halberstadt, but it was probably supported through local donations as well.[181] A broad range of other monastic institutions appear to have been founded with primarily local support, such as the male houses Bücken, Münsterdorf, Niggenkerke, Ramesloh, Seligenstedt and Wildeshausen, and the female houses of Bassum, Böddeken, Essen, Freckenhorst, Gandersheim, Herzebrock, Lamspringe, Liesborn, Meschede, Metelen, Möllenbeck, Neuenheerse, Nottuln, Ridigippi, Vreden, Wendhausen and Wunstorf.[182]

Unfortunately, little information has been preserved about many of these foundations. Only four or five of these communities, that is, Gandersheim, Niggenkerke, Wendhausen, Wildeshausen and possibly

---

[179] The recent work of Caspar Ehlers has, however, rightly stressed the role played by local founders: see Ehlers, *Die Integration Sachsens*, pp. 158–87, 193, 388.

[180] The figures quoted in this paragraph do not count institutions which were re-founded subsequently in the ninth century, such as Hethis and Müdehorst, which were re-founded, respectively, as Corvey and Herford.

[181] Cf. Ehlers, *Die Integration Sachsens*, pp. 63, 157.

[182] For this, see also Ehlers, *Die Integration Sachsens*, pp. 158–87.

Neuenheerse, composed or commissioned (surviving) works of hagiography; a further eight houses are attested in contemporary charters.[183] For other foundations, the historian is reliant upon archaeological traces, manuscript evidence, chance attestations and later sources. Save for charter evidence, no proprietary sources, such as cartularies, *traditiones* or polyptychs, survive from this period.

Despite these difficulties, a few general remarks may be ventured. Many of these 'local' foundations were established in the mid-ninth century. Over half may tentatively be dated to the reign of Louis the German (840/843–876). This is a trend which points to the growing resources of the Saxon elite in this period.[184] These foundations appear, with a few exceptions, to have been relatively small in scale, often constituting little more than familial houses, which may be seen to reflect the relative absence of social stratification in Saxony in this period. Sometimes, as in the case of Werden, they additionally served as family necropolises.[185] These institutions were often founded with the cooperation and assistance of local bishops, and some counted tithe districts as part of their endowments. Finally, the majority of these foundations were for female communities. These female foundations were concentrated, in contrast to male houses, in southern Saxony, alongside main transport routes, possibly a reflection of the areas in which Carolingian rulers had first confiscated and then re-granted land.[186] Even more interestingly, they were often placed within 5–10 kilometres of extant fortifications.[187] It seems probable that this placement of such

---

[183] For the works of hagiography that have been associated with the communities of Gandersheim, Niggenkerke, Wendhausen, and Wildeshausen, see, respectively, Agius of Corvey, *Vita et obitus Hathumodae*, ed. G. H. Pertz, *MGH SS* 4 (Hanover: Hahn, 1841), pp. 165–89; *Sermo sancti Marsi*, ed. K. Honselmann 'Eine Essener Predigt zum Predigt zum Feste des hl. Marsus aus dem 9. Jahrhundert', *WZ* 110 (1960), 199–221; *Vita Liutbirgae virginis*, ed. O. Menzel, *Das Leben der Liutbirg: Eine Quelle zur Geschichte der Sachsen in karolingischer Zeit* (Deutsches Mittelalter 3) (Leipzig: K. W. Hiersemann, 1937); Rudolf and Meginhard, *Translatio sancti Alexandri*, ed. Pertz. Ian Wood has further suggested that the *Vita Rimberti* may be connected to the female community at Neuenheerse: see Wood, *The Missionary Life*, pp. 134–5. For the charter evidence, see *D LD*, ed. Kehr, nos. 137, 140, 142, 150, pp. 190–2, 195–6, 198–200, 210–12; *D LJ*, ed. Kehr, nos. 3–4, pp. 335–9; *D Karl*, ed. Kehr, no. 169, p. 273–4; *D Arn*, ed. Kehr, nos. 41, 59, 107, 107a, 147, pp. 59–60, 85–7, 157–9, 223–5.

[184] For the connection of these foundations to the *Stellinga* revolt, see the remarks of Ehlers, *Die Integration Sachsens*, p. 239.

[185] For Werden, see Angenendt, *Liudger*, p. 119; P. Engelbert, 'Liudger und das fränkische Mönchtum seiner Zeit' in Freise, *Vita*, pp. 151–66, here p. 165; von Padberg, *Mission und Christianisierung*, p. 94.

[186] For the hypothesis that royal fiscal lands in Saxony were located alongside major roads, see Metz, 'Probleme der fränkischen Reichsgutforschung', 78–9.

[187] U. Lobbedy, 'Zur archäologischen Erforschung westfälischer Frauenklöster des 9. Jahrhunderts (Freckenhorst, Vreden, Meschede, Herford)', *Frühmittelalterliche Studien*, 4 (1970), 320–40; see further W. Kohl, 'Bemerkungen zur Typologie sächsischer Frauenklöster in karolingischer Zeit'

houses near forts relates to the concentration of elite property holdings around such structures, and that it is therefore coincidental, rather than deliberate. Certainly, in contrast to missionary centres, female houses were never placed inside such structures.

In some cases, foundations were made on a larger scale. Wildeshausen, Essen and, above all, Gandersheim appear to have been sizeable communities. Yet here too it is nigh on impossible to gain a sense of how these communities were endowed, and whether they were the result of a single family endowment or the result of more general local patronage. In the case of Gandersheim, the only precise information we have about its holdings comes from the donations of Louis the Younger (who had married into the founding family) and Arnulf: while it is known that the Liudolfings, and more specifically Liudolf and Oda, provided the landed endowment for the foundation, the extent and productivity of the donated lands cannot be reconstructed.

Despite these regrettable lacunae, these foundations nonetheless attest to the activism of local donors. So too, despite the apparent contradiction, do the array of institutions traditionally regarded as 'outside' foundations, for although the initial impetus may have stemmed from Carolingian rulers or missionaries, their subsequent development, endowment and expansion may be cautiously attributed to local patronage and support. The bishoprics of Bremen, Halberstadt, Hamburg, Hildesheim, Minden, Münster, Osnabrück, Paderborn and Verden may have begun as Frankish foundations, although they had little in the way of endowments apart from tithe to show for it. Admittedly, there is little evidence for the local support of Saxon bishoprics. Only two local donations to bishoprics survive from ninth-century Saxony: a charter detailing the renewed gift of the 'illustrious' Sidag to Paderborn, and the donation of Liuthard, bishop of Paderborn and his sister, Waldburg, of all their property likewise to Paderborn.[188] The latter donation, moreover, was intricately bound up with the foundation of a female monastic community at Neuenheerse. Yet the Saxon bishoprics cannot be dismissed as less successful than their monastic counterparts.[189]

in *Untersuchungen zu Kloster und Stift* (SzGS 14) (Göttingen: Vandenhoeck & Ruprecht, 1980), pp. 113–39, here pp. 113–19; W. Kohl, *Das Bistum Münster 8: Das (freiweltliche) Damenstift Nottuln* (GSNF 44) (Berlin: W. de Gruyter, 2005), pp. 25–7, here especially p. 27; Last, 'Zur Einrichtung geistlicher Konvente', 344–5; H. Müller, *Das Bistum Münster 5: Das Kanonissenstift und Benediktinerkloster Liesborn* (GSNF 23) (Berlin: W. de Gruyter, 1987), p. 62.

[188] H. A. Erhard, *Regesta historiae Westfaliae: accedit codex diplomaticus*, 2 vols. (Münster: F. Regensberg, 1847), no. 20, p. 16; *D LD*, ed. Kehr, no. 137, pp. 190–2; see also Carroll, 'The bishoprics of Saxony', 222–3.

[189] Contrast to Carroll, 'The archbishops and church provinces of Mainz and Cologne', pp. 279–82.

Bishops appear to have founded or co-founded between eight and eleven monasteries in Carolingian Saxony; evidence suggests a high degree of involvement with a further seven houses.[190] Bishops were not in competition with local monasteries: rather, as the donation of Liuthard and Waldburg suggests, they were directly involved in, and directly benefited from, these establishments.

The absence of evidence for donations to bishoprics should not be taken for an absence of patronage.[191] By the end of the ninth century, the resources upon which bishops could draw had expanded dramatically. Münster had developed from an *honestum monasterium* to a full-fledged bishopric, boasting a diocesan clergy some fifty men strong; by the early tenth century, the bishop of Paderborn commanded a diocesan clergy of sixty-six men.[192] The bishops of Hamburg, Hildesheim, Minden and Verden, meanwhile, had amassed military followings.[193] Both the support of such sizeable communities and the maintenance of armed forces required landed wealth. This wealth does not appear to have stemmed from the Carolingians or Frankish sponsors, but rather from a broad spectrum of local donors.[194]

* * *

By the end of the ninth century, the missionary centres founded around a century earlier had changed beyond all recognition. The resultant institutions, and the economic endowments that underpinned them, cannot simply be attributed to Carolingian and Frankish initiative. Rather, these structures are the result of gradual development, made possible above all by local support.

The context of compulsion in the midst of the Saxon wars in which Saxony was converted to Christianity has understandably caused some to view the introduction of Christianity and Christian structures as a foreign imposition, 'a colonial venture, whose very existence depended on the threat of force that lay behind it'.[195] Yet while Christianity was instituted forcibly in Saxony, Christian structures were not. Initial missionary centres were, admittedly, constructed with Carolingian and Frankish backing. There is little evidence, however, for Carolingian rulers taking an active role in the establishment or material endowment of Saxon

---

[190] See below, pp. 227–30.   [191] Contrast to Carroll, 'The bishoprics of Saxony', 224–7.
[192] Schieffer, 'Die Anfänge', 187.   [193] Cf. Carroll, 'The bishoprics of Saxony', 239–40.
[194] See, for example, the following detailed discussion of Münster's growth through local patronage: Balzer, 'Frühe Mission', parts 1 and 2.
[195] R. Collins, *Charlemagne* (Basingstoke: Macmillan, 1998), p. 53.

religious institutions following the conclusion of the Saxon war. This absence of evidence is in itself revealing. Throughout the ninth century, Saxon authors attempted to connect their centres, whether bishoprics or monasteries, to Carolingian rulers – and specifically to Charlemagne himself – through any means available, however tenuous or outright false. If Carolingian rulers had provided material support to these centres, it would have been commemorated.

Saxon religious institutions were not, then, the product of some top-down strategy. Rather, they developed gradually and drew primarily upon local support, both in the form of donations and of tithes. This is demonstrated not only by the large number of local foundations but also by the evidence from Corvey and Werden, which suggests a far greater degree of local support and engagement in institutions previously considered to be 'outside' foundations. It is moreover attested by the unique developmental trajectory of Saxon Christian institutions, and it is to this, and to the resultant distinctiveness of Saxon Christianity itself, that I shall now turn.

Chapter 4

RELIGION AND SOCIETY

Saxony became Christian during the reign of Charlemagne. Yet the circumstances of forced baptisms under military duress have led many to question this apparent reorientation. Scholars have tended to view the Christianization of Saxony as a foreign imposition, advanced by Carolingian kings and outside missionaries; the region's continuing anti-Christian and anti-Carolingian sentiments, meanwhile, are extrapolated from the *Stellinga* 'revolt' of 841 to 842/3. Consequently, many have hypothesized the widespread presence of latent paganism in Saxony, especially among the lower orders of society. Upon reconsideration, however, the *Stellinga* appear to have been neither anti-Christian nor anti-Carolingian; moreover, the development of Christian infrastructure in Carolingian Saxony may be attributed to the patronage of local Saxons drawn from the elite and sub-elite alike. Previous chapters have addressed each of these in turn; this chapter will bring these various strands together, directly confronting the issue of lingering paganism before going on to discuss what being Christian meant in Carolingian Saxony, the distinctive forms which Christianity and Christian institutions assumed and how becoming Christian was remembered throughout the ninth century.

The overwhelming majority of the extant evidence for Carolingian Saxony points towards the successful conversion and political integration of the region. Notably, accusations of paganism in post-conquest Saxony are exceptionally rare and appear chiefly as rhetorical tools, for example to promote saintly relics or to cast aspersions on political opponents. The archaeological record, likewise, cannot be used to reconstruct 'pagan' religious affiliations: Saxon burial customs were in fact largely consistent with Christian practice by the early ninth century. There may have been some who persisted in the observance of traditional belief or custom in post-conquest Saxony, but they are not attested in the surviving sources. By contrast, contemporaries were clear in their categorization of the

Saxons as Christian. Christian authors sought to admonish and instruct Saxon audiences according to Scriptural teachings and, further, to shape their moral behaviour in accordance with contemporary Christian teaching. Crucially, the Saxons were regarded as a Christian *populus* in need of instruction, and not as a pagan *gens* in need of conversion.[1]

Saxon Christianity is generally understood to be distinctive only insofar as it betrays syncretism or lingering pagan sympathies. Yet there is little evidence for syncretism, and still less for outright paganism: according to the extant narrative sources, Saxony was Christian, as signalled not only by the apparent absence of paganism, but also by the positive introduction of Christian moral standards and observances. This is not to suggest that Christianity and Christian institutions in Saxony were just like the rest of the Frankish world. On the contrary, the Saxon religious landscape differed from other regions of the Carolingian world in a variety of ways, notably, in the language and form in which Scripture was disseminated; the placement and function of its bishoprics, the predominance of female institutions, in the more flexible provision of pastoral care and in the specific ways that local communities commemorated their past. Christianization produced a distinctive, but nonetheless distinctly Christian, Saxony.

Naturally, there were limits to such distinctiveness. Saxony cannot be considered as a wholly separate Christian unit: on a strictly organizational level, there was no 'Saxon church' separate from wider ecclesiastical structures. The Saxon bishoprics of Bremen and Münster held territory in Frisia, just as the Frankish archbishop of Cologne held territory in Saxony, and all Saxon bishoprics (with the eventual exception of Hamburg-Bremen) were subject to the authority of the metropolitans of Cologne and Mainz.[2] More significantly, some of the features outlined above were not strictly confined to Saxony. Some of the peculiarities in the Saxon religious landscape were parallelled in Frisia, which followed a similar course of development to that of Saxony in this period. Similarities to Anglo-Saxon England may also be noted. The use of vernacular texts in pastoral settings, meanwhile, may further be observed

---

[1] I. Rembold, 'Quasi una gens: Saxony and the Frankish world, c. 772–888', *History Compass*, 15(6) (2017).

[2] C. J. Carroll, 'The archbishops and church provinces of Mainz and Cologne during the Carolingian period, 751–911', unpublished Ph.D. thesis, University of Cambridge (1999), pp. 37–8; J. T. Palmer, 'Beyond Frankish authority: Frisia and Saxony between the Anglo-Saxons and Carolingians' in H. Sauer and J. Story (eds.), *Anglo-Saxon England and the Continent* (Essays in Anglo-Saxon Studies 3) (Tempe: Arizona Center for Medieval and Renaissance Studies, 2011), pp. 139–62, here pp. 148–9; H. Röckelein, *Reliquientranslationen nach Sachsen im 9. Jahrhundert: über Kommunikation, Mobilität und Öffentlichkeit im Frühmittelalter* (Beihefte der Francia 48) (Sigmaringen: J. Thorbecke, 2002), pp. 20–1.

more widely throughout East Francia, albeit in different forms and to different ends. Nonetheless, taken in aggregate, Christianity in Saxony may be considered distinctive not only insofar as its institutions and observances differed from those elsewhere in East Francia and in the wider Carolingian world, but also insofar as its Christian communities perceived themselves as distinct, and, more specifically, as distinctly Saxon.

To call Christianity in Saxony distinctive is not to suggest a different form of exceptionalism. For Saxony was not the only region to exhibit a peculiar set of Christian practices: there was no 'normative' Carolingian-wide observance. Christianity was, and will always be shaped by local societies. It exists in many regional forms, or 'micro-Christendoms', to use the coinage of Peter Brown.[3] In the observance of Christianity, as in the structures of governance,[4] regional differences were normal in the early medieval world. In considering the peculiar features of Christian institutions and observance in Saxony, this chapter will seek to understand better the essential variation of Christian practices across the Carolingian empire, and, in so doing, to highlight the significance of that diversity in the construction of local Christian identities.

PAGANS AND PAGANISM IN CAROLINGIAN SAXONY

Religious affiliation is, at root, subjective. Pagans and Christians are not diametrically opposed religious groups with rigid parameters.[5] Rather, the categories are malleable, and open to contestation.[6] Debates over what correct Christianity constitutes are as old as Christianity itself. Such debates have consisted of defining not merely what true Christianity was, but also what it was not: hence the oppositional categories of 'heretics' and 'pagans'.

---

[3] P. Brown, *The Rise of Western Christendom: Triumph and Diversity, 200–1000* (Oxford: Blackwell, 1996), see especially pp. 231–2.

[4] For studies on Carolingian governance in the localities, see among others W. C. Brown, *Unjust Seizure: Conflict, Interest, and Authority in an Early Medieval Society* (Ithaca: Cornell University Press, 2001); H. J. Hummer, *Politics and Power in Early Medieval Europe: Alsace and the Frankish Realm, 600–1000* (Cambridge: Cambridge University Press, 2005); M. Innes, *State and Society in the Early Middle Ages: The Middle Rhine Valley, 400–1000* (Cambridge: Cambridge University Press, 2000).

[5] See especially É. Rebillard, *Christians and Their Many Identities in Late Antiquity, North Africa, 200–450 CE* (Ithaca: Cornell University Press, 2012), pp. 1–2; see also the pertinent comments of Rogers Brubaker on 'group' identity: R. Brubaker, 'Ethnicity without groups', *European Journal of Sociology*, 43(2) (2002), 163–89.

[6] I. N. Wood, 'The pagans and the other: varying presentations in the early middle ages', *Networks and Neighbours*, 1(1) (2013), 1–22, here especially 19.

Paganism is fundamentally a Christian construct, a polemical term used to group together non-adherents to Christianity.[7] It was a label applied externally, an umbrella term used to create a clear dichotomy: the Christians and the other; us and them. The people to whom it was applied most probably did not perceive themselves as belonging to a homogeneous religious group; they may have practised a wide variety of customs and held differing, and at times contradictory, beliefs. Whether they even perceived these customs and beliefs as constituent parts of a religion is unclear. These distinctions were lost upon, or deliberately ignored by, contemporary Christian authors, whose concerns, in any case, did not match up to those of the present-day historian. Pagans were useful insofar as they provided a clear oppositional category, whether for didactic or rhetorical grounds, to include or to exclude.[8]

There are, then, many issues with the term 'pagan'. It cannot be applied straightforwardly to individuals or groups in early medieval society, for those who externally imposed the label did not use an objective set of criteria to do so; rather, the categories of 'pagan' and 'Christian' were applied to a broad spectrum of belief and practice, without doing justice to the countless shades of grey. Nevertheless, these are the terms that the largely Christian textual sources employ. They are essential to charting the perception of religious change in Carolingian Saxony.

Archaeology and Religious Change in Carolingian Saxony

Before turning to the textual sources, however, it is worth briefly discussing the archaeological record. The material evidence from early medieval burials, alongside other finds, has often been employed to analyse contemporary religious affiliations, despite the problems inherent in such attempts at classification.

By the ninth century, Saxon burial practice had come to be performed in a manner generally consistent with Christianity. In the Saxon heartland, inhumation in row-grave cemeteries with north–south or east–west alignment had already largely replaced cremation by the early years of the eighth century; by the mid- to late eighth century,

---

[7] See especially J. T. Palmer, 'Defining paganism in the Carolingian world', *EME*, 15(4) (2007), 402–25; see further, among others, J. Maxwell, 'Paganism and Christianization' in S. F. Johnson (ed.), *The Oxford Handbook of Late Antiquity* (Oxford: Oxford University Press, 2012), pp. 849–75, here p. 852; Wood, 'The pagans and the other', 1–22.

[8] Palmer, 'Defining paganism', 410, 425.

east–west alignment had become standard.[9] Around the beginning of the ninth century, grave goods began to disappear,[10] although some personal ornaments, including the occasional saint or cross fibula,[11] appear in ninth-century graves. Further to the north and east, and in areas remote from transportation routes, outside influences could take longer to penetrate traditional practices.[12] North–south inhumations, alongside pyre burials, persisted up to the late eighth century; only in the first quarter of the ninth century did east–west interment without grave goods become the norm.[13] There also appears to have been an increase in the number of infant burials around this time, a trend which has been connected to increasing Christianization.[14] Nevertheless, traditional row-grave cemeteries continued to be used throughout Saxony,[15] a fact that cannot be wholly attributed to the scarcity of local churches.[16] In Tostedt, where the remains of two wooden churches have been found dating to circa 800 and circa 850 respectively, a small graveyard appeared in the second half of the ninth century, but many continued to use old burial sites in the area well into the tenth century, thus paralleling broader trends in the region.[17]

By the early ninth century, then, Saxon burial practice roughly resembled Frankish, or 'Christian', practice.[18] Some have taken this as evidence

---

[9] See especially F. Laux, 'Sächsische Gräberfelder zwischen Weser, Aller und Elbe. Aussagen zur Bestattungssitte und religiösem Verhalten' in Hässler, Jarnut and Wemhoff, *Sachsen*, pp. 143–71, here pp. 148–58; see further T. Capelle, *Die Sachsen des frühen Mittelalters* (Stuttgart: Theiss, 1998), pp. 118–21; F. Laux, 'Nachklingendes heidnisches Brauchtum auf spätsächsischen Reihengräber-friedhöfen und an Kultstätten der nördlicher Lüneburger Heide in frühchristlicher Zeit', *Die Kunde*, 38 (1987), 179–98, here 179–81; K. Weidemann, 'Die frühe Christianisierung zwischen Schelde und Elbe im Spiegel der Grabsitten des 7. bis 9. Jahrhunderts' in W. Lammers (ed.), *Die Eingliederung der Sachsen in das Frankenreich* (Wege der Forschung 185) (Darmstadt: Wissenschaftliche Buchgesellschaft, 1970), pp. 389–415, here p. 393.

[10] Capelle, *Die Sachsen*, p. 127; Laux, 'Nachklingendes heidnisches Brauchtum', 181.

[11] Capelle, *Die Sachsen*, p. 121; F. Laux, 'Karolingische "Heiligenfibeln" aus Bardowick und Ochtmissen, Stadt Lüneburg, im Landkreis Lüneburg', *Die Kunde*, 46 (1995), 123–36.

[12] Capelle, *Die Sachsen*, pp. 118–19.

[13] Laux, 'Sächsische Gräberfelder', p. 158; Weidemann, 'Die frühe Christianisierung', p. 397; cf. F. W. Wulf, 'Karolingische und ottonische Zeit' in H.-J. Hässler (ed.), *Ur- und Frühgeschichte in Niedersachsen* (Stuttgart: Theiss, 1991), pp. 321–68, here p. 363.

[14] Capelle, *Die Sachsen*, p. 128; Laux, 'Sächsisches Gräberfelder', p. 152.

[15] Laux, 'Nachklingendes heidnisches Brauchtum', 181.

[16] Contrast to A. Genrich, 'Archäologische Aspekte zur Christianisierung im nördlichen Niedersachsen' in W. Lammers (ed.), *Die Eingliederung der Sachsen in das Frankenreich* (Wege der Forschung 185) (Darmstadt: Wissenschaftliche Buchgesellschaft, 1970), pp. 470–86, here p. 483; Wulf, 'Karolingische und ottonische Zeit', p. 363.

[17] H. Drescher, *Tostedt: die Geschichte einer Kirche aus der Zeit der Christianisierung im nördlichen Niedersachsen bis 1880* (Materialhefte zur Ur- und Frühgeschichte Niedersachsens 19) (Hildesheim: Lax, 1985), pp. 231–2; cf. Laux, 'Sächsische Gräberfelder', p. 153.

[18] Laux, 'Nachklingendes heidnisches Brauchtum', 191.

of the conversion of Saxony,[19] despite the fact that the shift to oriented graves preceded Charlemagne's conquest, though this too could be taken as evidence for pre-conquest Christian observance.[20] Traditionally, burial archaeology has been used to illustrate the processes of conversion and Christianization from the bottom up, thus providing a counter-weight to the extant written sources and their inherent Christian biases. More recent scholarship has however offered a substantial and persuasive reappraisal, arguing that the links once posited between burial archaeology and religion may be more tenuous than previously supposed.[21]

Guy Halsall in particular has offered an important corrective in a study that encompasses not only the Metz region but also Anglo-Saxon England. Conversion periods were accompanied by different archaeological phenomena in different regions: there was no pan-European archaeology of conversion.[22] In the Metz region, for instance, the Christian church was remarkably uninvolved in the ritual of burial for much of the early medieval period.[23] Grave goods, far from acting as a clear sign of paganism, were regularly buried with Christians, and without any inter-ference from the Church.[24] Their disappearance, Halsall argued, cannot be connected to either conversion or Christianization, but rather to wider social changes.[25]

More fundamentally, attempting to determine religious affiliation through burial patterns encounters the same difficulty identified above: that 'pagans' and normative Christians, rather than existing as wholly separate entities, formed part of a spectrum.[26] Christians might bury their

---

[19] See, for example, Genrich, 'Archäologische Aspekte', pp. 470–86; J. Hines, 'The conversion of the Old Saxons' in Green and Siegmund, *Saxons*, pp. 299–328, here pp. 303–5; Laux, 'Sächsische Gräberfelder', p. 153. Contrast to Capelle, *Die Sachsen*, p. 121.

[20] For pre-conquest Saxon contact with Christianity, see I. N. Wood, 'Before or after mission: social relations across the middle and lower Rhine the seventh and eighth centuries' in I. L. Hansen and C. Wickham (eds.), *The Long Eighth Century: Production, Distribution and Demand* (The Trans-formation of the Roman World 11) (Leiden: Brill, 2000), pp. 149–66.

[21] See especially G. Halsall, *Cemeteries and Society in Merovingian Gaul: Selected Studies in History and Archaeology, 1992–2009* (Brill's Series on the Early Middle Ages 18) (Leiden: Brill, 2010), pp. 261–84; see further D. Frankfurter, *Religion in Roman Egypt: Assimilation and Resistance* (Princeton: Princeton University Press, 1998), pp. 10–11; Rebillard, *Christians and Their Many Identities*, pp. 3, 17; É. Rebillard, 'Conversion and burial in the late Roman empire' in K. Mills and A. Grafton (eds.), *Conversion in Late Antiquity and the Early Middle Ages: Seeing and Believing* (Rochester: University of Rochester Press, 2003), pp. 61–83. The last of these offers many strong points, though I disagree with its interpretation of the Saxon evidence.

[22] Halsall, *Cemeteries and Society in Merovingian Gaul*, especially pp. 278–80.   [23] *Ibid*, p. 267.

[24] *Ibid*, pp. 263, 267.

[25] *Ibid*, pp. 275–6; E. James, *The Merovingian Archaeology of South-West Gaul* (British Archaeological Reports Supplementary Series 25), 2 vols. (Oxford: British Archaeological Reports, 1977), vol. I, especially p. 179.

[26] Halsall, *Cemeteries and Society in Merovingian Gaul*, pp. 269–70.

dead in churchyard cemeteries with east–west alignment, without grave goods, while 'pagans' might hold pyre ceremonies with ritual feasting; both might also, however, inter their dead in oriented graves with grave goods in large row-grave cemeteries.[27] It is also possible that other concerns, such as social status, gender or familial ties, may have out-weighed religious considerations in burial practice.

Often, then, the evidence with which we are presented is ambiguous. Friedrich Laux noted that the north–south alignment of an infant burial in Oldendorf could be taken as evidence for a 'pagan' burial, but further observed that the very fact of the child's burial could also be interpreted as revealing Christian influence.[28] The infant at Oldendorf was, more-over, buried in a cemetery where the majority of contemporary burials had east–west alignment, including that of a woman, possibly his mother, directly beside whom he was placed.[29] The discovery of other north–south infant burials in otherwise east–west cemeteries, such as that found in Ketzendorf, raises the question of whether ninth-century north–south burial might denote death before baptism.[30] Sometimes, however, grave alignment may simply be traced back to convenience. In grave thirteen at Ketzendorf, a woman was interred with north–south alignment in a section with multiple east–west burials, but there are signs that this was not necessarily a 'religious' choice. A coin of Louis the Pious had been sewn onto her clothing, seemingly as jewellery, with the side featuring the cross turned towards the front.[31] In this case, the grave alignment may simply have been determined by practicalities: she was buried in a crowded part of the cemetery, possibly in the vicinity of her kin-group, in the remaining space available.[32]

This is not to say that there was no connection between religion and burial practice: some contemporaries considered certain burial practices to be anti-Christian. Indeed, in the *First Saxon Capitulary*, two chapters are devoted to banning certain graveside rites.[33] Chapter 7 prescribes death to any man who, 'according to the rites of pagans, arranges for the corpse of a man to be consumed by flame and his bones reduced to ash'; chapter 22, meanwhile, orders that 'the bodies of Saxon Christians ought

[27] See here also the comments of E. James, 'Cemeteries and the problem of Frankish settlement in Gaul' in P. H. Sawyer (ed.), *Names, Words and Graves: Early Medieval Settlement* (Leeds: The School of History, University of Leeds, 1979), pp. 55–89, here especially pp. 68–70.

[28] Laux, 'Nachklingendes heidnisches Brauchtum', 187.   [29] *Ibid*, 187.   [30] *Ibid*, 187.

[31] Wulf, 'Karolingische und ottonische Zeit', p. 367.

[32] Laux, 'Nachklingendes heidnisches Brauchtum', 189.

[33] For more on this, cf. B. Effros, '*De partibus Saxoniae* and the regulation of mortuary custom: A Carolingian campaign of Christianization or the suppression of Saxon identity?' *Revue belge de philologie et d'histoire*, 75(2) (1997), 267–86.

to be interred in church cemeteries, and not in the mound (*tumulus*) of pagans'.[34] This capitulary was issued in the most contested phase of the Saxon wars; it was intended to identify 'pagan' practices by means of reference to objective criteria.[35] Yet, as Bonnie Effros has observed, the identification of such burial practices as 'pagan' was itself a novelty: cremation and mound burial first became a target of legislation in the reign of Charlemagne himself.[36] The chapters on burial practice should thus be read as part of a larger effort to delineate clearly the boundaries of Christian observance, rather than as a reaction to specifically 'pagan' practices.[37]

Moreover, the line the *First Saxon Capitulary* drew between pagan and Christian practices does not appear to have been uncontested. Paschasius Radbertus' *Life of Saint Adalhard*, written soon after Adalhard's death in 826, concludes with an *Eclogue* which details an imaginary dialogue between 'Philis' and 'Galathea', personifications of the monasteries Corbie and its Saxon daughter-house, Corvey, respectively. The *Eclogue* opens with 'Galathea' (i.e. Corvey) exhorting all men to mourn for Adalhard, and instructing 'Philis' on the solemnities surrounding his interment:

> Mourn, I beseech, o men, mourn piously with me for the father,
> And let each successive age ask for indulgence.
> Shower the earth with tears, sow fields with flowers:
> Let all henceforth keep his vigil with weeping.
> Let crying hearts find release by the office of speaking,
> That they might resound everywhere while the heavens rumble.
> Let this one eulogize in the language of homespun Romance and Latin,
> Let the Saxon, equally lamenting, speak a verse,
> Turn all to this place, for a great man has sung his last,
> And build a *tumulus*, and place a verse above the *tumulus*.
> Collect in a casket the blessed limbs of the venerable man,
> Who strove to make warm the blood within our veins.[38]

---

[34] *Capitulatio de partibus Saxoniae*, ed. C. von Schwerin, *MGH Fontes iuris* 4 (Hanover: Hahn, 1918), pp. 37–44, here cc. 7, 22, pp. 38, 41: 'Si quis corpus defuncti hominis secundum ritum paganorum flamma consumi fecerit et ossa eius ad cinerem redierit, capitae punietur'; 'iubemus ut corpora christianorum Saxanorum ad cimiteria ecclesiae deferantur et non ad tumulus paganorum.'

[35] For the dating of this text, see above, pp. 24–5.   [36] Effros, 'De partibus Saxoniae', 279, 283.

[37] Palmer, 'Defining paganism', 414; see also É. Rebillard, *The Care of the Dead in Late Antiquity* (Cornell Studies in Classical Philology 59) (Ithaca: Cornell University Press, 2009), p. xii.

[38] Paschasius Radbertus, *Vita sancti Adalhardi*, ed. J. P. Migne, *Patrologia Latina* 120 (Paris, 1852), pp. 1507–56, here *Ecloga duarum sanctimonialium*, 1553A–B: 'Plangite, quaeso, viri, mecum pie plangite Patrem,/Omnis et imploret veniam provectior aetas./Spargite humum lacrymis, componite floribus arva:/Patris ad excubias hinc fletibus omnia sudent./Officio linguae prodant sic corda vagitus,/Ut passim resonent etiam simul astra mugitum./Rustica concelebret Romana Latinaque lingua/Saxo quo pariter plangens, pro carmine dicat:/Vertite huc cuncti cecinit quam

Paschasius' *Eclogue* is, of course, infused with Virgilian echoes; the line in which the Saxon orders a *tumulus* to be constructed is, in fact, plucked directly from Virgil's fifth *Eclogue* (*et tumulum facite, et tumulo superaddite carmen*).[39] Yet the redeployment of this particular verse and its placement in the mouth of a Saxon suggests a deliberate choice – an inversion, so to speak, of the negative associations surrounding Saxon Christian observance and, more specifically, Saxon burial practice. *Tumulus* carried the older, more generic meaning of a 'tomb', but it was also the word used to denote Saxon burial mounds in Carolingian legislation.[40] Paschasius did not, evidently, view such *tumuli* as inherently anti-Christian.

In any case, whether interment in *tumuli* was viewed as an aggressively 'pagan' act, or, on the other hand, as an appropriate form of commemoration for a founding saint, it was, by this point, largely the product of Frankish imagination. With the exception of some areas along the northern coast, which had hitherto existed in relative isolation from their Frankish neighbours, cremation and mound burials had almost entirely disappeared by the early eighth century.[41] As Effros writes, the capitulary's provisions on these subjects thus appear to have been based on 'outdated assumptions about traditional Saxon mortuary practices'.[42] This is a tendency that can be found paralleled more generally in Carolingian anti-pagan rhetoric, as we shall see below.

Naturally, there are some exceptions to these trends. There is at least one site with mound burials from the mid-ninth century,[43] and there are also isolated instances of pyre burials in cemeteries otherwise dominated by oriented graves.[44] For instance, in a row-grave cemetery in Old-endorf, oriented inhumation was a feature of burial practice from the mid-eighth century onwards. There are however, rather incongruously, two pyre burials among the rest. Grave eighty-six dates from the second half of the eighth century and overlies two previous east–west-aligned

---

maximus ille,/Et tumulum facite, et tumulo superaddite carmen,/Membra beata senis celebri conferre locello,/Qui nobis studuit venas aperire calentes.'

[39] Publius Vergilius Maro, *Eclogae*, ed. R. A. B. Mynors, *Oxford Classical Texts: P Vergili Maronis: Opera* (Oxford: Clarendon, 1969), *Ecloga* V line 42, p. 13.

[40] See the entries for 'tumulus' in T. Lewis and C. Short, *A Latin Dictionary Founded on Andrews' Edition of Freund's Latin Dictionary* (Oxford: Clarendon, 1896); A. Souter, *A Glossary of Later Latin to 600 A.D.* (Oxford: Clarendon, 1964); and A. Sleumer, *Deutsch-kirchenlateinisches Wörterbuch* (Bonn: F. Dümmler, 1962); see also Springer, *Die Sachsen*, p. 226.

[41] For these earlier practices, see further K. Helm, *Altgermanische Religionsgeschichte*, 2 vols. (Heidelberg: C. Winter, 1953), vol. II:2, pp. 24–30. Contrast with Effros, 'De partibus Saxoniae', 279.

[42] Effros, 'De partibus Saxoniae', 279; see below, pp. 197–8.

[43] Laux, 'Nachklingendes heidnisches Brauchtum', 191.

[44] Genrich, 'Archäologische Aspekte', pp. 483–4. See further R. M. Karras, 'Pagan survivals and syncretism in the conversion of Saxony', *The Catholic Historical Review*, 72(4) (1986), 553–72, here 560–1.

burials; grave 158, even more intriguingly, can be roughly dated to the mid-ninth century.[45] These, along with the mound graves, may be 'pagan' burials, but if so, they are buried amid graves in outward conformity with contemporary Christian practice. They can just as easily be taken to represent a conscious deployment of age-old tradition, whether for political or social reasons.

Other instances of paganism are equally difficult to pin down in the archaeological record. There are some instances of continuing traditional practice. Laux has, in particular, drawn attention to the hundreds of eighth- through tenth-century potsherds found in a Neolithic tomb in Hamburg-Fischbeck, presumably as some type of offering.[46] Whether these offerings were left by unreconstructed 'pagans' or by people who considered themselves to be Christians remains uncertain.

The archaeological record, then, cannot be used to reconstruct religious affiliation in Carolingian Saxony. While Saxon burial customs may have been largely consistent with Christian practice by the early ninth century, they cannot be taken to indicate Christianity, just as deviations from such customs cannot be interpreted as signs of enduring paganism.

Pagans in Carolingian Saxony

Just as paganism is ambiguous in the material remains of Carolingian Saxony, so too is it elusive in the textual record. No single text has survived that can be attributed to a ninth-century Saxon pagan; rather, the only versions of paganism to which we have access are the 'imagined paganisms' constructed by contemporary Christian authors.[47] Thus paganism emerges from the sources as a fluid concept, employed in particular contexts to particular ends. The practices attributed to pagan religion in contemporary Christian writings vary considerably. While the *First Saxon Capitulary* discusses penalties for swearing oaths at groves, believing in witches and participating in cannibalism and human sacrifices, the deviant practices ascribed to pagans in the mid-eighth-century *List of Superstitions and Pagan Practices* are far more tame: for instance, performing songs for the dead and celebrating festivals honouring Jove and Mercury.[48] The latter serves to demonstrate the author's debt to literary tradition. When Rudolf of Fulda attempted to describe Saxon paganism some sixty years after the conquest, there were some commonalities with earlier reports, most

---

[45] Laux, 'Nachklingendes heidnisches Brauchtum', 181–5.   [46] *Ibid*, 191–2.
[47] For the term 'imagined paganisms', see Palmer, 'Defining paganism', 410.
[48] *Capitulatio de partibus Saxoniae*, ed. von Schwerin, cc. 6, 9, 21, pp. 38–9, 41; *Indiculus superstitionum et paganiarum*, in *Cap. 1*, ed. A. Boretius, *MGH Cap.* 1 (Hanover: Hahn, 1883), pp. 233–4.

notably with the *List*: both discuss divination by horses and birds and holy groves.[49] Yet these same features were also described in the first century AD in Tacitus' *Germania*, Rudolf's chief source.[50] There was no static, unchanging 'pagan religion': there were simply convenient literary formulae.

The concept of paganism could be employed by Christian writers for a wide variety of purposes. For instance, as James Palmer has recently argued, descriptions of paganism could be used to reinforce normative Christian beliefs and behaviours through negative illustration and can therefore be understood within the framework of Christian 'alterity motifs'.[51] When Boniface decried contemporary paganism in Hessia, for instance, he did so before a Christian audience in order to define the set contours of Christian religion; so too did the *List of Superstitions and Pagan Practices* define correct Christian behaviour by what it was not.[52] In such contexts, as Palmer writes, 'the principal target of description is not paganism in any form, but rather the imaginative *mundus* ['world'] of strict forms of Christianity'.[53] Similarly, descriptions of pagans could be linked into the tradition of ethnography, in which explorations of the often fantastical 'other' evoked comparison, whether implicit or explicit, to one's own society. Tacitus' *Germania* certainly fits inside such a category, and while Rudolf's motives may have differed from that of his exemplar, it is important to remember the original

---

[49] Rudolf and Meginhard, *Translatio sancti Alexandri*, ed. G. H. Pertz, *MGH SS* 2 (Hanover: Hahn, 1829), pp. 673–81, here c. 2, p. 675.

[50] Tacitus Cornelius, *Germania*, ed. A. Önnerfors, *De origine et situ Germanorum liber* (Stuttgart: Teubner, 1983), c. 10, pp. 8–9 Palmer, 'Defining paganism', 405, 420.

[51] Palmer, 'Defining paganism', 410; J. M. H. Smith, *Europe after Rome: A New Cultural History 500–1000* (Oxford: Oxford University Press, 2005), pp. 232–3.

[52] *Indiculus superstitionum et paganiarum* in *Cap. 1*, ed. Boretius, pp. 233–4; see especially Palmer, 'Defining paganism', 407–8; Smith, *Europe after Rome*, pp. 237–8; see further Brown, *The Rise of Western Christendom*, pp. 271–2; A. Dierkens, 'Superstitions, christianisme et paganisme à la fin de l'époque mérovingienne: A propos de l'*Indiculus superstitionum et paganiarum*' in H. Hasquin (ed.), *Magie, sorcellerie, parapsychologie* (Laïcité. Série "Recherches" 5) (Brussels: Université de Bruxelles, 1984), pp. 9–26, here especially pp. 23–6; Y. Hen, *Culture and Religion in Merovingian Gaul, A.D. 481–751* (Cultures, Beliefs and Traditions 1) (Leiden: Brill, 1995), pp. 178–80; R. A. Markus, 'From Caesarius to Boniface: Christianity and paganism in Gaul' in J. Fontaine and J. N. Hillgarth (eds.), *Le septième siècle, changements et continuités: actes du colloque bilatéral franco-britannique tenu au Warburg Institute les 8–9 juillet 1988* (Studies of the Warburg Institute 42) (London: Warburg Institute, 1992), pp. 154–72, here pp. 164–5; I. N. Wood, 'Ideas of mission in the Carolingian world' in W. Fałkowski and Y. Sassier (eds.), *Le monde carolingien: bilan, perspectives, champs de recherches: actes du colloque international de Poitiers, Centre d'études supérieures de civilisation médiévale, 18–20 novembre 2004* (Culture et société médiévales 18) (Turnhout: Brepols, 2009), pp. 183–98, here p. 190; Wood, 'The pagans and the other', 7. Contrast with J. H. Clay, *In the Shadow of Death: Saint Boniface and the Conversion of Hessia, 721–54* (Cultural Encounters in Late Antiquity and the Middle Ages 11) (Turnhout: Brepols, 2010), pp. 289–91.

[53] Palmer, 'Defining paganism', 425.

context of his material. Finally, the attribution of paganism could be put to various discursive ends within a narrative. It could be used as a delegitimizing accusation, to highlight the 'otherness' of opponents, or, more positively, it could be located within the historical past in order to stress the Christianizing prowess of particular relics, who in their coming had freed the region from the darkness of perfidy.

While this approach to paganism has been fruitfully applied elsewhere, for example in relation to Boniface's activity on the continent, Carolingian Saxony has largely escaped such revisionist treatment.[54] Scholars still refer to pagans and Christians as separate religious groups, with clearly defined parameters; some suppose the existence of widespread paganism, culminating in the *Stellinga* revolt of 841 to 842/3. Such an approach is misguided, and not simply because it fails to consider paganism as a discursive category. More specifically, it misrepresents the evidential base.[55]

The most vaunted example of Saxon paganism is, without a doubt, the *Stellinga* revolt, which engulfed Saxony from 841 to 842/3. Yet, as I have argued in Chapter 2, there is little evidence to classify the *Stellinga* as pagan. Only two of the four contemporary sources for the revolt even imply that the movement was in any manner pagan; in both sources, the implication of paganism rests upon the conflation of law and religion, or of secular and religious fidelity. In both cases the implication of paganism served a clear narrative aim: by depicting the *Stellinga* as pagan, these authors, who were *fideles* of the West Frankish king Charles the Bald, sought to tarnish the reputation of his rival, the Emperor Lothar, who had allied with the movement. Any evidence for the 'pagan' nature of the *Stellinga* is, at best, equivocal.[56]

Apart from the *Stellinga*, references to contemporary paganism in post-conquest Saxony are scarce indeed, occurring in merely a handful of hagiographical sources. In the *Life of the Virgin Liutbirga*, Count Bernhard expresses concern at Liutbirga's habit of wandering to far-away churches overnight: he advises her that even 'armed men should fear, when day and night pagans and false Christians engage in banditry'.[57]

---

[54] An exception which applies this approach to Saxony is J. T. Palmer, *Anglo-Saxons in a Frankish World, 690–900* (Studies in the Early Middle Ages 19) (Turnhout: Brepols, 2009), pp. 113–44.

[55] For similar comments on the sources for Merovingian Gaul, see Hen, *Culture and Religion*, pp. 165, 175, 178, 205.

[56] See above, pp. 107–14.

[57] *Vita Liutbirgae virginis*, ed. O. Menzel, *Das Leben der Liutbirg: Eine Quelle zur Geschichte der Sachsen in karolingischer Zeit* (Deutsches Mittelalter 3) (Leipzig: K. W. Hiersemann, 1937), c. 12, p. 18: 'armatis pertimescendum est viris, cum diebus ac noctibus paganis et falso nomine Cristianis latrocinantibus'.

The combination of pagans and false Christians is in itself noteworthy. Bernhard's worries may moreover be seen as serving a narrative aim: in addition to demonstrating Liutbirga's Christian devotion, they set the stage for Liutbirga to offer a learned response, laced with Scriptural quotations, in which she places all her hopes not in transitory existence, but rather in the life eternal.[58] There are only two other references to paganism in the entire Saxon hagiographical corpus. In the *Translation of Saint Liborius*, we read of how 'the populace was hitherto unlearned in faith, and the majority of the common people were only with difficulty able to tear completely away from the gentile error, privately turning to certain traditions honoured by their ancestors'.[59] Similar sentiments are echoed in the *Translation of Saint Alexander*, which describes how the Saxons 'had been more entangled with pagan error, which threatened Christian religion'.[60] Later in the same text, a letter is included from Lothar in which he deplores how, along the border, 'because of the vicinity of the pagans, some of the Saxons stay firm in true religion, while others nearly defect, unless, with God's aid and your blessed protection, our weakness is reinforced'.[61]

These statements must, however, be read within their narrative context. Both of the hagiographical texts are translation narratives; in other words, they describe the movement of relics, and are written to convince a new audience of the relics' authenticity, efficacy and importance. By delaying the full Christian devotion of the Saxon *gens*, these texts are able to create a decisive role for the imported relics. They became the agents through which Saxony was brought to full Christian observance. Indeed, in both texts the eventual advent of the relics causes an outpouring of public piety: in the *Translation of Saint Liborius*, the clergy who were bearing the relics, once they had passed into Saxony, 'were barely able to move a step, meeting with an excessive crowd before

---

[58] *Ibid*, c. 13, pp. 18–9.

[59] Anonymus Paderbrunnensis, *Translatio sancti Liborii*, ed. V. de Vry, *Liborius, Brückenbauer Europas: die mittelalterlichen Viten und Translationsberichte: mit einem Anhang der Manuscripta Liboriana* (Paderborn: Schöningh, 1997), c. 9, p. 195: 'Quia uero rudis adhuc in fide populus, et maxime plebebium uulgus difficile poterat ab errore gentili perfectae diuelli, latenter ad auitas quasdans supersticiones colendas sese conuertens'. Contrast with S. Epperlein, 'Sachsen im frühen Mittelalter: Diskussionsbeitrag zur Sozialstruktur Sachsens im 9. Jahrhundert und seiner politischen Stellung im frühen Mittelalter', *Jahrbuch für Wirtschaftsgeschichte*, 7(1) (1966), 189–212, here 196.

[60] Rudolf and Meginhard, *Translatio sancti Alexandri*, ed. Pertz, c. 4, pp. 676–7: 'Erant enim adhuc gentili errore magis impliciti, quam christiana religione intenti'; cf. E. Shuler, 'The Saxons within Carolingian Christendom: post-conquest identity in the *translationes* of Vitus, Pusinna, and Liborius', *Journal of Medieval History*, 36(1) (2010), 39–54, here 44–5.

[61] Rudolf and Meginhard, *Translatio sancti Alexandri*, ed. Pertz, c. 4, p. 677: 'propter vicinitatem paganorum ex parte firma in vera religione constat, et ex parte iam pene defecta, nisi, Deo auxiliante et vestra sanctitate patrocinante, nostra corroboratur infirmitas'.

them'.[62] Descriptions of latent paganism are thus employed as narrative tools, to make the eventual, pious profession of Christian religion all the more dramatic.[63] Neither text relates that the Saxons had actually reverted to paganism. In the *Translation of Saint Liborius*, they are only 'with difficulty' able to renounce former errors; in the *Translation of Saint Alexander*, a part of the population is on the verge of lapsing, but has not lapsed yet. In fact, in both the *Translation of Saint Alexander* and the *Translation of Saint Liborius*, as well as in the *Life of the Virgin Liutbirga*, the conversion of the Saxons under Charlemagne is acknowledged and celebrated.[64] These sources certainly seek to cast aspersions on the proper Christianity of the Saxons, but the Saxons are still treated as Christians in these texts.[65]

The close proximity of pagans beyond the borders of Saxony did, admittedly, continue to be a matter of concern, particularly to Carolingian rulers: Saxony had long boasted strong connections to its neighbouring regions, as illustrated most poignantly by Saxon alliances in the conquest period.[66] Hence Louis the German's worries of an alliance between the *Stellinga*, Northmen and Slavs during the Carolingian civil war, as narrated by Nithard; hence too Lothar's fear that the presence of pagans across the border might undermine the as yet imperfect Christianity of the Saxons.[67] In a letter to Haimo, bishop of Halberstadt, Hrabanus Maurus sympathized with the challenges he imagined his Saxon colleague to face: 'I am not ignorant of what great vexations you endure, not only from the pagans who border you, but even from the disturbances of the populace, who through their insolence and improbity of customs force not inconsiderable trouble upon your paternity, and thereby do not permit you the leisure for frequent prayer or serious reading.'[68] Clearly,

---

[62] Anonymus Paderbrunnensis, *Translatio sancti Liborii*, ed. de Vry, c. 38, p. 218: 'prae nimia sibi obuiante turba uix gradum mouere poterant'.

[63] Cf. Karras, 'Pagan survivals and syncretism', 559, 570–1.

[64] Rudolf and Meginhard, *Translatio sancti Alexandri*, ed. Pertz, c. 3, p. 676; *Vita Liutbirgae virginis*, ed. Menzel, c. 1, p. 10 (this text only refers explicitly to the conversion of the leading Saxons); Anonymus Paderbrunnensis, *Translatio sancti Liborii*, ed. de Vry, cc. 2, 7, pp. 188–9, 193–4.

[65] Cf. Karras, 'Pagan survivals and syncretism', p. 559; contrast with E. J. Goldberg, 'Popular revolt, dynastic politics, and aristocratic factionalism in the Early Middle Ages: the Saxon *Stellinga* reconsidered', *Speculum*, 70(3) (1995), 467–501, here 480, which takes the *Translatio sancti Alexandri* as evidence for continuing paganism.

[66] See above, pp. 42–4.

[67] Nithard, *Historiae*, eds. P. Lauer and S. Glansdorff, *Histoire des fils de Louis le Pieux* (Les classiques de l'histoire au Moyen Âge 51) (Paris: Les Belles Lettres, 2012), IV:2, p. 134; Rudolf and Meginhard, *Translatio sancti Alexandri*, ed. Pertz, c. 4, p. 677. See also above, pp. 110–11.

[68] Hrabanus Maurus, *Epistolae*, ed. E. Dümmler, *MGH Epp.* 5:3 (Berlin: Weidemann, 1899), pp. 379–533, here no. 36, p. 471: 'Neque enim mihi ignotum est, qualem infestationem habeas, non solum a paganis, qui tibi confines sunt, sed etiam a populorum turbis, quae per insolentiam et inprobitatem morum tuae paternitati non parvam molestiam ingerunt, et ob hoc frequenti

in Hrabanus' view, a Christian people still young in the faith might pose problems, in a manner not dissimilar to their pagan counterparts. Yet in all three instances, cross-border pagans and imperfectly Christian Saxons are depicted as separate, distinct groups. Moreover, these concerns raised in such texts are not to be found paralleled in works composed at Saxon centres.

Finally, only one pastoral text from the post-conquest period employs the term 'heathen': the *Old Saxon Penitential*, a catalogue, in confession form, of potential sins. Here, among other confessions, the following is included: 'I listened to *hethinnussia* ("heathen things") and unclean mourning'.[69] To take this as evidence of lingering Saxon paganism would be a stretch:[70] rather, it should be read in a manner similar to Boniface's use of paganism, as an oppositional category to define correct Christian practice. *Hethinnussia* is best interpreted as referring to trad-itional epic poetry, which was enjoyed (and, at intervals, decried) throughout the Carolingian world: even Louis the Pious, Thegan writes, learned 'pagan songs' in his youth, which he soundly rejected upon his assumption of the crown.[71] The new moral climate ushered in by Louis and his episcopate, however, did not succeed in diminishing the enjoy-ment of such songs in either lay or religious circles: in the second half of the ninth century, Otfrid of Weissenburg, in Franconia, drafted a biblical epic in part – or so he states – to offer religious alternatives for those who delighted in such secular songs.[72] The 'unclean mourning', meanwhile, may simply have been songs sung to commemorate the dead, which was a common enough practice in Carolingian Europe to be addressed in a wide array of legislation.[73] Other features of the text recommend the text for primarily monastic penitents. Its potential sins include chanting

---

orationi atque assiduae lectioni te vacare non permittunt.' For this, see E. J. Goldberg, *Struggle for Empire: Kingship and Conflict under Louis the German, 817–876* (Ithaca: Cornell University Press, 2006), pp. 176–7.

[69] *Old Saxon Penitential*, ed. E. Wadstein, *Kleinere altsächsische Sprachdenkmäler* (Niederdeutsche Denkmäler 6) (Norden: Soltau, 1899), pp. 16–17, here p. 17: 'Ik gihorda hethinnussia endi unhrenia sespilon.' Cf. Helm, *Altgermanische Religionsgeschichte*, vol. II:2, pp. 15–17.

[70] H. Patze, 'Mission und Kirchenorganisation in karolingischer Zeit' in H. Patze (ed.), *Geschichte Niedersachsens: Grundlagen und frühes Mittelalter* (Veröffentlichungen der Historischen Kommission für Niedersachsen und Bremen 36, 5 vols.) (Hildesheim: Lax, 1977), vol. I: pp. 653–712, here p. 705.

[71] Thegan, *Gesta Hludovici imperatoris*, ed. E. Tremp, *MGH SRG* 64 (Hanover: Hahn, 1995), c. 19, p. 200: 'poetica carmina gentilia'.

[72] Otfrid von Weissenburg, *Evangelienbuch*, eds. O. Erdmann and L. Wolff, *Otfrids Evangelienbuch* (Altdeutsche Textbibliothek 49) (Tübingen: M. Niemeyer, 1965), *Praefatio*, p. 4; see also Hummer, *Politics and Power*, pp. 143–54, here especially p. 146.

[73] See, for example, *Capitula Treverensia*, ed. P. Brommer, *MGH Cap. episc.* 1 (Hanover: Hahn, 1984), c. 11, p. 56; Hincmar of Rheims, *Prima Capitula*, eds. R. Pokorny and M. Stratmann, *MGH Cap. episc.* 2 (Hanover: Hahn, 1995), c. 14, pp. 41–2; for these and further references, see M. Innes, 'Keeping it in the family: women and aristocratic memory, 700–1200' in E. M. C. van Houts (ed.),

wrongly, praying wrongly, reading wrongly and spilling consecrated food and drink. The *Penitential*, therefore, does not constitute evidence for continuing pagan practice: it merely betrays anxiety regarding the consumption at Saxon monasteries of heroic lays and songs commemorating the dead, both of which were a feature of life in religious houses throughout the Carolingian empire.

These are the only references to contemporary paganism in Carolingian Saxony, and can scarcely be taken as evidence of widespread paganism. In every case, contemporary authors' references to paganism can be seen to be subservient to a narrative goal. There may have been some who continued to observe traditional beliefs and practices in post-conquest Saxony, but they are not attested in the extant sources.

Conversion and Christianization

The textual record is clear: the Saxons were converted under Charlemagne and thereafter remained within the Christian fold. Such a view, while not expressly confirmed, is at least not contradicted by the archaeological evidence. In the Carolingian world, conversion was signified by baptism. This conception of conversion as a single, discrete action,[74] and the corresponding division of the world into Christians and non-Christians or pagans, may appear reductionist or, at the very least, minimalist to the modern observer.[75] Christianity is not, after all, a light switch which can be flipped on and off. The term 'Christianization' has

Medieval Memories: Men, Women and the Past, 700–1300 (Harlow: Longman, 2001), pp. 17–35, here p. 27; cf. Karras, 'Pagan survivals and syncretism', 564.

[74] I am employing the modern usage of the word 'conversion' to signal the assumption of a different religion: in a medieval context, *convertere* had many different connotations and meanings, and could also be used to signify the intensification of religious devotion, for example signalled by admission into a monastic community.

[75] For contemporaries' understanding of baptism, see especially S. A. Keefe, *Water and the Word: Baptism and the Education of the Clergy in the Carolingian Empire*, 2 vols. (Notre Dame: University of Notre Dame Press, 2002), vol. I; O. M. Phelan, *The Formation of Christian Europe: The Carolingians, Baptism, and the Imperium Christianum* (Oxford: Oxford University Press, 2014). See further J. van Engen, 'Christening, the kingdom of the Carolingians, and European humanity' in V. L. Garver and O. M. Phelan (eds.), *Rome and Religion in the Medieval World: Studies in Honor of Thomas F.X. Noble* (Farnham: Ashgate, 2014), pp. 101–28; H. Kuhn, 'Das Fortleben des germanischen Heidentums nach der Christianisierung' in *La Conversione al Cristianesimo nell'Europa dell'Alto Medioevo* (Settimane 14) (Spoleto: Il Centro, 1967), pp. 743–57, here p. 746; R. A. Markus, *The End of Ancient Christianity* (Cambridge: Cambridge University Press, 1990), pp. 9–10; Shuler, 'The Saxons within Carolingian Christendom', 43; see further D. Sorber, 'Carolingian concepts of conversion', unpublished M.Phil. thesis, University of Cambridge (2012), especially pp. 60–5.

been introduced into modern scholarship for precisely this reason: it casts the transition to Christian religion as an extended process, and in so doing accommodates the continually evolving standards of what it meant to be Christian. Such an approach pays clear dividends: it allows Christianity to be approached as a socially contingent phenomenon. Yet Carolingian clerics were far from viewing Christianity in such terms. In their minds, Christianity had defined, if contested, parameters: one was either in or out, a Christian or an unbeliever. After the conquest, the Saxons were, by and large, in, and were treated as such.

What 'conversion' actually entailed in day-to-day life, however, remains unclear. The church fathers may have conceptualized conversion as a complete spiritual and material realignment, but this was, and would always be, an ideal.[76] In practice, conversion could never represent a complete abnegation of what had come before.[77] Many scholars have thus rejected the traditional narrative of conversion and the clear reorientation it implies. Particularly interesting in this regard is Patrick Wormald's reexamination of *Beowulf* in the context of the Anglo-Saxon conversion. According to Wormald, *Beowulf*, far from being a normative 'pagan' or 'Christian' text, may be used as a mirror onto the conversion of the Anglo-Saxon aristocracy.[78] It provides a useful comparison to the more normative view of the Anglo-Saxon conversion offered by Bede, prompting a minimalist view of conversion. Wormald even went so far as to speak of 'the domination of the church by the values of the barbarian aristocracy'.[79]

More recently, the work of David Frankfurter has offered new insights on the process of conversion in Roman Egypt. Frankfurter approaches religion as a 'local, collective endeavor', which operated within the ideology of larger traditions.[80] In his writing, conversion appears merely as 'a complex process of embracing new idioms and ideologies in order to reinterpret them'.[81] While such an approach, in its drive to uncover continuous local religions, unnecessarily discounts the possibility of religious change and occasionally even verges towards geographic determinism, his idea of religion as an idiom within which rituals, behaviours and beliefs were articulated nonetheless remains compelling.

---

[76] Contrast to A. D. Nock, *Conversion: The Old and the New in Religion from Alexander the Great to Augustine of Hippo* (Oxford: Clarendon, 1933), pp. 1–16, especially p. 7.

[77] See, for example, Frankfurter, *Religion in Roman Egypt*, pp. 17–20; Maxwell, 'Paganism and Christianization', p. 852.

[78] P. Wormald, 'Bede, "Beowulf" and the conversion of the Anglo-Saxon aristocracy' in R. T. Farrell (ed.), *Bede and Anglo-Saxon England: Papers in Honour of the 1300th Anniversary of the birth of Bede, Given at Cornell University in 1973 and 1974* (British Archaeological Reports 46) (Oxford: British Archaeological Reports, 1978), pp. 32–95, here pp. 39–42.

[79] *Ibid*, p. 64.   [80] Frankfurter, *Religion in Roman Egypt*, pp. 5–6.   [81] *Ibid*, p. 6.

Indeed, Frankfurter's conception of conversion as a shift in paradigm may help to elucidate the surviving material from Carolingian Saxony. Following the conclusion of the conquest, references to paganism become rare indeed; the sources affirm that Saxony had become Christian. Not all Saxons were exemplary, pious Christians: there were also unschooled Christians, even Christians on the verge of lapsing. This is not to dismiss the conversion of Saxony as a rhetorical sleight of hand: rather, it is to explain the seamless transition depicted in the written sources, which overlay a more complex process of religious change.

There is simply insufficient evidence to postulate the widespread observance of traditional beliefs in Carolingian Saxony. The textual record is clear: during the reign of Charlemagne, Saxony became Christian. Precisely what this conversion to Christianity entailed, however, is far from clear. How was Christian doctrine disseminated in Carolingian Saxony, and what were the expectations of Christian observance? What forms and functions did fledgling Christian institutions assume? How did Christian Saxons conceptualize their membership within the wider *ecclesia*? It is to these questions that I shall now turn.

CHRISTIANS AND CHRISTIANITY IN CAROLINGIAN SAXONY

Just as the implication of Saxon paganism could be employed to rhetorical effect, so too could assertions of Saxon Christianity. Authors who stressed the pious Christian observance of the Saxons could have their own agenda, in a manner not altogether dissimilar from authors who decried their near-desertion of the faith.[82] The majority of the texts which describe Saxony in the post-conquest period were, unsurprisingly, composed at Saxon bishoprics or monasteries, often by Saxons. They had clear motives to depict Saxon Christianity in a positive light: the clergy were, after all, responsible for the care of the souls entrusted to them. Yet the sources' near uniformity in presenting the Saxons as a Christian *gens*, as discussed above, suggests that such depictions cannot simply be attributed to the aims of individual texts.[83] Rather, the Saxons were typically perceived to be Christian by contemporary (Christian) authors.

This is true not only insofar as Saxon Christianity fits into a broader, triumphal narrative, but also in the pastoral concerns these same narratives betray: when pastoral concerns do surface in Saxon hagiography, they appear to be connected to Carolingian *correctio*, rather than to any continuing struggle against paganism. This was not a self-evident choice.

---

[82] See here, and in what follows, Rembold, '*Quasi una gens*'.   [83] See above, pp. 82–4.

There were numerous precedents for the elision of *correctio* and the insinuation of paganism: the letters of Boniface, not to mention the *List of Superstitions and Pagan Practices*, employ accusations of paganism as part of a broader reforming strategy.[84] If Christian clerics of the ninth century had wished to conjure pagan phantasms haunting the Saxon religious landscape, the literary tradition was already in place. Yet, with the one exception noted above, clerics in post-conquest Saxony did not resort to such models: they simply did not depict themselves as battling paganism anymore.

Pastoral Concerns in Saxon Hagiography

Clerics who voiced pastoral concerns in their works did so without the invocation of paganism. Instead, the concerns they raised, such as respect for holy days, correct sexual behaviour and the correct treatment of Christian slaves, can be seen as part of a broader programme of Carolingian *correctio*. Of these, the most frequently recurring concern in Saxon hagiography was the observance of Sundays and feast days. In the *Third Life of Saint Liudger*, we read of how some peasants, 'because it was springtime and the labours of ploughing were at hand, having yoked an ox to the plough, persevered with their work until the iron, with which they were accustomed to plough, broke into several pieces'.[85] All halted save a certain Benno, who, 'with an obstinate mind', repaired his plough and drove his cows to the field once more, only to have the plough break once again, and his cows run off into the forest.[86] Likewise, in the *Life of Saint Anskar* (although this time the story is set just across the Frisian border, in Ostergau), Rimbert tells us of how certain 'proud and stupid' people, disregarding Anskar's admonition, collected hay into haystacks on the Sunday. The haystacks they had so boldly constructed were later destroyed by fire, while those which had been collected earlier in the week survived intact.[87] The leitmotif of obstinacy followed by repentance recurs in both tales.

---

[84] See above, p. 198; see also Dierkens, 'Superstitions, christianisme et paganisme', pp. 23–6; Palmer, 'Defining paganism', 407–8; Palmer, *Anglo-Saxons in a Frankish World*, pp. 113–44; Smith, *Europe after Rome*, pp. 236–8.

[85] *Vita tertia sancti Liudgeri*, ed. W. Diekamp, *Die vitae sancti Liudgeri* (Die Geschichtsquellen des Bisthums Münster 4) (Münster: Theissing, 1881), pp. 85–134, here II:10, p. 119: 'Et quia vernum tempus erat et arandi opera instabant, iunctus bubus ad arandum processerunt, cumque iam operi insisterent, ferrum, quo arari debuerat, singulis confractum est.'

[86] *Ibid*, II:10, p. 119: 'mente obstinata'; cf. Karras, 'Pagan survivals and syncretism', 557.

[87] Rimbert, *Vita sancti Anskarii*, ed. G. Waitz, MGH SRG 55 (Hanover: Hahn, 1884), c. 37, p. 72: 'contumaces et stolidi'.

The anxiety that some might violate the observance of Sundays and feast days through illicit sexual intercourse or judicial proceedings also surfaces in hagiography. In the *Life of the Virgin Liutbirga*, an infant who died before baptism is revealed to have been 'conceived on a Sunday, and consequently did not deserve to come to the grace of rebirth, but was assigned to the punishments of hell'.[88] In a different, albeit equally sobering fashion, the *Second Life of Saint Liudger* contains a story about how Liudger came upon a crowd preparing for a hanging on a Sunday:

He addressed them persuasively, demanding that they release the man or, if they insisted upon executing him, that they not do it on this day, but rather come together to church in order to hear mass. Although he did not procure either of these concessions from these rustics, for the place did not pertain to his parish, he only just prevailed to talk for a short while with the man about his penance. When he had finished, the bishop, the man of God, departed, and the man was hanged on a gibbet.[89]

The tale continues, and the condemned man miraculously survives his hanging and escapes.

These stories, while possibly born out of general rumour, nonetheless reflect the genuine pastoral concerns of the clerics who wrote them. They indicate a general anxiety over the observance of the Lord's day and feast days, which was one of the most basic tenets of the recently assumed faith. Such concerns were not just present on the Carolingian fringe, nor were they indicative of latent paganism.[90] Rather, the correct observance of holy days was a priority throughout the Carolingian world, addressed not only in the *General Admonition* but also in a wide variety of capitulary and conciliar legislation.[91] It had been a concern in

---

[88] *Vita Liutbirgae virginis*, ed. Menzel, c. 33, p. 39: 'die dominico conceptus est, et per hoc non meruit ad regenerationis gratiam pervenire, sed penis deputandus est inferorum'.

[89] *Vita secunda sancti Liudgeri*, ed. E. Freise, *Die Vita sancti Liudgeri: Vollständige Faksimile-Ausgabe der Handschrift Ms. Theol. lat. fol. 323 der Staatsbibliothek Berlin – Preußischer Kulturbesitz. Text, Übersetzung und Kommentar, Forschungsbeiträge* (Graz: Akadem. Druck- und Verlagsanstalt, 1999), pp. 9–24, here c. 28, p. 15: 'affatus est eos blande, postulans sibi concedi hominem. Aut si necesse esset eum interfici, hoc eo die non facerent, sed magis ad ęcclesiam missas audituri convenirent. Cumque nichil horum a rusticis impetrare potuisset – locus enim ille ad suam parrochiam non pertinebat –, vix optinere potuit, ut parumper cum homine super eius pęnitentia se loqueretur. Quod cum factum esset, vir Dei discessit antistes, et homo in patibulum suspensus est'.

[90] Holy day observance, is, however, especially highlighted in the *Capitulatio de partibus Saxoniae*, ed. von Schwerin, c. 18, p. 40.

[91] *Admonito Generalis*, c. 81, p. 61, and *Capitulare Missorum*, c. 46, p. 104, ed. A. Boretius, *MGH Cap.* 1 (Hanover: Hahn, 1883); *Concilium Arelatense*, c. 16, p. 252, *Concilium Francofurtense*, c. 21, p. 168, *Concilium Foroiuliense*, c. 13, pp. 194–5, *Concilium Remense*, c. 35, p. 256, *Concilium Moguntienense*, cc. 36–7, pp. 269–70, and *Concilium Turonense*, c. 40, p. 292, ed. A. Werminghoff, *MGH Conc.* 2:1 (Hanover: Hahn, 1906); *Concilium Parisiense*, ed. A. Werminghoff, *MGH Conc.* 2:2 (Hanover: Hahn, 1908), c. 50, pp. 643–4; for these references and more, see D. Haines, *Sunday Observance and the Sunday*

hagiographical writing since Gregory of Tours, who had included many similar stories within his voluminous works.[92]

The observance of holy days is, by far, the most pervasive pastoral concern in Saxon hagiography. Other anxieties surface as well: correct sexual behaviour was also a recurring theme in Saxon miracle stories, hence the miracle above, which concluded in the eternal damnation of the child conceived on a Sunday. And the timing of sexual acts was not the only cause for concern. Marriage was also a pre-requisite: in the *Life of the Virgin Liutbirga*, a man who attempts to seduce a maidservant outside wedlock was quickly dispatched by a grave and sudden illness.[93] Finally, the Christian taboo on incest was raised as a priority: Altfrid's *Life of Saint Liudger* contains a story in which a woman in an incestuous marriage attempts to bribe the saint, only to have her husband expelled from the country.[94] Here, too, such themes echo the programme of Carolingian *correctio*, which attempted to reform the sexual *mores* of the populace.[95]

The remaining pastoral concerns contained in Saxon hagiography, which tackle respect for Church lands and the prohibition on selling Christian slaves beyond the border, should likewise be connected to wider Carolingian priorities and *correctio*.[96] There is simply no indication that clerics were concerned about continuing pagan practices any longer: it was a brave new, ultimately Christian, world.

Vernacular Texts and Christian Instruction

An examination of Saxon vernacular texts largely complements this perspective.[97] While Latin hagiography may betray the concerns of

---

Letter in Anglo-Saxon England (Anglo-Saxon Texts 8) (Woodbridge: Boydell & Brewer, 2010), pp. 15–16.

[92] *Liber in gloria martyrum*, c. 15, p. 48, *Liber de passione et virtutibus sancti Iuliani martyris*, c. 11, p. 119, *Liber de virtutibus sancti Martini episcopi*, II:13, 57, III:3, 7, 29, 55, IV:45, pp. 163, 178, 183–4, 189, 195, 210–11, and *Liber in gloria confessorum*, c. 97, pp. 360–1, in Gregory of Tours, *Miracula et Opera Minora*, ed. B. Krush, *MGH SRM* 1:2 (Hanover: Hahn, 1885); for these references, see I. N. Wood, 'How popular was early medieval devotion?', *Essays in Medieval Studies: Proceedings of the Illinois Medieval Association*, 14 (1997); see further the comments of Markus, 'From Caesarius to Boniface', pp. 158–9.

[93] *Vita Liutbirgae virginis*, ed. Menzel, c. 30, pp. 34–7; see also F. S. Paxton, *Anchoress and Abbess in Ninth-Century Saxony: The Lives of Liutbirga of Wendhausen and Hathumoda of Gandersheim* (Washington, DC: Catholic University of America Press, 2009), pp. 53–4.

[94] Altfrid, *Vita sancti Liudgeri*, ed. W. Diekamp, *Die vitae sancti Liudgeri* (Die Geschichtsquellen des Bisthums Münster 4) (Münster: Theissing, 1881), pp. 3–53, here I:28, pp. 33–4.

[95] R. Stone, *Morality and Masculinity in the Carolingian Empire* (Cambridge: Cambridge University Press, 2011), pp. 255–61, 282–7.

[96] For the prohibition on selling Christian slaves beyond the border, see A. Rio, *Slavery after Rome, 500–1100* (Oxford: Oxford University Press, 2017), pp. 20–1.

[97] This section has been adapted from a forthcoming book chapter: see I. Rembold, 'The Christian message and the laity: the Heliand in post-conquest Saxony' in N. Edwards, M. Ni Mhaonaigh

Saxon clerics, these texts give a window onto the means by which the Christian message was communicated to a wider audience. These texts appear to have been intended not to convert but rather to instruct an already Christian elite in matters of Christian doctrine and to shape their moral behaviour according to Scriptural teachings. As such, these texts bear productive comparison to contemporary lay mirrors; they reflect the general Carolingian priorities of Christian instruction and encouragement towards moral rectitude and emendation.

One contemporary witness even went so far as to link these compositions directly to the imperial centre: the anonymous prose preface to the *Heliand* (*Saviour*), an Old Saxon biblical epic based on an earlier 'Gospel harmony' (a single narrative derived from the four Gospel accounts), narrates how 'the most pious Emperor Louis ... ordered a certain man from the Saxon people, who was held to be a most noble poet among his people, to translate the Old and New Testament into the German language poetically'.[98] Just as the *Heliand* represented the New Testament, the Old Saxon *Genesis*, a similar biblical epic, represented the Old.[99] Translations of further biblical books, whether into Old Saxon or into the closely related Old Frisian, may have been made: fragments of an Old Saxon *Commentary on the Psalms* survive and are complemented by the story of how the missionary Liudger taught the psalms to a Frisian bard, Bernlef, perhaps pointing to the vernacular performance of these texts.[100] Yet even if the *Heliand* and *Genesis* formed the full original corpus of Old Saxon biblical literature, together they featured the 'Christian highlights', so to speak. Indeed, Ermoldus Nigellus depicts Louis the Pious ordering Archbishop Ebo, newly appointed as the head of the northern mission, to instruct his audiences on the creation, the fall of man and the events leading up to the flood, as well as the life and death of Jesus.[101] In Saxony, the *Genesis* and *Heliand* covered these bases.

and R. Flechner (eds.), *Transforming Landscapes of Belief in the Early Medieval Insular World and Beyond* (Converting the Isles 2) (Turnhout: Brepols), in press.

[98] *Heliand*, eds. O. Behaghel and B. Taeger, *Heliand und Genesis* (Altdeutsche Textbibliothek 4), 9th edn (Tübingen: M. Niemeyer, 1984), *Praefatio A*, p. 1: 'Ludouicus piissimus Augustus ... Praecepit namque cuidem viro de gente Saxonum, qui apud suos non ignobilis vates habebatur, ut vetus ac novum Testamentum in Germanicam linguam poetice transferre studeret.'

[99] *Genesis*, ed. A. N. Doane, *The Saxon Genesis: An Edition of the West Saxon Genesis B and the Old Saxon Vatican Genesis* (Madison: University of Wisconsin Press, 1991).

[100] For the *Commentary on the Psalms*, see *Lectio psalmorum*, ed. E. Wadstein, *Kleinere altsächsische Sprachdenkmäler* (Niederdeutsche Denkmäler 6) (Norden: Soltau, 1899), pp. 4–15, 121–3; for Bernlef, see below, pp. 233–4.

[101] Ermoldus Nigellus, *In Honorem Hludowici*, ed. E. Faral, *Poème sur Louis le Pieux et épitres au Roi Pépin* (Les classiques de l'histoire de France au moyen age 14), 2nd edn (Paris: Société d'Édition "Les Belles Lettres", 1964), IV verses 1911–45, pp. 146–8; for this point, see R. E. Sullivan, 'The Carolingian missionary and the pagan', *Speculum*, 28(4) (1953), 705–40, here 715; R. E. Sullivan,

Accordingly, they were celebrated in the Latin prose preface, which connected their composition to the benevolent patronage of an 'Emperor Louis'.

The identity of this 'Emperor Louis' has been much debated. While the preface was originally assumed to refer to Louis the Pious, the pendulum of historical consensus has swung back and forth between the emperor and his son, King Louis the German.[102] In practice, however, the role of this 'Emperor Louis', whether Pious or German, was almost certainly restricted. The Latin prose preface was only added to the text at a later stage, as indicated by the inclusion of the Old Testament (the *Genesis* is considered to post-date the *Heliand*).[103] As such, it represents an attempt to associate both compositions with imperial grandeur and patronage post facto, in a manner similar to the many local foundations in Saxony which were later attributed to Charlemagne and his successors.

As discussed in the Introduction, the *Heliand* can be dated to the period between 821 and the mid-ninth century; it was probably composed at the monastery of Fulda, which had been closely associated with the Saxon mission and maintained monastic cells, Hameln and Brunshausen, within Saxony.[104] Its counterpart, the Old Saxon *Genesis*, has a less certain place of composition and date. It is first attested in the third quarter of the ninth century, when excerpts of both the *Heliand* and *Genesis* were copied into a manuscript associated with the archbishopric of Mainz.[105] In the absence of other information, the *Genesis* may tentatively be linked to the Fulda–Mainz axis; both institutions were closely linked, not only through Boniface, but also through the person of Hrabanus Maurus, who served near-consecutively as abbot of Fulda and archbishop of Mainz. Fulda in particular was deeply involved in the composition of vernacular texts, including the Old High German *Tatian* and a variety of shorter texts; Mainz, in turn, preserved the only copy of

---

'Carolingian missionary theories', *The Catholic Historical Review*, 42(3) (1956), 273–95, here 285. For a comparison of Ermoldus' account of this mission with that offered in Rimbert's *Vita sancti Anskarii*, see I. N. Wood, 'Christians and pagans in ninth-century Scandinavia' in B. Sawyer, P. H. Sawyer and I. N. Wood (eds.), *The Christianization of Scandinavia: Report of a Symposium held at Kungälv, Sweden, 4–9 August 1985* (Alingsås: Viktoria, 1987), pp. 36–67, here pp. 36–7.

[102] For arguments in favour of Louis the Pious, see especially H. J. Hummer, 'The identity of *Ludouicus piisimus augustus* in the *Praefatio in librum antiquum lingua Saxonica conscriptum*', *Francia*, 31 (1) (2004), 1–14. For arguments in favour of Louis the German, see especially W. Haubrichs, *Die Anfänge: Versuche volkssprachiger Schriftlichkeit im frühen Mittelalter, (ca. 700–1050/60)* (Geschichte der deutschen Literatur von den Anfängen bis zum Beginn der Neuzeit 1:1) (Frankfurt: Athenäum, 1988), pp. 336–38; see further R. Drögereit, *Werden und der Heliand: Studien zur Kulturgeschichte der Abtei Werden und zur Herkunft des Heliand* (Essen: Fredebeul & Koenen, 1951), pp. 106–7.

[103] Hummer, 'The identity of *Ludouicus piisimus augustus*', 1–2.   [104] See above, pp. 22–3.

[105] A. N. Doane, *The Saxon Genesis: An Edition of the West Saxon Genesis B and the Old Saxon Vatican Genesis* (Madison: University of Wisconsin Press, 1991), pp. 9–28.

the Old Saxon *Baptismal Vow* in an early ninth-century manuscript.[106] These institutions were not, however, the only centres of composition for Old Saxon texts. Other Old Saxon works, such as the Old Saxon *Penitential*, the *All Saints' Day Sermon* and the *Commentary on the Psalms*, have been associated, with greater or lesser degrees of plausibility, with the monasteries of Essen and Werden.[107] Some of these texts survive only by chance, entered in the white spaces or margins of manuscripts. This in turn raises the possibility of a larger original corpus of Old Saxon texts, and potentially of more centres of composition.

Nevertheless, the extant corpus is itself revealing. It points towards particular engagement in the production of Old Saxon texts on the periphery of Saxony: Fulda, of course, was located in nearby Hessia, while Essen and Werden were located on the Ruhr, a tributary of the Rhine in the Saxon–Frankish borderland. Both Fulda and Werden were eighth-century foundations and as such were closely involved in the Saxon mission; Essen, on the other hand, was founded in the mid-ninth century. Interestingly, however, Fulda and Werden's vernacular compositions largely post-date the early missionary period. Only one surviving Old Saxon text, namely the *Baptismal Vow*, a short set of six questions and responses, can be dated to the late eighth century; thereafter follows a large gap stretching to the second quarter of the ninth century (and even possibly up to circa 840).

The first surviving attempt at large-scale vernacular teaching in Saxony came with the composition of the *Heliand* and, following closely on its heels, the *Genesis*. Various audiences, both elite, lay and mixed, have been posited for the *Heliand* and thus, by extension, for the Old Saxon *Genesis* (which has largely been dealt with, somewhat unfairly, as an afterthought to its more famous cousin).[108] Yet there exists a general consensus, strengthened by the mid-ninth-century dating of these texts, that they were intended further to educate and instruct a Christian elite.[109] Similar arguments can be made for the *All Saints' Day Sermon*,

---

[106] For the Old Saxon Baptismal vow and its manuscript context, see *Abrenuntiatio diaboli et professio fidei*, ed. E. Wadstein, *Kleinere altsächsische Sprachdenkmäler* (Niederdeutsche Denkmäler 6) (Norden: Soltau, 1899), pp. 3, 119–21.

[107] *Old Saxon Penitential*, pp. 16–17, 123–6; *Sermo omnium sanctorum*, pp. 18, 126–7; *Lectio psalmorum*, p. 122, all ed. E. Wadstein, *Kleinere altsächsische Sprachdenkmäler* (Niederdeutsche Denkmäler 6) (Norden: Soltau, 1899). See further R. McKitterick, 'Werden im Spiegel seiner Handschriften (8./9. Jahrhundert)' in S. Patzold, A. Rathmann-Lutz and V. Scior (eds.), *Geschichtsvorstellungen: Bilder, Texte, und Begriffe aus dem Mittelalter: Festschrift für Hans-Werner Goetz zum 65. Geburtstag* (Vienna: Böhlau, 2012), pp. 326–53, here pp. 334–6.

[108] See, however, the excellent treatment of Doane, *The Saxon Genesis*.

[109] Within this general consensus, scholars have put forward a number of suggestions regarding the precise delineation of this Christian audience. For the suggestion of a lay elite audience, see

although its brevity precludes a full assessment. Meanwhile, the *Commentary on the Psalms* and the Old Saxon *Penitential* appear to have been composed for Saxon monastic audiences, as implied by the exegetical function of the former and the express instructions in the preface to the latter.[110] The thrust of Old Saxon composition, then, appears primarily to have been intended to Christianize an already Christian elite.[111]

This is especially the case for the *Heliand* and *Genesis*, both of which adapted their source material to be pertinent to the life of the male, secular elite. Even the style of these works points towards lay, elite consumption. The *Heliand* poet rendered his composition in alliterative verse, replete with epithets and with an eye to cadence; the *Genesis* poet, meanwhile, adapted this traditional style in closer accordance with written norms. Both works were presumably intended to be performed orally, in sections or *fitts*, if not in full.[112] In the case of the *Heliand*, this can be demonstrated by the presence of accents in two manuscripts and the inclusion of neumes in yet another, thereby indicating recitation and musical performance respectively; the Latin preface further employs the vocabulary of *cantilena* and *modulatio*, terms used to refer to singing.[113]

M. B. Gillis, *Heresy and Dissent in the Carolingian Empire: The Case of Gottschalk of Orbais* (Oxford: Oxford University Press, 2017), pp. 45–6; Goldberg, *Struggle for Empire*, p. 183; C. Zurla, 'Medium and message: the confluence of Saxon and Frankish values as portrayed in the Old Saxon Heliand', unpublished Ph.D. thesis, McGill University (2004), pp. 27–33. For a monastic and lay elite audience, see G. Mierke, *Memoria als Kulturtransfer: der altsächsische "Heliand" zwischen Spätantike und Frühmittelalter* (Ordo: Studien zur Literatur und Gesellschaft des Mittelalters und der frühen Neuzeit 11) (Cologne: Böhlau, 2008), especially p. 121; see further Haubrichs, *Die Anfänge*, p. 353; S. Matzner, 'Christianizing the epic – epicizing Christianity: Nonnus' paraphrasis and the Old-Saxon Heliand in a comparative perspective', *Millennium: Jahrbuch zu Kultur und Geschichte des ersten Jahrtausend n. Chr.* 5 (2008), 111–45, here 117. For a mixed (male and female) monastic audience, see R. Drögereit, 'Die schriftlichen Quellen zur Christianisierung der Sachsen und ihre Aussagefähigkeit' in W. Lammers (ed.), *Die Eingliederung der Sachsen in das Frankenreich* (Wege der Forschung 185) (Darmstadt: Wissenschaftliche Buchgesellschaft, 1970), pp. 451–69, here p. 465. For lay brothers and/or *conversi*, see K. Gantert, *Akkommodation und eingeschriebener Kommentar: Untersuchungen zur Übertragungsstrategie des Helianddichters* (ScriptOralia 111) (Tübingen: G. Narr, 1998), pp. 265–77; D. H. Green, 'Three aspects of the Old Saxon Biblical epic, the *Heliand*' in Green and Siegmund, *Saxons*, p. 255; H. Haferland, 'Was the Heliand poet illiterate?' in V. A. Pakis (ed.), *Perspectives on the Old Saxon Heliand: Introductory and Critical Essays, with an Edition of the Leipzig Fragment* (Medieval European Studies 12) (Morgantown: West Virginia University Press, 2010), pp. 167–207, here p. 167. Contrast to the approach taken in G.R. Murphy, *The Saxon Savior: The Germanic Transformation of the Gospel in the Ninth-Century Heliand* (Oxford: Oxford University Press, 1989).

[110] For the Latin preface to the text, see *Old Saxon Penitential*, ed. Wadstein, pp. 124–5.

[111] I have explored this issue at greater length in Rembold, 'The Christian message and the laity', in press; see also Mierke, *Memoria als Kulturtransfer*.

[112] For the division of these texts into songs, or *fitts*, see Doane, *The Saxon Genesis*, pp. 27–8; Gantert, *Akkommodation und eingeschriebener Kommentar*, pp. 123–4.

[113] For the presence of accents and neumes, see especially B. Taeger, 'Das Straubinger 'Heliand' Fragment: Philologische Untersuchungen (Fortsetzung)', *Beiträge zur Geschichte der deutschen Sprache und Literatur*, 103(3) (1981), 402–24; see further B. Bischoff, 'Die Straubinger Fragmente

Such performance would have rendered these works accessible to literate and illiterate audiences alike. The *Genesis* may have further been copied in a high-status, illustrated manuscript as would befit elite consumption: Barbara Raw has argued that the illustrations accompanying Old English translation of the Old Saxon text, *Genesis B*, appear to have been copied from a lost Carolingian exemplar.[114]

The argument for lay elite consumption of these texts lies not only in their form, but also in their content. Both the *Heliand* and *Genesis* represent an interpretation, as opposed to simply translation, of one or more biblical books. In the case of the *Heliand*, this was mediated by the *Codex Fuldensis*, a Latin translation of Tatian's gospel harmony; it was to this source, rather than to the Gospels themselves, that the anonymous poet turned.[115] In this process of interpretation and versification, the poets took substantial liberties with their sources, adapting their exemplars so as to aid the understanding of their audience and to sharpen these texts' relevance to their audiences' daily lives. They reordered their material, expanding some sections while omitting or minimizing others; they added glosses and extended explanations, sometimes relating biblical teaching directly to present-day life; they recast the language of the Vulgate, drawing upon traditional motifs and modes of expression; the poet of the *Genesis* presumably drew upon a range of apocrypha in addition to his biblical source. Some have taken this 'artistic license' as evidence of syncretism, of a Christianity laced with purportedly 'pagan' elements. Yet such an interpretation not only ignores the monastic context for the composition and, in part, reception of these texts; it also presupposes a normative, non-syncretic Christianity, distinct from its cultural context, which simply cannot be demonstrated to exist. Instead, it seems better to approach these works as studies in inter-cultural communication, designed to instruct their audiences in Christian doctrine while also driving home the relevance and applicability of biblical texts to the lives of Saxon elites.[116]

---

einer Heliand-Handschrift', *Beiträge zur Geschichte der deutschen Sprache und Literatur*, 101(2) (1979), 171–80, here 174; B. Taeger, 'Ein vergessener handschriflicher Befund: Die Neumen in Münchener "Heliand"', *Zeitschrift für deutsches Altertum und deutsche Literatur*, 107(3) (1978), 184–93. For the use of the Latin terms in the preface, see *Heliand*, eds. Behaghel and Taeger, *Praefatio A*, p. 2; Green, 'Three aspects', p. 253.

[114] B. C. Raw, 'The probable derivation of most of the illustrations in Junius 11 from an illustrated Old Saxon *Genesis*', *Anglo-Saxon England*, 5 (1976), 133–48.

[115] Tatian, *Diatessaron*, in Victor of Capua, *Codex Fuldensis*, ed. E. Ranke, *Codex Fuldensis: Novum Testamentum Latine interprete Hieronymo* (Marburg, 1868). David R. Smith has compiled a translation of Tatian's Diatessaron by excerpting the relevant sections of the Douay-Rheims translation: see D. R. Smith, tr., *The Forgotten Gospel: The Latin Diatessaron* (ebook, 2008).

[116] Gantert, *Akkommodation und eingeschriebener Kommentar*; Mierke, *Memoria als Kulturtransfer*. Cf. Murphy, *The Saxon Savior*, here especially p. 28.

Gesine Mierke in particular has drawn attention to the emphasis placed upon elite lay piety in the *Heliand*, comparing it to lay mirrors such as Alcuin's *De virtutibus et vitiis*.[117] This is especially the case in the *Heliand* poet's rendering of the Sermon on the Mount.[118] The degree to which the poet has adapted the text of his exemplar is clear from a comparison of the two works. Take, for example, their respective views on justice:

TATIAN: Blessed are they that hunger and thirst after justice: for they shall have their fill.[119]

HELIAND: Blessed also are the men who strove for virtue here, and so judged rightly. For this they may be fulfilled in the kingdom of the Lord for their devout deeds.[120]

TATIAN: Blessed are the peacemakers, for they shall be called the children of God.[121]

HELIAND: He also said that blessed were those who live peacefully among the people and do not wish to create any strife or disputes with their own actions: they may be called sons of the Lord, for he will wish to be merciful to them.[122]

TATIAN: Judge not.[123]

HELIAND: You shall not render man anything unjust or hostile.[124]

The *Heliand* poet wrote for an audience composed of judges and would-be litigants, not the wronged and oppressed. Accordingly, Tatian's passive conception of justice was transformed into one of active judgement and dispute resolution.[125] Similarly, in other areas the poet significantly altered his source to bring out themes pertinent to the life of the male, secular elite. A particularly striking example is his inclusion of moral commentary on the blood feud, a subject not to be found in

---

[117] Mierke, *Memoria als Kulturtransfer*, especially pp. 115–16.   [118] *Ibid*, pp. 230–5.

[119] Tatian, *Diatessaron*, in Victor of Capua, *Codex Fuldensis*, ed. Ranke, c. 23, p. 45: 'beati qui esuriunt et sitiunt iustitiam quoniam ipsi saturabuntur'.

[120] *Heliand*, eds. Behaghel and Taeger, XVI: 1308–10, p. 52: 'Sâlige sind ôc, the sie hîr frumono gilustid, | ricos, that sie rehto adômien. Thes môtun sie uuerðan an them rîkia drohtines | gifullit thurh iro ferhton dâdi'. Please note that my translations of passages from the *Heliand* are greatly indebted to the excellent translation of Tonya K. Dewey: T. K. Dewey, tr., *An Annotated English Translation of the Old Saxon Heliand: A Ninth-Century Biblical Paraphrase in the Germanic Epic Style* (Lewiston: Edwin Mellen, 2011).

[121] Tatian, *Diatessaron*, in Victor of Capua, *Codex Fuldensis*, ed. Ranke, c. 23, p. 45: 'beati pacifici. quoniam filii dei uocabuntur'.

[122] *Heliand*, eds. Behaghel and Taeger, XVI: 1316–19, p. 52: 'Quað that ôc sâlige uuârin, | thie the friðusamo undar thesumu folke libbiod endi ni uuilliad êniga fehta geuuirken, | saca mid iro selboro dâdiun: thie môtun uuesan suni drohtines genemnide | huuande he im uuil genâdig uuerðen.'

[123] Tatian, *Diatessaron*, in Victor of Capua, *Codex Fuldensis*, ed. Ranke, c. 40, p. 50: 'nolite iudicare'.

[124] *Heliand*, eds. Behaghel and Taeger, XX: 1691–92, p. 66: 'Ne sculun gi ênigumu manne uhrehtes uuiht, | derbies adêlean.'

[125] Murphy, *The Saxon Savior*, pp. 85–8.

the Sermon or even in the wider Gospels. Here, the poet recasts provisions on avoiding adultery and granting forgiveness as warnings against those who seek vengeance: Tatian's injunction that 'if thy right eye scandalize thee, pluck it out and cast it from thee, for it is expedient for thee that one of thy members should perish, rather than thy whole body be cast into hell' is embellished in the *Heliand* with the following commentary:[126]

This affliction, then, means that no one should follow his friend, his own man, if he urges him towards sin, towards crimes: then he is not so closely related to him by family-ties, nor is their relationship so important, if he drives him to murder and forces him to commit evil deeds: the other thing is better for him, that he reject the friend far away from him and that he avoid the relative and not love him, in order that he alone may rise to the high kingdom of heaven, lest they both bewail the force of hell, great eternal punishment, evil suffering.[127]

The *Heliand* poet returns to address the subject at a later junction, expanding upon Tatian's original teaching:

TATIAN: For if you will forgive men their offences, your heavenly Father will forgive you also your offences. But if you will not forgive men, neither will your Father forgive your offences.[128]

HELIAND: If you wish, then, to forgive every person for the crimes and sins which they angrily carry out against you yourself here, then ruler God, the father almighty, forgives you for your great crimes, your many sins. But if you become too hard in your mind, so that you do not wish to forgive other men for their sins, then ruler God will also not wish to forgive you for your evil deeds, and you shall take his payment, a very ruinous punishment for a longer time, for all

---

[126] Tatian, *Diatessaron*, in Victor of Capua, *Codex Fuldensis*, ed. Ranke, c. 29, p. 47: 'Quodsi oculus tuus dexter scandalizat te. erue eum et proice abs te. expedit enim tibi ut pereat unum membrorum tuorum quam totum corpus tuum mittatur in gehennam.'

[127] *Heliand*, eds. Behaghel and Taeger, XVII: 1492–502, p. 59: 'Than mênid thiu lêfhêd, that ênig liudeo ni scal | farfolgan is friunde, ef he ina an firina spanit, | suâs man an saca: than ne sî he imu eo sô suuîðo an sibbiun bilang, | ne iro mâgskepi sô mikil, ef he ina an morð spenit, | bêdid baluuuerco; betera is imu than ôðar, | that he thana friund fan imu fer faruuerpa, | mîðe thes mâges endi ni hebbea thar êniga minnea tô, | that he môti êno up gistîgan | hô himilrîki, than sie heligethuing, | brêd baluuuîti bêðea gisôkean, | ubil albidi.' See also P. Augustyn, *The Semiotics of Fate, Death, and the Soul in Germanic Culture: The Christianization of Old Saxon* (Berkeley Insights in Linguistics and Semiotics 50) (New York: P. Lang, 2002), p. 150.

[128] Tatian, *Diatessaron*, in Victor of Capua, *Codex Fuldensis*, ed. Ranke, c. 35, p. 49: 'si enim dimiseritis hominibus peccata eorum dimittet et uobis pater uester caelestis delicta uestra. Si autem non dimiseritis hominibus nec pater uester dimittet uobis peccata uestra'.

that you accomplish unjustly against others here in this
world and because you did not reconcile crimes with the
children of men before you men pass from this world.[129]

Those who engage in the blood feud are thus roundly condemned.
At other points, too, the elite audience whom the poet envisaged are
sharply admonished, notably in regard to the use of wealth and the need
to give charity. The poet did not coddle his audience: on the contrary, he
strove to instruct them in their duties and to urge emendation.

The *Heliand* poet's pointed revision of Tatian's gospel harmony is most
apparent in the Sermon on the Mount: this formed, after all, one of Jesus'
main statements on moral instruction. In many other sections of the work,
though, the poet adapted, expanded and reordered his exemplar so as to
render it comprehensible and relevant to his intended audience. When we
shift our gaze to the Old Saxon *Genesis*, by contrast, there is no such
'programmatic statement' of Christian teaching. This is a feature that it
shares with its biblical namesake. The absence of a clear source text renders
such an assessment of the poet's role more difficult: the poet clearly diverges
from the biblical Genesis, but the extent to which his innovations are to
be attributed to his own imagination as opposed to lost or unidentified
apocryphal sources is uncertain. Nevertheless, there are signs that he too
actively shaped his work to have resonances with his Saxon audiences.
For example, he depicts the events leading up to Satan's fall in a manner
not dissimilar to earthly rebellion, fleshing out his narrative with reference
to retainers and vassals: as the poet narrates, Satan could not

find it in his mind to serve as a vassal of Lord God. It appeared to him that he
had a greater strength and larger army than Holy God might have comrades-in-
arms for himself ... He said that his spirit was pulling him to begin to work in
the West and North, to build up a structure. He said that it seemed doubtful to
him that he would be subject to God. 'Why should I toil?' he asked. "By no
means do I need to have a lord ... I have great power to construct a more
splendid throne, higher in heaven. Why should I serve according to his favour
or submit to him in such vassalage? I may be God as much as He! Strong
retainers stand with me, hardened warriors who will not withdraw from me in
the battle. Brave warriors have chosen me as lord; with such men one can devise

---

[129] *Heliand*, eds. Behaghel and Taeger, XIX: 1616–28, pp. 63–4: 'Ef gi than uilliad alâtan liudeo
gehuuilicun | thero sacono endi thero sundeono, the sie uuið iu selbon hîr | uurêða geuuirkeat,
than alâtid iu uualand god, | fadar alamahtig firinuuerk mikil, | managoro mênsculdeo. Ef iu than
uuirðid iuuua môd te starc, | that gi ne uuilleat ôðrun erlun alâtan, | uueron uuamdâdi, than ne uuil
iu ôc uualdand god | grimuuerc fargeban, ac gi sculun is geld niman, | suîðo lêðlic lôn te languru
huuîlu, | alles thes unrehtes, thes gi ôðrun hîr | gilêstead an thesumu liohte endi than uuið liudeo
barn | thea saca ne gisônead, êr gi an thana sîð faran, | uueros fon thesoro uueroldi.'

a plan, with such men can one begin a following. My friends are eager, loyal in their hearts. I may be their lord and rule in this kingdom.[130]

When Satan's plan is discovered and duly punished, the poet conceives of such punishment in terms of earthly dispossession: Satan is made to bewail that man will possess 'the prosperity and dominion which we should rightly hold in Heaven'.[131] At other points, the poet narrates more successful relationships between a lord (the Lord) and his men, such as in the following speech by Abraham to the Lord:

Whither do you want now, my Ruler Lord, almighty Father? I am your one servant, loyal and obedient. You are so good to me, Lord, so generous with treasure. Would you like to have anything of mine, Lord? Whatever you choose is yours. I live by your gift, and I believe in you, my good Lord.[132]

While this work lacks the clear moral agenda of the *Heliand*, the poet nevertheless reworks his narrative so as to render it more explicable and relatable to the life of the secular elite.

An examination of the vernacular evidence, then, may be seen broadly to parallel that of contemporary Latin hagiography. There is nothing to suggest that Christian authors were ever confronted by, or even worried about, lingering paganism. What concerned contemporary authors was not how to draw the Saxon laity away from paganism, but rather how to make them into better Christians. They worried about how best to educate them in Christian doctrine and to shape their moral behaviour according to Christian teaching. In so doing, they were participating in an empire-wide process of *correctio* and Christian reform. After all, as

---

[130] *Genesis*, ed. Doane, lines 266–89, pp. 208–9: 'ne meahte he æt his hige findan | þaet he gode wolde geongerdome | þeodne þeowian. þuhte him sylfum | þaet he mægyn and cræft maran hæfde | þonne se halga god habban mihte | folcgestælna... | ... cwæð þæt hine his hige speonne | þæt he west and norð wyrcean ongunne, | trymede getrimbro. cwæð him tweo þuhte | þæt he gode wolde geongra weorðan. | 'hwæt sceal ic winnan?' cwæð he. 'nis me wihtæ þearf | hearran to habbanne... | ... ic hæbbe geweald micel | to gyrwanne godlecran stol, | hearran on heofne. hwy sceal ic æfter his hyldo ðeowian, | bugan him swilces geongordomes? ic mæg wesan god swa he. | bigstandað me strange geneatas þa ne willað me æt þam striðe geswican, | hæleþas heardmode. hie habbað me to hearran gecorene, | rofe rincas. mid swilcum mæg man ræd geþencean, | fon mid swilcum folcgesteallan. frynd synd hie mine georne, | holde on hyra hygesceaftum. ic mæg hyra hearra wesan, | rædan on þis rice.'

[131] *Ibid*, lines 422–4, p. 215: 'þone welan agan | þe we on heofonrice habban sceoldon, | rice mid rihte'.

[132] *Ibid*, lines 168–74, p. 244: ' "Uuarod uuilthu nu, uualdand fro min, | alomatig fadar? ik biun thin egan scalc, | hold endi gehorig. thu bist mi, erro, so guod, | meðmo mildi. uuilthu minas uuiht, | drotin, hebbian? huat, it all an thinum duoma sted. | Ik libbio bi thinum lehene endi ik gilobi" an thi, fro | min the gouda'. See also Doane, *The Saxon Genesis*, pp. 167, 170; J. K. Bostock, K. C. King and D. McLintock (eds.), *A Handbook on Old High German Literature* (Oxford: Clarendon, 1976), p. 185.

Einhard wrote, the Saxons were one *populus* with the Franks, with all the Christian connotations that such a word implied.[133]

TOWARDS A SAXON 'MICRO-CHRISTENDOM'

The Saxons, then, were broadly understood to form part of the Christian *ecclesia*, an institution with distinctly universalist pretensions. They were instructed and admonished in line with contemporary *correctio*, which set out a programme of moral emendation and general Christian improvement across the length and breadth of the Carolingian empire. Yet within these larger units, there was also room for diversity, for micro-Christendoms within both the Carolingian empire and the universal church. The observance of Christianity in Saxony differed significantly from that in other regions of the Carolingian world. This was not only in the language (Old Saxon) of scriptural teaching, but also in the very forms which Christian institutions assumed.

The roots of this distinctive form of 'Saxon' Christianity are unsurprising. Saxony's economy and social structure differed dramatically from that of the Frankish world; not only is there no evidence of cities or monetization prior to the Saxon conquest, but Saxon society also appears far less stratified than that of Francia throughout the Carolingian period. The region had its own unique legal codes and customs, its own language and oral traditions; moreover, the introduction of Christianity had taken a substantially different course in Saxony than elsewhere in the early medieval world. These differences necessarily affected the forms that Christianity took and the ways in which Christian communities perceived themselves and their past in Saxony.

In the Absence of Cities

The creation of a Christian landscape in Saxony was not a straightforward process. Christian institutional structures had hitherto developed in primarily urban contexts; even the great rural monasteries of the Frankish world had been supported by developed agricultural systems, capable of producing surpluses sufficient in size to maintain large communities.[134] In Saxony, by contrast, there is no evidence of urbanization prior to the conquest, and it is generally assumed that manorial organization was only

---

[133] Einhard, *Vita Karoli Magni*, ed. O. Holder-Egger, *MGH SRG* 25 (Hanover: Hahn, 1911), c. 7, p. 10; see also above, p. 1.

[134] For a wider discussion of how a lack of urban centres impeded missionary work more generally, see Sullivan, 'The Carolingian missionary', 706–9.

introduced in the course of the ninth century. These conditions posed challenges for the establishment of Christian structures and further influenced the patterns of Christian observance in Saxony for decades to come.

Certainly, the lack of cities or even significant towns raised questions regarding missionary strategy; bishoprics were, after all, customarily placed in urban contexts, thereby fulfilling canonical stipulations that bishops were only to be established to serve sizeable populations. This was a tradition that was clearly untenable in this Saxon context. In the end, the author of the *Translation of Saint Liborius* relates how, as we have seen above, Charlemagne chose to place missionary centres in 'those places which seemed more suitable than the others both in terms of their natural excellence and the number of people'.[135] Further detail is offered in the case of Paderborn, to whose clergy the author belonged. The site's agricultural capacity, with its ample springs, mild climate and fertile fields and forests, is highlighted; it was 'not dissimilar to that region, which sacred Scripture calls the land of flowing milk and honey'.[136] The author draws further attention to Paderborn's fortifications, its occasional role in hosting assemblies, the proximity of rivers and the peaceful coexistence of Franks and Saxons in the larger region. He even commented on the Saxons' receptiveness to Christianity in the region.

The *Translation of Saint Liborius* may be unique in explaining why Paderborn was selected as the seat of a bishopric so exactly, albeit from a later and biased perspective.[137] Certain patterns may nonetheless be detected. In the absence of cities, missionary centres evolved at fortified sites with extant settlements and good transportation routes. This is clearly demonstrated by the missionary centres, and later bishoprics, of Bremen, Verden, Osnabrück, Paderborn, Münster and Minden.[138]

---

[135] Anonymus Paderbrunnensis, *Translatio sancti Liborii*, ed. de Vry, c. 2, p. 189: 'loca tamen ad hoc, quae et naturali quadam excellentia et populi frequentia prae caeteris oportuna uidebantur'. See further the comments of E. Schubert, *Geschichte Niedersachsens: Politik, Verfassung, Wirtschaft vom 9. bis zum ausgehenden 15. Jahrhundert* (Veröffentlichungen der historischen Kommission für Niedersachsen und Bremen 36), 5 vols. (Hanover: Hahn, 1997), vol. II.1, p. 59; for the lack of early urbanization in Paderborn, see U. Lobbedy, 'Anmerkungen zur archäologischen Stadtkernforschung in Paderborn' in H. Jäger (ed.), *Stadtkernforschung* (Cologne: Böhlau, 1987), pp. 149–60, here especially pp. 152–3. See also above, pp. 146–7.

[136] Anonymus Paderbrunnensis, *Translatio sancti Liborii*, ed. de Vry, c. 4, p. 190: 'non dissimilis ... regioni quam sacrae litterae uocant terram lactae et maellae manantem'. See further R., Flierman, *Saxon Identities, AD 150–900* (London: Bloomsbury Academic, 2017), p. 134. Contrast to Helm, *Altgermanische Religionsgeschichte*, vol. II:2, p. 179.

[137] See above, pp. 146–7. For the contemporary aims of the *Translatio sancti Liborii*, see I. Rembold, 'The Poeta Saxo at Paderborn: episcopal authority and Carolingian rule in late ninth-century Saxony', *EME*, 21(2) (2013), 169–96.

[138] For transportation routes and fortifications, see F. Wilschewski, *Die karolingischen Bischofssitze des sächsischen Stammesgebietes bis 1200* (Studien der internationalen Architektur- und Kunstgeschichte

Given the uncertainties inherent in missionary endeavours, such a placement appears easily explicable: clerics were afforded a certain degree of protection, while roads and water routes offered the possibility of travel or relief.

Nonetheless, the absence of concentrated populations in the early ninth century had certain clear consequences, the most obvious of which was the size of the bishop's congregation. A bishop's flock might be only slightly larger than that of a local priest, as can be shown evocatively by a comparison of the archaeological remains of episcopal and parish churches.[139] The dimensions of a mid-ninth-century wooden parish church in Tostedt, which measured some eighteen by seven metres, are of a similar magnitude to those of the episcopal churches of Bremen (twenty-four by eight metres) and Münster (twenty-three by eight metres) in around the same period.[140] Parish churches and episcopal churches were not interchangeable: the former were sometimes constructed in wood, as in the case of Tostedt above, while the latter tended to be built in stone, and were often dramatically expanded over the course of the ninth century. A three-aisled church at Paderborn was rebuilt before the pope's visit in 799 to measure some forty-three by twenty-one metres – the *Lorsch Annals* note its 'remarkable dimensions'; in the ninth century it was expanded again to include a western transept and apse and an ambulatory crypt.[141] Yet the papal visit makes Paderborn an exceptional case. Even the size of its church building may be more reflective of Paderborn's intermittent function as a royal centre than its stable population: its regular congregation may have numbered few more

---

46) (Petersberg: M. Imhof, 2007), especially pp. 240–4, 249–56; see further E. Freise, 'Die Sachsenmission Karls des Großen und die Anfänge des Bistums Minden' in *An Weser und Wiehen: Beiträge zur Geschichte und Kultur einer Landschaft. Festschrift für Wilhelm Brepohl* (Mindener Beiträge 20) (Minden: Mindener Geschichtsverein, 1983), pp. 57–100, here p. 70; H. Steuer, 'The beginnings of urban economies among the Saxons', in Green and Siegmund, *Saxons*, pp. 159–92, here pp. 173–4. For the existence, size and importance of pre-Carolingian period settlements at these sites, see especially Wilschewski, *Die karolingischen Bischofssitze*, pp. 244–6; see further, among others, M. Balzer, 'Siedlungsgeschichte und topographische Entwicklung Paderborns im Früh- und Hochmittelalter' in H. Jäger (ed.), *Stadtkernforschung* (Cologne: Böhlau, 1987), pp. 103–47, here pp. 110–13; O. Ellger, 'Mimigernaford: Von der sächsischen Siedlung zum karolingischen Bischofssitz Münster', pp. 386–93, W. Schlüter, 'Osnabrück in karolingisch-ottonischer Zeit', pp. 394–400, and E. Treude, 'Minden im frühen Mittelalter', pp. 380–5, all in Stiegemann and Wemhoff, *799*, vol. III.

[139] 'Parish church' is used here as a term of convenience to designate non-episcopal and non-monastic local churches.

[140] Drescher, *Tostedt*, p. 22; Wilschewski, *Die karolingischen Bischofssitze*, pp. 24, 247.

[141] *Annales Laureshamenses*, ed. G. H. Pertz, *MGH SS* I (Hanover: Hahn, 1826), pp. 22–39, here 799, p. 38: 'mira magnitudinis'; Balzer, 'Siedlungsgeschichte und topographische Entwicklung', pp. 120–1.

than that of Tostedt, with very real consequences for the nature of episcopal governance and for the Christianization of the region.

Accordingly, the lives of ninth-century Saxon bishops take pains to emphasize the role that bishops played in their dioceses more widely, beyond simply their principal seat.[142] Bishops' achievements within their own town are listed as well. Hagiographers note that Liudger constructed a *monasterium* in Münster, while Willehad and Anskar both contributed to the development of Bremen, constructing a church and hospital respectively.[143] Yet these are rather small feats compared to the lavish building programmes of Frankish colleagues recorded in their *vitae*. By comparison, Saxon *vitae* are keen to stress the extent to which bishops were active throughout their regions, most notably through their construction of parish churches, in the cases of Willehad and Liudger, and in their annual visits to all churches within the dioceses. Such visits receive an unusual degree of focus, being mentioned prominently in all three *vitae*, and not once but four times in the *Life of Saint Willehad*.[144] Altfrid's *Life of Saint Liudger* is especially remarkable in this regard: he is depicted as constantly in motion, to the extent that he preached in two separate villages on the day of his death.[145] Willehad is likewise reported to have been visiting a parish church on the occasion of his death.[146] Bishops' flocks were even more dispersed than usual, rendering such visits of critical importance.

Bishoprics were not the only institutions affected by Saxony's rural and undeveloped character. Monasteries could also be affected, insofar as large communities were always dependent upon local agricultural surpluses. This could pose acute problems, as demonstrated by the cases of Corvey and Werden. Both of these institutions were founded following the failure of attempted monastic foundations at other locations, namely at Hethis and Wichmond/Ad Cruces, respectively.[147] To these may also be added the comparative, and considerably more

[142] Sullivan, 'The Carolingian missionary', 708–9.
[143] Altfrid, *Vita sancti Liudgeri*, ed. Diekamp, I:23, pp. 27–8; *Vita sancti Willehadi*, eds. C. de Smedt, F. van Ortroy, H. Delehaye, A. Poncelet and P. Peeters, *Acta Sanctorum III Novembris* (Brussels, 1910), pp. 842–6, here c. 9, p. 845E; Rimbert, *Vita sancti Anskarii*, ed. Waitz, c. 35, p. 69.
[144] *Vita sancti Willehadi*, eds. de Smedt, van Ortroy, Delehaye, Poncelet, and Peeters, cc. 5, 8–10, 844A–845F; Altfrid, *Vita sancti Liudgeri*, ed. Diekamp, I:23, p. 28; Rimbert, *Vita sancti Anskarii*, ed. Waitz, c. 35, p. 69.
[145] Altfrid, *Vita sancti Liudgeri*, ed. Diekamp, I:25, 27–9, 31, pp. 30–7.
[146] *Vita sancti Willehadi*, eds. de Smedt, van Ortroy, Delehaye, Poncelet and Peeters, c. 10, pp. 845E–846B.
[147] See also H. Röckelein, 'Bairische, sächsische und mainfränkische Klostergründungen im Vergleich (8. Jahrhundert bis 1100)' in E. Schlotheuber, H. Flachenecker and I. Gardill (eds.), *Nonnen, Kanonissen und Mystikerinnen: religiöse Frauengemeinschaften in Süddeutschland* (SzGS 31) (Göttingen: Vandenhoeck & Ruprecht, 2008), pp. 23–55, here p. 28.

complicated, experience of the missionary community at Hamburg, which was likewise displaced to the already extant bishopric of Bremen following a period of shortage and want.[148]

The most detailed account of a monastic dislocation is that provided by the *Translation of Saint Vitus* for the relocation of the community at Hethis.[149] The main problem with the initial site, the anonymous author relates, was a lack of water. Even after 'they had worked for more than six years, they were able accomplish nothing' in that 'deserted place'.[150] The rapidly increasing number of monks at the site soon demanded urgent action, and the community divided into three parts, each subject to a separate prior.[151] Eventually the restoration of Adalhard of Corbie to the emperor's good graces brought about a change in fortune, and a site in Höxter was chosen for the foundation of Corvey.[152] The necessity of dividing the initial community into three separate parts is a clear indication of the constraints of local agricultural organization.

Similar concerns could have lain behind the movement of the communities at Wichmond and Ad Cruces, in Frisia, to Werden in the Saxon-Frankish borderland. The *Second Life of Saint Liudger* relates how 'two places appeared suitable for monastic foundations, one in Wichmond next to the Yssel River, the other, called Ad Cruces, next to the Erft River'.[153] The seriousness with which these foundations were pursued is demonstrated by the landed donations and acquisitions at these sites prior to the establishment of a monastery at Werden: a donation is recorded in the vicinity of Wichmond as early as 794, while a later donation charter even refers to 'the relics of the blessed Saviour and other saints which have been placed in Wichmond by abbot Liudger'.[154] Even as late as 800 land was donated in Wichmond for the construction

---

[148] See above, pp. 156–9. For further examples, see C. Ehlers, Die zweifache Integration: Sachsen zwischen Karolingern und Ottonen. Überlegungen zur Erschließung von Diözesen mit Klöstern und Stiften in Westfalen und Sachsen bis 1024' in K. Bodarwé and T. Schilp (eds.), *Herrschaft, Liturgie und Raum: Studien zur mittelalterlichen Geschichte des Frauenstifts Essen* (Essener Forschungen zum Frauenstift 1) (Essen: Klartext, 2002), pp. 24–50, here pp. 27–8.

[149] For a more detailed summary of these successive foundations, see K. H. Krüger, *Studien zur Corveyer Gründungsüberlieferung* (Abhandlungen zur Corveyer Geschichtsschreibung 9) (Münster: Aschendorff, 2001), pp. 103–15.

[150] *Translatio sancti Viti*, ed. I. Schmale-Ott, *Übertragung des hl. Märtyrers Vitus* (Fontes minores 1) (Münster: Aschendorff, 1979), c. 3, p. 40: 'per sex et eo amplius annos laborassent, nihil proficere potuerunt'; 'loco deserto'.

[151] *Ibid*, c. 3, p. 42.   [152] *Ibid*, c. 3, p. 42.

[153] *Vita secunda sancti Liudgeri*, ed. Freise, c. 29, p. 16: 'Duo autem loca construendis apta monasteriis videbantur, unus in Widmundi iuxta fluvium Isla, alter, qui Ad Cruces dicitur, secus fluvium Arnapa'. See also W. Stüwer, *Das Erzbistums Köln 3: Die Reichsabtei Werden an der Ruhr* (GSNF 12) (Berlin: W. de Gruyter, 1980), p. 88.

[154] *Cartularium Werthinense*, ed ed. D. P. Blok, 'Een diplomatisch onderzoek van de oudste particuliere oorkonden van Werden', unpublished Ph.D. thesis, University of Amsterdam (1960),

of a church there, and in 801 a deed was witnessed there.[155] Meanwhile, the first recorded donation at Ad Cruces was in 795, with land being once again granted to the relics for the use of the church; the last deed transacted here was in 818.[156] By contrast, the first donation in the general vicinity of Werden is recorded in 796.[157] It was three years and several land trades and donations later that Liudger began to show any special interest in this site.

In the end, Liudger's movement of the monastery was attributed to divine revelation. No other reasons were provided for this relocation. Nevertheless, the comparative case of Hethis/Corvey, placed alongside the general lack of developed agricultural organization, suggests that the economic insufficiency of the initial sites may be tentatively postulated as a proximate cause. Liudger belonged to the elite but is not known to have been particularly wealthy; in the absence of other clear motivations to undertake such a difficult and arduous move, economic sustainability may well have been the deciding factor.

The constraints of the Saxon (and also Frisian) landed economy thus appear to have posed, at least initially, substantial barriers to missionaries and founders alike. Over time, these problems eased. Missionary centres and, later, bishoprics contributed to urban development. By the end of the ninth century there were towns, if not cities, at the sites of most bishoprics, most probably a result of their careful placement, certain fiscal and trade privileges, and the wealth of bishops in local society. So too did monasteries gradually develop the structures of a manorial economy, as is visible in the proprietary sources from Werden and Corvey.[158] Despite these changes, Saxony remained underdeveloped by Frankish standards throughout the Carolingian period due to the continued absence of cities and its relatively simple, and substantially unmonetized, economy.

The Predominance of Female Monasticism

The placement of episcopal seats and the dislocations of early monastic foundations were far from constituting the only peculiarities of Saxon ecclesiastical life: another unusual feature of the Saxon religious landscape

---

nos. 4, 10, pp. 158–9, 166–7: 'reliquias sancti saluatoris ceterorumque sanctorum quę a Liudgero abbate in UUithmundi constitute sunt'.

[155] *Ibid*, nos. 18, 25, pp. 175–7, 183–4.　　[156] *Ibid*, nos. 5–6, 38, pp. 159–62, 194–5.

[157] *Ibid*, no. 7, pp. 162–3.

[158] W. Rösener, 'Zur Struktur und Entwicklung der Grundherrschaft in Sachsen in karolingischer und ottonischer Zeit' in A. Verhulst (ed.), *Le grand domaine aux époques mérovingienne et carolingienne* (Ghent: Belgisch Centrum voor Landelijke Geschiedenis, 1985), pp. 173–207.

was the predominance of female monasteries.[159] The number and influence of female monasteries in Ottonian Saxony has long been the focus of scholarly enquiry.[160] Between 918 and 1024, a staggering thirty-six female houses were founded in Saxony, but the emergence of this trend towards female foundations lies firmly in the Carolingian period. Indeed, in the course of the ninth century, some nineteen female houses were founded, compared to some ten male houses, with significant consequences for patterns of religious observance in Carolingian Saxony.

There is no single explanation that can wholly account for this preference for female monasticism.[161] Yet one can reconstruct the motivations of the various actors who were involved in these foundations, of which the most important appears to have been concern for female family members. In the early decades of the ninth century, Saxon religious institutions were, much like the earlier Frankish mission, almost exclusively male. By circa 825, the Saxon religious landscape consisted of bishoprics equipped with sizeable *monasteria*, or cathedral chapters; the large male monasteries of Corvey and Werden; the sole female monastery of Herford; and various parish churches. These institutions were first filled with Frankish clerics and monks, but gradually, and certainly by the second third of the ninth century, elite Saxon families began to give their sons to these institutions. By contrast, there were almost no available options for female monasticism.

---

[159] It is worth noting that while this predominance was unusual, it was not unparalleled: female monasteries were also extremely prominent in Anglo-Saxon England. For more on female institutions in Anglo-Saxon England, see especially S. Foot, *Veiled Women*, 2 vols. (Aldershot: Ashgate, 2000); B. A. E. Yorke, *Nunneries and the Anglo-Saxon Royal Houses* (London: Continuum, 2003).

[160] For studies of Ottonian female houses, see, among others, K. Bodarwé, *Sanctimoniales litteratae: Schriftlichkeit und Bildung in den ottonischen Frauenkommunitäten Gandersheim, Essen und Quedlinburg* (Quellen und Studien 10) (Münster: Aschendorff, 2004); L. Körntgen, 'Zwischen Herrschern und Heiligen: Zum Verhältnis von Königsnähe und Eigeninteresse bei den Frauengemeinschaften Essen und Gandersheim' in K. Bodarwé and T. Schilp (eds.), *Herrschaft, Liturgie und Raum: Studien zur mittelalterlichen Geschichte des Frauenstifts Essen* (Essener Forschungen zum Frauenstift 1) (Essen: Klartext, 2002), pp. 7–23; K. Leyser, *Rule and Conflict in an Early Medieval Society: Ottonian Saxony* (London: Arnold, 1979), pp. 63–73 (p. 63 for the number of female foundations in the Ottonian period offered above); C. Moddelmog, 'Stiftung oder Eigenkirche? Der Umgang mit Forschungskonzepten und die sächsischen Frauenklöster im 9. und 10. Jahrhundert' in W. Huschner and F. Rexroth (eds.), *Gestiftete Zukunft im mittelalterlichen Europa: Festschrift für Michael Borgolte zum 60. Geburtstag* (Berlin: Akademie, 2008), pp. 215–43; M. Parisse, 'Die Frauenstifte und Frauenklöster in Sachsen vom 10. bis zur Mitte des 12. Jahrhunderts' in S. Weinfurter (ed.), *Die Salier und das Reich: Das Reichskirche in der Salierzeit*, 3 vols. (Sigmaringen: J. Thorbecke, 1992), vol. II: pp. 465–501.

[161] For some suggestions, see here especially the insightful observations of Röckelein, 'Bairische, sächsische und mainfränkische Klostergründungen', 50–5; see also I. Crusius, '*Sanctimoniales quae canonicas vocant*. Das Kannonissenstift als Forschungsproblem' in I. Crusius (ed.), *Studien zum Kanonissenstift* (SzGS 24) (Göttingen: Vandenhoeck & Ruprecht, 2001), pp. 9–38, here pp. 20–5; Leyser, *Rule and Conflict*, pp. 64, 72–3.

If a family wished to entrust a daughter to a religious life, they had to found a monastery themselves: and indeed, the houses of Gandersheim, Herzebrock, Lamspringe, Möllenbeck, Neuenheerse and Wendhausen all appear to have been founded on behalf of unmarried female relatives.[162]

Saxon elite families had but slender means in this period. We should envisage a relatively large and modestly endowed elite, without much internal stratification. Consequently, the early female foundations were small 'familial monasteries': their endowments (sometimes comprising a mere ten *mansi*, supplemented by tithe districts) were not sufficient to support large communities, nor were they intended to do so.[163] The continued familial control over such institutions, meanwhile, could be guaranteed by charter clauses guaranteeing the communities' right to elect 'freely' any candidates from inside the founding family.[164]

Once this pattern of female foundations had been established, it was self-reinforcing. Elite families chose to make their own arrangements rather than place their daughters in another family's institution. The profusion of such houses can be largely explained by the needs of family strategy and, further, by intra-elite competition: one can certainly imagine an element of 'keeping up with the Joneses' to be at play. Elite competition and religious patronage centred on the foundation of female institutions, and when the Saxon elite became rich in the early Ottonian period, they continued to express their status and religious devotion in this traditional manner.

Another contributory factor in this development may have been the inheritance rights of women supposedly expressed in Saxon law. As Hedwig Röckelein has argued, women had more control over property, and thus may have been more easily able to found female institutions.[165]

---

[162] For Gandersheim, see Agius of Corvey, *Vita et obitus Hathumodae*, G. H. Pertz, *MGH SS* 4 (Hanover: Hahn, 1841), pp. 165–89, here c. 4, p. 168; for Herzebrock (which is also only attested in later sources), see E. Klueting, *Das Bistum Osnabrück 1: Das Kanonissenstift und Benediktiner-innenkloster Herzebrock* (GSNF 21) (Berlin: W. de Gruyter, 1986), pp. 49–51; for Lamspringe, see *D LD*, ed. P. Kehr, *MGH, Die Urkunden Ludwigs des Deutschen, Karlmanns und Ludwigs der Jüngeren* (Berlin: Weidemann, 1934), no. 150, pp. 210–12; for Möllenbeck, see *D Arn*, ed. P. Kehr, *MGH, Die Urkunden Arnolfs* (Berlin: Weidemann, 1940), no. 147, pp. 223–5; for Neuenheerse, see *D LD*, ed. Kehr, no. 137, pp. 190–2; for Wendhausen, see *Vita Liutbirgae virginis*, ed. Menzel, c. 2, p. 11. For Gandersheim see further Bodarwé, *Sanctimoniales litteratae*, pp. 15–31, here especially pp. 16–17. Cf. Leyser, *Rule and Conflict*, p. 64.

[163] See, for example, *D LD*, ed. Kehr, no. 140, pp. 195–6.

[164] *D LJ*, ed. P. Kehr, *MGH, Die Urkunden Ludwigs des Deutschen, Karlmanns und Ludwigs der Jüngeren* (Berlin: Weidemann, 1934), no. 3, pp. 335–7; *D Arn*, ed. Kehr, nos. 59, 147, pp. 85–7, 223–5. For the question of how whether these foundations actually constituted an alienation of property, or whether they can be better understood as 'Eigenkirche', see Moddelmog, 'Stiftung oder Eigenkirche?', pp. 215–43.

[165] Röckelein, 'Bairische, sächsische und mainfränkische Klostergründungen', p. 53. For a comparative view of female agency in monastic profession in Anglo-Saxon England, see D. B.

Certainly, the *Law of the Saxons* suggests that women enjoyed some legal privileges. In the absence of sons, daughters could inherit land (a privilege shared with their Frankish counterparts); under certain conditions, women could retain their dowries after their husbands' deaths; and lastly, in Westphalia, widows could retain half of their husband's acquired property.[166] It is worth observing, however, the emphasis that the law places upon appointing male 'protectors' for widows and unmarried daughters, whose duties may well have included the management of female property, even though this is not explicitly stated.[167] Even more fundamentally, it is unclear how far the *Law of the Saxons* was representative of Saxon legal practice, as has been explored at length above.[168]

In fact, while women were involved in the foundation of roughly half of these houses, it is extremely difficult to find examples of women founding monasteries independently in Carolingian Saxony.[169] The foundations of Bassum, Essen, Möllenbeck and Neuenheerse appear to have been carried out by women in conjunction with local bishops and, in the case of Möllenbeck, with a priest; in Gandersheim and Lamspringe, by married couples; and in Herzebrock, by a woman and her son.[170] The monasteries of Wendhausen and Metelen may stand as exceptions to this general trend. The former was founded by Gisla for her daughter Bilihild, but even here it appears that local bishops may have been intricately involved in the foundation: the *Life of the Virgin Liutbirga*, a work of hagiography describing an anchoress whose cell was attached to the abbey's church, allots ample attention to her episcopal supervision.[171] A charter for Metelen, meanwhile, shows the lengths to which

---

Baltrusch-Schneider, 'Klosterleben als alternative Lebensform zu Ehe?' in H. W. Goetz (ed.), *Weibliche Lebensgestaltung im frühen Mittelalter* (Cologne: Böhlau, 1991), pp. 45–64.

[166] *Lex Saxonum*, ed. C. von Schwerin, *MGH Fontes iuris* 4 (Hanover: Hahn, 1918), pp. 9–36, here cc. 54, 57–8, pp. 29–30.

[167] *Ibid*, cc. 52–5, pp. 28–9. See here also the excellent discussion of these issues in J. L. Nelson, 'The wary widow' in W. Davies and P. Fouracre (eds.), *Property and Power in the Early Middle Ages* (Cambridge: Cambridge University Press, 1995), pp. 82–113.

[168] See above, pp. 25–6.   [169] Moddelmog, 'Stiftung oder Eigenkirche?', p. 223.

[170] For Bassum, see Adam of Bremen, *Gesta Hammaburgensis ecclesiae pontificum*, ed. B. Schmeidler, *MGH SRG* 2 (Hanover: Hahn, 1917), I:30, pp. 35–6; for Essen, see H. Röckelein, 'Altfrid, Gründer des Stifts Essen und international agierender Kirchenmann?' in T. Schilp (ed.), *Frauen bauen Europa: Internationale Verflechtungen des Frauenstifts Essen* (Essener Forschungen zum Frauenstift 9) (Essen: Klartext, 2011), pp. 27–64, here p. 29; for Möllenbeck, see *D Arn*, ed. Kehr, no. 147, pp. 223–5; for Neuenheerse, see *D LD*, ed. Kehr, no. 137, pp. 190–2; for Gandersheim, whose foundation is primarily, if not solely, attributed to Liudolf and Oda, see *D LJ*, ed. Kehr, no. 3, pp. 335–9; Agius of Corvey, *Vita et Obitus Hathumodae*, ed. Pertz, c. 4, p. 187; see further Bodarwé, *Sanctimoniales litteratae*, pp. 16–17; for Lamspringe, see *D LD*, ed. Kehr, no. 150, pp. 210–2; for Herzebrock, see Klueting, *Das Kanonissenstift und Benediktinerinnenkloster Herzebrock*, pp. 49–51.

[171] *Vita Liutbirgae virginis*, ed. Menzel, cc. 16–22, 35, pp. 21–6, 43–4.

its founder, Friduwi, had to go to secure its establishment. Friduwi approached King Arnulf and volunteered to transfer all her property into his power if she were permitted to build a monastery on the land. This licence was duly granted.[172]

This is not to say that female inheritance was entirely divorced from these foundations: indeed, Bassum, Metelen, Möllenbeck and Wendhausen all appear to have to have been primarily endowed with lands from their female founders.[173] Rather, it is to note that female monastic foundations cannot be ascribed to female activism alone, even if this was an important component of their success. Almost all of these institutions were founded with male involvement, whether on the part of male relatives, bishops or even male relative bishops. Particularly remarkable in this regard is the activism of bishops in female monastic foundations, and the degree of control they exercised over the resultant institutions.

The involvement of bishops in the foundation and governance of male houses is perhaps easier to explain: such monasteries, particularly if they followed a canonical rule, could supplement the cathedral clergy and perform a variety of pastoral functions in the localities. Indeed, bishops appear to have been involved in the foundation or later governance of the male communities of Bücken, Helmstedt, Münsterdorf, Ramesloh, Seligenstedt and Werden.[174] These comprised all but three of the male monasteries in Saxony. Yet bishops were also deeply implicated in the foundation of female institutions in Carolingian Saxony as well, and with less clear cause.[175] The foundations of a handful of communities, namely

---

[172] *D Arn*, ed. Kehr, no. 59, pp. 85–7.

[173] For Bassum, see Adam of Bremen, *Gesta Hammaburgensis Ecclesiae Pontificum*, ed. Schmeidler, I:30, p. 36; for Metelen, see *D Arn*, ed. Kehr, no. 59, pp. 85–7; for Möllenbeck, see *D Arn*, ed. Kehr, no. 147, pp. 223–5; for Wendhausen, see *Vita Liutbirgae virginis*, ed. Menzel, cc. 2–4, pp. 10–13.

[174] For Bücken, see Patze, 'Mission und Kirchenorganisation', p. 698; for Helmstedt, see H. Röckelein, 'Halberstadt, Helmstedt und die Liudgeriden' in J. Gerchow (ed.), *Das Jahrtausend der Mönche: Kloster Welt Werden, 799–1803* (Cologne: Wienand, 1999), pp. 65–73; for Münsterdorf, see C. Ehlers, *Die Integration Sachsens in das fränkische Reich (751–1024)* (Veröffentlichungen des Max-Planck-Instituts für Geschichte 231) (Göttingen: Vandenhoeck & Ruprecht, 2007), p. 69; for Ramesloh, see Adam of Bremen, *Gesta Hammaburgensis Ecclesiae Pontificum*, ed. Schmeidler, I:23, 30, pp. 29, 35; for Seligenstedt, see H. Goetting, *Das Bistum Hildesheim 3: Die Hildesheimer Bischöfe von 815 bis 1221 (1227)* (GSNF 20) (Berlin: W. de Gruyter, 1984), p. 89; for Werden, see I. Rembold, 'Rewriting the founder: Werden on the Ruhr and the uses of hagiography', *Journal of Medieval History*, 41(4) (2015), 363–87. Some have argued that one of the remaining male monasteries, Bardowick, may have served an episcopal function, but there is simply not enough evidence to say: see the instructive comments of M. Last, 'Die Bedeutung des Klosters Amorbach für Mission und Kirchenorganisation im sächsischen Stammesgebiet' in F. Oswald and W. Störmer (eds.), *Die Abtei Amorbach im Odenwald: neue Beiträge zur Geschichte und Kultur des Klosters und seines Herrschaftsgebietes* (Sigmaringen: J. Thorbecke, 1984), pp. 33–53, here pp. 40–4.

[175] Parisse, 'Die Frauenstifte und Frauenklöster', pp. 468–70; Röckelein, 'Bairische, sächsische und mainfränkische Klostergründungen', pp. 44–5. Contrast with Carroll, 'The bishoprics of Saxony', 226–7.

those of Neuenheerse, Ridigippi and Wunstorf, were carried out primarily by bishops.[176] Further foundations, including those of Bassum, Böddeken, Essen, Freckenhorst, Gandersheim, Herzebrock, Lamspringe, Möllenbeck, Nottuln and Wendhausen, appear to have been dependent on their local bishops to varying degrees, although here too, caution must˙be advised: the cases of Essen, Gandersheim and Lamspringe suggest that later attempts by local bishops to establish control at these houses could be retrojected into the earlier periods.[177]

The relationships between bishops and female monasteries may have been, in certain contexts, mutually beneficial. In many cases, we can imagine the involvement of a bishop to have worked, at least in part, to a monastery's advantage: bishops not only performed certain important functions, such as the consecration of church buildings or the organization of relic translations, but could also guarantee the protection of the institution, and in some cases grant tithe districts for the community's support.[178] In return, royal charters record that bishops received a nominal annual rent, generally in the region of some four to ten *solidi*; the nuns of Möllenbeck, for example, owed an annual payment of five silver or gold *solidi* to their protector, the bishop of Minden.[179] Charters could further bestow the right of confirming elections and sometimes

---

[176] For Neuenheerse, see *D LD*, ed. Kehr, no. 137, pp. 190–2; for Ridigippi, see *D Arn*, ed. Kehr, no. 41, pp. 59–60; for Wunstorf, see *D LD*, ed. Kehr, no. 140, pp. 195–6. For Neuenheerse, see further Leyser, *Rule and Conflict*, p. 67.

[177] See especially Röckelein, 'Altfrid', pp. 27–64. For Bassum, see Adam of Bremen, *Gesta Hammaburgensis ecclesiae pontificum*, ed. Schmeidler, I:30, pp. 35–6; for Böddeken, see *Vita sancti Meinolfi*, ed. K. Honselmann, 'Die älteste Vita Meinolfi: Brevierlesungen zu den Festen des Heiligen aus dem Ende des 9. Jahrhunderts', *WZ*, 137 (1987), 185–206, here 198–200; for Essen, see Bodarwé, *Sanctimoniales litteratae*, pp. 33–8, 41–3; for Freckenhorst, see *Annales Xantenses*, ed. B. Simpson, *MGH SRG* 12 (Hanover: Hahn, 1909), 861, p. 19; W. Kohl, *Das Bistum Münster 3: Das (freiweltliche) Damenstift Freckenhorst* (GSNF 10) (Berlin: W. de Gruyter, 1975), p. 55; for Gandersheim, see H. Goetting, *Das Bistum Hildesheim 1: Das reichsunmittelbare Kanonissenstift Gandersheim* (GSNF 7) (Berlin: W. de Gruyter, 1973), pp. 81–5, 216–17; cf. C. Ehlers, 'Das Damenstift Gandersheim und die Bischöfe von Hildesheim', *Die Diözese Hildesheim in Vergangenheit und Gegenwart. Jahrbuch des Vereins für Geschichte und Kunst im Bistum Hildesheim*, 70 (2002), 1–31; for Herzebrock, see Klueting, *Das Kanonissenstift und Benediktinerinnenkloster Herzebrock*, p. 50; for Lamspringe, see *D LD*, ed. Kehr, no. 150, pp. 210–2; for Möllenbeck, see *D Arn*, ed. Kehr, no. 147, pp. 223–5; for Nottuln, see W. Kohl, *Das Bistum Münster 8: Das (freiweltliche) Damenstift Nottuln* (GSNF 44) (Berlin: W. de Gruyter, 2005), pp. 32–3; Parisse, 'Die Frauenstifte und Frauenklöster', p. 468; for Wendhausen, see above, p. 226.

[178] For the episcopal consecration of buildings, see, for example, *Vita Liutbirgae virginis*, ed. Menzel, c. 22, p. 25; for bishops' involvement in relic translations to these institutions, see *Annales Xantenses*, ed. Simpson, 861, p. 19; for the granting of episcopal protection, see *D LD*, ed. Kehr, no. 137, pp. 190–2; *D Arn*, ed. Kehr, no. 147, pp. 223–5; for the granting of tithe districts, see *D LD*, ed. Kehr, nos. 137, 140, pp. 190–2, 195–6; *D Arn*, ed. Kehr, nos. 41, 147, pp. 59–60, 223–5.

[179] For Möllenbeck, see *D Arn*, ed. Kehr, no. 147, pp. 223–5; for rent payments more generally, see *D LD*, ed. Kehr, nos. 137, 140, pp. 190–2, 195–6; *D Arn*, ed. Kehr, no. 41, pp. 59–60.

even the legal right of ownership.[180] This is clearly attested in the case of Neuenheerse, in whose foundation source Liuthard of Paderborn and his sister Waldburg 'gave their property permanently to the aforementioned blessed church of Paderborn, which was constructed in honour of the blessed mother of God, Mary, provided that that property may remain perpetually in the power of that monastery'.[181] In his capacity as diocesan bishop, Liuthard granted a further ten *mansi* to the monastery's perpetual use, as well as tithe revenues from four towns, an endowment that was later augmented under his successor Biso.[182] Despite this transfer of property to the institution's protector, it does not appear that the bishops of Paderborn profited directly from these transactions: rather, they gained the right to nominal ownership while voluntarily forgoing revenues.[183] Liuthard and his successors nonetheless retained a significant measure of control over Neuenheerse, insofar as they were guaranteed the right to confirm elections at the monastery.

On the other hand, the examples of Metelen and Gandersheim, which went to such great lengths to exclude their local bishops, suggest that some institutions viewed episcopal interest as predatory, or, at the very least, undesirable.[184] The community at Möllenbeck, although grateful for the protection and material support of Bishop Drogo of Minden, left a clause in their agreement stipulating that 'should the aforementioned bishop or his successors demand or plunder any more than this agreement stipulates for their own uses, the canonesses may sequester their property from the episcopal property and seek protection wherever they may wish'.[185] Both Wunstorf and Ridigippi, meanwhile, were founded by bishops but placed under royal protection.[186] The former came under royal protection on the request of the founder himself; the latter sought immunity a mere two years after its founder's death, so that 'neither bishop, nor public judge, nor advocate, nor relative of the bishop who

---

[180] *D LD*, ed. Kehr, no. 137, pp. 190–2.

[181] *Ibid*, no. 137, p. 191: 'permanens tradiderunt suam proprietatem ad praefatam sanctam ecclesiam Padrabrunnensem, quae est constructa in honore sanctae dei genitricis Mariae, quatenus easdem res perpetualiter in eiusdem monasterii potesate consisterunt'.

[182] *Ibid*, no. 137, p. 191; *D Karl*, ed. Kehr, no. 169, pp. 273–4. See further Moddelmog, 'Stiftung oder Eigenkirche?', pp. 226–8.

[183] *D Arn*, ed. Kehr, no. 59, pp. 85–7; see further Moddelmog, 'Stiftung oder Eigenkirche?', p. 231.

[184] For Gandersheim, see Goetting, *Das Reichsunmittelbare Kanonissenstift Gandersheim*, pp. 82–3; for Metelen, see *D Arn*, ed. Kehr, no. 59, pp. 85–7.

[185] *D Arn*, ed. Kehr, no. 147, p. 225: 'si episcopus supra scriptus magis suis usibus vel sui successores quam hic insertum continetur, quaesierint aut depredaverint, praelibatae sanctimoniales feminae licentiam habeant suas res a rebus episcopii sequestrandi et mundipurdum quaerere ubicumque voluerint'.

[186] *D LD*, ed. Kehr, no. 140, pp. 195–6.

founded this place, might attempt to infringe on or change anything'.[187]
Such clauses highlight, at the very least, the potential for profiteering
on the part of local bishops.

Female monasticism, then, was advanced by a multiplicity of interests.
First, families who wished to commit a female relative to a religious life,
even if only temporarily, were best served, in the absence of alternatives, by
founding small familial houses. Second, Saxon women who hoped to
safeguard their property rights had the opportunity to do so through
the act of monastic foundation. Finally, bishops who founded female
communities appear to have wielded a considerable degree of authority
over such houses and their landholdings. The last of these is of particular
interest. Many scholars, most prominently Christopher Carroll, have seen
bishops as the ecclesiastical underdogs in Carolingian Saxony when compared to local monasteries, with whom they are assumed to have been in
competition.[188] Such a characterization, however, fails to capture the
extent to which bishops were involved in and benefited from the development of monasticism in Saxony. The appeal of Bishop Egilmar of Osnabrück, who, as we have seen above, sought to retain the tithes from the lands
of Corvey and Herford which lay inside his diocese, is generally interpreted
to be the desperate plea of an obscure bishop pitted against more wealthy
and politically connected monastic opponents.[189] Yet it may also be worth
considering the scene from an alternative perspective, in which an ambitious young bishop attempted to impose some measure of his authority
upon those institutions and, in so doing, to emulate his episcopal colleagues
who had benefited so much from their associations with monasteries.

Form and Function

Egilmar did not simply resent Corvey and Herford's possession of tithes; he
further resented the autonomy with which the former performed various
priestly functions within his diocese. As he wrote to Pope Stephen V,

When the office of bishop was enjoined upon my unworthy self, I discovered,
among other various neglected matters, too long to enumerate, many unconse-
crated churches, and even some churches stained with homicides, and various
other instances of filth and shame which had not been cleansed. Unknown
priests, coming from Western regions and subject to the aforementioned monastery, whose consecration we call into question, celebrated holy offices in such

---

[187] *D Arn*, ed. Kehr, no. 41, pp. 59–60, here p. 60: 'neque episcopus neque iudex publicus neque
advocatus neque episcopi qui eundem primum locum fundavit propinquus aliquid umquam
infringere vel immutare temptet'.

[188] Carroll, 'The bishoprics of Saxony', 225–7.   [189] See above, pp. 172–4.

places. I have forbidden divine mysteries to be celebrated by those ones until I have consulted you, venerable fathers and teachers, about this thing.[190]

Despite his obvious displeasure regarding this, the arrangements which Egilmar described appear to have been far from unusual. Indeed, the monastic cells Brunshausen and Hameln, both of which were subject to the Hessian monastery of Fulda, appear to have played a largely pastoral and educational role. Their membership, as listed in a mid-ninth century source, correlates far more closely to that of a cathedral clergy or missionary cell than to that of a Benedictine house: at Hameln, some nine priests (six of whom were also monks), two monks and eleven students were numbered, while at Brunshausen the tally came to fourteen priests and five deacons (all of whom were also monks), four monks and sixteen students.[191] The personnel present at these Benedictine cells can only be explained insofar as they were intended to supplement the sacramental functions of bishops and their clergy in the region.[192]

Much scholarship on the development of Christian structures in Carolingian Saxony has employed categories or typologies such as bishoprics, male monasteries or female monasteries, and, in so doing, has assumed that these categories represented certain distinct forms of religious organization which served a clearly delineated set of functions. The extant evidence for the early development of church structures in Saxony, however, clearly belies such category-based analysis. Saxon bishoprics were not homogeneous or discrete as a group. They developed alongside, or even out of, *monasteria*; they were integrally involved in the governance of monasteries inside their dioceses; their congregations, meanwhile, may have been similar in size to those of parish churches, as noted above.[193]

---

[190] Stephanus V papa, *Epistolae*, ed. G. Laehr, *MGH Epp.* 7:5 (Berlin: Weidemann, 1928), pp. 354–65, here no. 3, p. 361: 'cum mihi indigno eiusdem episcopatus cura fuisset iniuncta et inter varias negligentias, quas perlongum est enucleare, plures ecclesias inconsecratas, aliquantas etiam homicidiis perpetratis infectas variisque spurcitiis et flagitiis minime purgatas repperissem, in quibus praedictorum monasteriorum subiugati de plaga occidentali advenientes presbyteri ignoti, de quorum consecratione ambigimus, officia celebrant, ne ibi divina mysteria ab ipsis celebrarentur, inhibendo interdixi, donec vos vernabiles patres et magistros super hac re consulerem'.

[191] *Annales necrologici Fuldenses*, ed. G. Waitz, *MGH SS* 13 (Hanover: Hahn, 1881), pp. 161–218, here p. 218. See also H. Goetting, *Das Bistum Hildesheim 2: Das Benediktiner(innen)kloster Brunshausen, das Benediktinerinnenkloster St. Marien vor Gandersheim, das Benediktinerkloster Clus, das Franziskanerkloster Gandersheim* (GSNF 8) (Berlin: W. de Gruyter, 1974), pp. 25–6; J. Raaijmakers, *The Making of the Monastic Community of Fulda, c.744–c.900* (Cambridge: Cambridge University Press, 2012), pp. 187–8, 223.

[192] Freise, 'Die Sachsenmission Karls des Großen', p. 65.

[193] See above, pp. 220–1. Compare to the 'minster hypothesis' for Anglo-Saxon England: among many other contributions, see especially J. Blair, 'Debate: ecclesiastical organization and pastoral care in Anglo-Saxon England', *EME*, 4(2) (1995), 193–212; J. Blair, *The Church in Anglo-Saxon Society* (Oxford: Oxford University Press, 2005); E. Cambridge and D. Rollason, 'Debate: the

These observations suggest that episcopal foundations should be considered not as a separate category, but rather within the wider context of ecclesiastical and monastic development, and crucially without recourse to teleological trends. By the end of the ninth century, episcopal churches may well have provided different functions than monasteries and parish churches. In the late eighth and early ninth centuries, by contrast, there is very little evidence of such 'ecclesiastical specialization'.

Just as bishoprics have been largely considered as a separate category, so too have monasteries. If anything, monasteries have been subjected to more strict category-based analysis: male and female institutions are rarely considered together, and much attention is paid to the distinctions between Benedictine and canonical observance, although it is often impossible to reconstruct which rule a community followed in this early period.[194] More fundamentally, these categories obscure not only the many commonalities between different 'types' of monasteries in Carolingian Saxony, but also the similarities between these institutions and other contemporary forms of ecclesiastical organization. As observed above, Saxon bishoprics and their associated cathedral chapters had evolved out of missionary *monasteria*; monasteries located in the countryside, meanwhile, appear to have served the function of parish churches for neighbouring settlements.

This flexibility in pastoral provision appears to have stemmed from the particular way in which Saxon ecclesiastical structures developed and the shortage of churches and clerics in Saxony. Even if Rimbert's lament on the mere four baptismal churches in his diocese is apocryphal, it is nonetheless evocative of limited Christian infrastructure. In a religious landscape where female monastic institutions were so predominant, where parish church provision remained inadequate and where episcopal churches, far from boasting large urban congregations, were located in small, relatively undeveloped villages, such flexibility was clearly necessary. In Carolingian Saxony, religious institutions appear to have served their surroundings no matter their type, and no matter the gender of their members.

---

pastoral organization of the Anglo-Saxon church: a review of the "minster hypothesis"', *EME*, 4(1) (1995), 87–104.

[194] For debates about Benedictine or canonical observance, see especially Crusius, '*Sanctimoniales quae canonicas vocant*', pp. 29–35; W. Kohl, 'Bemerkungen zur Typologie sächsischer Frauenklöster in karolingischer Zeit' in *Untersuchungen zu Kloster und Stift* (SzGS 14) (Göttingen: Vandenhoeck & Ruprecht, 1980), pp. 113–39, here pp. 127–36; J. Semmler, 'Corvey und Herford in der benediktinischen Reformbewegung des 9. Jahrhunderts', *Frühmittelalterliche Studien*, 4 (1970), 289–319.

Indeed, even female figures and institutions performed active pastoral functions in the community. This is perhaps most remarkably illustrated in a miracle story from the *Life of the Virgin Liutbirga*, in which the anchoress Liutbirga requests, and receives, permission to perform a baptism: the priests who had been called in 'approved the woman's plan and determined that it might take place if the resources of the place permitted'.[195] In the end, the baptism is prevented by the death of the infant, but it is nonetheless striking that permission was so readily granted, and that the priests had exhibited more concern over the limitations of Liutbirga's anchorhold than over her gender.[196] The female monastery which her cell adjoined, meanwhile, held daily masses in which the local laity could partake of the sacraments.[197]

In extreme circumstances, the laity could be drafted into pastoral service, as demonstrated by a case in nearby Frisia. The *Third Life of Saint Liudger* records how, when all the clergy sought refuge elsewhere during the second Frisian and Saxon rebellion, Bishop Liudger, fearing for the souls of infants who would die in his absence, sought the aid of one of his associates, a married layman and formerly blind bard named Bernlef:

Hence, because Bernlef was loved by many and, inasmuch as he was a layman, he could not be held in any suspicion, Liudger ordered him to travel to each house giving lessons, so that, having persuaded the women, whose innate natural disposition is known to be more easily able to believe, he might baptize simply their infants who were about to die with sacred water in the name of the Lord and with the invocation of the blessed trinity. He obeyed these orders gladly and baptized eighteen infants, all of whom died in white [baptismal gowns], except two who the blessed priest, after peace had returned once more, confirmed by anointing with sacred oil and by the laying on of hands.[198]

---

[195] *Vita Liutbirgae virginis*, ed. Menzel, c. 31, p. 38: 'propositum mulieris laudantes, si loci sineret facultas, fieri decreverunt'. For Liutbirga's instruction of women from her anchorhold, see V. L. Garver, 'Learned women? Liutberga and the instruction of Carolingian women' in P. Wormald and J. L. Nelson (eds.), *Lay Intellectuals in the Carolingian World* (Cambridge: Cambridge University Press, 2007), pp. 121–38; H. Röckelein, *Schriftlandschaften, Bildungslandschaften und religiöse Landschaften des Mittelalters in Norddeutschland* (Wolfenbütteler Hefte 33) (Wiesbaden, 2015), p. 10.

[196] *Vita Liutbirgae virginis*, ed. Menzel, cc. 31–3, pp. 37–40.   [197] *Ibid*, c. 35, p. 40.

[198] Universitätsbibliothek Kassel, 4°, Nr. 29, fos 26v–27r: 'Proinde quia a multis diligebatur et de eo utpute laico nulla huiusmodi suspicio haberi poterat per singulorum domos eum discurrere iussit . dato precepto . ut persuasis matronis quarum ingenium naturali conditione . ad credendum esse facilius nouerat . morituros earum infantulos benedicta simpliciter aqua . in nomine domini . cum inuocatione sanctae trinitatis baptizaret . Cuius ille iussis libenter obtemperans . xviii infantes baptizauit, qui omnes in albis defuncti sunt . exceptis duobus quos sanctus sacerdos pace denuo reddita . sancti krismatis in unctione et manuum impositione firmauit .' See also the incomplete edition of this text by Diekamp, which includes most of this passage: *Vita tertia sancti Liudgeri*, ed. Diekamp, I:29, pp. 104–5.

Even in peacetime, it is possible that Bernlef continued to fulfil a pastoral role. Altfrid's *Life of Saint Liudger* describes Bernlef's fame as a bard with considerable detail, a skill which might have helped him disseminate the Scripture to new audiences.[199] Much attention has focused upon a passage in the *Third Life of Saint Liudger*, which notes that 'after he received his sight, he was accustomed to consort with erudite men and to learn the psalms from them, along with whatever other bits of the scripture he was able to master'.[200] Although there is simply insufficient evidence to conclude that Bernlef was the author of vernacular biblical epics such as the Old Saxon *Heliand*, as some have suggested, one can speculate that Bernlef may have used his facility with language to the benefit of the newly established church.[201]

Naturally, this 'ecclesiastical flexibility' was circumscribed in certain important ways: there were clear (if contested) limits to what was considered acceptable. One such example is detailed in the *Xanten Annals*, which describe how

In Saxony, two ignorant priests dressed themselves in monastic habit and imitated men of great sanctity under the pretext of religion, so that they presented themselves as very blessed men to all the bishops and priests of that province. At first they led a solitary life together in hypocrisy. Later, in the midst of spiritual discord, they separated from one another and sought remote dwellings. They always bragged that they had seen angelic visions and performed miracles. A great multitude of that people, both rich and poor alike, flocked to them bearing diverse gifts, and the priests heard their confessions and offered new judgements.[202]

The matter was duly brought before a synod and the priests were defrocked. It is nonetheless noteworthy that the men in question were initially approved by local bishops and priests despite their unusual

---

[199] Altfrid, *Vita sancti Liudgeri*, ed. Diekamp, I:25–6, pp. 30–2.

[200] *Vita tertia sancti Liudgeri*, ed. Diekamp, I:29, p. 104: 'post suam inluminationem tamen eriditos quosque viros frequentare et psalmos ab eis, vel si quid aliud ex scripturis poterat, discere consuevit.' For attention devoted to Bernlef in modern scholarship, see, among others, Haubrichs, *Die Anfänge*, p. 84; G. Quispel, *Tatian and the Gospel of Thomas: Studies in the History of the Western Diatessaron* (Leiden: Brill, 1975), pp. 2, 13–14; J. fon Weringha, *Heliand and Diatessaron* (Studia Germanica 5) (Assen: Van Gorcum, 1965), p. 10, footnote 51.

[201] For the identification of Bernlef as author, see, for example, fon Weringha, *Heliand and Diatessaron*, p. 10, footnote 51.

[202] *Annales Xantenses*, ed. Simpson, 867, p. 24: 'Duo presbiteri, qui se monachico habitu in Saxonia, quamvis inperiti, nimiae sanctitatis viros sub obtentu religionis simulabant, ita ut episcopis et presbiteris omnibus eiusdem provintiae sanctiores se esse prefigurabant. Nam solitariam vitam in hipocrisi primum duxere simul. Sed postea, mediante inter illos spiritu discordiae, separati sunt ab invicem, et tamen remota querentes habitacula semper iactitabant etiam se visiones angelicas vidisse et signa fecisse. Et confluebat ad eos multitudo magna gentis huius, tam divitum quam etiam ceterorum, diversa munera deferentes. Quorum confessiones suscipientes nova iudicia pretulerunt.'

arrangements, until their penchant for handing out extra-canonical judgements was made known.

From monastic priests stepping up to fill the shortage of trained clergy, to laymen and religious women performing baptisms, religious structures in Carolingian Saxony exhibit far greater flexibility than their Frankish counterparts. This was necessitated above all by the distinctive development of the Saxon ecclesiastical landscape, namely the preponderance of female institutions and the rural nature of episcopal seats, which were to have a decisive impact upon Saxon religious life for centuries to come.

REWRITING CONQUEST AND CONVERSION

The peculiarities of Saxon religious development did not simply manifest themselves in the forms and functions of its ecclesiastical life: they also shaped the ways in which Christian communities came to understand themselves and their past. The Saxons had converted to Christianity under duress; at the conclusion of the conquest, they had no local Christian traditions, no local saints. They had nothing, in fact, to create a sense of local Christian community.

Over the course of the ninth century, Saxon saints began to be commemorated and venerated; further relics, meanwhile, were imported from across the Carolingian world and established as local patrons. Central to these developments were the texts which sought not only to establish these saintly patrons in the localities but, further, to create a shared local past, and in so doing to forge a sense of community. Although these texts were firmly grounded in specific Christian centres, the themes they tackled, notably conquest and conversion, were also of wider regional significance. This distinctively 'Saxon' hagiography sought to produce a sense of a Saxon Christian past of which its audiences could be proud. This was in stark contrast to earlier Frankish depictions of that formative period. Indeed, as Helmut Beumann has argued, Saxon hagiographical sources constitute a reinterpretation of the Saxons' role in their own conversion, and in so doing recast a humiliating defeat, that is, political incorporation following conquest, as a crowning triumph.[203]

---

[203] H. Beumann, 'Die Hagiographie 'bewältigt': Unterwerfung und Christianisierung der Saschen durch Karl den Grossen' in *Cristianizzazione ed organizzazione ecclesiastica delle campagne nell'Alto Medioevo: espansione e resistenze: 10–16 aprile 1980* (Settimane 28:1) (Spoleto: Il Centro, 1982), pp. 129–68; see also Flierman, *Saxon Identities*, pp. 119–62; H. Mayr-Harting, 'Charlemagne, the Saxons, and the imperial coronation of 800', *The English Historical Review*, 111 (1996), 1113–33, here especially 1129; Shuler, 'The Saxons within Carolingian Christendom', 39–54. See further the topical comments of Joachim Ehlers, who reacts to the earlier argument by Henry Mayr-Harting: J. Ehlers, 'Die Sachsenmission als heilsgeschichtlichen Ereignis' in F. J. Felten and

In the case of local saints who lived during the conquest period, such a focus is relatively unsurprising. The *vitae* of Willehad and Liudger understandably deal with themes of conquest and conversion; if their depictions of the Saxons fall short of positive, they are nevertheless more favourable than earlier Frankish depictions, and their miracle stories, appended subsequently in the case of the *Life of Saint Willehad*, serve to display the later outpouring of devotion on the part of local congregations. What is more remarkable is the extent to which all other saints – both those active in Saxony in later periods and those imported from other regions – are connected explicitly to the period of conquest and conversion, and often directly to Charlemagne himself.[204] The translations of saints Vitus, Pusinna, and Alexander are depicted as the consummation of the conversion begun by Charlemagne.[205] The later *Life* of Meinolf, meanwhile, is tied directly back to Charlemagne, however improbably: Meinolf, a deacon of Paderborn and founder of Böddeken, was allegedly raised from the baptismal font by Charlemagne himself.[206] Even the one local saint who pre-dated the conquest period, Lebuin, is linked to this later history in his *Life*: his divinely inspired speech foresaw the conquest and conversion that would follow.[207] The conversion of the Saxons under Charlemagne was cast as the central point in Saxon history, to which all local religious traditions, regardless of period, context or relevance, necessarily connected.[208]

Although these Saxon hagiographies built upon one another, they did not operate within a closed 'textual community': rather, they reacted and responded to earlier Frankish annalistic and historiographical accounts of the Saxon war, most notably Einhard's *Life of Charlemagne*, the *Royal Frankish Annals* and the latter's revision.[209] Often, authors drew content from these earlier works, sometimes even lifting entire clauses verbatim. The interpretations these texts offered were, however, substantially different from their Frankish predecessors. The first section of the

---

N. Jaspert (eds.), *Vita religiosa im Mittelalter: Festschrift für Kaspar Elm zum 70. Geburtstag* (Berliner historische Studien 31) (Berlin: Duncker & Humblot, 1999), pp. 37–53.

[204] See here the comments of E. Knibbs, *Ansgar, Rimbert and the Forged Foundations of Hamburg-Bremen* (Farnham: Ashgate, 2011), p. 49.

[205] See further the comments of Krüger, *Studien zur Corveyer Gründungsüberlieferung*, pp. 91–2.

[206] *Vita sancti Meinolfi*, ed. Honselmann, 194.

[207] *Vita sancti Lebuini antiqua*, ed. A. Hofmeister, *MGH SS* 30:2 (Leipzig: K. W. Hiersemann, 1934), pp. 789–95, here c. 6, pp. 793–4; see also Beumann, 'Die Hagiographie 'bewältigt'', pp. 157–63; Flierman, *Saxon Identities*, pp. 98–9.

[208] See also the comments of Flierman, *Saxon Identities*, pp. 123–4.

[209] This is a significant theme in Beumann, 'Die Hagiographie 'bewältigt'', pp. 129–63; see also M. Becher, *Rex, Dux und Gens: Untersuchungen zur Entstehung des sächsischen Herzogtums im 9. und 10. Jahrhundert* (Historische Studien 444) (Husum: Matthiesen, 1996), pp. 41–50.

Translation of Saint Alexander, composed by Rudolf of Fulda for the monastery of Wildehausen sometime before his death in 865, certainly borrows from both works extensively, but with significant changes.[210] First, Einhard's comments regarding the conclusion of the war are placed in a far more Christian context than before: having reiterated Einhard's summary of the peace, namely that the Saxons 'were united to the Franks and made one *populus* with them', Rudolf notes that 'after this, the Saxons received preachers, bishops, and presbyters of the truth and, having been given initial instruction in the sacraments of the true faith, were baptized in the name of the Father, Son, and Holy Ghost. With growing faith and true religion, they have been united with the people of God continuously up to the present day'.[211] Second, and more importantly, the chronology of the Saxon war was recast so as to give greater prominence to the actions of Widukind.[212] Having recounted Einhard's comments on the deportations and peace settlement of 804, Rudolf continued on, as if chronologically, to recount Widukind's baptism of 785, which is presented as the culmination of this peace:

Likewise Widukind, who was eminent among them both in renown of birth and in the greatness of his power, and who was the inciter and unwearied author of many defections of those ones, coming to the faith of Charlemagne of his own free will, was baptized at Attigny and was accepted by the king from the sacred font, and all Saxony was subjugated.[213]

Here, Rudolf's language draws upon the *Lorsch Annals* and the *Royal Frankish Annals*, but with two conspicuous additions: the positive comments about Widukind's power and ancestry (which anticipate later positive commemoration, most notably in the *Third Life of Saint Liudger*) and the crucial detail that he came to Attigny *sua sponte* ('of his own free will').[214]

---

[210] Beumann, 'Die Hagiographie 'bewältigt'', pp. 145–8. Contrast with Shuler, 'The Saxons within Carolingian Christendom', 42–5, who views the *Translatio sancti Alexandri* as being written from a hostile Frankish perspective.

[211] Rudolf and Meginhard, *Translatio sancti Alexandri*, ed. Pertz, c. 3, p. 676: 'Francis adunati unus cum eis populis efficerentur'; 'Posthaec susceptis praedicatoribus veritatis episcopis et presbiteris, imbuti verae fidei sacramentis, baptizati sunt in nomine Patris et Filii et Spiritus sancti, et crescente fide ac vera religione, adunati sunt populo Dei usque in hodiernum diem.' See also Einhard, *Vita Karoli Magni*, ed. Holder-Egger, c. 7, p. 10.

[212] For this, and for what follows, see Flierman, *Saxon Identities*, pp. 153–4.

[213] Rudolf and Meginhard, *Translatio sancti Alexandri*, ed. Pertz, c. 3, p. 676: 'Witukind quoque, qui inter eos et claritate generis et opum amplitudine eminebat, et qui perfidiae atque multimodae defectionis eorum auctor et indefessus erat incentor, ad fidem Karoli sua sponte veniens, Attiniaci baptizatus et a rege de fonte sacro susceptus est et Saxonia tota subacta.'

[214] See *Annales Laureshamenses*, ed. Pertz, 785, p. 32; *Annales Regni Francorum*, ed. F. Kurze, *MGH SRG 6* (Hanover: Hahn, 1895), 785, p. 70; *Vita tertia sancti Liudgeri*, ed. Diekamp, I:18, p. 95. For these points, see also Flierman, *Saxon Identities*, pp. 153-4.

The conclusion of the Saxon war thus appears to have resulted from the voluntary submission of the renowned Saxon leader. In the continuation of the text by Rudolf's student Meginhard, the full conversion of the Saxons is depicted as having been achieved through the activism of a certain Waltbraht, the grandson of Widukind, and specifically through his translation of Roman relics to his Saxon foundation at Wildeshausen.

The *Translation of Saint Alexander* drew heavily upon previous Frankish sources, but it shaped them to a new end. Many of its motifs and emphases, above all the extent to which conversion is stressed above conquest and the positive role played by the Saxons in their own conversion, recur in other hagiographical works. The *Translation of Saint Vitus*, for example, appears to have viewed conquest primarily as a means to conversion. Its anonymous author wrote as follows:

The Saxon people, who once had rebelled against the Franks, were not only conquered under his lordship, but also earned the right to say the sweet name of Christ. Therefore we believe Charlemagne to be to be the most powerful in war of all Christian kings, because those whom he subjected to his lordship dedicated themselves to the name of Christ. When the Lord provided him with respite from his many enemies, he called together all of the mighty under his dominion, both priests and lords, and inquired most earnestly as to how he might strengthen the true faith and the true religion throughout his kingdom.[215]

The secular motivations for war recounted by Einhard and reiterated by Rudolf are passed over entirely. The *Translation of Saint Pusinna*, a text composed at the monastery of Herford after 864, went further still:

It is the promise of our Lord and Saviour: 'Behold, I am with you all days, even to the consummation of the world.' It is so evident that this is the case that no one may doubt it. For it has now come to pass through his servants and through the church which he acquired with his blood that he not only rules, but even expands his territory. There are many examples, but we will direct our attention to our purpose. The noble, vigorous, and – according to the quality of their character – most wise people of the Saxons, commemorated even in ancient writings, having been subdued by the power of the Emperor Charlemagne, most glorious and illustrious in our memory, through the diverse fate of wars

---

[215] *Translatio sancti Viti*, ed. Schmale-Ott, c. 3, pp. 34–6: 'ut gentem Saxonicam, quae olim contra Francos rebellabat, non solum suo dominio subegisset, sed et mellifluo Christi nomini dicare meruisset. Nam et hunc ideo prae omnibus christianis regibus potentissimum in bellis fuisse credimus, quia, quos suo dominio subiugabat, Christi nomini dedicabat. Cum autem requiem praestitisset ei Dominus a compluribus inimicis suis, convocavit omnes, qui sub ditione sua erant maiores, sacerdotes et principes, atque studiossime quaesivit, quomodo veram fidem veramque religionem in universo regno suo firmavit.' See also the comments of Shuler, 'The Saxons within Carolingian Christendom', 45–6.

over the course of thirty years, with God willing, accepted a treaty of the divine word, faith in God, and the hope of eternal beatitude.[216]

Here, Charlemagne is presented as little more than an agent of divine will; his conquest is reduced simply to a means of extending the Christian faith.

The culmination of this trend is to be found in the *Translation of Saint Liborius* and the Saxon Poet's *Deeds of the Emperor Charlemagne*, both of which were composed in the late ninth century at the bishopric of Paderborn.[217] The former of these, as in the examples above, explicitly depicts the Saxon war as being waged for purely Christian motivations: following the conclusion of the war, its anonymous author relates, Charlemagne set about building churches 'in order that he might reveal this hard assault to be more for the sake of Christian religion than for the expansion of his kingdom'.[218] Yet, notably, it goes further still, casting Charlemagne as an apostle for his role in the conversion of the Saxons:

I believe him to be called deservedly of our apostles; by whom swords preached as if they were tongues, so that the entrance to faith opened. When, victories having been secured so many times, as often as pitching for battle, he subjected many peoples and kingdoms to himself, still it is evident that he had triumphed even over the devil, from whom so many thousands of souls, previously captive under his tyranny, were rescued in the conversion of our people, and acquired for Lord Christ.[219]

---

[216] *Translatio sanctae Pusinnae*, ed. R. Wilmans, *Die Kaiserurkunden der Provinz Westfalen, 777–1313*, 2 vols. (Münster: F. Regensberg, 1867), vol. I: pp. 539–46, here c. 1, p. 541: 'Salvatoris ac Domini nostri promissio est: Ecce ego vobiscum sum omnibus diebus usque ad consummationem seculi. Hoc ita esse, tam manifestum est, ut nulli facultas ulla sit dubitandi. Operatur enim nunc per famulos suos et ecclesiam, quam acquisivit sanguine suo, non modo regit, sed etiam propagando dilatat. Sunt exempla plurima, sed nos ad institutum intendamus. Nobilis et strenua, iuxtaque dotem naturae sagacissima gens Saxonum, ab antiquis etiam scriptoribus memorata, summi et gloriossimi nostra memoria imperatoris Caroli auspiciis varia sorte bellorum vix per triginta annos Deo volente subdita, verbi divini foedera, et fidem in Deum et spem beatudinis suscepit aeternae.' See further the comments of Beumann, 'Die Hagiographie 'bewältigt', pp. 156–7; Ehlers, 'Die Sachsenmission', p. 46; Flierman, *Saxon Identities*, p. 143; Shuler, 'The Saxons within Carolingian Christendom', 47–8.

[217] See here especially Rembold, 'The Poeta Saxo at Paderborn', 169–96.

[218] Anonymus Paderbrunnensis, *Translatio sancti Liborii*, ed. de Vry, c. 2, p. 189: 'Et ut se magis christianae religionis, quam regni sua dilatandi causa, tantae rei difficultatem aggressum ostenderet.'

[219] *Ibid*, c. 7, p. 194: 'Quem arbitror nostrum iure apostolum nominari, quibus, ut ianuam fidei aperiret, ferrea quodammodo lingua praedicauit. Qui cum tociens uictoria potitus quotiens in procinctu positus multas sibi gentes, multa regna subiecerit, constat tamen eum gloriosissime etiam de diabolo triumphasse, cui tot animarum milia prius sub eius tyrannide captiua, in conuersione nostrae gentis eripuit et Christo Domino adquisiuit.' See further Becher, *Rex, Dux und Gens*, p. 31; Beumann, 'Die Hagiographie 'bewältigt'', pp. 143–4; Ehlers, 'Die Sachsenmission', pp. 41–2.

This motif was expanded upon and given greater prominence in the historiographical undertaking of the Saxon Poet. Indeed, it forms the conclusion to his 2,693-line versified history: at the end of a long train of apostles and converted peoples appears Charlemagne, leading 'a rejoicing crowd of Saxons . . . a glory of perpetual joy to him', up to heaven – a very clear departure from the revised version of the *Royal Frankish Annals* and Einhard's *Life of Charlemagne*, from which the poet drew his historical content.[220] Depicting Charlemagne as an apostle highlighted his religious victories far above mere worldly triumphs, a representation which reaped clear dividends for Saxon audiences.[221]

Saxon hagiographical writing did not merely seek to elide the history of conquest with a history of triumphal conversion: it also sought to revise the Saxons' role in their own conversion. In contrast to Frankish accounts, these narratives underscored the active role that Saxons played in the introduction of the Christianity to the region.[222] As we have seen above, the *Translation of Saint Vitus* attributes the initial push to found the monastery of Corvey to the Saxon hostages resident at Corbie; the *Translation of Saint Alexander* likewise credits the Saxon Waltbraht for importing the relics 'through whose miracles and signs his countrymen were converted away from pagan rite and superstition to the true religion'.[223] Similarly, the *Translation of Saint Liborius* emphasizes the efficacious work of the Saxon bishops Hathumar and Badurad, while the *Life of Meinolf* stresses the Christian works undertaken by its title saint.[224] As mentioned above, the efforts of all of these Christians and saints were depicted as accomplishing the last stages of that great work undertaken by Charlemagne: no less than the establishment of true Christian observance in Saxony.

---

[220] Poeta Saxo, *Annalium de gestis Caroli magni imperatoris libri V*, ed. P. Winterfeld, *MGH Poet.* 4:1 (Berlin: Weidemann, 1899), pp. 1–71, here V, lines 687–8, p. 71: 'gaudens Saxonum turma. . ./ Illi perpetuae gloria laeticiae.' See also Beumann, 'Die Hagiographie 'bewältigt'', pp. 139–43.

[221] See also the pertinent comments of M. de Jong, 'The state of the church: *ecclesia* and early medieval state formation' in W. Pohl and V. Wieser (eds.), *Der frühmittelalterliche Staat: europäische Perspektiven* (Forschungen zur Geschichte des Mittelalters 16) (Vienna: Verlag der Österreichischen Akademie der Wissenschaften, 2009), pp. 241–54, here pp. 253–4; see further Ehlers, 'Die Sachsenmission', p. 42.

[222] For this, see especially Shuler, 'The Saxons within Carolingian Christendom', 39–54.

[223] *Translatio sancti Viti*, ed. Schmale-Ott, c. 3, p. 36; Rudolf and Meginhard, *Translatio sancti Alexandri*, ed. Pertz, c. 4, p. 676: 'quatenus earum signis et virtutibus, sui cives a paganico ritu et superstitione ad veram religionem converterentur'; see also above, p. 124. See further D. F. Appleby, 'Spiritual progress in Carolingian Saxony: a case from ninth-century Corvey', *The Catholic Historical Review*, 82(4) (1996), 599–613, here 605–6; Shuler, 'The Saxons within Carolingian Christendom', 46.

[224] Anonymus Paderbrunnensis, *Translatio sancti Liborii*, ed. de Vry, cc. 7–8, pp. 193–5; see also Shuler, 'The Saxons within Carolingian Christendom', 51–2.

Despite this emphasis on the recent introduction of full Christian observance, the present-day observance of Christianity in Saxony is not denigrated in these texts. Instead, it is celebrated, and in some cases it is even compared favourably to Frankish Christianity. In the Saxon translation narratives, the transported relics are venerated throughout their journey through Francia – but when the relics are brought into Saxon territory, the greater devotion and Christian adoration of the Saxon populace becomes clearly apparent: hence the crowds which awaited the relics of Liborius beyond the Saxon border.[225] In the *Translation of Saint Vitus*, the reaction was somewhat more gradual, but no less dramatic:

and truly after all of these [miracles] had been divulged and revealed in every region, people – whether noble or obscure, rich or destitute, healthy or infirm – began to assemble here more and more, to the extent that no one was thought to remain in all of the province, who was not coming or had not come for the grace of worshiping there.[226]

The greater devotion of the Saxons is thus a recurring motif. Even the fact that the Saxons needed to import their relics, the *Sermon of Saint Marsus* asserts, can be seen as a sign of their superior Christianity:

You are clearly blessed, and always must be blessed, you who, not tarnished with the blood of saints, have merited their protection. Although Germany, Gaul, Italy and especially Rome, abundant in the ashes of saints, appear full of glory, nevertheless they turn a bloody red through their deaths. How much more will you be proclaimed to be blessed, Saxony, you who have acquired such a boon without sin?[227]

In the *Translation of Saint Pusinna*, for instance, the initial reluctance of the Saxons to accept Christ, attributed to their respect for their ancestors, made them better Christians in the end: 'any people marked with such cleverness and innate acuity become firmer in the faith . . . the more they

---

[225] See above, pp. 200–1; see also Röckelein, *Reliquientranslationen nach Sachsen*, pp. 336–7, 341, 363.

[226] *Translatio sancti Viti*, ed. Schmale-Ott, c. 29, p. 64: 'Ac vero post haec, ut divulgata sunt et in omni regione manifestata, ceperunt magis ac magis undique concurrere tam nobiles quam ignobiles, divites et pauperes, sani atque infirmi, in tantum, ut nullus remansisse putaretur in omni illa provincia, qui non illuc gratia orandi veniret sive venisset.' See also Gillis, *Heresy and Dissent*, pp. 43–4.

[227] *Sermo sancti Marsi*, ed. K. Honselmann 'Eine Essener Predigt zum Predigt zum Feste des hl. Marsus aus dem 9. Jahrhundert', *WZ* 110 (1960), 199–221, here c. 9, p. 212: 'Beata plane et semper beatificanda, quę nullo sanctorum sanguine polluta eorum patrocinia meruisti. Nam quamvis Germania, Gallia, Italia et precipue Roma sanctorum cineribus fertiles gloriosę prorsus existant, ipsorum tamen mortibus cruentatę rubescunt. Quo magis tua, Saxonia, beatitudo predicabitur, quę sine scelere tantum bonum adquisisti.' See further the comments of Ehlers, 'Die Sachsenmission', p. 45; Röckelein, *Reliquientranslationen nach Sachsen*, p. 366.

had been led away earlier from Christian religion by natural influence, thus the more fervently they eventually surrendered themselves to it'.[228]

These depictions of the 'historical' Saxon conversion and of present Saxon Christianity had real impact. Hagiographical texts did not operate solely within the walls of the cloister: rather, they could be remarkably influential in both lay and religious circles. In designating saintly patrons, and in creating a local past with which people could identify, hagiographical texts played a pivotal role in the formation of Christian communities. Yet these Saxon texts did not simply create a local history of individual Christian centres and communities; crucially, they also undertook to rewrite the Christian history of the region at large. They acknowledged the unique trajectory of Saxon Christian history and, hence, the singularity of Saxon Christianity itself. In so doing, they further cemented the importance of these differences in the identities of local Saxon communities.

Christianity was, and is, a local and universal religion, both distinctive and at the same time homogeneous. Christianity in Saxony, as elsewhere in the Carolingian world, was distinctive in the forms that its institutions took, the roles those institutions fulfilled, the ways in which Christian teaching was disseminated and the ways in which Christian communities conceived of themselves and their past. Yet the substance of that Christian teaching was notably unexceptional by contemporary standards, impossible to distinguish from Carolingian Christianity at large. Saxon Christianity was both different and the same. It was simultaneously a micro-Christendom and a beacon of Christian universalism.

---

[228] *Translatio sanctae Pusinnae*, ed. Wilmans, c. 1, p. 541: 'nationem aliquam bono solertiae et ingenita sibi subtilitate magis illa callere ... quo magis efficacia naturali abducebatur prius a religione christiana, ita ferventissime demum eidem sese mancipavit'. See also the comments of Flierman, *Saxon Identities*, p. 144; Shuler, 'The Saxons within Carolingian Christendom', 47–8.

CONCLUSION

Saxony has sometimes been viewed by historians as a failure of the Carolingian experiment. The *Stellinga*, in particular, have been taken to signify the region's ongoing hostility towards Carolingian rule and Christian religion, while other differences, such as the region's distinctive social landscape and underdeveloped economy, have further contributed towards the sense that Saxony fell outside the 'normal' course of Carolingian development. As a result, the region's history has been marginalized in accounts of Carolingian Europe. It has been labelled as exceptional, and thereby excused the necessity of explanation.

As recent work on Carolingian governance has revealed, however, there was no 'normative' experience of Carolingian rule. Power was not delegated through institutions and officials to be applied uniformly across the length and breadth of the empire; rather, governance was predicated upon extant power relations and local networks, and rulers relied upon local elites, and vice versa, for the routine exercise of their power. The resultant picture of Carolingian governance is one of regional diversity writ large. Carolingian Saxony need no longer stand as an exception. The peculiarities of Saxon politics and elite power, as revealed through the *Stellinga* 'revolt', were not innately anti-Carolingian: rather, they embody the regionalism inherent in Carolingian politics at large.

By contrast, Carolingian Christianity continues to be approached largely as a normative phenomenon. Christianization and Christian reform are conceived of as top-down processes, their courses set by the centre and experienced in the localities. This book has attempted to undercut this narrative of top-down Christianization and Christian reform and, in so doing, to highlight the potential for similar diversity within Carolingian Christianity and the structures which underpinned it.

In Saxony, Christianity and Christian structures have long been assumed to have been imposed by Carolingian rulers and Frankish missionaries, thus leading to the ultimate apostasy of the Saxons. Yet following the conquest, Saxon appears to have remained Christian throughout the Carolingian period; the Christianization of the region appears to have been advanced chiefly through local mechanisms. The resultant Christianity was in some ways distinctive, particularly in regard to the means by which Christian teachings were propagated, to the forms and functions its Christian institutions assumed, and to the ways in which Christian communities understood and commemorated their past. This distinctiveness, however, should not be confused with inferiority. Rather, it is a marker of the rich variety to be found within the early medieval world.

BIBLIOGRAPHY OF PRIMARY SOURCES IN ENGLISH TRANSLATION

Allott, S., tr., *Alcuin of York: His Life and His Letters* (York: William Sessions Ltd, 1974)

Bachrach, B. S. and Bachrach, D. S., tr., *Widukind of Corvey: Deeds of the Saxons* (Washington, DC: Catholic University of America Press, 2014)

Cabaniss, A., tr., *Charlemagne's Cousins: Contemporary Lives of Adalard and Wala* (Syracuse: Syracuse University Press, 1967): contains the *Life of Adalhard* and the *Epitaph of Arsenius*

Collins, R. and McClure, J., tr., *Bede: The Ecclesiastical History of the English People* (Oxford: Oxford University Press, 2008)

Dewey, T. K., tr., *An Annotated English Translation of the Old Saxon Heliand: A Ninth-Century Biblical Paraphrase in the Germanic Epic Style* (Lewiston, NY: Edwin Mellen, 2011)

Dutton, P. E., tr., *Carolingian Civilization: A Reader*, 2nd edn (Peterborough: Broadview, 2004): contains the *List of Superstitions and Pagan Practices*, Einhard's *Life of Charlemagne*, the *First Saxon Capitulary*, selected letters of Alcuin, Thegan's *Life of Louis*, Nithard's *Histories*, a section of the *Xanten Annals*, Rimbert's *Life of Anskar* and a section of the Saxon Poet's *Deeds of the Emperor Charlemagne*

tr., *Charlemagne's Courtier: The Complete Einhard* (Readings in Medieval Civilizations and Cultures 3) (Toronto: University of Toronto Press, 2009)

Ganz, D., *Two Lives of Charlemagne* (Harmondsworth: Penguin, 2008): contains the lives of Einhard and Notker

Kennedy, C. W., tr., *The Caedmon Poems: Translated into English Prose* (London: Routledge, 1916): contains the *Old Saxon Genesis* (*Genesis B*)

King, P. D., tr., *Charlemagne: Translated Sources* (Kendal: P. D. King, 1987): contains the *Royal Frankish Annals* and their revised version; sections of the *Lorsch Annals*, *Moselle Annals*, and *Moissiac Chronicle*, as well as individual entries from other assorted annals; the *First* and *Second Saxon Capitularies*; and the *Caroline Code*

McKinney, M. E., tr., *The Saxon Poet's Life of Charles the Great* (New York: Pageant, 1956)

Murphy, G. R., tr., *The Heliand: the Saxon Gospel* (New York: Oxford University Press, 1992)

Nelson, J. L., tr., *The Annals of St-Bertin* (Ninth-Century Histories 1) (Manchester: Manchester University Press, 1991)

Noble, T. F. X., tr., *Charlemagne and Louis the Pious: The Lives by Einhard, Notker, Ermoldus, Thegan, and the Astronomer* (University Park: Pennsylvania State University Press, 2009)

Paxton, F. S., tr., *Anchoress and Abbess in Ninth-Century Saxony: The Lives of Liutbirga of Wendhausen and Hathumoda of Gandersheim* (Washington, DC: Catholic University of America Press, 2009)

Rabe, S. A., *Faith, Art, and Politics at Saint-Riquier: The Symbolic Vision of Angilbert* (Philadelphia: University of Pennsylvania Press, 1995): contains the *Poem Concerning the Conversion of the Saxons*

Reuter, T., tr., The Annals of Fulda *(Ninth-Century Histories 2)* (Manchester: Manchester University Press, 1992)

Robinson, C. H., tr., *Anskar: The Apostle of the North, 801–865* (London: The Society for the Propagation of the Gospel in Foreign Parts, 1921)

Scholz, B. W., tr., *Carolingian Chronicles: Royal Frankish Annals and Nithard's Histories* (Ann Arbor: University of Michigan Press, 1972, reprinted 2000)

Scott, M., tr., *The Heliand* (Chapel Hill: University of North Carolina Press, 1966)

Smith, D. R., tr., *The Forgotten Gospel: The Latin Diatessaron* (ebook, 2008)

Talbot, C. H., tr., *The Anglo-Saxon Missionaries in Germany: Being the Lives of SS. Willibrord, Boniface, Sturm, Leoba and Lebuin, together with the Hodoeporicon of St. Willibald and a Selection from the Correspondence of St. Boniface* (London: Sheed and Ward, 1954)

Tschan, F. J., tr., *History of the Archbishops of Hamburg-Bremen* (New York: Columbia University Press, 1959, reprinted 2002)

Thorpe, L., tr., *Two Lives of Charlemagne: Einhard and Notker the Stammerer* (Harmondsworth: Penguin, 1969)

Wallace-Hadrill, J. M., tr., *The Fourth Book of the Chronicle of Fredegar with Its Continuations* (London: Nelson, 1960)

Wood, R. F., tr., 'The three books of the deeds of the Saxons', unpublished Ph.D. thesis (University of California, Los Angeles, 1949)

BIBLIOGRAPHY OF WORKS CITED

MANUSCRIPTS

Dresden, Sächsische Landesbibliothek – Staats- und Universitätsbibliothek mscr. Dresd. R.147 (facsimile), ed. L. Schmidt (Dresden: Tamme, 1905)
Kassel, Universitätsbibliothek 4°, Nr. 29
Paris, Bibliothèque nationale de France lat. 9768

PRINTED PRIMARY SOURCES

Abrenuntiatio diaboli et professio fidei, ed. E. Wadstein, *Kleinere altsächsische Sprachdenk-mäler* (Niederdeutsche Denkmäler 6) (Norden: Soltau, 1899), p. 3

Adam of Bremen, *Gesta Hammaburgensis ecclesiae pontificum*, ed. B. Schmeidler, *MGH SRG* 2 (Hanover: Hahn, 1917)

Agius of Corvey, *Versus computistici*, ed. K. Strecker, *MGH Poet.* 4:2.3 (Berlin: Weidemann, 1923), pp. 937–43

    Versus computistici, ed. E. Könsgen, 'Eine neue komputistische Dichtung des Agius von Corvey', *Mittellateinisches Jahrbuch*, 14 (1979), 66–75

    Vita et obitus Hathumodae, ed. G. H. Pertz, *MGH SS* 4 (Hanover: Hahn, 1841), pp. 165–89

Alcuin, *Epistolae*, ed. E. Dümmler, *MGH Epp.* 4:2 (Berlin: Weidemann, 1895), pp. 1–481

Alpertus, *De diversitate temporum*, eds. H. van Rij and A. S. Abulafia, *Alpertus van Metz, Gebeurtenissen van deze tijd en Een fragment over bisschop Diederik I van Metz* (Amsterdam: Verloren, 1980)

Altfrid, *Vita sancti Liudgeri*, ed. W. Diekamp, *Die vitae sancti Liudgeri* (Die Geschichts-quellen des Bisthums Münster 4) (Münster: Theissing, 1881), pp. 3–53

Annales Alamannici, ed. G. H. Pertz, *MGH SS* 1 (Hanover: Hahn, 1826), pp. 22–30, 40–4, 47–60

Annales Augienses, ed. G. H. Pertz, *MGH SS* 1 (Hanover: Hahn, 1826), pp. 67–9

Annales Bertiniani, eds. F. Grat, J. Vielliard and S. Clémencet, *Annales de Saint-Bertin* (Paris: C. Klincksieck, 1964)

Annales Corbeienses, ed. J. Prinz, *Die Corveyer Annalen* (Abhandlungen zur Corveyer Geschichtsschreibung 7) (Münster: Aschendorff, 1982)

Annales Fuldenses, ed. F. Kurze, *MGH SRG* 7 (Hanover: Hahn, 1891)

247

Annales Guelferbytani, ed. G. H. Pertz, *MGH SS* 1 (Hanover: Hahn, 1826), pp. 23–31, 40–6

Annales Iuvavenses maximi, ed. H. Bresslau, *MGH SS* 30:2 (Leipzig: K. W. Hiersemann, 1934), pp. 732, 734, 736, 738, 740

Annales Laubacenses, ed. G. H. Pertz, *MGH SS* 1 (Hanover: Hahn, 1826), pp. 7, 9–10, 12, 15, 52–5

Annales Laureshamenses, ed. G. H. Pertz, *MGH SS* 1 (Hanover: Hahn, 1826), pp. 22–39

Annales Lobienses, ed. G. Waitz, *MGH SS* 13 (Hanover: Hahn, 1881), pp. 224–35

Annales Laurissenses minores, ed. G. H. Pertz, *MGH SS* 1 (Hanover: Hahn, 1826), pp. 112–23, 630

Annales Maximiani, ed. G. Waitz, *MGH SS* 13 (Hanover: Hahn, 1881), pp. 19–25

Annales Mettenses priores, ed. B. Simpson, *MGH SRG* 10 (Hanover: Hahn, 1905)

Annales Mosellani, ed. J. M. Lappenberg, *MGH SS* 16 (Hanover: Hahn, 1859), pp. 491–9

Annales Nazariani, ed. G. H. Pertz, *MGH SS* 1 (Hanover: Hahn, 1826), pp. 23–31, 40–4

Annales necrologici Fuldenses, ed. G. Waitz, *MGH SS* 13 (Hanover: Hahn, 1881), pp. 161–218

Annales Petaviani, ed. G. H. Pertz, *MGH SS* 1 (Hanover: Hahn, 1826), pp. 7, 9, 11, 13, 15–18

Annales Quedlinburgenses, ed. M. Giese, *MGH SRG* 72 (Hanover: Hahn, 2004)

Annales qui dicuntur Einhardi, ed. F. Kurze, *MGH SRG* 6 (Hanover: Hahn, 1895)

Annales Regni Francorum, ed. F. Kurze, *MGH SRG* 6 (Hanover: Hahn, 1895)

Annales sancti Amandi, ed. G. H. Pertz, *MGH SS* 1 (Hanover: Hahn, 1826), pp. 6, 8, 10, 12, 14

Annales Sangallenses Baluzii, ed. G. H. Pertz, *MGH SS* 1 (Hanover: Hahn, 1826), p. 63

Annales Sangallenses breves, eds. G. H. Pertz and I. ab Arx, *MGH SS* 1 (Hanover: Hahn, 1826), pp. 64–5

Annales Sangallenses maiores, ed. I. ab Arx, *MGH SS* 1 (Hanover: Hahn, 1826), pp. 72–85

Annales Tiliani, ed. G. H. Pertz, *MGH SS* 1 (Hanover: Hahn, 1826), pp. 6, 8, 219–24

Annales Xantenses, ed. B. Simpson, *MGH SRG* 12 (Hanover: Hahn, 1909)

Anonymus Paderbrunnensis, *Vita et Translatio sancti Liborii*, ed. V. de Vry, *Liborius, Brückenbauer Europas: die mittelalterlichen Viten und Translationsberichte: mit einem Anhang der Manuscripta Liboriana* (Paderborn: Schöningh, 1997)

Anskar, *Miracula sancti Willehadi*, eds. C. de Smedt, F. van Ortroy, H. Delehaye, A. Poncelet and P. Peeters, *Acta Sanctorum III Novembris* (Brussels, 1910), pp. 847–5

Astronomus, *Vita Hludowici imperatoris*, ed. E. Tremp, *MGH SRG* 64 (Hanover: Hahn, 1995)

Avranches, *Translatio sancti Liborii*, ed. F. Baethgen, *MGH SS* 30:2 (Leipzig: K. W. Hiersemann, 1934), pp. 806–13

Bede, *Historica Ecclesiastica*, ed. C. Plummer, *Venerabilis Baedae opera historica*, 2 vols. (Oxford: Clarendon, 1896)

Benedict, *Chronicon*, ed. G. H. Pertz, *MGH SS* 3 (Hanover: Hahn, 1839), pp. 197–213

Cap. 1, ed. A. Boretius, *MGH Cap.* 1 (Hanover: Hahn, 1883)

Cap. 2, eds. A. Boretius and V. Krause, *MGH Cap.* 2 (Hanover: Hahn, 1897)

Cap. episc. 1, ed. P. Brommer, *MGH Cap. episc.* 1 (Hanover: Hahn, 1984)

Cap. episc. 2, eds. R. Pokorny and M. Stratmann, *MGH Cap. episc.* 2 (Hanover: Hahn, 1995)

Capitulare Saxonicum, ed. C. von Schwerin, *MGH Fontes iuris* 4 (Hanover: Hahn, 1918), pp. 45–9

Capitulatio de partibus Saxoniae, ed. C. von Schwerin, *MGH Fontes iuris* 4 (Hanover: Hahn, 1918), pp. 37–44

Carmen de conversione Saxonum, ed. E. Dümmler, *MGH Poet.* 1 (Berlin: Weidemann, 1881), pp. 380–1

Cartularium Werthinense, ed. D. P. Blok, 'Een diplomatisch onderzoek van de oudste particuliere oorkonden van Werden' (unpublished Ph.D. thesis, University of Amsterdam, 1960)

Catalogus abbatum et fratrum Corbeiensium, ed. K. Honselmann, *Die alten Mönchslisten und die Traditionen von Corvey* (Abhandlungen zur Corveyer Geschichtsschreibung 6), 2 vols. (Paderborn: Bonifatius, 1982), vol. I

Chronicon Hildesheimense, ed. G. H. Pertz, *MGH SS* 7 (Hanover: Hahn, 1846), pp. 845–73

Chronicon Moissiacense, ed. G. H. Pertz, *MGH SS* 1 (Hanover: Hahn, 1826), pp. 280–313

Codex Carolinus, ed. W. Gundlach, *MGH Epp.* 3:1 (Berlin: Weidemann, 1892), pp. 469–657

Codex Eberhardi, ed. H. Meyer zu Ermgassen, *Der Codex Eberhardi des Klosters Fulda* (Veröffentlichungen der Historischen Kommission für Hessen 58), 3 vols. (Marburg: Elwert, 1996)

Conc. 2:1, ed. A. Werminghoff, *MGH Conc.* (Hanover: Hahn, 1906)

Conc. 2:2, ed. A. Werminghoff, *MGH Conc.* (Hanover: Hahn, 1908)

Conc. 3, ed. W. Hartmann, *MGH Conc.* (Hanover: Hahn, 1984)

Concilium Magontiacensis, ed. M. Stimming, *Mainzer Urkundenbuch: Die Urkunden bis zum Tode Erzbischof Adalberts I (1137)*, 2 vols. (Darmstadt: Hessische Historische Kommission, 1972), vol. I

D Arn, ed. P. Kehr, *MGH, Die Urkunden Arnolfs* (Berlin: Weidemann, 1940)

D Kar. 1, ed. E. Mühlbacher, *MGH, Die Urkunden Pippins, Karlmanns, und Karls des Grossen* (Hanover: Hahn, 1906)

D Kar. 2, ed. T. Kölzer, *MGH, Die Urkunden Ludwigs des Frommen*, 3 vols. (Wiesbaden: Harrassowitz, 2016)

D Karl, ed. P. Kehr, *MGH, Die Urkunden Karls III* (Berlin: Weidemann, 1937)

D LD, ed. P. Kehr, *MGH, Die Urkunden Ludwigs des Deutschen, Karlmanns und Ludwigs der Jüngeren* (Berlin: Weidemann, 1934)

D LJ, ed. P. Kehr, *MGH, Die Urkunden Ludwigs des Deutschen, Karlmanns und Ludwigs der Jüngeren* (Berlin: Weidemann, 1934)

D LK, ed. T. Schieffer, *MGH, Die Urkunden Zwetibolds und Ludwigs des Kindes* (Berlin: Weidemann, 1960)

D Lo I, ed. T. Schieffer, *MGH, Die Urkunden Lothars I. und Lothars II* (Berlin: Weidemann, 1966)

Bibliography of Works Cited

D O I, ed. T. Sickel, *MGH, Die Urkunden Konrad I., Heinrich I. und Otto I.* (Hanover: Hahn, 1884)

D Zw, ed. T. Schieffer, *MGH, Die Urkunden Zwetibolds und Ludwigs des Kindes* (Berlin: Weidemann, 1960)

De Karolo rege et Leone papa, ed. W. Hentze, *De Karolo rege et Leone papa: der Bericht über die Zusammenkunft Karls des Grossen mit Papst Leo III. in Paderborn 799 in einem Epos für Karl den Kaiser* (Studien und Quellen zur westfälischen Geschichte 36) (Paderborn: Bonifatius, 1999)

Eigil of Fulda, *Vita sancti Sturmi*, ed. P. Engelbert, *Die Vita Sturmi des Eigil von Fulda: literarkritisch-historische Untersuchung und Edition* (Veröffentlichungen der Historischen Kommission für Hessen und Waldeck 29) (Marburg: N. G. Elwert, 1968)

Einhard, *Epistolae*, ed. K. Hampe, *MGH Epp.* 5:3 (Berlin: Weidemann, 1899), pp. 105–49

Vita Karoli Magni, ed. O. Holder-Egger, *MGH SRG* 25 (Hanover: Hahn, 1911)

Epistolae variorum inde a morte Caroli Magni usque ad divisionem imperii collectae, ed. E. Dümmler, *MGH Epp.* 5:3 (Berlin: Weidemann, 1899), pp. 299–350

Erconrad, *Translatio sancti Liborii*, eds. A. Cohausz, V. Mellinghoff-Bourgerie and R. Latouche, *La Translation de Saint Liboire (836) du diacre Erconrad: Un Document de l'époque carolingienne récemment découvert et les Relations déjà connues du Transfert des Reliques* (Archives historiques du Maine 14) (Le Mans: Société historique de la province du Maine, 1967)

Erhard, H. A., *Regesta historiae Westfaliae: accedit codex diplomaticus*, 2 vols. (Münster: F. Regensberg, 1847), vol. I

Ermoldus Nigellus, *In honorem Hludowici*, ed. E. Faral, *Poème sur Louis le Pieux et épitres au Roi Pépin* (Les classiques de l'histoire de France au moyen age 14), 2nd edn (Paris: Société d'Édition "Les Belles Lettres", 1964)

Flodoard, *Historia Remensis ecclesiae*, ed. M. Stratmann, *MGH SS* 36 (Hanover: Hahn, 1998)

Formulae imperiales, ed. K. Zeumer, *MGH Formulae Merowingici et Karolini aevi* I (Hanover: Hahn, 1886), pp. 285–328

Fredegar, *Chronicon*, ed. J. M. Wallace-Hadrill, *The Fourth Book of the Chronicle of Fredegar with Its Continuations* (London: Nelson, 1960)

Fredegarii continuationes, ed. J. M. Wallace-Hadrill, *The Fourth Book of the Chronicle of Fredegar with Its Continuations* (London: Nelson, 1960)

Genesis, ed. A. N. Doane, *The Saxon Genesis: An Edition of the West Saxon Genesis B and the Old Saxon Vatican Genesis* (Madison: University of Wisconsin Press, 1991)

Gesta Aldrici episcopi Cenomannensis, ed. G. Waitz, *MGH SS* 15:1 (Hanover: Hahn, 1887), pp. 304–27

Gregory of Tours, *Miracula et Opera Minora*, ed. B. Krush, *MGH SRM* 1:2 (Hanover: Hahn, 1885)

Libri Historiarum X, eds. B. Krush and W. Levison, *MGH SRM* 1:1 (Hanover: Hahn, 1951)

Heliand, eds. O. Behaghel and B. Taeger, *Heliand und Genesis* (Altdeutsche Textbibliothek 4), 9th edn (Tübingen: M. Niemeyer, 1984)

Hrabanus Maurus, *Liber de oblatione puerorum*, ed. J. P. Migne, *Patrologia Latina 107* (Paris: Imprimerie Catholique, 1851), pp. 419–40

Bibliography of Works Cited

Epistolae, ed. E. Dümmler, *MGH Epp.* 5:3 (Berlin: Weidemann, 1899), pp. 379–533

Hucbald, *Vita secunda sancti Lebuini*, ed. G. H. Pertz, *MGH SS* 2 (Hanover: Hahn, 1829), pp. 360–4

Indiculus obsidum Saxonum Moguntiam deducendorum, ed. A. Boretius, *MGH Cap.* 1 (Hanover: Hahn, 1883), pp. 233–4

Lampert, *Annales*, ed. O. Holder-Egger, *MGH SRG* 38 (Hanover: Hahn, 1894)

Lectio psalmorum, ed. E. Wadstein, *Kleinere altsächsische Sprachdenkmäler* (Niederdeutsche Denkmäler 6) (Norden: Soltau, 1899), pp. 4–15

Lex Saxonum, eds. K. von Richthofen and K. F. von Richthofen, *MGH Leges (in Folio)* 5 (Hanover: Hahn, 1889), pp. 47–84

Lex Saxonum, ed. C. von Schwerin, *MGH Fontes iuris* 4 (Hanover: Hahn, 1918), pp. 9–36

Liudger, *Vita sancti Gregorii*, ed. O. Holder-Egger, *MGH SS* 15:1 (Hanover: Hahn, 1887), pp. 63–79

Lupus, *Epistolae*, ed. P. K. Marshall, *Servati Lupi Epistulae* (Leipzig: Teubner, 1984)

Publius Vergilius Maro, *Eclogae*, ed. R. A. B. Mynors, *Oxford Classical Texts: P Vergili Maronis: Opera* (Oxford: Clarendon, 1969)

Miracula sancti Liudgeri, ed. W. Diekamp, *Die vitae sancti Liudgeri* (Die Geschichtsquellen des Bisthums Münster 4) (Münster: Theissing, 1881), pp. 229–36

Miracula sanctae Pusinnae, ed. K. Honselmann, 'Berichte des 9. Jahrhunderts über Wunder am Grabe der hlg. Pusinna in Herford' in J. Bauermann, ed., *Dona Westfalica: Georg Schreiber zum 80 Geburtstage* (Schriften der Historischen Kommission für Westfalen 4) (Münster: Aschendorff, 1963), pp. 128–30

Miracula sancti Wandregisili, eds. J. B. Sollerius, J. Pinius, G. Cuperus and P. Boschius, *Acta Sanctorum V Julii* (Antwerp, 1727), pp. 281–91

Nithard, *Historiae*, eds. P. Lauer and S. Glansdorff, *Histoire des fils de Louis le Pieux* (Les classiques de l'histoire au Moyen Âge 51) (Paris: Les Belles Lettres, 2012)

Notitiae fundationis monasterii Corbeiensis, ed. O. Holder-Egger, *MGH SS* 15:2 (Hanover: Hahn, 1888), pp. 1043–5

Notker Babulus, *De Carolo Magno*, ed. H. F. Haefele, *MGH SRG Nova series* 12 (Berlin: Weidemann, 1959)

Old Saxon Penitential, ed. E. Wadstein, *Kleinere altsächsische Sprachdenkmäler* (Niederdeutsche Denkmäler 6) (Norden: Soltau, 1899), pp. 16–17

Otfrid von Weissenburg, *Evangelienbuch*, eds. O. Erdmann and L. Wolff, *Otfrids Evangelienbuch* (Altdeutsche Textbibliothek 49) (Tübingen: M. Niemeyer, 1965)

Paschasius Radbertus, *Vita sancti Adalhardi*, ed. J. P. Migne, *Patrologia Latina 120* (Paris, 1852), pp. 1507–56

Epitaphium Arsenii, ed. E. Dümmler, *Radbert's Epitaphium Arsenii* (Abhandlungen der Kgl. Akademie der Wissenschaft zu Berlin, Phil.-hist. Classe II) (Berlin: W. de Gruyter, 1900)

Poeta Saxo, *Annalium de gestis Caroli magni imperatoris libri V*, ed. P. Winterfeld, *MGH Poet.* 4:1 (Berlin: Weidemann, 1899), pp. 1–71

Praeceptum diui Ludevvici imperatoris, ed. P. Caesar, *Triapostolatus septemtrionis: vita et gesta S. Willehadi, S. Ansgarii, S. Rimberti* (Cologne: Metternich, 1642), pp. 173–9

Privilegium Werthinense A, B, ed. W. Diekamp, *Die vitae sancti Liudgeri* (Die Geschichtsquellen des Bisthums Münster 4) (Münster: Theissing, 1881), pp. 286–94

Bibliography of Works Cited

Rimbert, *Vita sancti Anskarii*, ed. G. Waitz, *MGH SRG* 55 (Hanover: Hahn, 1884)

Rudolf and Meginhard, *Translatio sancti Alexandri*, ed. G. H. Pertz, *MGH SS* 2 (Hanover: Hahn, 1829), pp. 673–81

Sermo omnium sanctorum, ed. E. Wadstein, *Kleinere altsächsische Sprachdenkmäler* (Niederdeutsche Denkmäler 6) (Norden: Soltau, 1899), p. 18

Sermo sancti Marsi, ed. and tr. K. Honselmann 'Eine Essener Predigt zum Predigt zum Feste des hl. Marsus aus dem 9. Jahrhundert', *WZ* 110 (1960), 199–221

Stephanus V papa, *Epistolae*, ed. G. Laehr, *MGH Epp.* 7:5 (Berlin: Weidemann, 1928), pp. 354–65

Symeon, *Historia regum*, ed. T. Arnold, *Symeonis monachi opera omnia*, 2 vols. (London: Longman, 1885), vol. II

Tacitus Cornelius, *Germania*, ed. A. Önnerfors, *De origine et situ Germanorum liber* (Stuttgart: Teubner, 1983)

Thegan, *Gesta Hludovici imperatoris*, ed. E. Tremp, *MGH SRG* 64 (Hanover: Hahn, 1995)

Thietmar of Merseburg, *Chronicon*, ed. R. Holtzmann, *MGH SRG Nova Series* 9 (Berlin: Weidemann, 1935)

Traditiones Corbeienses, ed. K. Honselmann, *Die alten Mönchslisten und die Traditionen von Corvey* (Abhandlungen zur Corveyer Geschichtsschreibung 6), 2 vols. (Paderborn: Bonifatius, 1982), vol. I

Translatio sanctae Pusinnae, ed. R. Wilmans, *Die Kaiserurkunden der Provinz Westfalen, 777–1313*, 2 vols. (Münster: F. Regensberg, 1867), vol. I: pp. 539–46

Translatio sancti Viti, ed. and tr. I. Schmale-Ott, *Übertragung des hl. Märtyrers Vitus*, (Fontes minores 1) (Münster: Aschendorff, 1979)

Urbare Werthinense, ed. R. Kötzschke, *Die Urbare der Abtei Werden a.d. Ruhr: Die Urbare vom 9.-13. Jahrhundert* (Rheinische Urbare: Sammlung von Urbaren und anderen Quellen zur Rheinischen Wirtschaftsgeschichte 2) (Bonn: H. Behrendt, 1906)

Victor of Capua, *Codex Fuldensis*, ed. E. Ranke, *Codex Fuldensis: Novum Testamentum Latine interprete Hieronymo* (Marburg: N. G. Elwert, 1868)

Vita Liutbirgae virginis, ed. O. Menzel, *Das Leben der Liutbirg: Eine Quelle zur Geschichte der Sachsen in karolingischer Zeit* (Deutsches Mittelalter 3) (Leipzig: K. W. Hiersemann, 1937)

Vita sanctae Idae, ed. R. Wilmans, *Die Kaiserurkunden der Provinz Westfalen 777–1313*, 2 vols. (Münster: F. Regensberg, 1867), vol. I: pp. 469–88

Vita sancti Lebuini antiqua, ed. A. Hofmeister, *MGH SS* 30:2 (Leipzig: K. W. Hiersemann, 1934), pp. 789–95

Vita sancti Meinolfi, ed. and tr. K. Honselmann, 'Die älteste Vita Meinolfi: Brevierlesungen zu den Festen des Heiligen aus dem Ende des 9. Jahrhunderts', *WZ*, 137 (1987), 194–205

Vita sancti Rimberti, ed. G. Waitz, *MGH SRG* 55 (Hanover: Hahn, 1884)

Vita secunda sancti Liudgeri, ed. and tr. E. Freise, *Die Vita sancti Liudgeri: Vollständige Faksimile-Ausgabe der Handschrift Ms. Theol. lat. fol. 323 der Staatsbibliothek Berlin – Preußischer Kulturbesitz. Text, Übersetzung und Kommentar, Forschungsbeiträge* (Graz: Akadem. Druck- und Verlagsanstalt, 1999), pp. 9–24

Vita sancti Willehadi, eds. C. de Smedt, F. van Ortroy, H. Delehaye, A. Poncelet and P. Peeters, *Acta Sanctorum III Novembris* (Brussels: Société des Bollandistes, 1910), pp. 842–6

Bibliography of Works Cited

Vita tertia sancti Liudgeri, ed. W. Diekamp, *Die vitae sancti Liudgeri* (Die Geschichts-quellen des Bisthums Münster 4) (Münster: Theissing, 1881), pp. 85–134

Widukind of Corvey, *Res Gestae Saxonicae*, eds. P. Hirsch and H. E. Lohmann, *MGH SRG* 60 (Hanover: Hahn, 1935)

SECONDARY WORKS

Airlie, S., 'The world, the text and the Carolingian: royal, aristocratic and masculine identities in Nithard's *Histories*' in P. Wormald and J. L. Nelson (eds.), *Lay Intellectuals in the Carolingian World* (Cambridge: Cambridge University Press, 2007), pp. 51–76

Althoff, G., *Family, Friends and Followers: Political and Social Bonds in Early Medieval Europe* (Cambridge: Cambridge University Press, 2004)

Angenendt, A., *Liudger: Missionar – Abt – Bischof im frühen Mittelalter* (Münster: Aschendorff, 2005)

Appleby, D. F., 'Spiritual progress in Carolingian Saxony: a case from ninth-century Corvey', *The Catholic Historical Review*, 82(4) (1996), 599–613

Arndt, M., *Die Goslarer Kaiserpfalz als Nationaldenkmal: eine ikonographische Untersuchung* (Hildesheim: Lax, 1976)

Augustyn, P., *The Semiotics of Fate, Death, and the Soul in Germanic Culture: The Christianization of Old Saxon* (Berkeley Insights in Linguistics and Semiotics 50) (New York: P. Lang, 2002)

Bachrach, B. S., *Charlemagne's Early Campaigns (768–777): A Diplomatic and Military Analysis* (History of Warfare 82) (Leiden: Brill, 2013)

Bachrach, B. S., and Bachrach, D., 'Saxon military revolution, 912–973? Myth and reality', *EME*, 15(2) (2007), 186–222

Baesecke, G., 'Fulda und die altsächsischen Bibelepen' in J. Eichhoff and I. Rauch (eds.), *Der Heliand* (Wege der Forschung 321) (Darmstadt: Wissenschaftliche Buchgesellschaft, 1973), pp. 54–92

Baltrusch-Schneider, D. B., 'Klosterleben als alternative Lebensform zu Ehe?' in H. W. Goetz (ed.), *Weibliche Lebensgestaltung im frühen Mittelalter* (Cologne: Böhlau, 1991), pp. 45–64

Balzer, E., 'Frühe Mission, adelige Stifter und die Anfänge des Bischofssitzes in Münster', *WZ*, 160 and 161 (2010–11), 9–50, 9–59

Balzer, M., 'Siedlungsgeschichte und topographische Entwicklung Paderborns im Früh- und Hochmittelalter' in H. Jäger (ed.), *Stadtkernforschung* (Cologne: Böhlau, 1987), pp. 103–47

'Paderborn – Zentralort der Karolinger in Sachsen des späten 8. und frühen 9. Jahrhunderts' in C. Stiegemann and M. Wemhoff (eds.), *799: Kunst und Kultur der Karolingerzeit. Karl der Grosse und Papst Leo III. in Paderborn: Katalog der Ausstellung, Paderborn 1999*, 3 vols. (Mainz: von Zabern, 1999), vol. I: pp. 116–23

Barnwell, T. 'Fragmented identities: otherness and authority in Adam of Bremen's *History of the Archbishops of Hamburg-Bremen*' in C. Gantner, R. McKitterick and S. Meeder (eds.), *The Resources of the Past in Early Medieval Europe* (Cambridge: Cambridge University Press, 2015), pp. 206–22

Bartmuss, H. J., 'Zur Frage der Bedeutung des Stellingaaufstandes', *Wissenschaftliche Zeitschrift der Martin-Luther-Universität Halle-Wittenberg*, 7(1) (1957), 113–23

Bibliography of Works Cited

'Ursachen und Triebkräfte im Entstehungsprozeß des "frühfeudalen deutschen Staates"', *ZfG*, 10(7) (1962), 1591–1625

Bauer, K., 'Die Quellen für das sogenannte Blutbad von Verden' in W. Lammers (ed.), *Die Eingliederung der Sachsen in das Frankenreich* (Archäologische Aspekte 185) (Darmstadt: Wissenschaftliche Buchgesellschaft, 1970), pp. 109–50

Becher, M., *Eid und Herrschaft: Untersuchungen zum Herrscherethos Karls des Großen* (Vorträge und Forschungen 39) (Sigmaringen: J. Thorbecke, 1993)

Rex, Dux und Gens: Untersuchungen zur Entstehung des sächsischen Herzogtums im 9. und 10. Jahrhundert (Historische Studien 444) (Husum: Matthiesen, 1996)

'Vitus von Corvey und Mauritius von Magdeburg: zwei sächsische Heilige in Konkurrenz', *WZ*, 147 (1997), 235–49

'Die Sachsen im 7. Und 8. Jahrhundert: Verfassung und Ethnogenese' in C. Stiegemann and M. Wemhoff (eds.), *799: Kunst und Kultur der Karolingerzeit. Karl der Grosse und Papst Leo III. in Paderborn: Katolog der Ausstellung, Paderborn 1999*, 3 vols. (Mainz: von Zabern, 1999), vol. I: pp. 188–94

'Karl der Große und Papst Leo III. Die Ereignisse der Jahre 799 und 800 aus der Sicht der Zeitgenossen' in C. Stiegemann and M. Wemhoff (eds.), *799: Kunst und Kultur der Karolingerzeit. Karl der Grosse und Papst Leo III. in Paderborn: Katolog der Ausstellung, Paderborn 1999*, 3 vols. (Mainz: von Zabern, 1999), vol. I: pp. 22–36

'Non enim habent regem idem Antiqui Saxones . . . Verfassung und Ethnogenese in Sachsen während des 8. Jahrhunderts' in H. J. Hässler, J. Jarnut and M. Wemhoff (eds.), *Sachsen und Franken in Westfalen: zur Komplexität der ethnischen Deutung und Abgrenzung zweier frühmittelalterlicher Stämme* (Studien zur Sachsenforschung 12) (Oldenbourg: Isensee, 1999), pp. 1–31

'Volksbildung und Herzogtum in Sachsen während des 9. und 10. Jahrhunderts', *Mitteilungen des Instituts für österreichische Geschichtsforschung*, 108(1) (2000), 67–84

Beumann, H., 'Die Hagiographie 'bewältigt': Unterwerfung und Christianisierung der Saschen durch Karl den Grossen' in *Cristianizzazione ed organizzazione ecclesiastica delle campagne nell'Alto Medioevo: espansione e resistenze: 10–16 aprile 1980* (Settimane 28:1) (Spoleto: Il Centro, 1982), pp. 129–68

Bigott, B., *Ludwig der Deutsche und die Reichskirche im Ostfränkischen Reich (826–876)* (Historische Studien 470) (Husum: Matthiesen, 2002)

Bischoff, B., 'Der Schriftheimat der Münchener Heliand-Handschrift', *Beiträge zur Geschichte der deutschen Sprache und Literatur*, 101(2) (1979), 161–70

'Die Straubinger Fragmente einer Heliand-Handschrift', *Beiträge zur Geschichte der deutschen Sprache und Literatur*, 101(2) (1979), 171–80

Blair, J., 'Debate: ecclesiastical organization and pastoral care in Anglo-Saxon England', *EME*, 4(2) (1995), 193–212

The Church in Anglo-Saxon Society (Oxford: Oxford University Press, 2005)

Bodarwé, K., *Sanctimoniales litteratae: Schriftlichkeit und Bildung in den ottonischen Frauenkommunitäten Gandersheim, Essen und Quedlinburg* (Quellen und Studien 10) (Münster: Aschendorff, 2004)

Bostock, J. K., King, K. C. and McLintock, D. (eds.), *A Handbook on Old High German Literature* (Oxford: Clarendon, 1976)

Brown, P., *The Rise of Western Christendom: Triumph and Diversity, 200–1000* (Oxford: Blackwell, 1996)

Brown, W. C., *Unjust Seizure: Conflict, Interest, and Authority in an Early Medieval Society* (Ithaca: Cornell University Press, 2001)

Brown, W. C., Costambeys, M., Innes, M. and Kosto, A. J. (eds.), *Documentary Culture and the Laity* (Cambridge: Cambridge University Press, 2013)

Brubaker, R., 'Ethnicity without groups', *European Journal of Sociology*, 43(2) (2002), 163–89

Büttner, H., 'Mission und Kirchenorganisation des Frankenreiches bis zum Tode Karls des Großen' in H. Beumann (ed.), *Karl der Grosse: Lebenswerk und Nachleben: Persönlichkeit und Geschichte*, 5 vols. (Düsseldorf: L. Schwann, 1965) vol. I: pp. 454–87

Büttner, H., and Dietrich, I., 'Weserland und Hessen im Kräftespiel der karolingischen und frühen ottonischen Politik', *Westfalen*, 30(3) (1952), 133–49

Cabaniss, A., tr., *Charlemagne's Cousins: Contemporary Lives of Adalard and Wala* (Syracuse: Syracuse University Press, 1967)

Cambridge, E. and Rollason, D., 'Debate: the pastoral organization of the Anglo-Saxon church: a review of the "minster hypothesis"', *EME*, 4(1) (1995), 87–104

Capelle, T., *Die Sachsen des frühen Mittelalters* (Stuttgart: Theiss, 1998)

Carroll, C. J., 'The bishoprics of Saxony in the first century after Christianization', *EME*, 8(1) (1999), 219–46

Clay, J. H., *In the Shadow of Death: Saint Boniface and the Conversion of Hessia, 721–54* (Cultural Encounters in Late Antiquity and the Middle Ages 11) (Turnhout: Brepols, 2010)

Collins, R., *Charlemagne* (Basingstoke: Macmillan, 1998)

'The 'reviser' revisited: another look at the alternative version of the *Annales Regni Francorum*' in A. C. Murray (ed.), *After Rome's Fall: Narrators and Sources of Early Medieval History: Essays Presented to Walter Goffart* (Toronto: University of Toronto Press, 1998), pp. 191–213

'Charlemagne's Imperial Coronation and the Annals of Lorsch' in J. Story (ed.), *Charlemagne: Empire and Society* (Manchester: Manchester University Press, 2005), pp. 52–70

Conant, J., 'Louis the Pious and the contours of empire', *EME*, 22(3) (2014), 336–60

Constable, G., *Monastic Tithes: From Their Origins to the Twelfth Century* (Cambridge: Cambridge University Press, 1964)

Coupland, S., 'From poachers to gamekeepers: Scandinavian warlords and Carolingian kings', *EME*, 7(1) (1998), 85–114

Crusius, I., '*Sanctimoniales quae canonicas vocant*. Das Kannonissenstift als Forschungsproblem' in I. Crusius (ed.), *Studien zum Kanonissenstift* (SzGS 24) (Göttingen: Vandenhoeck & Ruprecht, 2001), pp. 9–38

Davies, W., 'People and places in dispute in ninth-century Brittany' in W. Davies and P. Fouracre (eds.), *The Settlement of Disputes in Early Medieval Europe* (Cambridge: Cambridge University Press, 1986), pp. 65–84

Small Worlds: The Village Community in Early Medieval Brittany (London: Duckworth, 1988)

Davis, J. R., *Charlemagne's Practice of Empire* (Cambridge: Cambridge University Press, 2015)

de Cazanove, C., 'Construire l'identité communautaire, les abbayes de Werden et Wissembourg du IXe au début Xe siècle', *Circé: Histoires, Cultures et Sociétés*, 5 (2014)

de Jong, M., *In Samuel's Image: Child Oblation in the Early Medieval West* (Brill's Studies in Intellectual History 12) (Leiden: Brill, 1996)
  The Penitential State: Authority and Atonement in the Age of Louis the Pious, 814–840 (Cambridge: Cambridge University Press, 2009)
  'The state of the church: *ecclesia* and early medieval state formation' in W. Pohl and V. Wieser (eds.), *Der frühmittelalterliche Staat: europäische Perspektiven* (Forschungen zur Geschichte des Mittelalters 16) (Vienna: Verlag der Österreichischen Akademie der Wissenschaften, 2009), pp. 241–54
de Vry, V., 'Die Gründung des Bistums Paderborn im Spiegel der Berichte über die Translatio des Bischofs Liborius von Le Mans' in T. M. Buck and J. Herrmann (eds.), *Quellen, Kritik, Interpretation: Festgabe zum 60. Geburtstag von Hubert Mordek* (Frankfurt: P. Lang, 1999), pp. 117–26
Depreux, P., 'L'intégration des élites aristocratiques de Bavière et de Saxe au royaume des francs – crise ou opportunité?' in F. Bougard, L. Feller and R. Le Jan (eds.), *Les élites au haut moyen âge: Crises et renouvellements* (Haut Moyen Âge 1) (Turnhout: Brepols, 2006), pp. 225–52
  'Défense d'un statut et contestation d'un modèle de société. Conjuration, révolte et répression dans l'Occident du Haut Moyen Âge' in P. Depreux (ed.), *Revolte und Sozialstatus von der Spätantike bis zur Frühen Neuzeit* (Pariser Historische Studien 87) (Munich: Oldenbourg, 2008), pp. 93–109
Diebold, W. J., 'The early middle ages in the exhibition *Deutsche Größe* (1940–1942)' in J. T. Marquardt and A. A. Jordan (eds.), *Medieval Art and Architecture after the Middle Ages* (Newcastle upon Tyne: Cambridge Scholars, 2011), pp. 363–86
Dierkens, A., 'Superstitions, christianisme et paganisme à la fin de l'époque mérovingienne: A propos de l'*Indiculus superstitionum et paganiarum*', in H. Hasquin (ed.), *Magie, sorcellerie, parapsychologie* (Laïcité. Série "Recherches" 5) (Brussels: Université de Bruxelles, 1984), pp. 9–26
Doane, A. N., *The Saxon Genesis: An Edition of the West Saxon Genesis B and the Old Saxon Vatican Genesis* (Madison: University of Wisconsin Press, 1991)
Drescher, H., *Tostedt: die Geschichte einer Kirche aus der Zeit der Christianisierung im nördlichen Niedersachsen bis 1880* (Materialhefte zur Ur- und Frühgeschichte Niedersachsens 19) (Hildesheim: Lax, 1985)
Drögereit, R., *Werden und der Heliand: Studien zur Kulturgeschichte der Abtei Werden und zur Herkunft des Heliand* (Essen: Fredebeul & Koenen, 1951)
  'Die schriftlichen Quellen zur Christianisierung der Sachsen und ihre Aussagefähigkeit' in W. Lammers (ed.), *Die Eingliederung der Sachsen in das Frankenreich* (Wege der Forschung 185) (Darmstadt: Wissenschaftliche Buchgesellschaft, 1970), pp. 451–69
  'Erzbistum Hamburg, Hamburg-Bremen oder Erzbistum Bremen? Studien zur Hamburg-Bremer Frühgeschichte. Friedrich Prüser (1892–1974) zum Gedächtnis. Erster Teil', *AfD*, 21 (1975), 136–230
Effros, B., '*De partibus Saxoniae* and the regulation of mortuary custom: A Carolingian campaign of Christianization or the suppression of Saxon Identity?', *Revue belge de philologie et d'histoire*, 75(2) (1997), 267–86
Eggert, W., 'Rebelliones servorum. Bewaffnete Klassenkämpfe im Früh- und frühen Hochmittelalter und ihre Darstellung in zeitgenössischen erzählenden Quellen', *ZfG*, 23(10) (1975), 1147–64

Bibliography of Works Cited

'"Franken und Sachsen" bei Notker, Widukind und anderen. Zu einem Aufsatz von Josef Semmler' in A. Scharer and G. Scheibelreiter (eds.), *Historiographie im frühen Mittelalter* (Veröffentlichungen des Instituts für Österreichische Geschichtsforschung 32) (Vienna: Oldenbourg, 1994), pp. 514–30

Ehlers, C., 'Das Damenstift Gandersheim und die Bischöfe von Hildesheim', *Die Diözese Hildesheim in Vergangenheit und Gegenwart. Jahrbuch des Vereins für Geschichte und Kunst im Bistum Hildesheim*, 70 (2002), 1–31

'Die zweifache Integration: Sachsen zwischen Karolingern und Ottonen. Überlegungen zur Erschließung von Diözesen mit Klöstern und Stiften in Westfalen und Sachsen bis 1024' in K. Bodarwé and T. Schilp (eds.), *Herrschaft, Liturgie und Raum: Studien zur mittelalterlichen Geschichte des Frauenstifts Essen* (Essener Forschungen zum Frauenstift 1) (Essen: Klartext, 2002), pp. 24–50

'Könige, Klöster, und der Raum. Die Entwicklung der kirchlichen Topographie Westfalens und Ostsachsens in karolingischer und ottonischer Zeit', *WZ*, 153 (2003), 189–216

Die Integration Sachsens in das fränkische Reich (751–1024) (Veröffentlichungen des Max-Planck-Instituts für Geschichte 231) (Göttingen: Vandenhoeck & Ruprecht, 2007)

Ehlers, J., 'Die Sachsenmission als heilsgeschichtlichen Ereignis' in F. J. Felten and N. Jaspert (eds.), *Vita religiosa im Mittelalter: Festschrift für Kaspar Elm zum 70. Geburtstag* (Berliner historische Studien 31) (Berlin: Duncker & Humblot, 1999), pp. 37–53

Ellger, O., 'Mimigernaford: Von der sächsischen Siedlung zum karolingischen Bischofssitz Münster' in C. Stiegemann and M. Wemhoff (eds.), *799: Kunst und Kultur der Karolingerzeit. Karl der Grosse und Papst Leo III. in Paderborn: Katalog der Ausstellung, Paderborn 1999*, 3 vols. (Mainz: von Zabern, 1999), vol. III: pp. 386–93

Engelbert, P., 'Liudger und das fränkische Mönchtum seiner Zeit', in E. Freise (ed.), *Die Vita sancti Liudgeri: Vollständige Faksimile-Ausgabe der Handschrift Ms. Theol. lat. fol. 323 der Staatsbibliothek Berlin – Preußischer Kulturbesitz. Text, Übersetzung und Kommentar, Forschungsbeiträge* (Graz: Akadem. Druck- und Verlagsanstalt, 1999), pp. 151–66

Epperlein, S., 'Sachsen im frühen Mittelalter: Diskussionsbeitrag zur Sozialstruktur Sachsens im 9. Jahrhundert und seiner politischen Stellung im frühen Mittelalter', *Jahrbuch für Wirtschaftsgeschichte*, 7(1) (1966), 189–212

Herrschaft und Volk im karolingischen Imperium: Studien über soziale Konflikte und dogmatisch-politische Kontroversen im fränkischen Reich (Forschungen zur mittelalterlichen Geschichte 14) (Berlin: Akademie, 1969)

'Die Kämpfe zwischen Slawen, Franken und Sachsen und die fränkische Eroberungspolitik' in J. Herrmann (ed.), *Die Slawen in Deutschland: Geschichte und Kultur der slawischen Stämme westlich von Oder und Neisse vom 6. bis 12. Jahrhundert: ein Handbuch* (Veröffentlichungen des Zentralinstituts für Alte Geschichte und Archäologie der Akademie der Wissenschaften der DDR 14, new edn) (Berlin: Akademie, 1985), pp. 326–33

Faulkner, T., *Law and Authority in the Early Middle Ages: The Frankish Leges in the Carolingian Period* (Cambridge: Cambridge University Press, 2016)

Bibliography of Works Cited

Fischer, B., 'Bibelausgaben des frühen Mittelalters' in *La Bibbia nell'Alto Medioevo* (Settimane 10) (Spoleto: Il Centro, 1963), pp. 519–600

Flierman, R., '*Gens perfida* or *populus Christianus*? Saxon (in)fidelity in Frankish historical writing' in C. Gantner, R. McKitterick and S. Meeder (eds.), *The Resources of the Past in Early Medieval Europe* (Cambridge: Cambridge University Press, 2015), pp. 188–205

'Religious Saxons: paganism, infidelity and biblical punishment in the *Capitulatio de partibus Saxoniae*' in R. Meens, D. van Espelo, B. van den Hoven van Genderen, J. Raaijmakers, I. van Renswoude and C. van Rhijn (eds.), *Religious Franks: Religion and Power in Honour of Mayke de Jong* (Manchester: Manchester University Press, 2016), pp. 181–201

Saxon Identities, AD 150–900 (London: Bloomsbury Academic, 2017)

fon Weringha, J., *Heliand and Diatessaron* (Studia Germanica 5) (Assen: Van Gorcum, 1965)

Foot, S., *Veiled Women*, 2 vols. (Aldershot: Ashgate, 2000)

Frankfurter, D., *Religion in Roman Egypt: Assimilation and Resistance* (Princeton: Princeton University Press, 1998)

Freise, E., 'Die Sachsenmission Karls des Großen und die Anfänge des Bistums Minden' in *An Weser und Wiehen: Beiträge zur Geschichte und Kultur einer Landschaft. Festschrift für Wilhelm Brepohl* (Mindener Beiträge 20) (Minden: Mindener Geschichtsverein, 1983), pp. 57–100

'Vom vorchristlichen Mimigernaford zum *honestum monasterium* Liudgers' in F. J. Jakobi (ed.), *Geschichte der Stadt Münster*, 3 vols. (Münster: Aschendorff, 1993), vol. I: pp. 1–53

Gadberry, G. W., 'An "ancient German rediscovered": The Nazi Widukind plays of Forster and Kiß' in H. H. Rennert (ed.), *Essays on Twentieth Century German Drama and Theater: An American Reception, 1977–1999* (New German-American Studies 19) (New York: P. Lang, 2004), pp. 155–66

Ganshof, F. L., *The Carolingians and the Frankish Monarchy* (London: Longman, 1971)

Gantert, K., *Akkommodation und eingeschriebener Kommentar: Untersuchungen zur Übertragungsstrategie des Helianddichters* (ScriptOralia 111) (Tübingen: G. Narr, 1998)

Garver, V. L., 'Learned women? Liutberga and the instruction of Carolingian women' in P. Wormald and J. L. Nelson (eds.), *Lay Intellectuals in the Carolingian World* (Cambridge: Cambridge University Press, 2007), pp. 121–38

Genrich, A., 'Archäologische Aspekte zur Christianisierung im nördlichen Niedersachsen' in W. Lammers (ed.), *Die Eingliederung der Sachsen in das Frankenreich* (Wege der Forschung 185) (Darmstadt: Wissenschaftliche Buchgesellschaft, 1970), pp. 470–86

Gfrörer, A. F., *Geschichte der ost- und westfränkischen Carolinger vom Tode Ludwigs des Frommen bis zum Ende Conrads I. (840–918)* (Freiburg: Herder, 1848)

Gillis, M. B., 'Noble and Saxon: the meaning of Gottschalk of Orbais' ethnicity at the Synod of Mainz, 829' in R. Corradini, M. B. Gillis, R. McKitterick and I. van Renswoude (eds.), *Ego Trouble: Authors and Their Identities in the Early Middle Ages* (Forschungen zur Geschichte des Mittelalters 15) (Vienna: Verlag der Österreichischen Akademie der Wissenschaften, 2010), pp. 197–210

Gillis, M. B., *Heresy and Dissent in the Carolingian Empire: the Case of Gottschalk of Orbais* (Oxford: Oxford University Press, 2017)

Goetting, H., *Das Bistum Hildesheim 1: Das reichsunmittelbare Kanonissenstift Gandersheim* (GSNF 7) (Berlin: W. de Gruyter, 1973)

Das Bistum Hildesheim 2: Das Beneditiner(innen)kloster Brunshausen, das Benediktinerinnenkloster St. Marien vor Gandersheim, das Benediktinerkloster Clus, das Franziskanerkloster Gandersheim (GSNF 8) (Berlin: W. de Gruyter, 1974)

Das Bistum Hildesheim 3: Die Hildesheimer Bischöfe von 815 bis 1221 (1227) (GSNF 20) (Berlin: W. de Gruyter, 1984)

Goetz, H. W., *Life in the Middle Ages: From the Seventh to the Thirteenth Century* (Notre Dame: University of Notre Dame Press, 1993)

Goldberg, E. J., 'Popular revolt, dynastic politics, and aristocratic factionalism in the Early Middle Ages: the Saxon *Stellinga* reconsidered', *Speculum*, 70(3) (1995), pp. 467–501

Struggle for Empire: Kingship and Conflict under Louis the German, 817–876 (Ithaca: Cornell University Press, 2006)

Gollancz, I., *The Caedmon Manuscript of Anglo-Saxon Biblical Poetry, Junius XI in the Bodleian Library* (Oxford: Oxford University Press, 1927)

Goosmann, E., 'Politics and penance: transformations in the Carolingian perception of the conversion of Carloman (747)' in C. Gantner, R. McKitterick and S. Meeder (eds.), *The Resources of the Past in Early Medieval Europe* (Cambridge: Cambridge University Press, 2015), pp. 51–67

Gowers, B., '966 and all that: the Norman peasants' revolt reconsidered', *EME*, 21(1) (2013), 71–98

Green, D. H., 'Three aspects of the Old Saxon Biblical epic, the Heliand', in D. H. Green and F. Siegmund (eds.), *The Continental Saxons from the Migration Period to the Tenth Century: An Ethnographic Perspective* (Studies in Historical Archaeoethnology 6) (Woodbridge: Boydell, 2003), pp. 247–69

Haferland, H., 'Was the *Heliand* poet illiterate?' in V. A. Pakis (ed.), *Perspectives on the Old Saxon Heliand: Introductory and Critical Essays, with an Edition of the Leipzig Fragment* (Medieval European Studies 12) (Morgantown: West Virginia University Press, 2010), pp. 167–207

Haines, D., *Sunday Observance and the Sunday Letter in Anglo-Saxon England* (Anglo-Saxon Texts 8) (Woodbridge: Boydell & Brewer, 2010)

Halsall, G., *Warfare and Society in the Barbarian West, 450–900* (London: Routledge, 2003)

Cemeteries and Society in Merovingian Gaul: Selected Studies in History and Archaeology, 1992–2009 (Brill's Series on the Early Middle Ages 18) (Leiden: Brill, 2010)

Haubrichs, W., *Die Anfänge: Versuche volkssprachiger Schriftlichkeit im frühen Mittelalter, (ca. 700–1050/60)* (Geschichte der deutschen Literatur von den Anfängen bis zum Beginn der Neuzeit 1:1) (Frankfurt: Athenäum, 1988)

Hauck, K., *Karolingische Taufpfalzen im Spiegel hofnaher Dichtung: Überlegungen zur Ausmalung von Pfalzkirchen, Pfalzen und Reichsklöstern* (Nachrichten der Akademie der Wissenschaften in Göttingen: I. Philologisch-Historische Klasse 1985:1) (Göttingen: Vandenhoeck & Ruprecht, 1985)

Helm, K., *Altgermanische Religionsgeschichte*, 2 vols. (Heidelberg: C. Winter, 1953), vol. II:2

Hen, Y., *Culture and Religion in Merovingian Gaul, A.D. 481–751* (Cultures, Beliefs and Traditions 1) (Leiden: Brill, 1995)

'The Annals of Metz and the Merovingian past' in Y. Hen and M. Innes (eds.), *The Uses of the Past in the Early Middle Ages* (Cambridge: Cambridge University Press, 2000), pp. 175–90

'Charlemagne's jihad', *Viator*, 37 (2006), 33–51

Hengst, K., 'Die Ereignisse der Jahre 777/78 und 782: Archäologie und Schriftüberlieferung' in P. Godman, J. Jarnut and P. Johanek (eds.), *Am Vorabend der Kaiserkrönung: das Epos "Karolus Magnus et Leo papa" und der Papstbesuch in Paderborn 799* (Berlin: Akademie, 2002), pp. 57–74

Herlihy, D., 'The Carolingian mansus', *The Economic History Review*, 13(1) (1960), 79–89

Herrmann, J., 'Sozialökonomische Grundlagen und gesellschaftliche Triebkräfte für die Herausbildung des deutschen Feudalstaates', *ZfG*, 19(6) (1971), 752–89

Hildebrandt, M. M., *The External School in Carolingian Society* (Education and Society in the Middle Ages and Renaissance 1) (Leiden: Brill, 1992)

Hines, J., 'The conversion of the Old Saxons' in D. H. Green and F. Siegmund (eds.), *The Continental Saxons from the Migration Period to the Tenth Century: An Ethnographic Perspective* (Studies in Historical Archaeoethnology 6) (Woodbridge: Boydell, 2003), pp. 299–328

Hollander, A. d., and Schmid, U., 'The *Gospel of Barnabas*, the *Diatessaron*, and method', *Vigiliae Christianae*, 61(1) (2007), 1–20

Honselmann, K., 'Die Urkunde Erzbischof Liudberts von Mainz für Corvey-Herford von 888"', *WZ*, 89(2) (1932), 130–9

'Die Annahme des Christentums durch die Sachsen im Lichte sächsischer Quellen des 9. Jahrhunderts', *WZ*, 108 (1958), 201–19

'Eine Essener Predigt zum Predigt zum Feste des hl. Marsus aus dem 9. Jahrhundert', *WZ*, 110 (1960), 199–221

'Reliquientranslationen nach Sachsen' in V. H. Elbern (ed.), *Das erste Jahrtausend: Kultur und Kunst im werdenden Abendland an Rhein und Ruhr*, 3 vols. (Düsseldorf: L. Schwann, 1962), vol. I: pp. 159–93

'Berichte des 9. Jahrhundert über Wunder am Grabe der hl. Pusinna in Herford' in J. Bauermann (ed.), *Dona Westfalica: Georg Schreiber zum 80 Geburtstage* (Schriften der Historischen Kommission für Westfalen 4) (Münster: Aschendorff, 1963), pp. 128–36

'Der Bericht des Klerikers Ido von der Übertragung der Gebeine des hl. Liborius', *WZ*, 119 (1969), 189–265

'Die Bistumsgründungen in Sachsen unter Karl dem Großen, mit einem Ausblick auf spätere Bistumsgründungen und einem Excurs zur Übernahme der christlichen Zeitrechnung im frühmittelalterlichen Sachsen', *AfD*, 30 (1984), 1–50

'Die Gründung der sächsischen Bistümer 799: Sachsens Anschluß an das fränkische Reich', *AfD*, 34 (1988), 1–2

Hummer, H. J., 'The identity of *Ludouicus piisimus augustus* in the *Praefatio in librum antiquum lingua Saxonica conscriptum*', *Francia: Forschungen zur westeuropäischen Geschichte*, 31(1) (2004), 1–14

Politics and Power in Early Medieval Europe: Alsace and the Frankish Realm, 600–1000 (Cambridge: Cambridge University Press, 2005)

Innes, M., *State and Society in the Early Middle Ages: The Middle Rhine Valley, 400–1000* (Cambridge: Cambridge University Press, 2000)

'Keeping it in the family: women and aristocratic memory, 700–1200' in E. M. C. van Houts (ed.), *Medieval Memories: Men, Women and the Past, 700–1300* (Harlow: Longman, 2001), pp. 17–35

'Property, politics and the problem of the Carolingian state' in W. Pohl and V. Wieser (eds.), *Der frühmittelalterliche Staat: europäische Perspektiven* (Forschungen zur Geschichte des Mittelalters 16) (Vienna: Verlag der Österreichischen Akademie der Wissenschaften, 2009), pp. 299–313

'Charlemagne, justice and written law' in A. Rio (ed.), *Law, Custom, and Justice in Late Antiquity and the Early Middle Ages: Proceedings of the 2008 Byzantine Colloquium* (London: Centre for Hellenic Studies, 2011), pp. 155–203

'Rituals, rights and relationships: some gifts and their interpretation in the Fulda cartulary, c. 827', *Studia Historica: Historia Medieval*, 31 (2013), 25–50

Innes, M., and McKitterick, R., 'The writing of history' in R. McKitterick (ed.), *Carolingian Culture: Emulation and Innovation* (Cambridge: Cambridge University Press, 1994), pp. 193–220

Isenberg, G., 'Kulturwandel einer Region: Westfalen im 9. Jahrhundert' in C. Stiegemann and M. Wemhoff (eds.), *799: Kunst und Kultur der Karolingerzeit. Karl der Grosse und Papst Leo III. in Paderborn: Katalog der Ausstellung, Paderborn 1999*, 3 vols. (Mainz: von Zabern, 1999), vol. I: pp. 314–23

James, E., *The Merovingian Archaeology of South-West Gaul* (British Archaeological Reports Supplementary Series 25), 2 vols. (Oxford: British Archaeological Reports, 1977), vol. I

'Cemeteries and the problem of Frankish settlement in Gaul' in P. H. Sawyer (ed.), *Names, Words and Graves: Early Medieval Settlement* (Leeds: The School of History, University of Leeds, 1979), pp. 55–89.

Jenkis, A., 'Die Eingliederung "Nordalbingiens" in das Frankenreich' in W. Lammers (ed.), *Die Eingliederung der Sachsen in das Frankenreich* (Darmstadt: Wissenschaftliche Buchgesellschaft, 1970), pp. 29–58

Johanek, P., 'Der Ausbau der sächsischen Kirchenorganisation' C. Stiegemann and M. Wemhoff (eds.), *799: Kunst und Kultur der Karolingerzeit. Karl der Grosse und Papst Leo III. in Paderborn: Katalog der Ausstellung, Paderborn 1999*, 3 vols. (Mainz: von Zabern, 1999), vol. II: pp. 494–506

Kahl, H.-D., 'Karl der Große und die Sachsen. Stufen und Motive einer historischen "Eskalation"' in H. Ludat and R. C. Schwinges (eds.), *Politik, Gesellschaft, Geschichtsschreibung: Giessener Festgabe für František Graus zum 60. Geburtstag* (Beihefte zum Archiv für Kulturgeschichte 18) (Cologne: Böhlau, 1982), pp. 49–130

Karras, R. M., 'Pagan survivals and syncretism in the conversion of Saxony', *The Catholic Historical Review*, 72(4) (1986), 553–72

Kaschke, S., 'Sachsen, Franken und die Nachfolgeregelung Ludwigs des Deutschen: *unus cum eis populus efficerentur*?', *NJ*, 79 (2007), 147–86

Kasten, B., *Adalhard von Corbie: die Biographie eines karolingischen Politikers und Klostervorstehers* (Studia humaniora 3) (Düsseldorf: Droste, 1986)

Keefe, S. A., *Water and the Word: Baptism and the Education of the Clergy in the Carolingian Empire*, 2 vols. (Notre Dame: University of Notre Dame Press, 2002), vol. I

Klueting, E., *Das Bistum Osnabrück 1: Das Kanonissenstift und Benediktinerinnenkloster Herzebrock* (GSNF 21) (Berlin: W. de Gruyter, 1986)

Bibliography of Works Cited

Knibbs, E., *Ansgar, Rimbert and the Forged Foundations of Hamburg-Bremen* (Farnham: Ashgate, 2011)

Kohl, W., *Das Bistum Münster 3: Das (freiweltliche) Damenstift Freckenhorst* (GSNF 10) (Berlin: W. de Gruyter, 1975)

'Bemerkungen zur Typologie sächsischer Frauenklöster in karolingischer Zeit' in *Untersuchungen zu Kloster und Stift* (SzGS 14) (Göttingen: Vandenhoeck & Ruprecht, 1980), pp. 113–39

'Honestum monasterium in loco Mimigernaefor: Zur Frühgeschichte des Doms in Münster' in N. Kamp and J. Wollasch (eds.), *Tradition als historische Kraft: interdisziplinäre Forschungen zur Geschichte des früheren Mittelalters* (Berlin: W. de Gruyter, 1982), pp. 156–80

Das Bistum Münster 7: Die Diözese (GSNF 37), 4 vols. (Berlin: W. De Gruyter, 1999–2004)

Das Bistum Münster 8: Das (freiweltliche) Damenstift Nottuln (GSNF 44) (Berlin: W. de Gruyter, 2005)

Kölzer, T., 'Die Urkunden Ludwigs des Frommen für Halberstadt (BM2 535) und Visbek (BM2 702) und ein folgenreiches Mißverständnis', *AfD*, 58 (2012), 103–23

'Zum angeblichen Immunitätsprivileg Ludwigs des Frommen für das Bistum Hildesheim', *AfD*, 59 (2013), 11–24

'Ludwigs des Frommen "Gründungsurkunde" für das Erzbistum Hamburg', *AfD*, 60 (2014), 35–68

Körntgen, L., 'Zwischen Herrschern und Heiligen: Zum Verhältnis von Königsnähe und Eigeninteresse bei den Frauengemeinschaften Essen und Gandersheim' in K. Bodarwé and T. Schilp (eds.), *Herrschaft, Liturgie und Raum: Studien zur mittelalterlichen Geschichte des Frauenstifts Essen* (Essener Forschungen zum Frauenstift 1) (Essen: Klartext, 2002), pp. 7–23

Kosto, A. J., 'Hostages in the Carolingian world (714–840)', *EME*, 11(2) (2002), 123–47

Hostages in the Middle Ages (Oxford: Oxford University Press, 2012)

Krogmann, W., 'Die Praefatio in librum antiquum lingua Saxonica conscriptum' in J. Eichhoff and I. Rauch (eds.), *Der Heliand* (Wege der Forschung 321) (Darmstadt: Wissenschaftliche Buchgesellschaft, 1973), pp. 20–53

Krüger, K. H., 'Zur Nachfolgeregelung von 826 in den Klöstern Corbie und Corvey' in N. Kamp and J. Wollasch (eds.), *Tradition als historische Kraft: interdisziplinäre Forschungen zur Geschichte des früheren Mittelalters* (Berlin: W. de Gruyter, 1982), pp. 181–96

'Neue Beobachtungen zur Datierung von Einhards Karlsvita', *Frühmittelalterliche Studien*, 32 (1998), 124–45

Studien zur Corveyer Gründungsüberlieferung (Abhandlungen zur Corveyer Geschichtsschreibung 9) (Münster: Aschendorff, 2001)

'Die ältern Sachsen als Franken. Zum Besuch des Kaisers Arnulf 889 im Kloster Corvey', *WZ*, 151/152 (2001/2002), 225–44

Krüger, S., *Studien zur Sächsischen Grafschaftsverfassung im 9. Jahrhundert* (Göttingen: Vandenhoeck & Ruprecht, 1950)

Kuhn, H., 'Das Fortleben des germanischen Heidentums nach der Christianisierung' in *La Conversione al Cristianesimo nell'Europa dell'Alto Medioevo* (Settimane 14) (Spoleto: Il Centro, 1967), pp. 743–57

La giustizia nell'alto Medioevo (secoli v–viii) (Settimane 42) (Spoleto: Il Centro, 1995)

La giustizia nell'alto Medioevo (secoli ix–xi) (Settimane 44) (Spoleto: Il Centro, 1997)

Lambert, P., 'Duke Widukind and Charlemagne in twentieth-century Germany: myths of origin and constructs of national identity' in C. Raudvere, K. Stala, and T. S. Willert (eds.), *Rethinking the Space for Religion: New Actors in Central and Southeast Europe on Religion, Authenticity and Belonging* (Lund: Nordic Academic Press, 2012), pp. 97–125

'The immediacy of a remote past: the afterlife of Widukind in the Third Reich', *British Academy Review*, 22 (2013), 13–16

'Widukind or Karl der Große? Perspectives on historical culture and memory in the Third Reich and post-war West Germany' in J. H. Lim, B. Walker and P. Lambert (eds.), *Mass Dictatorship and Memory as Ever Present Past* (Basingstoke: Palgrave Macmillan, 2014), pp. 139–61

Lampen, A., 'Sachsenkriege, sächischer Widerstand und Kooperation' in C. Stiegemann and M. Wemhoff (eds.), *799: Kunst und Kultur der Karolingerzeit. Karl der Grosse und Papst Leo III. in Paderborn: Katalog der Ausstellung, Paderborn 1999*, 3 vols. (Mainz: von Zabern, 1999), vol. I: pp. 264–72

Landwehr, G., 'Die Liten in den altsächsischen Rechtsquellen. Ein Diskussionsbeitrag zur Textgeschichte der *Lex Saxonum*' in G. Landwehr (ed.), *Studien zu den germanischen Volksrechten. Gedächtnisschrift für Wilhelm Ebel* (Rechtshistorische Reihe 1) (Frankfurt: P. Lang, 1982), pp. 117–42

Last, M., 'Zur Einrichtung geistlicher Konvente in Sachsen während des frühen Mittelalters (Ein Diskussionsbeitrag)', *Frühmittelalterliche Studien*, 4 (1970), 341–7

'Niedersachsen in der Merowinger- und Karolingerzeit' in H. Patze (ed.), *Geschichte Niedersachsens: Grundlagen und frühes Mittelalter* (Veröffentlichungen der Historischen Kommission für Niedersachsen und Bremen 36), 5 vols. (Hildesheim: Lax, 1977), vol. I: pp. 543–652

'Die Bedeutung des Klosters Amorbach für Mission und Kirchenorganisation im sächsischen Stammesgebiet' in F. Oswald and W. Störmer (eds.), *Die Abtei Amorbach im Odenwald: neue Beiträge zur Geschichte und Kultur des Klosters und seines Herrschaftsgebietes* (Sigmaringen: J. Thorbecke, 1984), pp. 33–53

Laux, F., 'Nachklingendes heidnisches Brauchtum auf spätsächsischen Reihengräberfriedhöfen und an Kultstätten der nördlicher Lüneburger Heide in frühchristlicher Zeit', *Die Kunde*, 38 (1987), 179–98

'Karolingische "Heiligenfibeln" aus Bardowick und Ochtmissen, Stadt Lüneburg, im Landkreis Lüneburg', *Die Kunde*, 46 (1995), 123–36

'Sächsische Gräberfelder zwischen Weser, Aller und Elbe. Aussagen zur Bestattungssitte und religiösem Verhalten' in H. J. Hässler, J. Jarnut and M. Wemhoff (eds.), *Sachsen und Franken in Westfalen: zur Komplexität der ethnischen Deutung und Abgrenzung zweier frühmittelalterlicher Stämme* (Studien zur Sachsenforschung 12) (Oldenbourg: Isensee, 1999), pp. 143–71

Leleu, L., 'Les sources saxones et la spatialisation du pouvoir en Saxe, IXe-XIe siècles. Première résultats', *Territorium* (2012), 1–39, available at https://publika tionen.uni-tuebingen.de/xmlui/handle/10900/47064

Lewis, T., and Short, C., *A Latin Dictionary founded on Andrews' Edition of Freund's Latin Dictionary* (Oxford: Clarendon, 1896)

Bibliography of Works Cited

Leyser, K., *Rule and Conflict in an Early Medieval Society: Ottonian Saxony* (London: Arnold, 1979)

Medieval Germany and Its Neighbours, 900–1250 (London: Hambledon, 1982)

Communications and Power in Medieval Europe: The Gregorian Revolution and Beyond (London: Hambledon, 1994)

Linde, R., 'Externsteine, Verden und Enger: Der völkische Sachsenkult in der Zeit der Nationalsozialismus' in C. Stiegemann, M. Kroker and W. Walter (eds.), *Credo: Christianisierung Europas im Mittelalter*, 2 vols. (Petersberg: M. Imhof, 2013), vol. I: pp. 475–82

Lintzel, M., 'De Capitulatio de partibus Saxoniae', 'Die Entstehung der Lex Saxonum', 'Die Stände der deutschen Volksrechte, hauptsächlich der Lex Saxonum', 'Die Unterwerfung Sachsens durch Karl den Großen und der sächsische Adel', 'Die Vita Lebuini antiqua', 'Die Vorgänge in Verden im Jahre 782', all in M. Lintzel (ed.), *Ausgewählte Schriften*, 2 vols. (Berlin: Akademie, 1961), vol. I

Lobbedy, U., 'Zur archäologischen Erforschung westfälischer Frauenklöster des 9. Jahrhunderts (Freckenhorst, Vreden, Meschede, Herford)', *Frühmittelalterliche Studien*, 4 (1970), 320–40

'Anmerkungen zur archäologischen Stadtkernforschung in Paderborn' in H. Jäger (ed.), *Stadtkernforschung* (Cologne: Böhlau, 1987), pp. 149–60

Löwe, H., 'Studien zu den Annales Xantenses', *DA*, 8 (1951), 59–99

'Die Entstehungszeit der *Vita Karoli* Einhards', *DA*, 39 (1983), 85–103

Markey, T. L., *A North Sea Germanic Reader* (Munich: Fink, 1976)

Markus, R. A., *The End of Ancient Christianity* (Cambridge: Cambridge University Press, 1990)

'From Caesarius to Boniface: Christianity and paganism in Gaul' in J. Fontaine and J. N. Hillgarth (eds.), *Le septième siècle, changements et continuités: actes du colloque bilatéral franco-britannique tenu au Warburg Institute les 8–9 juillet 1988* (Studies of the Warburg Institute 42) (London: Warburg Institute, 1992), pp. 154–72

Martindale, J., 'The kingdom of Aquitaine and the "dissolution of the Carolingian fisc"', *Francia: Forschungen zur westeuropäischen Geschichte*, 11 (1983), 131–91

Matzner, S., 'Christianizing the epic – epicizing Christianity: Nonnus' paraphrasis and the Old-Saxon Heliand in a comparative perspective', *Millennium: Jahrbuch zu Kultur und Geschichte des ersten Jahrtausend n. Chr.* 5 (2008), 111–45

Maxwell, J., 'Paganism and Christianization' in S. F. Johnson (ed.), *The Oxford Handbook of Late Antiquity* (Oxford: Oxford University Press, 2012), pp. 849–75

Mayr-Harting, H., 'Two abbots in politics: Wala of Corbie and Bernard of Clairvaux', *Transactions of the Royal Historical Society*, 40 (1990), 217–37

'Charlemagne, the Saxons, and the imperial coronation of 800', *The English Historical Review*, 111 (1996), 1113–33

McKitterick, R., *The Frankish Church and the Carolingian Reforms, 789–895* (London: Royal Historical Society, 1977)

The Carolingians and the Written Word (Cambridge: Cambridge University Press, 1989)

'The illusion of royal power in Carolingian annals', *The English Historical Review*, 115(460) (2000), 1–20

Bibliography of Works Cited

History and Memory in the Carolingian World (Cambridge: Cambridge University Press, 2004)

Perceptions of the Past in the Early Middle Ages (Notre Dame: University of Notre Dame Press, 2006)

Charlemagne: The Formation of a European Identity (Cambridge: Cambridge University Press, 2008)

'The uses of literacy in Carolingian and post-Carolingian Europe: literate conventions of memory' in *Scrivere e leggere nell'alto medioevo* (Settimane 59:1) (Spoleto: Il Centro, 2012), pp. 179–211

'Werden im Spiegel seiner Handschriften (8./9. Jahrhundert)' in S. Patzold, A. Rathmann-Lutz and V. Scior (eds.), *Geschichtsvorstellungen: Bilder, Texte, und Begriffe aus dem Mittelalter: Festschrift für Hans-Werner Goetz zum 65. Geburtstag* (Vienna: Böhlau, 2012), pp. 326–53

Metz, W., 'Probleme der fränkischen Reichsgutforschung im sächsischen Stammesgebiet', *NJ*, 31 (1959), 77–126

Das karolingische Reichsgut: eine verfassungs- und verwaltungsgeschichtliche Untersuchung (Berlin: W. de Gruyter, 1960)

Mierke, G., *Memoria als Kulturtransfer: der altsächsische "Heliand" zwischen Spätantike und Frühmittelalter* (Ordo: Studien zur Literatur und Gesellschaft des Mittelalters und der frühen Neuzeit 11) (Cologne: Böhlau, 2008)

Moddelmog, C., 'Stiftung oder Eigenkirche? Der Umgang mit Forschungskonzepten und die sächsischen Frauenklöster im 9. und 10. Jahrhundert' in W. Huschner and F. Rexroth (eds.), *Gestiftete Zukunft im mittelalterlichen Europa: Festschrift für Michael Borgolte zum 60. Geburtstag* (Berlin: Akademie, 2008), pp. 215–43

Morimoto, Y., 'Aspects of the early medieval peasant economy as revealed in the polyptych of Prüm' in P. Linehan and J. L. Nelson (eds.), *The Medieval World* (London: Routledge, 2001), pp. 605–20

Muir, B. J., *A Digital Facsimile of Oxford, Bodleian Library, MS. Junius 11* (Bodleian Digital Texts 1) (Oxford: Bodleian Library, 2004)

Müller, E., *Die Entstehungsgeschichte der sächsischen Bistümer unter Karl dem Grossen* (Quellen und Darstellungen zur Geschichte Niedersachsens 47) (Hildesheim: Lax, 1938)

Müller, H., *Das Bistum Münster 5: Das Kanonissenstift und Benediktinerkloster Liesborn* (GSNF 23) (Berlin: W. de Gruyter, 1987)

Müller-Mertens, E., 'Vom Regnum Teutonicum zum Heiligen Römischen Reich Deutscher Nation: Reflexionen über die Entwicklung des deutschen Staates im Mittelalter', *ZfG*, 11(2) (1963), 319–46

'Der Stellingaufstand: Seine Träger und die Frage der politischen Macht', *ZfG*, 20(7) (1972), 818–42

Murphy, G. R., *The Saxon Savior: The Germanic Transformation of the Gospel in the Ninth-Century Heliand* (Oxford: Oxford University Press, 1989)

Naß, K., 'Fulda und Brunshausen: Zur Problematik der Missionsklöster in Sachsen', *NJ*, 59 (1987), 1–62

Nelson, J. L., 'Public and private history in the work of Nithard', *Speculum*, 60(2) (1985), 251–93

Charles the Bald (London: Longman, 1992)

265

Bibliography of Works Cited

'History-writing at the courts of Louis the Pious and Charles the Bald' in A. Scharer and G. Scheibelreiter (eds.), *Historiographie im frühen Mittelalter* (Veröffentlichungen des Instituts für Österreichische Geschichtsforschung 32) (Vienna: Oldenbourg, 1994), pp. 435–42

'The wary widow' in W. Davies and P. Fouracre (eds.), *Property and Power in the Early Middle Ages* (Cambridge: Cambridge University Press, 1995), pp. 82–113

'Charlemagne and empire', in J. R. Davis and M. McCormick (eds.), *The Long Morning of Medieval Europe: New Directions in Early Medieval Studies* (Aldershot: Ashgate, 2008), pp. 223–34

Niemeyer, G., 'Die Herkunft der Vita Willehadi', *DA*, 12 (1956), 17–35

Noble, T. F. X., 'Lupus of Ferrières in his Carolingian context' in A. C. Murray (ed.), *After Rome's Fall: Narrators and Sources of Early Medieval History: Essays Presented to Walter Goffart* (Toronto: University of Toronto Press, 1998), pp. 232–50

Nock, A. D., *Conversion: The Old and the New in Religion from Alexander the Great to Augustine of Hippo* (Oxford: Clarendon, 1933)

Oexle, O. G., 'Die mittelalterlichen Gilden: ihre Selbstbedeutung und ihr Beitrag zur Formung sozialer Strukturen' in A. Zimmerman (ed.), *Soziale Ordnungen im Selbstverständnis des Mittelalters* (Miscellanea Mediaevalia 12) (Berlin: W. de Gruyter, 1979), vol. I: pp. 203–26

'Gilden als soziale Gruppen in der Karolingerzeit' in H. Jankuhn, W. Janssen, R. Schmidt-Wiegand and H. Tiefenbach (eds.), *Das Handwerk in vor- und frühgeschichtlicher Zeit* (Abhandlungen der Akademie der Wissenschaften in Göttingen: Philologisch-Historische Klasse. Dritte Folge 122) (Göttingen: Vandenhoeck & Ruprecht, 1981), vol. I: pp. 284–354

'*Conjuratio* und Gilde im frühen Mittelalter. Ein Beitrag zum Problem der sozialgeschichtlichen Kontinuität zwischen Antike und Mittelalter' in B. Schwineköper (ed.), *Gilden und Zünfte: Kaufmännische und gewerbliche Genossenschaften im frühen und hohen Mittelalter* (Vorträge und Forschungen 29) (Sigmaringen: J. Thorbecke, 1985), pp. 151–214

'Kulturwissenschaftliche Reflexionen über soziale Gruppen in der mittelalterlichen Gesellschaft: Tönnies, Simmel, Durkheim und Max Weber', *Historische Zeitschrift. Beihefte*, 17 (1994), 115–59

'Die Kultur der Rebellion: Schwureinungen und Verschwörung im früh- und hochmittelaltlichen Okzident' in M. T. Fögen (ed.), *Ordnung und Aufruhr im Mittelalter: historische und juristische Studien zur Rebellion* (Studien zur Europäischen Rechtsgeschichte 70) (Frankfurt: V. Klostermann, 1995), pp. 119–37

'Peace through conspiracy' in B. Jussen (ed.), *Ordering Medieval Society: Perspectives on Intellectual and Practical Modes of Shaping Social Relations* (Philadelphia: University of Pennsylvania Press, 2001), pp. 285–322

Pakis, V. A., '(Un)Desirable origins: the *Heliand* and the Gospel of Thomas' in V. A. Pakis (ed.), *Perspectives on the Old Saxon Heliand: Introductory and Critical Essays, with an Edition of the Leipzig Fragment* (Medieval European Studies 12) (Morgantown: West Virginia University Press, 2010), pp. 120–63

Palmer, J. T., 'Rimbert's *Vita Anskarii* and Scandinavian mission in the ninth century', *Journal of Ecclesiastical History*, 55(2) (2004), 235–56

'Defining paganism in the Carolingian world', *EME*, 15(4) (2007), 402–25

Anglo-Saxons in a Frankish World, 690–900 (Studies in the Early Middle Ages 19) (Turnhout: Brepols, 2009)

'Anskar's imagined communities' in H. Antonsson and I. H. Garipzanov (eds.), *Saints and Their Lives on the Periphery* (Cursor mundi 9) (Turnhout: Brepols, 2010), pp. 171–88

'Beyond Frankish authority: Frisia and Saxony between the Anglo-Saxons and Carolingians' in H. Sauer and J. Story (eds.), *Anglo-Saxon England and the Continent* (Essays in Anglo-Saxon Studies 3) (Tempe: Arizona Center for Medieval and Renaissance Studies, 2011), pp. 139–62

Parisse, M., 'Die Frauenstifte und Frauenklöster in Sachsen vom 10. bis zur Mitte des 12. Jahrhunderts' in S. Weinfurter (ed.), *Die Salier und das Reich: Das Reichskirche in der Salierzeit*, 3 vols. (Sigmaringen: J. Thorbecke, 1992), vol. II: pp. 465–501

Patze, H., 'Mission und Kirchenorganisation in karolingischer Zeit' in H. Patze (ed.), *Geschichte Niedersachsens: Grundlagen und frühes Mittelalter* (Veröffentlichungen der Historischen Kommission für Niedersachsen und Bremen 36, 5 vols.) (Hildesheim: Lax, 1977), vol. I: pp. 653–712

Patzold, S., 'Einhards erste Leser: zu Kontext und Darstellungsabsicht der "Vita Karoli",' *Viator multilingual*, 42 (2011), 33–55

Paxton, F. S., *Anchoress and Abbess in Ninth-Century Saxony: The Lives of Liutbirga of Wendhausen and Hathumoda of Gandersheim* (Washington, DC: Catholic University of America Press, 2009)

Phelan, O. M., *The Formation of Christian Europe: The Carolingians, Baptism, and the Imperium Christianum* (Oxford: Oxford University Press, 2014)

Pohlsander, H. A., *National Monuments and Nationalism in 19th Century Germany* (New German-American Studies 31) (Oxford: P. Lang, 2008)

Quispel, G., *Tatian and the Gospel of Thomas: Studies in the History of the Western Diatessaron* (Leiden: Brill, 1975)

Raaijmakers, J., *The Making of the Monastic Community of Fulda, c.744–c.900* (Cambridge: Cambridge University Press, 2012)

Rabe, S. A., *Faith, Art, and Politics at Saint-Riquier: The Symbolic Vision of Angilbert* (Philadelphia: University of Pennsylvania Press, 1995)

Raw, B. C., 'The probable derivation of most of the illustrations in Junius 11 from an illustrated Old Saxon *Genesis*', *Anglo-Saxon England*, 5 (1976), 133–48

Rebillard, É., 'Conversion and burial in the late Roman empire' in K. Mills and A. Grafton (eds.), *Conversion in Late Antiquity and the Early Middle Ages: Seeing and Believing* (Rochester: University of Rochester Press, 2003), pp. 61–83

The Care of the Dead in Late Antiquity (Cornell Studies in Classical Philology 59) (Ithaca: Cornell University Press, 2009)

Christians and Their Many Identities in Late Antiquity, North Africa, 200–450 CE (Ithaca: Cornell University Press, 2012)

Rembold, I., 'The Poeta Saxo at Paderborn: episcopal authority and Carolingian rule in late ninth-century Saxony', *EME*, 21(2) (2013), 169–96

'Rewriting the founder: Werden on the Ruhr and the uses of hagiography', *Journal of Medieval History*, 41(4) (2015), 363–87

'The Christian message and the laity: the Heliand in post-conquest Saxony' in N. Edwards, M. Ni Mhaonaigh, and R. Flechner (eds.), *Transforming Landscapes of*

Bibliography of Works Cited

Belief in the Early Medieval Insular World and Beyond (Converting the Isles 2) (Turnhout: Brepols), in press

'Quasi una gens: Saxony and the Frankish world, c. 772–888', *History Compass*, 15(6) (2017)

Renard, É., 'La politique militaire de Charlemagne et la paysannerie franque', *Francia: Forschungen zur westeuropäischen Geschichte*, 36 (2009), 1–33

Reuter, T., 'Assembly politics in Western Europe from the eighth century to the twelfth' in P. Linehan and J. L. Nelson (eds.), *The Medieval World* (London: Routledge, 2001), pp. 432–50

'Charlemagne and the world beyond the Rhine' in J. Story (ed.), *Charlemagne: Empire and Society* (Manchester: Manchester University Press, 2005), pp. 183–94

Reynolds, S., *Kingdoms and Communities in Western Europe, 900–1300* (Oxford: Clarendon, 1997)

Rio, A., 'Freedom and unfreedom in early medieval Francia: the evidence of the legal formulae', *Past & Present*, 193 (2006), 7–40

'High and low: ties of dependence in the Frankish kingdoms', *Transactions of the Royal Historical Society*, 18 (2008), 43–68

Legal Practice and the Written Word in the Early Middle Ages: Frankish Formulae, c. 500–1000 (Cambridge: Cambridge University Press, 2009)

'Self-sale and voluntary entry into unfreedom', *Journal of Social History*, 45(3) (2012), 661–85

'"Half-free" categories in the early middle ages: fine status distinctions before professional lawyers' in P. Dresch and J. Scheele (eds.), *Legalism: Rules and Categories* (Oxford: Oxford University Press, 2015), pp. 129–52

Slavery after Rome, 500–1100 (Oxford: Oxford University Press, 2017)

Roach, L., 'Law codes and legal norms in later Anglo-Saxon England', *Historical Research*, 86(233) (2013), 465–86

Röckelein, H., 'Miracle collections of Carolingian Saxony: literary tradition versus original creation', *Hagiographica*, 3 (1996), 267–76

'Zur Pragmatik hagiographischer Schriften im Frühmittelalter' in H. Keller, T. Scharff and T. Behrmann (eds.), *Bene vivere in communitate: Beiträge zum italienischen und deutschen Mittelalter: Hagen Keller zum 60. Geburtstag überreicht von seinen Schülerinnen und Schülern* (Münster: Waxmann, 1997), pp. 225–38

'Miracles and horizontal mobility in the early middle ages: some methodological reflections' in J. Hill and M. Swan (eds.), *The Community, the Family and the Saint: Patterns of Power in Early Medieval Europe: Selected Proceedings of the International Medieval Congress, University of Leeds, 4–7 July 1994, 10–13 July 1995* (Turnhout: Brepols, 1998), pp. 181–97

'Halberstadt, Helmstedt und die Liudgeriden' in J. Gerchow (ed.), *Das Jahrtausend der Mönche: Kloster Welt Werden, 799–1803* (Cologne: Wienand, 1999), pp. 65–73

'"Pervenimus mirificum ad sancti Medardi oraculum". Der Anteil westfränkischer Zellen am Aufbau sächsischer Missionszentrum' in P. Godman, J. Jarnut and P. Johanek (eds.), *Am Vorabend der Kaiserkrönung: das Epos "Karolus Magnus et Leo Papa" und der Papstbesuch in Paderborn 799* (Berlin: Akademie, 2002), pp. 145–62

Reliquientranslationen nach Sachsen im 9. Jahrhundert: über Kommunikation, Mobilität und Öffentlichkeit im Frühmittelalter (Beihefte der Francia 48) (Sigmaringen: J. Thorbecke, 2002)

'Eliten markieren den sächsischen Raum als christlichen: Bremen, Halberstadt, und Herford (8.-11. Jahrhundert)' in P. Depreux, F. Bougard and R. Le Jan (eds.), *Les élites et leurs espaces: mobilité, rayonnement, domination (du VIe au XIe siècle)* (Collection Haut Moyen Âge 5) (Turnhout: Brepols, 2007), pp. 273–98

'Bairische, sächsische und mainfränkische Klostergründungen im Vergleich (8. Jahrhundert bis 1100)' in E. Schlotheuber, H. Flachenecker and I. Gardill (eds.), *Nonnen, Kanonissen und Mystikerinnen: religiöse Frauengemeinschaften in Süddeutschland* (SzGS 31) (Göttingen: Vandenhoeck & Ruprecht, 2008), pp. 23–55

'Altfrid, Gründer des Stifts Essen und international agierender Kirchenmann?' in T. Schilp (ed.), *Frauen bauen Europa: Internationale Verflechtungen des Frauenstifts Essen* (Essener Forschungen zum Frauenstift 9) (Essen: Klartext, 2011), pp. 27–64

Schriftlandschaften, Bildungslandschaften und religiöse Landschaften des Mittelalters in Norddeutschland (Wolfenbütteler Hefte 33) (Wiesbaden: Harrassowitz, 2015)

Rösener, W., 'Zur Struktur und Entwicklung der Grundherrschaft in Sachsen in karolingischer und ottonischer Zeit' in A. Verhulst (ed.), *Le grand domaine aux époques mérovingienne et carolingienne* (Ghent: Belgisch Centrum voor Landelijke Geschiedenis, 1985), pp. 173–207

Schaller, D., 'Der Dichter des "Carmen de conversione Saxonum"' in G. Bernt, F. Rädle and G. Silagi (eds.), *Tradition und Wertung: Festschrift für Franz Brunhölzl zum 65. Geburtstag* (Sigmaringen: J. Thorbecke, 1989), pp. 27–45

Schieffer, R., *Die Entstehung von Domkapiteln in Deutschland* (Bonner historische Forschungen 43) (Bonn: Röhrscheid, 1976)

'Die Anfänge der westfälischen Domstifte', *WZ*, 138 (1988), 175–91

'Reliquientranslationen nach Sachsen' in C. Stiegemann and M. Wemhoff (eds.), *799: Kunst und Kultur der Karolingerzeit. Karl der Grosse und Papst Leo III. in Paderborn: Katalog der Ausstellung, Paderborn 1999*, 3 vols. (Mainz: von Zabern, 1999), vol. III: pp. 484–97

Schlüter, W., 'Osnabrück in karolingisch-ottonischer Zeit' in C. Stiegemann and M. Wemhoff (eds.), *799: Kunst und Kultur der Karolingerzeit. Karl der Grosse und Papst Leo III. in Paderborn: Katalog der Ausstellung, Paderborn 1999*, 3 vols. (Mainz: von Zabern, 1999), vol. III: pp. 394–400

Schmidt, H., 'Über Christianisierung und gesellschaftliches Verhalten in Sachsen und Friesland', *NJ*, 49 (1977) 1–44

Schubert, E., 'Die Capitulatio de partibus Saxoniae' in D. Brosius, C. van der Heuvel, E. Hinrichs and H. van Lengen (eds.), *Geschichte in der Region. Zum 65. Geburtstag von Heinrich Schmidt* (Hanover: Hahn, 1993), pp. 3–28

Geschichte Niedersachsens: Politik, Verfassung, Wirtschaft vom 9. bis zum ausgehenden 15. Jahrhundert (Veröffentlichungen der historischen Kommission für Niedersachsen und Bremen 36), 5 vols. (Hanover: Hahn, 1997), vol. II.1

Screen, E., 'The importance of the emperor: Lothar I and the Frankish civil war, 840–843', *EME*, 12(1) (2003), 25–51

Semmler, J., 'Corvey und Herford in der benediktinischen Reformbewegung des 9. Jahrhunderts', *Frühmittelalterliche Studien*, 4 (1970), 289–319

'Francia Saxoniaque oder Die ostfränkische Reichsteilung von 865/76 und die Folgen', *DA*, 46(2) (1990), 337–74

Bibliography of Works Cited

Shuler, E., 'The Saxons within Carolingian Christendom: post-conquest identity in the *translationes* of Vitus, Pusinna, and Liborius', *Journal of Medieval History*, 36(1) (2010), 39–54

Siegmund, F., 'Social relations among the Old Saxons' in D. H. Green and F. Siegmund (eds.), *The Continental Saxons from the Migration Period to the Tenth Century: An Ethnographic Perspective* (Studies in Historical Archaeoethnology 6) (Woodbridge: Boydell, 2003), pp. 77–111

Sievers, E., *Der Heliand und die angelsächsische Genesis* (Halle: M. Niemeyer, 1875)

Sleumer, A., *Deutsch-kirchenlateinisches Wörterbuch* (Bonn: F. Dümmler, 1962)

Smith, J. M. H., *Europe after Rome: A New Cultural History 500–1000* (Oxford: Oxford University Press, 2005)

Sobel, L., 'Ruler and society in early medieval Western Pomerania', *Antemurale*, 25 (1981), 19–142

Souter, A., *A Glossary of Later Latin to 600 A.D.* (Oxford: Clarendon, 1964)

Spicker-Wendt, A., *Die querimonia Egilmari episcopi und die responsio Stephani papae: Studien zu den Osnabrücker Quellen der Karolingerzeit* (Studien und Vorarbeiten zur Germania pontificia 8) (Cologne: Böhlau, 1980)

Springer, M., 'Geschichtsbilder, Urteile und Vorurteile: Franken und Sachsen in den Vorstellungen unserer Zeit und in der Vergangenheit' in C. Stiegemann and M. Wemhoff (eds.), *799: Kunst und Kultur der Karolingerzeit. Karl der Grosse und Papst Leo III. in Paderborn: Katalog der Ausstellung, Paderborn 1999*, 3 vols. (Mainz: von Zabern, 1999), vol. III: pp. 224–32

Springer, M., 'Was Lebuins Lebensbeschreibung über die Verfassung Sachsens wirklich sagt oder warum man sich mit einzelnen Wörtern beschäftigen muß' in H. J. Hässler, J. Jarnut and M. Wemhoff (eds.), *Sachsen und Franken in Westfalen: zur Komplexität der ethnischen Deutung und Abgrenzung zweier frühmittelalterlicher Stämme* (Studien zur Sachsenforschung 12) (Oldenbourg: Isensee, 1999), pp. 223–39

'Location in space and time' in D. H. Green and F. Siegmund (eds.), *The Continental Saxons from the Migration Period to the Tenth Century: An Ethnographic Perspective* (Studies in Historical Archaeoethnology 6) (Woodbridge: Boydell, 2003), pp. 11–36

Die Sachsen (Stuttgart: W. Kohlhammer, 2004)

Staab, F., 'Die Wurzel des zisterziensischen Zehntprivilegs, zugleich zur Echtheitsfrage der "Querimonia Egilmari episcopi" und der "Responsio Stephani V papae"', *DA*, 40 (1984), 21–54

Steuer, H., 'The beginnings of urban economies among the Saxons' in D. H. Green and F. Siegmund (eds.), *The Continental Saxons from the Migration Period to the Tenth Century: An Ethnographic Perspective* (Studies in Historical Archaeoethnology 6) (Woodbridge: Boydell, 2003), pp. 159–92

Stone, R., *Morality and Masculinity in the Carolingian Empire* (Cambridge: Cambridge University Press, 2011)

Story, J., *Carolingian Connections: Anglo-Saxon England and Carolingian Francia, c. 750–870* (Aldershot: Ashgate, 2003)

Stüwer, W., *Das Erzbistums Köln 3: Die Reichsabtei Werden an der Ruhr* (GSNF 12) (Berlin: W. de Gruyter, 1980)

Sullivan, R. E., 'The Carolingian missionary and the pagan', *Speculum*, 28(4) (1953), 705–40

'The papacy and missionary activity in the early middle ages', *Mediaeval Studies*, 17 (1955), 46–106

'Carolingian missionary theories', *The Catholic Historical Review*, 42(3) (1956), 273–95

Taeger, B., 'Ein vergessener handschriflicher Befund: Die Neumen in Münchener "Heliand"', *Zeitschrift für deutsches Altertum und deutsche Literatur*, 107(3) (1978), 184–93

'Das Straubinger 'Heliand' Fragment: Philologische Untersuchungen (Fortsetzung)', *Beiträge zur Geschichte der deutschen Sprache und Literatur*, 103(3) (1981), 402–24

Thompson, J. W., *Feudal Germany* (Chicago: University of Chicago Press, 1928)

Treude, E., 'Minden im frühen Mittelalter' in C. Stiegemann and M. Wemhoff (eds.), *799: Kunst und Kultur der Karolingerzeit. Karl der Grosse und Papst Leo III. in Paderborn: Katalog der Ausstellung, Paderborn 1999*, 3 vols. (Mainz: von Zabern, 1999), vol. III: pp. 380–5

Unterkircher, F., *Sancti Bonifacii epistolae. Codex Vindobonensis 751 der Oesterreichischen Nationalbibliothek. Faksimile-Ausg. der Wiener Handschrift der Briefe des heiligen Bonifatius* (Codices selecti phototypice impressi 24) (Graz: Akadem. Druck- und Verlagsanstalt, 1971)

van Engen, J., 'Christening, the kingdom of the Carolingians, and European humanity' in V. L. Garver and O. M. Phelan (eds.), *Rome and Religion in the Medieval World: Studies in Honor of Thomas F. X. Noble* (Farnham: Ashgate, 2014), pp. 101–28

Verhulst, A., *The Carolingian Economy* (Cambridge: Cambridge University Press, 2002)

Vogtherr, T., 'Visbek, Münster, Halberstadt: neue Überlegungen zu Mission und Kirchenorganisation im karolingischen Sachsen', *AfD*, 58 (2012), 125–45

von Padberg, L. E., *Mission und Christianisierung: Formen und Folgen bei Angelsachsen und Franken im 7. und 8. Jahrhundert* (Stuttgart: F. Steiner, 1995)

Heilige und Familie: Studien zur Bedeutung familiengebundener Aspekte in den Viten des Verwandten- und Schülerkreises um Willibrord, Bonifatius, und Liudger (Quellen und Abhandlungen zur mittelrheinischen Kirchengeschichte 83) (Mainz: Selbstverlag der Gesellschaft für mittelrheinische Kirchengeschichte, 1997)

Wagner, N., 'Der Name der Stellinga', *Beiträge zur Namenforschung*, 15(2) (1980), 128–33

Wallace-Hadrill, J. M., *The Frankish Church* (Oxford: Oxford University Press, 1983)

Wavra, B., *Salzburg und Hamburg: Erzbistumsgründung und Missionspolitik in karolingischer Zeit* (Giessener Abhandlungen zur Agrar- und Wirtschaftsforschung des Europäischen Ostens 179) (Berlin: Duncker & Humblot, 1991)

Weidemann, K., 'Die frühe Christianisierung zwischen Schelde und Elbe im Spiegel der Grabsitten des 7. bis 9. Jahrhunderts' in W. Lammers (ed.), *Die Eingliederung der Sachsen in das Frankenreich* (Wege der Forschung 185) (Darmstadt: Wissenschaftliche Buchgesellschaft, 1970), pp. 389–415

Weinrich, L., *Wala: Graf, Mönch und Rebell: Die Biographie eines Karolingers* (Historische Studien 386) (Lübeck: Matthiesen, 1963)

Wenck, W. B., *Das fränkische Reich nach dem Vertrage von Verdun (843–861)* (Leipzig: G. Wigand, 1851)

Bibliography of Works Cited

Wenskus, R., *Stammesbildung und Verfassung: das Werden der frühmittelalterlichen Gentes* (Cologne: Böhlau, 1961)

Sächsischer Stammesadel und fränkischer Reichsadel (Abhandlungen der Akademie der Wissenschaften in Göttingen. Philologisch-Historische Klasse 93) (Göttingen: Vandenhoeck & Ruprecht, 1976)

'Die ständische Entwicklung in Sachsen im Gefolge der fränkischen Eroberung' in *Angli e Sassoni al di qua e al di là del mare: 26 aprile-10 maggio 1984* (Settimane 32:2) (Spoleto: Il Centro, 1986), pp. 587–616

West, C., *Reframing the Feudal Revolution: Political and Social Transformation between Marne and Moselle, c. 800 to c. 1100* (Cambridge: Cambridge University Press, 2013)

Wickham, C., 'Space and society in early medieval peasant conflicts' in *Uomo e spazio nell'alto medioevo* (Settimane 50:1) (Spoleto: Il Centro, 2003), pp. 551–85

'Public court practice: the eighth and twelfth centuries compared' in S. Esders (ed.), *Rechtsverständnis und Konfliktbewältigung: gerichtliche und aussergerichtliche Strategien im Mittelalter* (Cologne: Böhlau, 2007), pp. 17–30

'Consensus and assemblies in the Romano-Germanic kingdoms: a comparative approach' in V. Epp and C. H. F. Meyer (eds.), *Recht und Konsens im frühen Mittelalter* (Vorträge und Forschungen 82) (Ostfildern: J. Thorbecke, 2017), pp. 389–426

Wilschewski, F., *Die karolingischen Bischofssitze des sächsischen Stammesgebietes bis 1200* (Studien der internationalen Architektur- und Kunstgeschichte 46) (Petersberg: M. Imhof, 2007)

Wood, I. N., 'Christians and pagans in ninth-century Scandinavia' in B. Sawyer, P. H. Sawyer and I. N. Wood (eds.), *The Christianization of Scandinavia: Report of a Symposium Held at Kungälv, Sweden, 4–9 August 1985* (Alingsås: Viktoria, 1987), pp. 36–67

'Pagans and holy men, 600–800' in P. N. Chatháin and M. Richter (eds.), *Irland und die Christenheit* (Stuttgart: Klett-Cotta, 1987), pp. 347–61

'How popular was early medieval devotion?', *Essays in Medieval Studies: Proceedings of the Illinois Medieval Association*, 14 (1997), available at www.illinoismedieval.org/ems/emsv14.html

'Before or after mission: social relations across the middle and lower Rhine in the seventh and eighth centuries' in I. L. Hansen and C. Wickham (eds.), *The Long Eighth Century: Production, Distribution and Demand* (The Transformation of the Roman World 11) (Leiden: Brill, 2000), pp. 149–66

The Missionary Life: Saints and the Evangelisation of Europe, 400–1050 (Harlow: Longman, 2001)

'An absence of saints? The evidence for the Christianization of Saxony' in P. Godman, J. Jarnut and P. Johanek (eds.), *Am Vorabend der Kaiserkrönung: das Epos "Karolus Magnus et Leo papa" und der Papstbesuch in Paderborn 799* (Berlin: Akademie, 2002) , pp. 335–52

'Beyond satraps and ostriches: political and social structures of the Saxons in the early Carolingian period' in D. H. Green and F. Siegmund (eds.), *The Continental Saxons from the Migration Period to the Tenth Century: An Ethnographic Perspective* (Studies in Historical Archaeoethnology 6) (Woodbridge: Boydell, 2003), pp. 271–97

'Ideas of mission in the Carolingian world' in W. Fałkowski and Y. Sassier (eds.), *Le monde carolingien: bilan, perspectives, champs de recherches: actes du colloque international de Poitiers, Centre d'études supérieures de civilisation médiévale, 18–20 novembre 2004* (Culture et société médiévales 18) (Turnhout: Brepols, 2009), pp. 183–98

'The pagans and the other: varying presentations in the early middle ages', *Networks and Neighbours*, 1(1) (2013), 1–22

Wormald, P., 'Bede, "Beowulf" and the conversion of the Anglo-Saxon aristocracy', in R. T. Farrell (ed.), *Bede and Anglo-Saxon England: Papers in Honour of the 1300th Anniversary of the Birth of Bede, Given at Cornell University in 1973 and 1974* (British Archaeological Reports 46) (Oxford: British Archaeological Reports, 1978), pp. 32–95

Wulf, F. W., 'Karolingische und ottonische Zeit' in H.-J. Hässler (ed.), *Ur- und Frühgeschichte in Niedersachsen* (Stuttgart: Theiss, 1991), pp. 321–68

Yorke, B. A. E., *Nunneries and the Anglo-Saxon Royal Houses* (London: Continuum, 2003)

Zöllner, W., *Karl oder Widukind? Martin Lintzel und die NS-"Geschichtsdeutung" in den Anfangsjahren der faschistischen Diktatur* (Wissenschaftliche Beiträge der Martin-Luther-Universität Halle-Wittenberg 10) (Halle: Martin-Luther-Universität, 1975)

UNPUBLISHED DISSERTATIONS, THESES, AND PRESENTATIONS

Carroll, C. J., 'The archbishops and church provinces of Mainz and Cologne during the Carolingian period, 751–911', unpublished Ph.D. thesis, University of Cambridge (1999)

Flierman, R., 'Pagan, pirate, subject, saint: defining and redefining Saxons, 150–900 A.D.', unpublished Ph.D. thesis, Universiteit Utrecht (2015)

Lamb, S., 'Francia and Scandinavia in the early Viking Age, c. 700–900', unpublished Ph.D. thesis, University of Cambridge (2009)

McComb, M., '"Each by the law of his choosing": resistance, memory, and the Saxon *Stellinga*' (2012), paper presented at the Graduate History Colloquium, Cornell University

Melleno, D., 'Before they were Vikings: Scandinavia and the Franks up to the death of Louis the Pious', unpublished Ph.D. thesis, University of California, Berkeley (2014)

Röckelein, H., 'Heilige als Medien der Christianisierung. Das Fallbeispiel des hl. Alexander', paper presented at 'Christianisierungsgeschichte der Region Oldenburger Münsterland', Cloppenburg, on 22 November 2014

Schulze, H. J., 'Der Aufstand der Stellinga in Sachsen und sein Einfluß auf den Vertrag von Verdun', unpublished Ph.D. thesis, Humboldt-Universität zu Berlin (1955)

Screen, E. M., 'The reign of Lothar I (795–855), emperor of the Franks, through the charter evidence', unpublished Ph.D. thesis, University of Cambridge (1998)

Sorber, D., 'Carolingian concepts of conversion', M.Phil. thesis, University of Cambridge (2012)

Zurla, C., 'Medium and message: the confluence of Saxon and Frankish values as portrayed in the Old Saxon Heliand', unpublished Ph.D. thesis, McGill University (2004)

INDEX

274

Index

Index

CPSIA information can be obtained
at www.ICGtesting.com
Printed in the USA
LVHW021741041222
734568LV00009B/542

9 781316 647202